AUDITORIA

Michael Forsyth

AUDITORIA
Designing for the Performing Arts

Mitchell · London

To Antonia Caroline

First published 1987

Typeset by Tameside Filmsetting Limited,
Ashton-under-Lyne, Lancashire
and printed in Great Britain by
Butler & Tanner Ltd
Frome, Somerset

Published by
The Mitchell Publishing Company Limited
4 Fitzhardinge Street, London W1H 0AH
A subsidiary of B.T. Batsford Limited

British Library Cataloguing in Publication Data

Forsyth, Michael
    Auditoria: designing for the performing
    arts.
    1. Music-halls—Construction   2. Theaters
    —Construction
    I. Title
    725'.81   NA6821

    ISBN 0-7134-4855-5

Contents

The colour plates appear between pages 96 and 97

Preface

This book does not attempt a geographical survey of auditoria, which carries with it the obligation to include the less interesting examples for the sake of completeness. Nor is it a technical handbook on their design, as I think the do-it-yourself overtones of such books are precarious for what is one of the most complex of building types, while at the same time being too detailed for the fundamental problems of the subject to be easily distilled. (It is assumed that the non-specialist architect will generally work with a theatre and acoustical consultant on all but the simplest of theatre spaces.) Rather, it is a personal selection of case studies, mostly in the light of the last ten years, classified thematically to illustrate the architectural problems involved, together with a range of current solutions. The book is intended primarily for architects, students, designers and others involved, or with an interest in, theatre and concert hall management, design and construction, as well as being a source of collected information for the specialist.

A couple of decades ago a book on recent theatres might have been straightforwardly classified into end stage theatres, thrust stage theatres, theatres-in-the-round and adaptable stage theatres (which were especially favoured when it seemed uncertain whether the proscenium stage would survive). Concert halls would have been strange bedfellows. And multi-purpose halls might justifiably have been avoided, being a depressing term in the 1950s and 60s, suggesting the over-large and unsatisfactory fan-shaped proscenium theatres that were built in North America and elsewhere from around 1910 onwards, or on a smaller scale the inadequate school or community assembly hall with a flat floor and picture frame stage—the latter being entirely invalidated by lack of equipment and overhead space—with poor sightlines, lighting and acoustics.

I have aimed instead to illustrate the striking changes in attitude to auditorium design that have taken place over the last decade, particularly in the area of multiple-use halls. These are fundamentally twofold. First, as the economic feasibility of building single-purpose auditoria has continued to diminish, architects have begun to tackle the problem of variability in multiple-use auditoria by using simple technology, without resorting to the prohibitively expensive and theatrically limiting stage machinery that was used to modify often just the stage end of many North American and some German halls of the previous decade. Several recent school and community multiple purpose theatres are especially interesting—while in the past the problem of providing adequately for different functions was virtually ignored altogether. Awareness of the acoustical and spatial needs of different types of activity has increased—partly through greater knowledge of historical precedent—and it is now more generally realized that a room for one purpose is seldom suitable for another, without some rearrangement of the form and the acoustics. For this reason, I have felt it essential to include separate sections on auditoria that are specifically for music on one hand, and primarily for speech on the other, in order to illustrate the problems and requirements of each.

Second, there has been new emphasis on the 'live' aspects of performance. Designers have attempted to increase the rapport between the audience and the performer by developing more successful auditorium forms. For theatres they have looked increasingly towards historical models, notably the Jacobean and Georgian 'courtyard' playhouse where the audience gathers around the stage in galleries on at least three sides. The old concert halls of Europe also were more intimate than those built in the mid-twentieth century, but often simply because they were smaller. Recent large concert halls—usually with between 2000 and 2800 seats—have about twice the seating area of their nineteenth-century forebears, but several have adopted a centralized plan to achieve a closer relationship between audience and performer. These are mainly variations on the successful Berlin Philharmonie, built in 1956–63. There, as the architect Herman Hertzberger has said of his own concert hall in Utrecht, the audience can see at close quarters 'the idols on the record sleeves at work in person', while being able also to see each other across the arena, adding perhaps to the emotional tension of the concert. Attention too has been given to acoustic as well as visual intimacy, through the careful positioning of sound-reflecting surfaces. (Much was learned on this about the advantages of nineteenth-century rectangular halls from Leo Beranek's now classic survey, *Music, Acoustics and Architecture*. Unfortunately, he failed to put this knowledge into effect, as the end product of the book was the disastrous and now demolished Philharmonic Hall at Lincoln Center, New York.) A major acoustical advance, again inspired by the successful concert halls of the past, has been the discovery that because of our binaural hearing, strong lateral sound reflections are vital for providing a 'stereophonic' impression of space; this theory has now profoundly influenced the approach to concert hall design.

Another characteristic of the last decade or so is that some of the most successful auditoria—as well as those most integrated with the communities which they serve—have been conversions of existing buildings, creative designs that have often resulted ironically from lack of funds for a new building; Manchester's Royal Exchange Theatre Company had planned to build a conventional new theatre over a shopping precinct until financial difficulties induced the present highly successful solution.

Finally, there is a section on temporary and mobile theatres, because although they are perhaps less a typical product of the 1980s than of the technologically optimistic 1960s, they represent a particular type— indeed the extreme—of adaptability, and for certain theatre companies and festivals these fulfil a need that a conventional theatre cannot.

While providing an overall outline for each building, I have attempted to stress the points of interest to auditorium design in general, rather than simply to present a series of descriptions relevant to the context of the individual case. For example, the main significance of the Barbican Theatre, London, is its overall shape, including a series of stepped galleries, in relation to certain stated aims. Whilst it is of some interest that the galleries are supported by a system of 4m (13ft) deep roof beams which also perform the different functions of containing the earth for trees in the rooftop conservatory, and providing walls for the Royal Shakespeare Company's offices, this is not significant for theatres in general, as the galleries could also have been cantilevered from the rear, as an earlier scheme had proposed.

The technical and dimensional information provided for each building is intended to be that which is most relevant to the overall architectural design. For instance, for theatres I have included the height of the gridiron and a note on the flying system, but not on the lighting system. Also, it provides some basis for comparison between the buildings discussed. The criterion of cost, without much greater analysis, is perhaps the least comparable because of the different floor area, cubic volume and facilities of each building, the variations in what the project cost includes (though wherever possible this is total, inclusive of professional fees), varying rates of monetary exchange, and, of course, inflation.

Acoustical information is the most difficult—and contentious—area in which to be useful to the non-specialist, without providing vast and complex technical detail. The only criteria given in the present book, apart from key architectural dimensions for each auditorium, are the reverberation time and the designed maximum background noise level of the ventilation system. Reverberation times are given for the middle frequencies

(500–1000 Hz.) with a full audience. However, the relative reverberation time at different frequencies substantially affects the tone of a hall. And it is even more important to note that although listeners' preferences undoubtedly relate to reverberation time, the latter is no longer regarded by designers as the sole, or even the most important, criterion. Reverberation time, for example, tells nothing about the position of sound reflecting surfaces in relation to the listener, which affects the impact, or apparent strength, of the sound and the acoustical 'scale' of the room; a bathroom and a lecture theatre may have the same reverberation time, but wholly different acoustics.

The maximum background noise level is generally given in the unit of the original design. This may be either: NC (Noise Criterion), the standard originally devised by the acoustician Leo Beranek; NR (Noise Rating), an internationally agreed figure which gave a more stringent rating at higher frequencies; or PNC (Preferred Noise Criterion), which was originally a measure for masking noise in landscaped offices, and then later adopted for auditoria, mainly in North America. They are roughly comparable at the rather low frequencies in auditorium ventilation noise, though much more information would be required in each case on the relative noise levels at different frequencies for the values to be transposed.

The criteria for selecting the auditoria themselves have been various. Some are included because they contain ideas for potentially wider application, such as the use of contractors' scaffolding for creating theatres for companies with shoestring budgets, or the idea of a kit of parts that can be sold like a 'Meccano' set to schools and colleges, or the projection of a particular acoustical idea into built form. Others are essentially individual solutions to particular situations that are instructive for their eloquence; one or two are interesting for being unique and unrepeatable, like the Institute for Coordination and Research in Acoustics and Music at the Centre Georges Pompidou, Paris, which was built at high cost around the approach of one man. All the buildings are either completed, under construction or about to be built, with the exception of the projects for the New Bubble Theatre, London, and the Lyric Theatre, Hammersmith, in Chapter 7, which are included because together they illustrate well certain points to be made about two types of temporary theatre. Most have been completed since 1975—the majority since 1980—though not exclusively: for instance, Christ's Hospital Theatre, Horsham (1974) is included because it was the first of several theatres of this type; the Maltings Concert Hall at Snape (1967; rebuilt after a fire, 1970) is a model of excellence for the conversion of an old building into an auditorium; and the Teatro Regio, Turin (1973), is unique in the stylistic questions it raises, as well as incidentally being, remarkably, the only major modern Italian theatre.

Acknowledgements

I should like to thank the many architects, theatre design consultants, acousticians, engineers, concert hall and theatre managers and technical staff, too numerous to mention individually, who have helped me in various ways during the preparation of this book. It would not have been possible without their kind assistance, during visits and in providing information. For permission to reproduce drawings, I am grateful to the architects and design consultants credited under each case study, and to The Architectural Press with regard to the Arena Theatre, Liverpool. I am particularly indebted to the following for their generous sponsorship of colour pages: Mr Russell Johnson of Artec Consultants, Inc., New York; Mr Iain Mackintosh of Theatre Projects Consultants Ltd, London; Arup Associates, London; Renton Howard Wood Levin Partnership, London; Ove Arup Partnership, London; Levitt Bernstein Associates, London; Chamberlin, Powell, Bon and Wood, London; Arthur Erickson Associates, Toronto; Mr Tim Foster, London; Onno Greiner Martien van Goor Architekten B.V., Amsterdam; John Laing Construction PLC, London; Benjamin Thompson and Associates, Inc., Cambridge, Massachusetts.

For permission to reproduce their photographs on the following pages I am indebted to: The Architectural Press, London, 177–179, (photo: Brecht Einzig) 87, 88 (top), (photo: Bruno de Hamel) 88 (bottom), (photo: Hans Wilde) 164; Arup Associates, London, 167, 168, (photo: John Donat) 165, colour plates 15, 16; Bochsler Studios Ltd, Hamilton, Ontario, 85; Jac. ten Broek, Amsterdam, 99, 101, colour plate 6; Buro Happold, Bath, 205–207; *Canadian Architect*, Don Mills, Ontario, 83; Cement and Concrete Association, London, 121; Chamberlin, Powell and Bon, colour plate 12; Martin Charles, London, 113, 115, 120, 139, 140, 157–159, colour plate 9; Concord Music Pavilion, California, 203, 204; Peter Cook, Bristol, 142, 143, 145, 153, 154, 209–211; W. Diepraam, Amsterdam, 22; van Dijk, Johnson and Partners, Cleveland, Ohio (photo: Douglas Dalton) 28, (photo: Bruce Kieffer) 26, (photo: David M. Thum) 27; John Donat, London, 90, 91; Frank Grant, Toronto, 62; Frank Greiner, Amsterdam, 100; Rupert Gretton, 105; Christopher D. Guerin, 107 (top); Fotografo Gyenes, Madrid, 50; Wilhelm Hauschile, Hanover, 127 (top); Timothy Hursley, Arkansas, colour plates 2, 7; I.R.C.A.M., Paris (photo: Jean-Pierre Amand), 95, 96; Izenour Archive, Stoney Creek, Connecticut, 111, 192–195; Russell Johnson, New York, 31, 122, colour plates 1 (Jack Singer Hall), 8, 10; Kurt Julius, Hanover, 172 (bottom); John Laing Construction PLC, London, 66–69, colour plates 3, 12; Landeshauptstadt Hannover, Presseampt (photo: Fritz Seimart) 173; Nathaniel Lieberman, New York, 77, colour plate 4; Mannering and Associates, Christchurch, N.Z., 38; Axel Dieter Mayen, Hanover, 174 (top); Norman McGrath, New York, 46, 47; Orange County Performing Arts Center, 72, 73; Photographics Colorado Springs, 107 (bottom); Richard Pilbrow, London, 32, 33, colour plate 1 (Max Bell Theatre, Martha Cohen Theatre); David Reed, 123; Steve Rosenthal, Auburndale, Mass., 147–149, colour plate 14; Mark Rhyne, 106; Schaubühne, Berlin, 181–183; Steve Stephens, London, 134 (top), colour plate 11; Studio Two, Hamilton, Ont., colour plate 5; John Sturrock/Network, London, 186; Shin Sugino, Toronto, 59–61, 63; Teatro Regio, Turin, 130, 131; Theatre Projects Consultants Ltd, London, colour plate 13; Chris Thomas, Calgary, 30; VBB, Stockholm (photo: Sune Sundahl), 55–57.

CHAPTER 1

Introduction

After being asked for his opinion on the Bösendorfer Hall in Vienna, the eminent Viennese architect Adolf Loos in 1912 was prompted to write an essay titled, 'Das Mysterium der Akustik', so that the secrets of the subject did not go with him to the grave. Even allowing that the science of room acoustics was still in infancy, he made the extraordinary assertion—pioneer Modern Rationalist that he was—that concert halls become acoustically excellent when fine music played in them is gradually absorbed by the walls. In the mortar, he said, live the sounds of the great composers. The music of our symphony orchestras and the voices of singers impregnate the building materials, causing mysterious changes in the molecular structure, as in the wood of old violins. But brass instruments, he warned, have a bad effect, and military music played in the Bösendorfer Hall could ruin its acoustics within a week. For the same reason, opera houses have poor acoustics on the side where the brass players sit. Encouraged by nonsensical speculation of this sort, various myths have surrounded the subject of auditoria and their acoustics, and even today are far from extinct (see p. 35). However quaint to the specialist, these myths have for most people shrouded real understanding of the reasons for an auditorium's success or failure.

For the auditorium designer, Loos's conclusions are scant advice indeed, even if—perhaps generously—we interpret his statements as referring to the beneficial effect that associations with great performers have on an auditorium's reputation. In a new hall an acquired reputation is intrinsically absent, while it is certainly true that the association of Milan's Teatro alla Scala with the leaders of nineteenth-century opera, or of the Grosser Musikvereinssaal with the Vienna Philharmonic and its famous conductors, have helped to make these buildings venerable. Reputation even compensates for practical shortcomings in older halls, such as a lack of facilities at the front and back of house or the penetration of street noise which in a new auditorium would rightly be inexcusable.

More usefully, the key to an auditorium's success—old or new—can be found through studying the 'fit' that evolved historically between theatre and concert hall types, and the purposes for which they were built—the spoken voice, instrumental music, opera, and so on. Auditorium design in the past relied largely on precedent: successful forms were repeated, and modified only as necessary by social and performing demands, and by technological change. Acoustically important characteristics—perhaps narrow width, shallow side galleries, particular construction materials and so on— were retained because they appeared to be beneficial. Halls that were unsuccessful were usually demolished or 'downgraded' within a few years of their construction.

Designers are becoming aware of these facts, and are looking increasingly at historical examples for inspiration. Several of the recent concert halls and theatres illustrated in this book, such as the Wilde Theatre, Bracknell, and the Eugene McDermott Concert Hall, Dallas, have strong historicist overtones as a result. (There is also, as with the Ordway Theatre, St Paul, Minnesota, the influence of architectural 'Postmodernism' in general, based on the idea that people identify more with familiar, known architectural languages of form and style than they did with the abstract forms of the Modern Movement.) Other halls pay no stylistic homage, such as the Orange County Performing Arts Center, California, even though the acoustical principles used also relate to the admired halls of the past.

One conclusion from studying this process of natural selection is clear: that an auditorium built for one purpose is not, as it stands, suitable for another purpose without some fundamental changes to its architectural form and acoustic characteristics. For the present-day architect and theatre designer this presents a major dilemma, because for the majority of today's auditoria the economics of management dictate some degree of multiple use. The fact is that halls more often than not have to be all things to all men, and they must be adaptable where this is required. Even in strictly single-purpose halls some capability for long term 're-tailoring' is desirable, for adapting to the taste or requirements of each theatre director or conductor during the lifetime of the building.

Amphitheatres in the landscape, courtyards in the town

The history of auditoria is fully documented elsewhere, though a nutshell summary will be useful at this point, even at the risk of some over-simplification. Two distinct auditorium types developed historically: rooms for the spoken word—theatres and opera houses—and rooms for concert music. These together, at least until the nineteenth century, also divide very roughly into two categories: those with courtly associations or sponsored by learned societies and usually purpose-designed by architects and influenced by known theory; and those with roots in popular and commercial drama and music-making where the building forms developed as a tradition, more a result of precedent than of purpose-design.

The oldest type of auditorium, the classical amphitheatre as described by the Roman architect, Vitruvius, originated in a simple arrangement of benches set in the bowl of a hillside, with the slope built up artificially where the hill was insufficient. With the rediscovery of classical drama in Renaissance Italy the amphitheatre came to be seen by Italian princes and learned academies as being the natural setting for plays. Theatres for this purpose were initially temporary structures built within existing palaces, and permanent theatres were built only from the mid-sixteenth century. The earliest surviving examples are Andrea Palladio's Teatro Olimpico in Vicenza of 1580–84, the small theatre at Sabbioneta of 1588–90 by Vincenzo Scamozzi, and the enormous Teatro Farnese, Parma, built in 1618–28 by Giovanni Battista Aleotti. These are like roofed-in Roman amphitheatres, the former being widened into a semi-ellipse because of site constraints, and the latter being elongated into a U. (All three are within reasonable travelling distance of each other and are exceedingly interesting for the modern visitor.) The enclosing colonnade behind the seats at Vicenza and Sabbioneta became at the Parma theatre a two storey facade of Venetian windows. In subsequent Italian theatres the enclosing auditorium wall became 'inhabited' by spectators in boxes, and the amphitheatre seating was omitted. The U-shape plan form then developed into a horseshoe to create a wider auditorium to accommodate a larger audience. The splayed fan shape of the side walls also enabled the ducal box at the rear to be seen from the side boxes—a view just as important as the stage itself. This, then, was the fully developed Italian baroque theatre, a form adopted by the great opera houses such as the Teatro San Carlo, Naples, Teatro alla Scala, Milan, La Fenice, Venice, and countless other theatres throughout the world down to the present day.

The humble playhouse, on the other hand, grew not from a body of theory such as that of Vitruvius but from certain dramatic traditions, out of which a vernacular form of theatre construction developed. In England, as well as on the continent, secular plays were originally performed in the houses of noblemen and in town halls and market squares. The early theatres of the Elizabethan and Jacobean periods built for popular drama (as opposed to court masques) were initially open air but were enclosed by the mid-seventeenth century, and they resembled the baiting yards and cockpits of the period, with which purpose they frequently doubled. In the seventeenth century many indoor tennis courts (constructed for the original 'royal' game), in Paris, London and elsewhere, were converted into theatres when this was found to be a more intensive commercial use for the site. If the form of the Elizabethan theatre contained some memory of the courtyards of the medieval inn, the rectangular tennis courts were conveniently similar in shape and size to the great halls of manor houses where strolling players often performed. (The Ballhof Theater, Hanover, Chapter 6, is a unique modern example of a converted former tennis court.) Both these types of theatre were the basis of a tradition of galleried playhouses that continued throughout the Restoration and Georgian periods. They illustrate how conventions can arise out of the constraints of certain given spaces—dimensions, audience-performer relationships, the arrangement of galleries—which are then carried over into new theatre buildings.

Concert hall design similarly sprang from two distinct sources, early concerts being either public commercial ventures, or private occasions at the ducal and princely courts of Europe. Initially, few rooms for public music-making were purpose built; of those that were, the influences on their forms were various. The still existing Holywell Room, Oxford, of 1748 was designed by a cleric, Dr Thomas Caplin, who was influenced by contemporary church architecture. The elliptical St Cecilia's Hall, Edinburgh, of 1762 is also still with us and has been restored but unfortunately without the original amphitheatre seating layout. This was influenced by the Teatro Farnese, Parma, which the architect Sir Robert Mylne knew from his travels. The famous Altes Gewandhaus, Leipzig of 1781 (demolished in 1894) by Johann Friedrich Dauthe, had a curious 'parliamentary' seating layout with the rows facing each other across a central aisle, and a balustraded orchestra platform, suggestive of the old coffee house layout. Private concerts, on the other hand, were held in palace ballrooms and music rooms, though the latter, even when purpose-built, were little different from other rooms except in decorative detail. The rectangular 'shoe box' concert hall, which was the most repeated and successful shape for the large public concert halls of the later nineteenth century, owes its formal origin to the palace ballroom. Eminent examples are the Grosser Musik-vereinssaal, Vienna, opened in 1870, designed by Theophil Ritter von Hansen, the Neues Gewandhaus, Leipzig, of 1886, by Martin Gropius and Heinrich Schmieden (now destroyed) and the Concertgebouw, Amsterdam, of 1887, by A. V. van Gendt, which is markedly broader than the others in shape. It is worth noting that in terms of architectural form the shoe box concert hall is somewhat related to the Georgian playhouse mentioned above, as the plan of the latter tended to be based roughly on a double square, and the former, a double cube.

The introduction in the late nineteenth century of steel as a building material in theatres and concert halls enabled deep, large span cantilevered galleries to be constructed, seating large numbers of people relatively close to the stage. The first English theatre with steel cantilevered galleries was the Palace Theatre, London, of 1891, by G. H. Hollway and T. E. Collcutt (originally the English Opera House, then D'Oyly Carte's Opera House). Among concert halls of this type, with large cantilevered galleries, were the Queen's Hall, Langham Place, London, of 1893, by T. E. Knightly, and the Usher Hall, Edinburgh, of 1914, by Stockdale Harrison and Sons and H. H. Thomson. In North America, after about 1910, the new construction method, together with the desire to accommodate very large audiences, led to the universal construction of vast fan-shape auditoria which were nominally multi-purpose but which were actually less than ideal for virtually everything except perhaps cinema.

Just as the introduction of steel revolutionized the auditorium, the development of lighting profoundly influenced the stage area in the nineteenth century. First of all the invention of limelight, gas lighting and the electric arc lamp in the first half of the century completed the retreat of the actor from the forestage to behind the proscenium arch. Spectacle and the realist-illusionist stage were then to dominate over the actor in importance throughout the remainder of the Victorian era. The development before the turn of the century of mains electricity led in turn to the demise of painted canvas flats, which ceased to be realistic under the electric lantern's steady glare. The subsequent development of three-dimensional stage design in the twentieth century was paralleled by the development of the thrust stage and the re-emergence of the actors into the main body of the auditorium. The thrust stage, with the audience on three sides, was made possible by the development of the focusing spotlight. One of the first modern thrust stages was the vast Grosses Schauspielhaus, Berlin, of 1919–20. This was a former circus building converted for the productions of Max Reinhardt but little used because it was acoustically a failure. The three-sided thrust stage was later adopted by the Irish theatre director Tyrone Guthrie, but at a far smaller and consequently more successful scale, first at the Assembly Hall, Edinburgh, in 1948, where he wanted to recreate an Elizabethan stage. Other examples are the Festival Theatre, Stratford, Ontario, of 1953–57, designed by Routhwaite and Fairfield, the Festival Theatre, Chichester, of 1961 by Powell and Moya, the Tyrone Guthrie Theatre, Minneapolis, of 1963 and the Crucible Theatre, Sheffield, of 1971. The Guthrie stage, together with the related open, or end stage and theatre-in-the-round, all have the advantage that they provide the audience with a close sense of involvement in the drama (although at Chichester the seating rake is too shallow), and in the 1950s and 60s it seemed that they would all but supplant the proscenium theatre. However, because of the limitations of the open stage, especially for touring shows, this was not to be the case. From the actor's viewpoint it is difficult in theatre-in-the-round to 'command' the audience over a wide angle, and also fire regulations strictly limit the materials that can be used for stage sets where the stage is not separated from the auditorium by a fire-resistant curtain. (The design of the safety curtain in relation to the stage at the Theatre Royal, Plymouth, p. 116, is interesting in this regard.) Nonetheless, the tendency in recent years, even with conventional proscenium stages, has been to reduce the sense of detachment of the stage from the auditorium, as in the old picture frame theatres.

Function, form and style

The unique role of the individual architect within this evolution has been to tailor his building to the specific needs of function and site, and to integrate these with his own vision of how best to provide for the performance of music or drama. This process may result in an existing auditorium type being refined, as when the seventeenth-century architect Carlo Fontana developed the U-shape plan into an elegant truncated ellipse for the Teatro Tordinona, Rome. (The elliptical plan was justified in the eighteenth century by the quaint assumption that the voice propagates itself in ellipsoidal waves—the position of the boxes on plan presumably being thought to reflect contours of equal loudness!) Or more rarely, the designer has steered the entire development of auditoria towards a new direction through a radical restatement of the problem. Such was the case with Richard Wagner at the Festspielhaus, Bayreuth, a theatre conceived specifically for performances of his own music. His fan-shape auditorium was to influence theatre design for the next 100 years, as well as introducing other innovatory aspects of theatre, including the idea of darkening the auditorium during the performance. Yet other notable, but usually unrealized (and sometimes unrealizable), projects have been based more on creative imagination than on any underlying principle of acoustics or buildability, for instance Hans Poelzig's fantastic and cavernous designs for the Salzburg Schauspielhaus of 1920–22.

Significant developments in auditorium history sometimes occur when the designer projects into built form a new theoretical idea—though the practical success of this naturally depends on the soundness of the initial theory. The Scottish engineer John Scott Russell in 1838 devised his ingeniously simple 'isacoustic curve' by projecting sight lines—and therefore 'sound lines'—from a sound source on stage to the head of each listener. The curve varies according to the relationship of performer and audience, and is a device that has had application ever since. The French piano manufacturer and amateur acoustician, Gustave Lyon, at the Salle Pleyel, Paris, of 1927 derived the flared shape of his auditorium from a 'reflected ray' diagram, in order to direct the sound outwards into the auditorium. Today this would be considered harmful to the retention of reverberant sound in the upper part of a concert hall, but in its day was an influential idea and successful in what it set out to achieve. Over two decades later in 1951 when the Royal Festival Hall, London, was opened, the auditorium was said to be a three-dimensional statement of known acoustical theory. Among the auditoria discussed in this book, Christchurch Town Hall, the Michael Fowler Centre, Wellington, Pikes Peak Center, Colorado Springs, and Orange County Performing Arts Center are significant present-day examples of halls that take account of recent acoustical discoveries, particularly the importance of laterally-arriving sound.

The difficulty of integrating into the design relatively intangible principles about which much is still unknown helps to make auditorium design one of the most complex of architectural problems. Just as problematic too are the all-important aspects of mood and character. But the designer's main difficulty is that the design criteria themselves tend to be contradictory and even incompatible. For example, economic demands may require a large hall, while acoustical preference is for a small hall. Upholstered seating is usually required for comfort, while hard seating is preferred acoustically. When a hall is used for chamber music the room is acoustically more reverberant with fewer people on stage than with a large symphony orchestra, yet the reverse would be desirable. Similarly, open air scenes on stage are often more reverberant than indoor scenes that have enclosing stage sets, while, in real life the opposite is the case. The criterion of visual intimacy generates a short, broad auditorium, yet the importance of sound reflective side walls implies that halls for music be long and narrow. Socially, the theatre-in-the-round plan might be best, but for musical balance is worst. For sightlines the raked fan-shape is ideal, but for theatre provides poor interaction between the actors and the audience, while for a concert hall the fan-shape does not accord with present-day acoustical concepts. The architect and structural engineer may wish to express visually the ceiling beams in the auditorium, while the acoustician may wish to conceal them in case of 'sound shadows' from uneven ceiling reflection. Again, several of the auditoria discussed illustrate interesting solutions to these difficulties. For instance, the Manuel de Falla Centre, Grenada, has a hybrid plan which combines the social aspects and visual intimacy of the 'surround' seating plan with the advantages of a traditional rectangular plan form. Galleried courtyard theatres, such as Christ's Hospital Theatre, Horsham, and the Martha Cohen Theatre at the Centre for Performing Arts, Calgary, take the stance that sightlines may be slightly compromised in return for greater rapport between actor and audience.

The translation in this way of design criteria or acoustical theory into three-dimensional form is quite distinct from 'Functional Expressionism', the stylistic device associated with the Modern Movement in architecture where the exterior form expresses the interior functions of the building. The origins of Functional Expressionism are found in eighteenth-century Neo-classical architecture, particularly in theatre buildings with their clearly defined internal elements. Friedrich Gilly's project of 1797–98 for the Schauspielhaus, Berlin, expresses the internal elements on the exterior, with a cubic stagehouse, half-cylindrical auditorium, and corresponding backstage areas, with a pedimented entrance. Charles Garnier's Paris Opéra, built in 1861–75 (a particular object of dislike to the arch-twentieth-century functionalist, Le Corbusier) displays clearly in the free-standing exterior massing a carefully considered plan of sequential spaces. The Brutalist style of the 1960s, for example the Queen Elizabeth Hall on London's South Bank, provided auditorium architects with particular opportunity to create abstract sculptural compositions in reinforced concrete that, with hindsight, are ugly expressions of an aesthetic code that had the most negative effects on our cities. Functional Expressionism particularly fails as a device for designing auditorium buildings when the exterior form is derived from initial schematic concepts for the interior. When the two aspects are developed structurally and acoustically they frequently depart from each other, and the exterior form loses its original 'meaning'. In the competition-winning design for the Sydney Opera House of 1956 by Jørn Utzon the parabolic shells, although conceived primarily as sculpture, were also intended to wrap around the profile of the two auditoria. However, during the period until Utzon's resignation in 1966, several unsuccessful attempts were made to relate the exterior shells to the interior boundaries of the halls.

The modern Italian architect Luigi Moretti devised a design method for auditoria (and other buildings besides) called 'parametric architecture', which he claimed generated forms that reflected function more truly than the so-called functionalist architecture of the Modern Movement. He demonstrated the theory of this with regard to stadium design, deriving the form of the audience arena from contours of 'seating desirability' which he devised from a photographic analysis of various spectator sports. The precise form of the stadium depended on the 'parameters' that the problem dictated; as the parameters change, so too does the form.

The building process

If an auditorium's success depends on the fit between certain stated needs and the resulting built form, the cause of failure or inadequacy in an otherwise competently designed hall can usually be traced back to the building process. This has to do with the method by which critical decisions are taken in arriving at the specification, size and form of the building, mainly with regard to the client body or appointed building committee and the user groups, and to the method of appointment of the design team.

If the precise needs of the client are not initially known, or if the requirements change midway, the building can fail exactly to meet the purpose. Where a hall is being designed for a resident theatre company or orchestra, the early participation of the user is essential. At the Royal Exchange Theatre, Manchester, and the Barbican Theatre, London, the respective theatre companies specified their requirements exactly, in the former case from philosophical concepts down to architectural detail, and in the latter, precise dimensions and a specially-designed stage. The result is that both buildings are remarkably successful projections of each user's specified needs. Several unique musical facilities have even been instigated and specified by individual composers: The Maltings Concert Hall, Snape, by Benjamin Britten, IRCAM, in Paris, by Pierre Boulez, and (not illustrated here but discussed in *Buildings for Music*—see Bibliography) the West German Pavilion at the Osaka World Fair in 1970, which was an auditorium built for the music of Karlheinz Stockhausen.

It is significant that behind the most successful auditoria there is generally an individual on the building committee—who is often, but not necessarily, the artistic or musical director—who has beneficially influenced the decision-making process, sometimes in the face of opposing demands, both at the project's inception and during the course of its design and construction. In other words, there must be a person 'in the driving seat'. For example, financial concerns often dictate a large seating capacity, while particularly for drama and opera (where acting is increasingly important) intimacy is necessary for the audience to gain a sense of involvement in the performance. At the Barbican Theatre, London, the Royal Shakespeare Company specified, and obtained, a maximum distance of 20m (65ft) from the stage to the rearmost seat, while in North American opera theatres 38m (125ft) is common; but, as the director at the time, Peter Hall, put it, despite electronic aids 'actors come between about five feet two and six feet two in size'. Also, it is rare for no economies to be made during the design or construction of an auditorium, and the ultimate reputation of the hall will depend on the selection of the cost-saving elements. Among the options will be 'visible' items—such as reducing the size of the lobbies or the standard of finishes—or items with management implications, like removing a rehearsal hall, which could restrict the main hall's availability for rental. Alternatively, there are less visible possibilities such as substituting, instead of a double, a single roof enclosure. From these, it may be the latter that is chosen ('the performing facility has been built under my direction without alteration to the space standards of the brief'), even though this item, above others, because of resulting noise penetration, may determine the actual excellence of the hall. The repercussions may be even wider and may affect—long after the project director has moved on—the long-term reputation of the orchestra. For instance, if recording could only be carried out when aircraft are not overhead, it may be prohibitively expensive—in the absence of other halls—to record that particular orchestra.

With regard to the design team itself, a critical aspect when the architect and his consultants are appointed is that the parties define precisely, and understand, each other's responsibilities in the area of acoustics, theatre design and theatre technology. The responsibility of each consultant may range from providing a 'second opinion' to executing full working drawings and contract documentation for the auditorium and related areas. Some architect-consultant teams have successfully established a happy collaboration which has extended over several projects; other relationships have been ones of missed opportunities. Often the specialist consultant tends very strongly to push his own point of view, promoting perhaps an aspect on which he has made a reputation or with which his work has been associated. An acoustician may emphasize the design of a reflecting canopy, a method of varying the reverberation time, or the overall shape or seating layout of a hall. When the architect is over-willing to accept his instructions verbatim the result can be a 'built acoustical sketch' which is architecturally unrefined and, even if in itself soundly based, does not address the total problem of the building. Of course, where the advice is plainly incorrect, then the result is disastrous—just as much, equally, as if the advice of the consulting team is insufficient, or ignored by the architect.

In addition to 'in-house' factors, larger auditorium projects are highly susceptible to government policy and ideology, and—arts centres being 'political footballs'—to policy change. The magnificent Dresden Opera House (*Semperoper*), which was bombed in February 1945, was re-opened in 1985 with a superbly reconstructed interior—except, however, that the auditorium is measurably larger in circumference than the original, and the character of the proscenium throat is consequently changed. This is because the auditorium walls are constructed on the foundations of a previously proposed interior, designed before the government of the German Democratic Republic switched its overall town-planning policy from one of 'brave new world' to conservationism. The famous Neues Gewandhaus, Leipzig, was also bombed, in 1944, but again not totally destroyed. The burnt-out building was made secure and a temporary roof erected, with a view to its reconstruction. However, it was replaced a few years ago by an ugly complex in reinforced concrete, bearing the same venerable name, and the shell of the old building was demolished. The renovation of the Schauspielhaus am Gendarmenmarkt, Berlin, of 1818–21 by Karl Friedrich Schinkel fell between the poles of this debate. The building was restored externally, but with a newly-built auditorium in the form of a concert hall, which does not attempt to reconstruct the original interior.

The success of an auditorium project is also related to the time it takes to be completed. Extremely long-term projects may become obsolete before they are finished, and as personnel or interest groups change the design becomes compromised and the clarity of the original relationship between intention and built form is lost; and of course the constraints increase as the structure of the building or the other parts of the project are defined and built. At the Barbican Arts Centre, London, the concert hall element was conceived in the architects' planning report of 1959 as a 1000–1300 seat symphony hall with a platform that could convert to a forestage for Elizabethan drama, or to a theatre-in-the-round. The auditorium finally opened in 1981 as a 2000 seat single use concert hall, home of the London Symphony Orchestra; however, the hall had failed on the way to incorporate the changes that had taken place in the concepts of auditorium design, partly because of the constraints of the auditorium boundary that imposed themselves as the project progressed. At the Sydney Opera House, following the resignation of Jørn Utzon as architect one decade after the original competition, the first task of the newly appointed administrative team was to revise the brief in relation to Sydney's current needs. But with the shells almost complete and the flytower to the main auditorium (originally the opera house) already constructed, the main question, in fact, was, what could be fitted under the shells? It was decided that Sydney's main need was to have a modern concert hall, and so the flytower was dismantled, the main auditorium was redesigned and the 1500 seat minor auditorium was 'upgraded' from a drama theatre to one for grand opera, with the acceptance that the constraint of the existing shells meant that the stage dimensions were not ideal. There is also the danger that lengthy building projects become stylistically dated by the time of their completion, as again is the case with the Barbican Arts Centre, and also with London's National Theatre Complex.

In competition

Despite the well-known problems surrounding the Sydney Opera House—which eventually toppled the New South Wales government—the building nonetheless gave to Australia a monumental landmark equivalent to London's Houses of Parliament and Paris's Eiffel Tower. As with these structures, and with several other of the world's famous opera houses, the design was the result of an architectural competition—a system which, as every competition sponsor is aware, has in the past produced outstanding, even visionary buildings that may not otherwise have been created. Important competitions also have the advantage of being able to promote brilliant but hitherto unrecognized talent. Such was the case with the 25 year old Harvey Lonsdale Elmes with the monumental St George's Hall, Liverpool, the result of a competition held in 1838; the 31 year old Charles Garnier with the Paris Opéra competition in 1861; and in our own day with Jørn Utzon, architect of the Sydney Opera House.

The risk with competitions is of course that during the development of the design and its construction the talent might not live up to the promise shown in the initial project, especially considering the formidable management and political skills an architect requires to carry out successfully any building of exceptional architectural quality. The assessment of competitions invariably requires an immense act of faith, together with a certain 'genius', on the part of the judges, particularly when the competition is in a single stage and entrants' names are not disclosed until the winner has been selected. At Sydney the winning scheme was chosen on the basis of an undeveloped sketch proposal. Occasionally the results have been unexpected, not to say notoriously irregular.

When Gottfried Semper was appointed to judge the competition to design the Burgtheater (originally Hofburg, or Court Theatre) in Vienna in 1869, he declared the entries to be unsatisfactory and successfully proposed to the Kaiser a design of his own. The proposal was accepted and he built the opera house in partnership with one of the unsuccessful contestants!

The nature of the winning scheme depends to some extent on the stylistic leanings of the assessors. In the competition for the West Yorkshire Playhouse in Leeds in 1985, none of the assessors, led by Peter Moro (himself a veteran theatre architect) 'thought that the rather old-fashioned architectural style of certain entrants' designs was appropriate for a brand new theatre'. On the other hand, the winning entry for the competition for the Teatro Carlo Felice, Genoa, held in 1981, by Ignazio Gardella, Aldo Rossi, Fabio Reinhardt and Angelo Sibilla, was externally a daring historicist essay in the classical revival (though surprisingly the auditorium plan form was conventional modernist).

The distinct disadvantage of competitions is that the basic design cannot be developed in the normal way in collaboration with the user groups, who have little say in the choice of design apart from representation on the board of assessors. The brief has therefore to be finalized to an extreme degree in advance. Competitions also do not allow for changing circumstances that may invalidate the original competition—usually to the justified fury of the unsuccessful contestants. For instance, the competition of 1959–60 for the Badisches Staatstheater in Karlsruhe was for a site adjacent to the castle, but in 1963 a second competition was announced when another site was chosen further away from the historic centre. The Philharmonie in Berlin, the subject of a limited competition won in 1956 by Hans Scharoun, was originally to be on a site near the centre of West Berlin, but in 1959 the site was transferred to the edge of the Tiergarten as the first of a planned group of cultural buildings. Fortunately, the architect was able to transfer the design, with very little change to his original brilliant conception.

For the architect the deterrent from entering design competitions is the substantial expenditure of resources involved, often together with the slenderest odds of winning. Limited, invited competitions obviate some of the disadvantages but of course preclude the discovery of latent talent. (Invited competitions are by no means of recent origin; the Teatro La Fenice, Venice, by Gianantonio Selva was the result of such a competition, which was launched at the very height of the French Revolution in 1789.) A selection system which overcame some of these criticisms was devised recently for the extensions to London's Royal Opera House, Covent Garden. A staged procedure of submissions, interviews and outline 'ideas' proposals was initially open to any architect, and a shortlist was drawn up. Essentially, the procedure had more to do with the selection of designers than of design solutions, and allowed the highly complex project to evolve in the normal way. The contest was won by Jeremy Dixon in association with Building Design

Partnership. Another approach to the competition problem was found for the design of the Opéra de la Bastille in Paris in 1983 which was won by the Canadian architect, Carlos Ott. Here, the auditorium configuration and many other technical and planning aspects were established in advance by a previously assembled technical team. This ensured that the client's requirements were met as well as reducing the risk of untried talent, but with the result that the architect's creative role extended little beyond 'façade architecture' where the task was to create an attractive wrapping around a predetermined package.

CHAPTER 2

The Temple and the Music Shop

Auditoria in context

The planning of an auditorium—indeed of any building type—has two basic facets: the functional considerations from the users' viewpoint, and the design of the building on its site. These are, as it were, the private and public faces of the building. If architectural design is analogous to modelling clay, then these influences are like pressures that determine the form. There are the pressures from inside that mould the spaces, together perhaps with their expression on the exterior; conversely, there are pressures from outside suggested by the building's context, its site and situation. As most theatres and concert halls are accessible to the public, both of these aspects are naturally important, though at different times historically greater emphasis has been placed on one or the other.

The first theatre to be built as a free-standing monumental building in a city was the Staatsoper in Berlin, built for Frederick the Great by the architect Georg Wenzeslaus von Knobelsdorff in 1742. Subsequently, theatres became favourite elements in grandiose city planning, and several of the great nineteenth-century opera houses, in Paris, Vienna and elsewhere, are essentially buildings with a public face. The interior spaces of the Paris Opéra in particular are a carefully considered extension of the building's urban context. Most Victorian commercial theatres are also strongly 'contextual', but in a much more modest way, and out of necessity, being typically infill buildings on tight city centre sites, part of a dense fabric of old-established commercial streets. The areas between the auditorium and the outer street façade take on the character of *pochés*—left-over spaces which form the lobbies, bars and back-of-house facilities. In the recent past, during the era of out-of-town campus planning in the 1950s and 60s when planners zoned city functions into discrete areas, major theatres and concert halls were generally planned as isolated—and in practice frequently desolate—buildings detached from the existing city centre and monumentally sited as 'cultural centres' on the outskirts or in parkland. With no existing street pattern with which to integrate, they were conceived architecturally not as creating urban spaces but as free-standing sculptural forms expressive only of their inner functions.

In North America, the tendency to site performing arts buildings away from the city centre arises largely from fears that the downtown core will remain shabby and run-down. However, experience has shown that the construction of a major arts facility invariably has sufficient impact to guarantee prosperity and renewal for the surrounding area. The act of faith on the part of the building owner to opt for a central but dilapidated part of town should also extend to the architect in creating the design. At the Jefferson Center in Birmingham, Alabama, the designer's instinct in the original competition design was to create an inward-looking 'fortress' building because of a hostile existing environment. Yet a few years later the adjacent areas have become re-vitalized and the building is now unnecessarily introverted. Theatres can themselves effectively form the basis of an entire programme of urban conservation and revitalization, as with the historic Playhouse Square, Cleveland, discussed below. In North America (and elsewhere) a developer is sometimes granted planning approval for a commercial development in return for constructing, or at least providing a site for, a performing arts facility. However, the converse is also possible and increasingly likely in the future, where a performing arts centre incorporates shopping and other commercial development of its own, on a scale larger than the usual foyer restaurant. This is because there is the growing realization that auditoria in North America, to be financially viable, are generally too large to be acoustically excellent, and commercial enterprise is one effective means of making up financially for the reduced box office revenue in the case of a smaller capacity hall. This can, in turn, then act as a catalyst for further, adjacent commercial growth. Interestingly, the integration of theatres and halls with commercial premises was historically traditional in North America. There are many existing examples, for instance the recently renovated fine old concert hall at Worcester, Massachusetts, and Wheeler Opera House in Aspen, Colorado, built above former bank premises.

The Dutch are particularly adept at integrating art with everyday life; at a number of community centres and town theatres in the Netherlands the cultural rubs shoulders with the commercial. The main auditorium space itself often doubles as the weekly market, and forms in itself a 'town square'. The buildings that the Dutch construct for the purpose tend to be modestly unassuming, and serve to emphasize this extension of the arts to the person in the street. Examples are De Meerpaal theatre in the polder village of Dronten, the community centres of the Karregat at Eindhoven and De Flint at Amersfoort (see Chapter 4), and the Speelhuis in the centre of Helmond. The latter is an arts and residential complex by the architect Piet Blom, and consists of a 700 seat theatre known as the Circus, a 150 seat recital hall, and facilities for ballet and other activities. These are surrounded by a 'forest' of 37 extraordinary 'tree-houses', consisting of cubes resting on their corners and raised on stems. In this chapter there is Muziekcentrum Vredenburg in Utrecht, the design of which is based principally around public accessibility, being meant, as the architect puts it, to be 'less of a music temple and more of a music shop'.

Plan at street level. Note the close connection between the hall and the shopping arcade which partly wraps around the foyer.

Muziekcentrum Vredenburg, Utrecht

Owner: Municipality of Utrecht and Hoog Catherijne

Architect: Herman Hertzberger

Acoustic consultants: P. A. de Lange and L. G. Booy

Structural engineers: Adviesbureau D3BN

Mechanical and electrical engineers: Installatie Techniek Bredero

Main contractor: Bredero's Bouwbedrÿf

Opened: 1979

Cost: f48 million (including Hoog Catherijne shops and offices, total 77,600 cub.m [2,700,000 cub.ft])

Principal use: concerts

Seats: 1700–1900 (depending on stage configuration)

Furthest seat from stage: 16m (53ft)

Stage: 168 sq.m (1810 sq.ft)

Volume: 17,000 cub.m (600,000 cub.ft)

Reverberation time: 1.9 sec. at middle frequencies with full audience

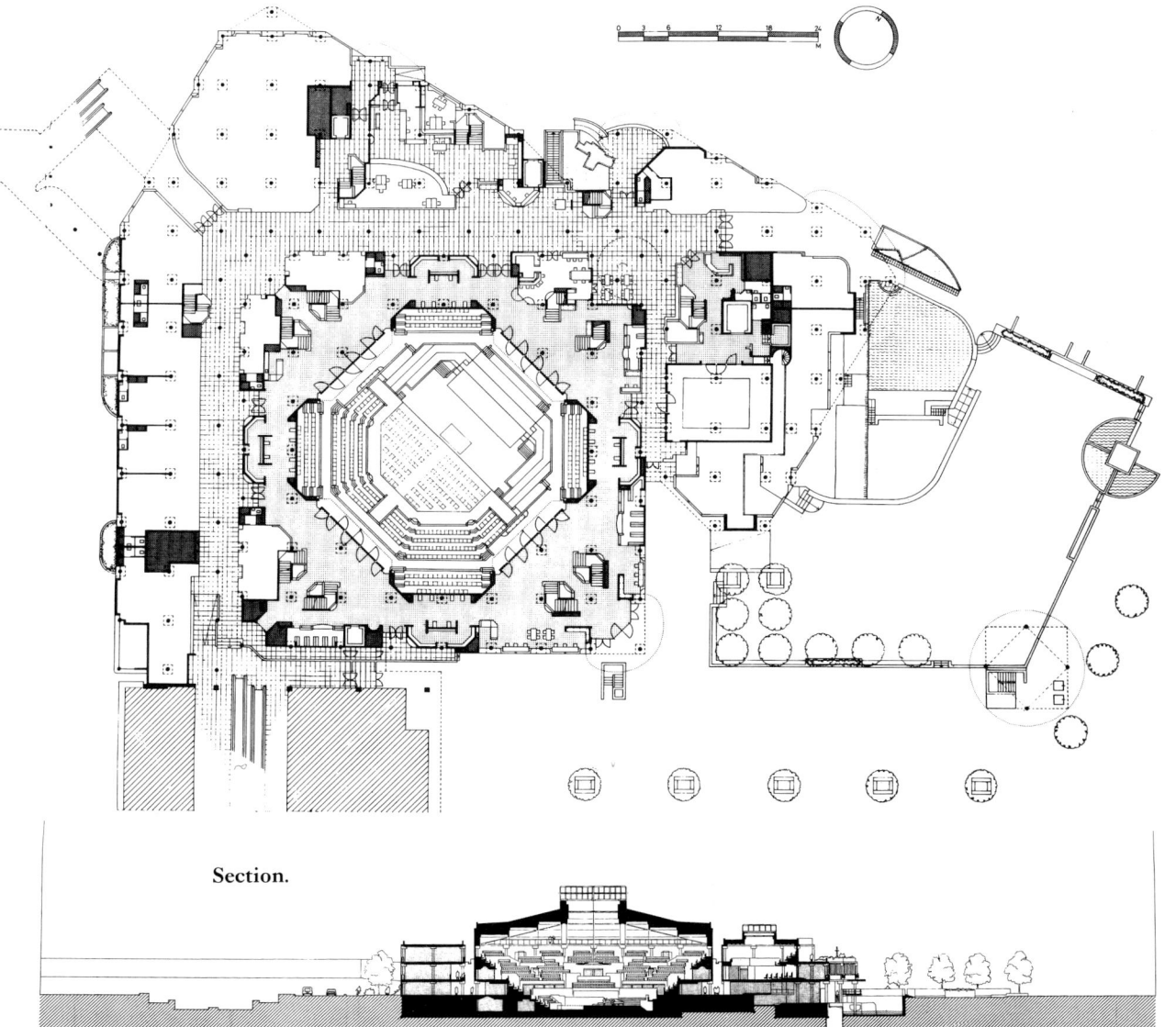

Section.

The unpretentious exterior is conceived as an integral extension of day to day street activity. Note the glazed roof lantern which admits daylight to the hall.

A covered 'street' links the shopping areas with the concert hall, so that the public can hear the music and stroll directly into daytime concerts.

The architect's aim was to make concertgoing highly accessible—even to those who would not normally attend musical events—by integrating the building with the existing town, extending the shopping and other day-to-day activities into the building itself to merge with the foyers—literally opening up the concert hall to the man in the street. The auditorium and foyers were conceived in terms of urban landscape as much as internal functioning, so that the music centre becomes a geographical as well as cultural focus of the town. It forms a transition between the small-scale medieval town centre of Utrecht with its cathedral, canals and old university, and a large and unsympathetic commercial and shopping complex beyond which forms part of the redevelopment and urban motorway programme that threatened to engulf the once sleepy provincial capital in the 1960s.

The main auditorium, which has an almost symmetrical octagonal form, is surrounded entirely by foyers and partly by internal galleried streets. These connect with the adjacent shopping centre and have the small-scale eventful character of the medieval alleyways of the old town. They contain shops, offices, an information centre, exhibition areas, a recital hall, a library and restaurants, and, in the square created in front of the building, a twice-weekly market takes place. Historical fragments—'memories' of buildings that formerly occupied the site—are left visible or are incorporated within the new construction—an ancient monastic wall, and pieces from one of a row of Jugendstil houses including a caryatid, a statue and decorative ironwork. During the free lunchtime concerts, large doors to the auditorium may be opened so that passers-by can hear the music and stroll inside.

The auditorium. The audience is seated around the stage, and no listener is far from the performers.

crete blockwork is used throughout, though this is the least successful aspect as the raw finishes, appropriate perhaps to a school or community hall, appear impoverished and reduce the sense of occasion which for many is an intrinsic part of concertgoing.

The auditorium has an unconventional theatre-in-the-round layout with steeply raked seats on all sides. Even the farthest seats feel surprisingly near the stage, so that all listeners have a considerable sense of involvement with the performance. Hertzberger describes the importance of close visual contact: 'Seeing music being made reinforces the ability to distinguish the various tonal nuances; this is especially helpful to those without a musical background. Moreover, the fact that individual members of the public are able to see each other may also contribute to the emotional tension of the audience as a whole, which may in turn be a source of inspiration for the musicians.' A central glazed lantern admits natural light for daytime rehearsals and concerts, such as the Sunday morning coffee concerts. Catwalks suspended between the main beams accommodate stage lighting and other installations for performances that have an element of theatre.

The concert hall has no less than 25 entrances and the foyers contain many alcoves and vantage points and several bars, in order to distribute large numbers of people evenly throughout the building. Hertzberger's architectural philosophy centres around the idea of the 'individual within a democracy'—the provision of small, almost domestic-scale spaces which the occupants can identify with and 'colonize' within the overall planning framework. At his housing and office projects, the buildings are without conventional finishes, to encourage the occupants to install their personal possessions; at the concert hall, with its transient population, 'humanizing' features and chance irregularities are instead built into the building itself, such as tables with lamps, semicircular alcove seats, shelves and concrete projections at seat and coffee cup height. To emphasize the building's extreme unselfconsciousness, exposed con-

Playhouse Square, Cleveland, Ohio

Client: Playhouse Square Foundation
Architects: Dalton, van Dijk, Johnson & Partners
Theatre consultants: Roger Morgan Studio Inc.
Acoustic consultants: Jaffe Acoustics Inc.
Structural engineer: Barber & Hoffman, Inc.
Mechanical and electrical engineer: Byers, Urban, Klug, White & Partners
Cost: approximately $27 million for the total project

Ohio Theater

General contractor: Dunbar Construction Company
Opened: 1981 (originally opened 1921, architect: Thomas Lamb)
Cost: $3.5 million
Principal uses: classic drama, also ballet, chamber music
Seats: 1035 (originally 1400)
Furthest balcony seat from front of stage: 23.8m (78ft)
Proscenium opening: width 12.6m (41.25ft), height 8.5m (28ft)
Stage: width 22.5m (74ft) left wing to right wing, depth 13.4m (44ft) from apron to rear wall, height to grid underside 19.7m (64.75ft)
Orchestra pit: 25 musicians

Plan (*left*) of the renovated Ohio Theater at orchestra level, with the larger State Theater (*right*) at mezzanine level, shown before renovation. Note the old stagehouse of the State Theater, which is far shallower than that of the smaller Ohio. The seating positions to the rear of the Ohio auditorium are for wheelchairs.

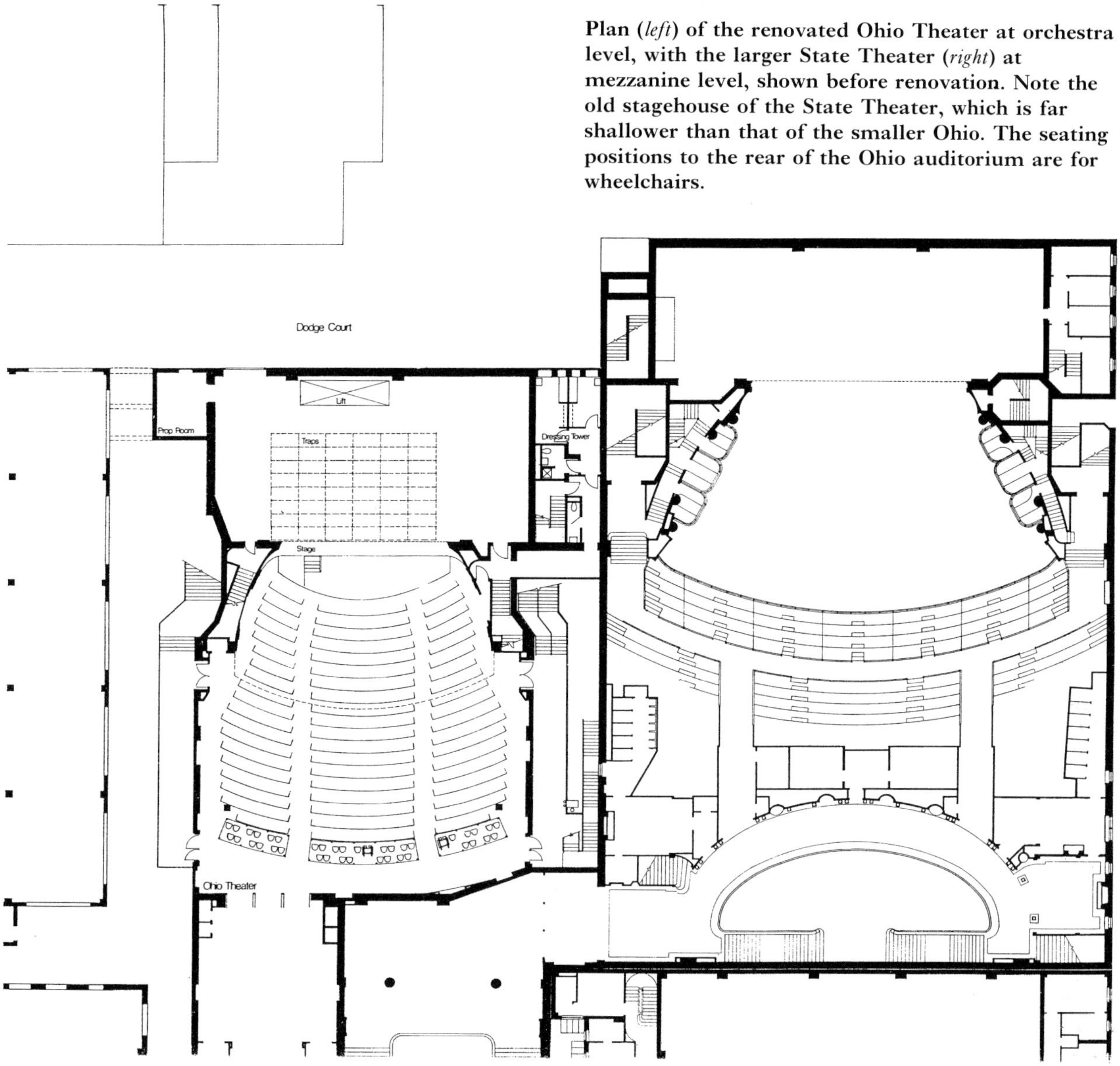

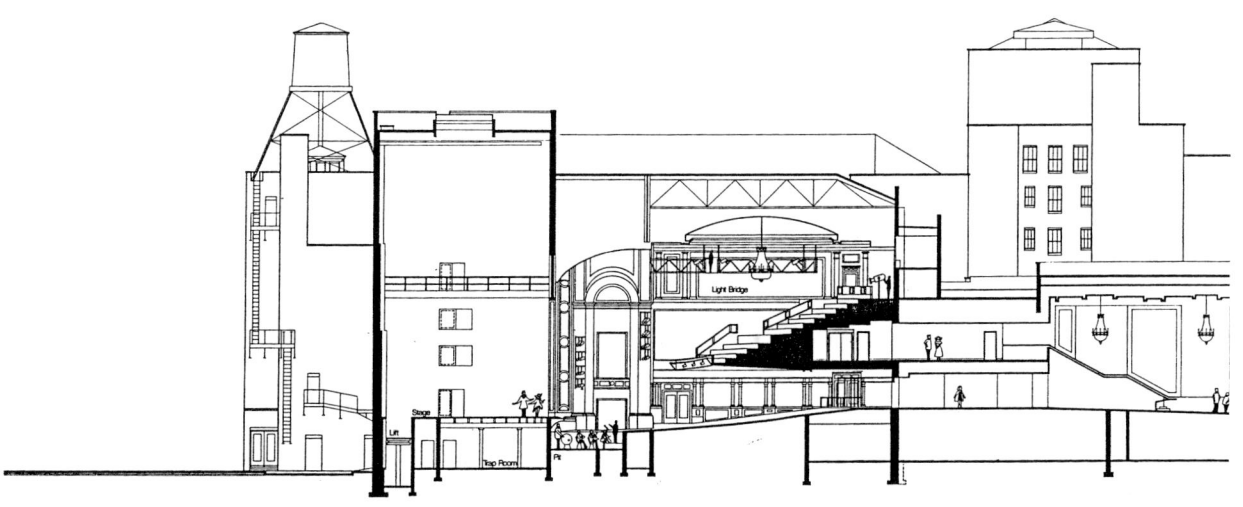

Dodge Court

Lift

Prop Room

Traps

Dressing Tower

Stage

Ohio Theater

Section through the renovated Ohio Theater. Note the profile of the old State Theater stagehouse extending behind the Ohio's.

Light Bridge

Stage

Lift

Trap Room

Pit

State Stagehouse

Ohio Theater

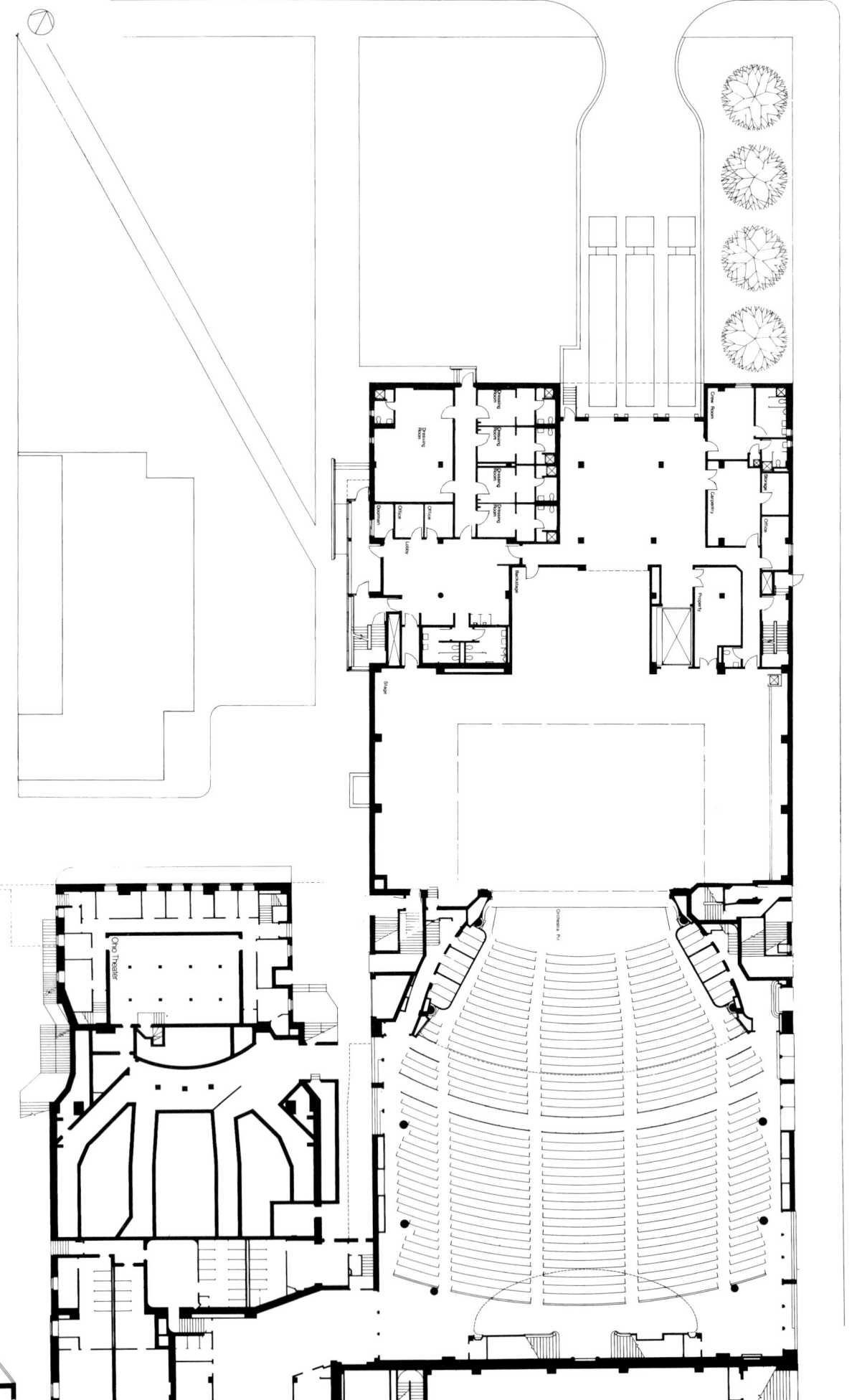

Chester Ave

E 17th St

Dressing Room

Dressing Room

Dressing Room

Dressing Room

Crew Room

Office

Office

Carpentry

Doorman

Lobby

Backstage

Property

Storage

Office

Stage

Orchestra Pit

Ohio Theater

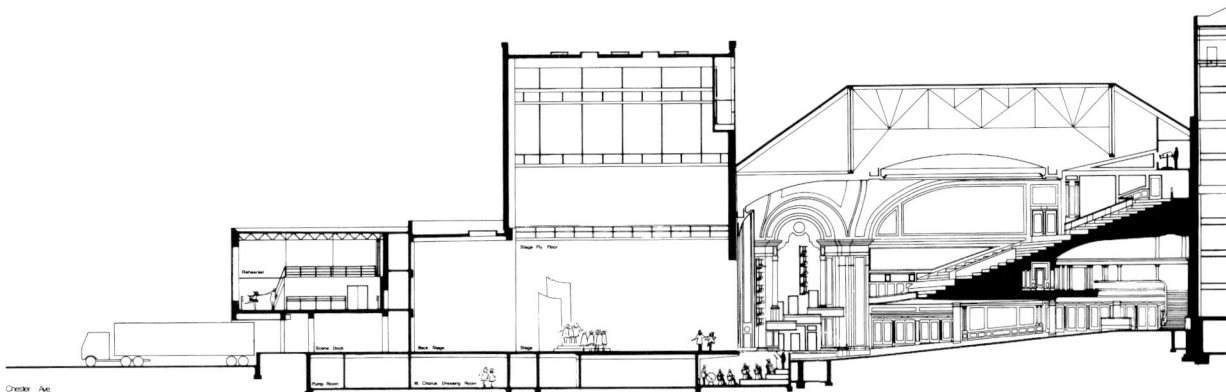

Section through the State Theater and the new stagehouse.

State Theater

General contractor: Hausmann & Johnson

Opened: 1984 (originally opened 1921, architect: Thomas Lamb)

Cost: auditorium renovation $3.5 million, new stagehouse $5.5 million, total $9 million

Principal uses: ballet, opera

Seats: 3150 (originally 3400)

Furthest balcony seat from front of stage: 43.8m (144ft)

Proscenium opening: width 15.8m (52ft), height 8.5m (28ft)

Stage: width 37.1m (122ft) left wing to right wing, depth 41.1m (135ft) from apron to rear wall, height to grid underside 24.4m (80ft)

Flying system: 82 rigging line sets (single purchase counterweight)

Orchestra pit: 8.2m by 14.9m (27ft by 49ft), 75 musicians

In 1972, four magnificent theatres that make up Cleveland's Playhouse Square were threatened with demolition to make way for a car park. They were reprieved at the last minute, and finally saved in 1976 by the creation of the Playhouse Square Foundation, with the vision of converting the four old theatres, which happened all to be grouped together, into a performing arts centre as large as New York's Lincoln Center. The Foundation purchased the theatres in 1977, when they were scheduled as being of historical interest by the government, and fund-raising began. The end result will perhaps be one third of the cost of equivalent new buildings. But, more significantly, the project has provided the cornerstone of a redevelopment effort that is transforming the entire district. Once a decaying urban

Plan of the State Theater with its new stagehouse, at stage level. Note the loading area and three truck bays.

centre with decaying buildings everywhere, Playhouse Square is being revitalized and has already attracted more than 2000 jobs. A major restaurant, office building and shops have opened on the square, and the flow of the population to the suburbs has begun to reverse. Playhouse Square is to date the most ambitious theatre renovation project in the United States, and is likely to be a catalyst to many more in the light of its impact on the urban context.

Two of the theatres at the time of writing have opened, the 1100 seat Ohio and the 3000 seat State, a former theatre and cinema respectively. The two auditoria were originally part of one complex, the Loew's Theater Building, which was completed in 1921 at the start of the movies' golden era, and at the tail end of vaudeville. They were designed by Thomas Lamb, America's leading theatre architect of the time, who built nearly 300 theatres across the country, including the old Madison Square Garden in New York.

The 'Adam neoclassical' style Ohio continued stage productions until the early 1930s. Its subsequent history is typical of such theatres: remodelled as a nightclub in 1935, the enterprise failed by 1938 and it remained dark until 1943, the only occupants being a Coast Guard recruiting office in the outer lobby during the early years of the Second World War. The Ohio then opened as a secondary cinema, and was successful until 1964 when fire destroyed the inner lobby with its paintings, vaulted ceilings and columns. It was 'repaired' with drywall lining and an acoustical tile false ceiling, and the auditorium was painted red throughout to disguise the smoke damage. It finally closed its doors in 1969, when it was later badly damaged by vandals.

The restoration of the Ohio, which took just one year, was largely a matter of bringing the theatre up to present-day standards. The ornamentation was refurbished, and, in the case of the Italian Renaisance style lobby, recreated from old newspaper descriptions. Five floors of dressing rooms were refitted; a sound-reflecting system was installed under the balcony and sound-absorbing fabric applied to the back wall on the orchestra level. A new rake for the orchestra floor was built to improve sightlines and new seating installed, coloured greenish-grey to recall the original colour scheme. Other additions included an orchestra pit for 25 musicians, a new stage lift and seating for the handicapped. One of the users of the building is

The interior of the Ohio Theater after renovation.

the Great Lakes Shakespeare Festival, the only professional classical theatre company in Ohio, and one of the few companies in the United States which plays in rotating repertory. Sophisticated technical systems were therefore required to accommodate the needs of rapid changeover and elaborate staging, and two light bridges were installed in the auditorium to provide the necessary lighting adaptability.

The State Theater was a much more difficult problem. One of the great American movie palaces of the 1920s, with 3400 seats, it has a 67m (320ft) long lobby elegantly decorated with a coffered ceiling, curved marble staircases, Tiffany-style backlit exit signs, chandeliers and spectacular murals by the early American modernist James Dougherty, including one entitled 'The Spirit of Cinema America'. Its size made it economically suitable for large-scale contemporary performing arts touring companies, except that, having been principally for film with only peripheral live theatre usage, the stage was too small.

The solution was to demolish the original stagehouse and build a completely new one, extending over a former car park to the rear, with rehearsal and backstage facilities suitable both for the resident companies, the Cleveland Ballet and the Cleveland Opera, and visitors such as the Cleveland and other, foreign, orchestras, the Metropolitan Opera and Broadway musicals. The stage is one of the largest in the United States, and incorporates a basketweave dance floor, to diffuse the impact of dancers' steps, transferring them layer by layer to the supporting floor slab. Side lighting is suspended directly from the grid. The stage is serviced by a three bay truck dock to the rear, which also connects with the other levels via an

State Theater auditorium after renovation.

New stagehouse to the State Theater, exterior looking at loading docks, with the rehearsal complex above.

fourth theatre, the Allen, was built solely as a movie palace, with virtually no stage at all. It will be several more years before its revival is complete.

elevator. A sunken 'Bayreuth style' orchestra pit for 75 musicians extends under the forestage and incorporates removable panels and curtains for adjusting the orchestral balance. Adjoining the pit at basement level to the rear are musicians' facilities, including a lounge, dressing rooms, office and music library. Above the loading bay and backstage area are two upper level 13.4m (44ft) by 15.8m (52ft) by 6m (20ft) high rehearsal rooms, which connect by a bridge to the adjacent Ohio Theater. Designed to approximate to the actual stage, they again have a five-layer basketweave resilient floor, with splayed walls and curtains for some acoustical variability, openable windows with panoramic views, and the requisite mirrors, hand-bars and associated changing rooms and locker facilities.

The third of the theatres, the Palace, originally seated 3368 and is nearly as grand a theatre as the State, but with a medium size stage that cannot be expanded. Current plans are for its use for popular music events, perhaps with a cabaret-type seating layout on the main floor. The

Centre for Performing Arts, Calgary

Owner: Calgary Center for Performing Arts
Architects: Raines Finlayson Barrett & Partners
Theatre design and technology consultants: Theatre Projects Consultants Ltd
Acoustic consultants: Artec Consultants Inc.
Structural, mechanical and electrical engineers: Reid Crowther & Partners
Construction manager: Cana Construction Co. Ltd
Opened: September 1985
Cost: Can $82 million

Jack Singer Concert Hall

Principal use: symphony concerts
Seats: Total 1846, orchestra and mezzanine 1050, dress circle 250, upper circle 162, balcony 308, loges 76

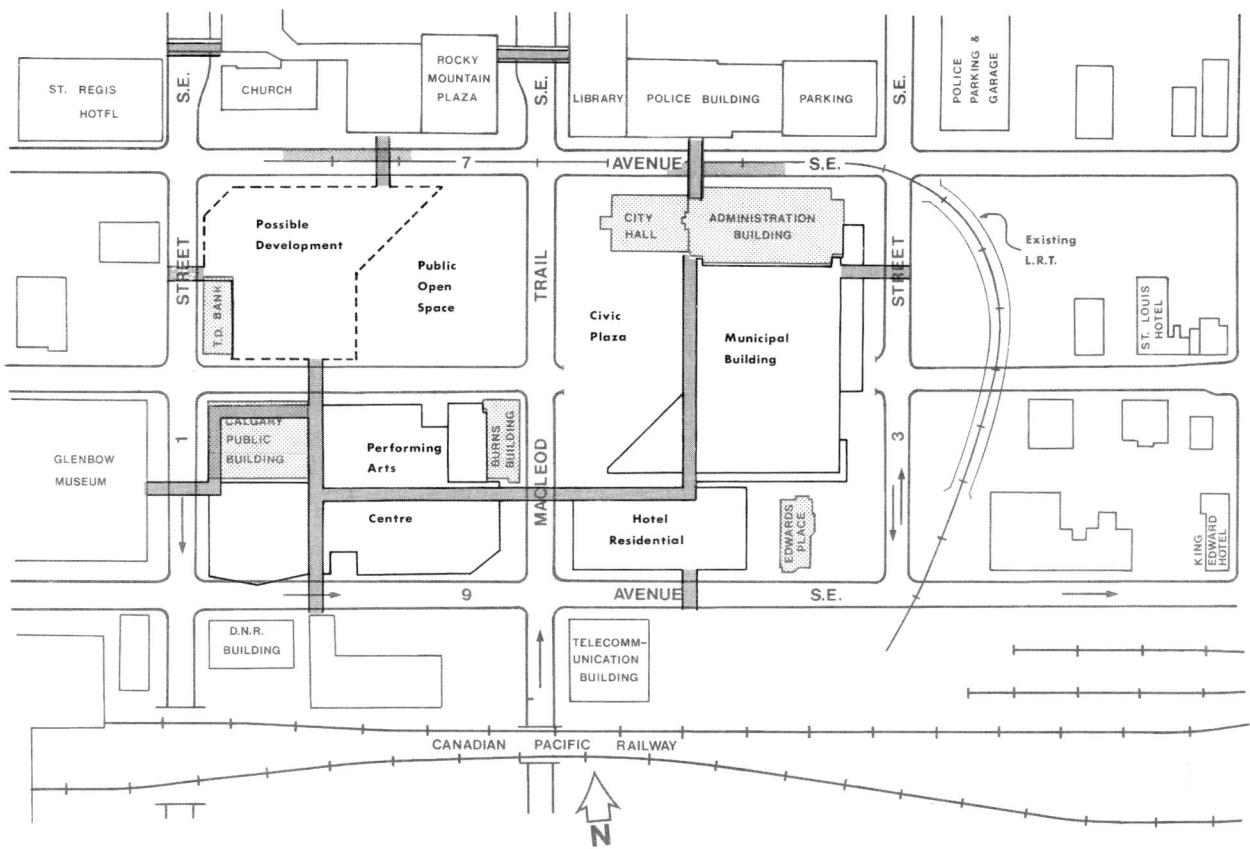

The Centre for Performing Arts in the context of the development plan for the east end of Calgary. The raised walkway system, which links all major downtown developments, can be seen connecting with adjacent buildings.

Plan of the complex, also at the level of the raised walkway, illustrating the relationship of the auditoria. From left to right are the Jack Singer Concert Hall, the Martha Cohen Theatre, and the Max Bell Theatre. In the north-west (*top left-hand*) corner is an existing building which forms a foyer to the concert hall. In the north-east (*top right-hand*) corner is the other historically scheduled building on the block, which is independent of the Centre.

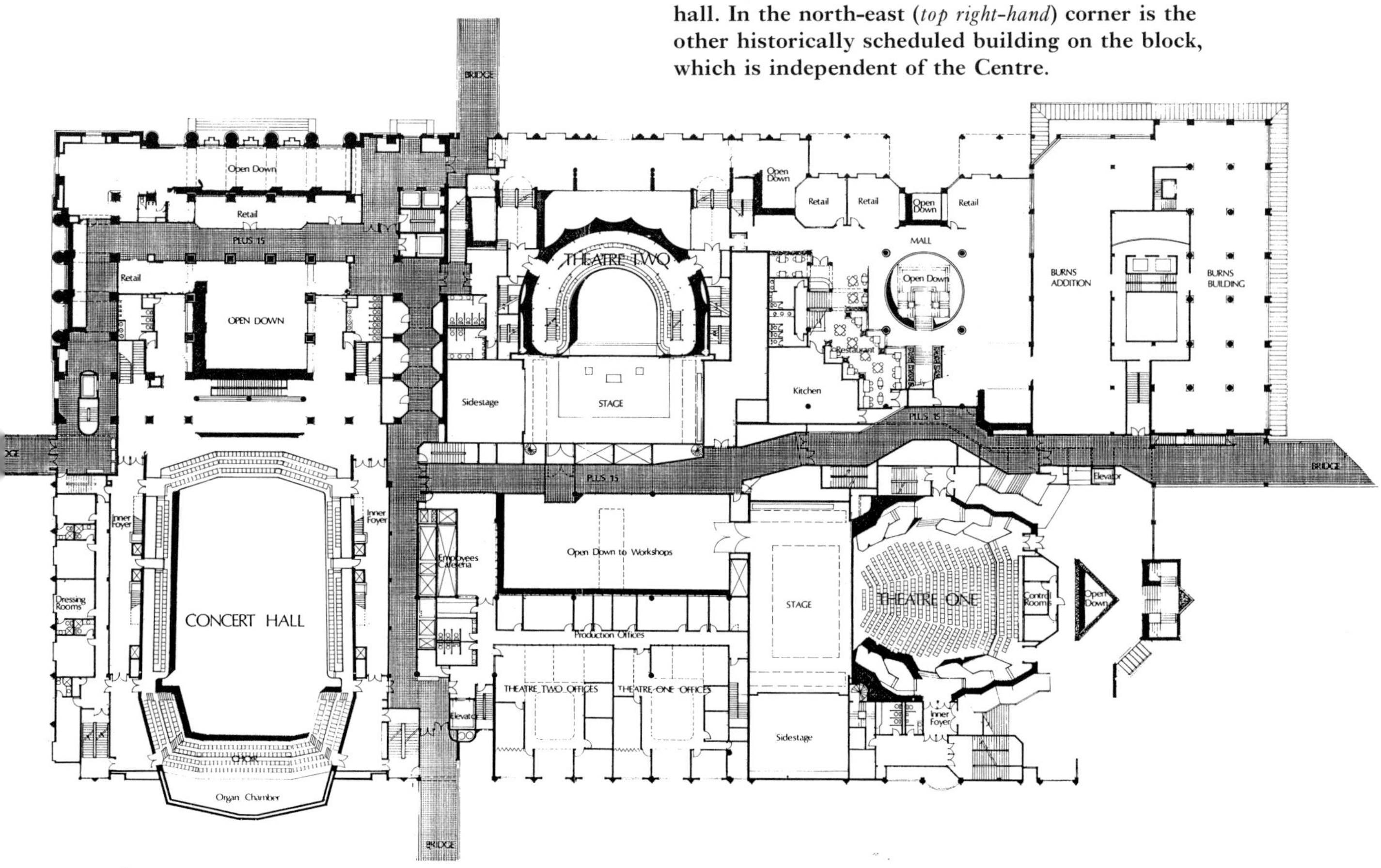

Furthest balcony seat from stage: 35m (115ft)

Stage: width 23m (75.6ft), depth 11.6m (34ft), depth with apron elevated 14.45m (47.4ft)

Orchestra pit: made up of three elevator sections, left, centre and right. Each section can move independently at three working levels: orchestra pit, stage apron, or audience seating. Width 6.8m (22.3ft), length 18m (59ft), depth below stage floor 3.6m (11.8ft), below auditorium floor 2.5m (8.2ft). Number of musicians 65–75.

Volume: 19,230 cub.m (680,000 cub.ft)

Reverberation time: 2.1 sec. at middle frequencies with full audience (estimate)

Maximum background noise level: PNC 15

Max Bell Theatre

Principal use: drama by resident company

Seats: total 750 approx., orchestra and mezzanine 466 approx., boxes 74 approx., first balcony 54, second balcony 67 approx., third balcony 89 approx.

Furthest balcony seat from stage: 22m (72ft)

Each of the auditoria has a separate entrance off the street. In the foreground is the entrance to the Max Bell Theatre, and behind the new construction is the former postal headquarters of 1932, containing an atrium at ground level which forms the entrance to the concert hall.

Proscenium opening: width variable by hinged 'caliper' boxes, maximum 19.2m (63ft), minimum 10m (33ft), height maximum 8.0m (26.25ft), minimum 5.5m (18ft)

Stage: width 34m (111.5ft), centreline to stage right wall 21.9m (72ft), depth 10.2m (33.3ft) from proscenium wall to upstage wall, with option for thrust stage projecting up to 4m (13ft) from edge of stage; height to grid underside 20.9m (68.5ft)

Flying system: 55 rigging line sets at 227mm (9in) centres (single purchase counterweight)

Orchestra pit: formed with lowered forestage elevator, width 2.4m (7.8ft) expandable to 4.85m (16ft) by removing infill scaffolding downstage of elevator, length 9.0m (29.5ft) maximum. Number of musicians 45

Volume: 4400 cub.m (155,370 cub.ft)

Reverberation time: 1.3 sec. at middle frequencies with full audience (estimate)

Maximum background noise level: PNC 15

Martha Cohen Theatre

Principal use: drama by resident company

Seats: total 450, orchestra 170, boxes 43, 1st balcony 46, 2nd balcony 117, 3rd balcony 96

Furthest balcony seat from stage: 11m (36ft)

Proscenium opening: width maximum to the side wall of the stage: 21.9m (72ft), minimum 10.5m (34.3ft), height maximum 7.8m (25.5ft), minimum 5.1m (16.75ft)

The Jack Singer Concert Hall is rectangular, like the old halls of Europe. The variable height canopy is set for different types of performance.

Stage: width 30.9m (101.5ft), centreline to stage left wall 20.8m (68.2ft), depth 9.25m (30.3ft) from proscenium wall to upstage wall, height to underside of grid 17.6m (57.75ft)

Flying system: 37 rigging line sets at 305mm (1ft) centres (single purchase counterweight)

Orchestra pit: formed with two lowered elevators; width 1.8m (5.9ft) using one elevator, 3.6m (1.8ft) using both elevators, length 10.5m (34.3ft), depth below stage floor 2.5m (8.2ft) maximum

Volume: 2160 cub.m (76,270 cub.ft)

Reverberation time: 1.0 sec. at middle frequencies with full audience (estimate)

Maximum background noise level: PNC 15

It is rare—and commendable—for a new performing arts centre to include, in one construction phase, two separate theatres and a full size concert hall. For a young city with

a population of 650,000, the decision to build three performance spaces—the ideal solution to multi-use requirements—was something of an act of faith: a vision conceived in the building boom of the 1970s when land values and the population in oil-rich Alberta soared, towards the time when the city's size and cultural life would fully support three separate auditoria, attracting in turn further businesses and professions to the community.

Unlike the isolated performing arts campuses of the 1960s, Calgary's auditoria are conceived as an urban 'theatre district'. The complex occupies an entire block in the formerly run-down east end of the city, and knits together with circulation and other public areas the three performance spaces and two existing buildings (of which one, the Burns Building, does not form part of the centre). The auditoria are themselves conceived like 'existing buildings', so that the result is more like a fragment of city than a single contained building. Like all large developments in Calgary, the Centre was required to link into the city's raised pedestrian walkway network which is elevated 4.75m (15ft) above street level (known locally as the Plus 15 System, being that many feet above grade), and which will extend to the adjacent City Hall in due course. The walkway plunges as an internal street through the building and, together with corresponding public circulation areas and foyers at ground floor level,

The Martha Cohen Theatre has the appearance of a
U-shaped, galleried Georgian playhouse.

links retail areas, a restaurant, cocktail lounge and a
viewing area from the upper level over the scenery
workshops backstage. The advantages of 24 hour public
access into the building have to be offset against
questions of security and responsibility for capital
payment and maintenance of the public malls.

This brave conception is unfortunately, however,
disappointing architecturally. Sitting between the two
existing large-scale buildings at either end of the block,
the building is an infill in brick, an *ad hoc* medley of
forms, intricately detailed with references to art deco, but
lacking the large-scale façade which the building's proud,
stone-clad neighbours demand.

There are three main auditoria: the 1800 seat Jack
Singer Concert Hall, home of the Calgary Philharmonic,
the 800 seat Max Bell Theatre, home of Calgary's largest
drama group, Theatre Calgary, and the 450 seat Martha
Cohen Theatre, designed to house the Theatre Projects
Alberta company. The Centre will also eventually
include a re-creation of the tiny 1911 Empress Theatre,
the oldest theatre in Calgary, which stood on the site and
whose interior was taken down to be incorporated in the
new building. The three main auditoria are grouped on
three sides around a large backstage area, which includes
common dressing rooms for the two theatres and a
scenery shop, property shop, paint area, costume shop,
laundry room and loading dock. Scenery, properties and
costumes are all provided by a production service
company known as JV Theatre Productions Ltd, jointly

owned by the two resident theatre companies. This
central service block, which also houses the mechanical
equipment—fans, pumps, boiler and chillers—is structurally separated from the performance spaces by
acoustic isolation joints extending from foundation level
to the roof.

In the north-east corner of the site is a substantial pre-
war limestone-clad building known as the Public
Building, which is retained as a heritage site. Originally a
post office from its construction in 1931 until 1961, when
it became government offices, it now serves as the concert
hall's main foyer. Its large central space, formerly the
mail sorting hall with a catwalk at mezzanine level for the
patrolling postal supervisors, now contains stairs and
escalators for access to the different levels of the concert
hall beyond. A third level contains the Centre's
administration, while government departments still
occupy the remainder.

The Jack Singer Concert Hall is orientated north-
south behind the old building, on the line of its central
axis. The hall, named after a local benefactor of the arts,
is a rectangular shoe box, whose shape and dimensions
derive from studies of the successful old halls at Vienna,
Boston, Amsterdam, Glasgow and Zurich. Uppermost in
the design was the desire to attain the strong lateral sound
reflection that is characteristic of the shoe box shape. In
particular, the side balconies are designed so that their
soffits reflect sound to the main floor. For amplified
speech and music the hall is equipped with manually-
operated sound-absorbing curtains and motorized
banners on the upper side walls. For amplified speech
and music these are fully extended to reduce the
reverberant sound level, so that the direct sound level is

more prominent. When the sound system is not in use (for instance for symphony concerts) the loudspeakers are fully retracted into storage pockets with tight-fitting doors. Above the orchestra platform and the front part of the hall is a gigantic vertically adjustable canopy which is set according to the needs of each performance. It is set at high level for large-scale works, allowing the sound to excite the entire cubic volume, and at low level for intimate chamber concerts, directing sound into the audience area, and increasing clarity and loudness. The least satisfactory element of the hall is the painted colour scheme—cool shades of ice blue and burgundy—which decreases the visual intimacy of the auditorium.

The Max Bell Theatre is at right angles to the concert hall, with its main access from the south-east corner of the site. It has a traditional horseshoe shape with a raked main floor surrounded by three tiers of boxes. The proscenium opening is variable, by pivoting the front three boxes on either side of the auditorium. This 'caliper' system of boxes was prompted not only by the need to stage productions of varying scale, but also by the desire of Theatre Calgary to present a large proportion of their work on a thrust stage. When design started the only true thrust stage in Canada was Guthrie's first, the Festival Theatre at Stratford, Ontario, although Edmonton opened the second, the McLab Theatre at the Citadel (November 1984). However, the Max Bell's thrust is slightly different in form from either, being closer in concept to the Elizabethan tradition of pitching a platform 'into the centre of the yard'.

To the north between these two auditoria is the Martha Cohen Theatre, a delightful U-shape theatre with three wood-fronted galleries, modelled on the Georgian playhouse at Bury St Edmunds, Suffolk. The structure is conceived as a 'theatre floating in space' like a stage set, and is freestanding from the enclosing walls. These form an elongated half drum of brickwork divided into a series of convex sections to prevent sound focusing. The galleries are reached by stairs inside the auditorium, as in an Elizabethan open-air theatre. The conventionally equipped flytower is protected by a safety curtain which extends the full width of the auditorium. The proscenium, which is adjustable, can totally retract beyond the side walls; thus there is no throat, and the side walls of the stage can be made to align with those of the apsidal auditorium to form a unified space. Two stage lifts in front of the proscenium offer either an extension to the seating, a forestage or an orchestra pit, and a flat floor at stage level can be formed throughout the space for 'promenade' and environmental productions. Stage lighting, sound equipment or scenery can be attached at any point of the auditorium structure. Over the central area there is a suspended ceiling of tensioned cable mesh with stage lighting above. Retractable fabric banners in the encircling space between the galleries and the outer walls of the auditorium provide variable sound absorption.

The Max Bell Theatre recalls an Italian opera house, with tiers of stepped boxes. The front boxes on either side pivot, to vary the size of the proscenium opening.

CHAPTER 3

Acoustics and the Building Form

Concert Hall Design: Reality and Myth

The later nineteenth century was the golden age of concert hall building. The Grosser Musikvereinssaal, Vienna, opened in 1870; the Stadt-Casino, Basel, in 1876; St Andrew's Hall, Glasgow, in 1877 (burnt in 1962); the Neues Gewandhaus, Leipzig, in 1886 (destroyed 1944); the Concertgebouw, Amsterdam, in 1887; the Atenuel Român, Bucharest, and the old Philharmonie, Berlin, in 1888 (destroyed 1944—both were conversions of existing buildings); the Grosser Tonhallesaal, Zurich, in 1895; Symphony Hall, Boston, in 1900, and the Philharmonic Hall, Warsaw, and the Large Hall of the Moscow Conservatory in 1901—to name but some. All these have a rectangular shoe box shape, and all of them are among the most admired concert halls. Although they cannot be directly imitated for present-day purposes—their seating standards and sightlines are generally poor and they are much smaller than most modern halls—designers have begun to look with increasing interest at the reasons for their excellence. At their best they provide a combination of full-toned blended sound with clarity and intimacy—a quality which can be enjoyed to an extreme degree on present day recordings made in a reverberant hall where the microcphones are positioned close to the orchestra. 'Front row' detail is combined with an overall reverberant sound—the impression in fact of sitting close and far away at the same time. It is a quality listeners have come to expect as a result, but which is difficult to achieve in a live concert.

There are, however, several points about these historic halls that inform our thinking today.

Rectangular halls have a substantial cubic volume relative to the sound-absorptive audience area, and there is also a large sound-reflective sidewall and ceiling area. Sound energy is retained and the reverberation time is relatively long—typically around two seconds at middle frequencies with a full audience, and longer in the bass frequencies. The theory of reverberation was developed as late as 1895–1900 by Wallace Clement Sabine, a young professor of physics at Harvard University. Reverberation is the 'ringing' which persists after the sound source in a room has stopped, and reverberation time is the time, in seconds, required for the average sound energy to decay beyond audibility, to one-millionth of its initial steady value. Reverberation time remained until the 1950s practically the sole criterion for determining a hall's acoustics, largely because it was one of the few aspects of room acoustics that could easily be measured.

Reverberation time, however, only partly determines the suitability of rooms for music or speech. The relative strength of direct and early-reflected sound to reverberant sound, and especially the position of sound-reflecting surfaces, are now regarded as more important to clarity, loudness and the acoustic 'scale' of a space. In a cathedral there may be excellent speech intelligibility for a small number of seats located near the pulpit, but very poor speech intelligibility for most seats located far from the preacher; the reverberation time for all seats, meanwhile, remains more or less the same. Imagine too a solo violinist practising at the front of the platform in a very large, empty concert hall with a reverberation time of more than two seconds. He may find the experience surprisingly like playing in the open air—where the reverberation time is more or less zero—because he is at a great distance from the walls and stage surround. Conversely, in a small, sound-absorptive Italian baroque opera house, the same musician may experience good 'response' from the acoustics as he hears the sound reflected from the nearby surfaces of the room. In such a theatre, where the reverberation time—perhaps less than one second when full of people—tends towards that of the open air, yet the voices and instruments are usefully reinforced by sound reflection from the balcony fronts and ceiling. In the open air itself, where the reverberation time is theoretically zero, we are still highly aware of the effect of sound reflection, as for instance when the chopping of a woodcutter's axe reflects off tree trunks and reverberates through the forest.

The particular advantage in this respect of the shoe-box hall is the direction from which the sound is reflected. Every listener receives strong early-reflected sound energy that is predominantly lateral rather than overhead. The reflections are returned from the wall-ceiling junction and from the sidewalls and gallery soffits. Through the binaural hearing process our two ears compare the time of arrival, loudness and tone of the laterally-arriving sound signals. For each 'particle' of arriving sound this provides the listener with a sense of its direction, and for multi-directional sound, a three-dimensional impression of space. This theory of sound perception as it relates to concert halls was only discovered in the late 1960s, and is now regarded as of such significance that it has come to dominate recent concert hall design.

In addition to the cubic volume of a hall and its shape, the other important variables are the construction materials. A popular myth has arisen during this century (which musicians in particular still generally believe) that concert halls are analogous to stringed instruments in that, if the walls are lined with thin wood panelling backed by an airspace, they will resonate and usefully reinforce the sound in the hall. In reality, these halls were constructed of heavy, sound-reflective materials—thick plaster, masonry, or heavy wood panelling that is rigid—which reflect sound energy at most frequencies, maximizing the strength and fullness of tone of sound in the hall. The vibration of thin panelling only causes the sound to be absorbed in the lower and middle frequencies, and reflected in the upper frequencies. Halls that are lined in this way have a bright, clear, non-reverberant sound quality, suited perhaps to speech and opera, but lacking the fullness of tone required for the repertoire of nineteenth-century orchestral music. (However, because of the popular belief to the contrary, there may be psychological advantage to be gained in using wood, provided it is totally rigid and perhaps veneered onto masonry!)

But the main acoustical advantage of most older halls is their small size compared with typical twentieth-century auditoria. The sound has great impact in such halls because of the short distances reflections have to travel to reinforce the direct sound. Also, because people are the principal sound-absorbing element, there is a slight loss of strength in a large hall through sound energy being absorbed. Most old halls are small not only because they have fewer seats but because the area per seat was less. If the historic halls were replanned to current standards of safety and seating comfort (assuming, say, an area of 0.71 square metres per seat, equivalent to Singer Hall at the new Calgary Centre for Performing Arts), their audience capacity would be little more than recital hall size. For instance, the 1680 seat Musikvereinssaal, Vienna, would seat only 1390 people. Similarly, the 1560 seat Neues Gewandhaus, Leipzig would have seated just 1270; the 2206 Concertgebouw, Amsterdam would seat 1600; the 1546 seat Tonhallesaal, Zurich, 1230; and the 2631 seat Symphony Hall, Boston, 1960. This means that in the larger halls of today the efficiency of the acoustical design has to be greater to maintain the same strength of sound.

Concert halls in the twentieth century developed very different acoustical qualities to their predecessors. This was largely the result, not of musical requirements, but of a financial demand for accommodating larger audiences. Greater seating comfort also came to be expected, with wider-spaced, upholstered seats. To avoid excessive distances from the front of the hall to the rear when accommodating the larger audiences, the designer's response was to push apart the acoustically 'useful' sidewalls to form a fan shape. The splayed angle of the walls, however, meant that they no longer reflected sound to the middle of the auditorium and the ceiling became the dominant sound-reflecting element in the hall. As such, the ceiling height was reduced, and the resulting high absorption and low cubic volume made the halls sound 'dead'.

The best recent concert halls have attempted to integrate the advantages of the shoe box hall with present-day needs of size, sightline, comfort and safety. It is not possible to reproduce the characteristics of the old rectangular halls simply by retaining their proportions but increasing the dimensions. This would have the effect of altering the arrival time of the direct and reflected sound, substantially reducing its impact. Instead, the design must be as efficient as possible; for instance, surfaces important for lateral reflection may be angled over the audience area to strengthen the sound in the middle of the main floor, and the auditorium walls or upper wall and ceiling surfaces may be angled into a reverse fan shape to increase the lateralness of reflected sound. These and other solutions are discussed in the context of the halls in this chapter.

Christchurch Town Hall and Michael Fowler Centre, Wellington

Christchurch Town Hall (Main auditorium)

Owner: Metropolitan Local Authorities of Christchurch

Architects: Warren & Mahoney

Acoustic consultant: A. Harold Marshall

Structural engineers: Holmes Wood & Poole

Mechanical and electrical engineers: Maindonald & Associates

Quantity surveyors: Russell Drysdale & Thomas

Main contractor: Chas S. Luney Ltd

Opened: 1972

Primary use: concerts, but capable of other uses such as exhibitions

Seats: total 2338 (the 400 choir seats can provide an additional 324 seats when not used by the choir), stalls 1428 (of which 650 are removable for a clear floor area), gallery 910

Stage: 186 sq.m (2000 sq.ft)

Furthest seat from stage front: 28m (92ft)

Volume: 20,700 cub.m (730,930 cub.ft)

Reverberation time: 2.4 sec. at middle frequencies with full audience (Barron)

Michael Fowler Centre, Wellington

Owner: Wellington City Council

Architects: Warren & Mahoney

Acoustic consultants: Harold Marshall and Associates and Jerald R. Hyde

**Christchurch
Town Hall**

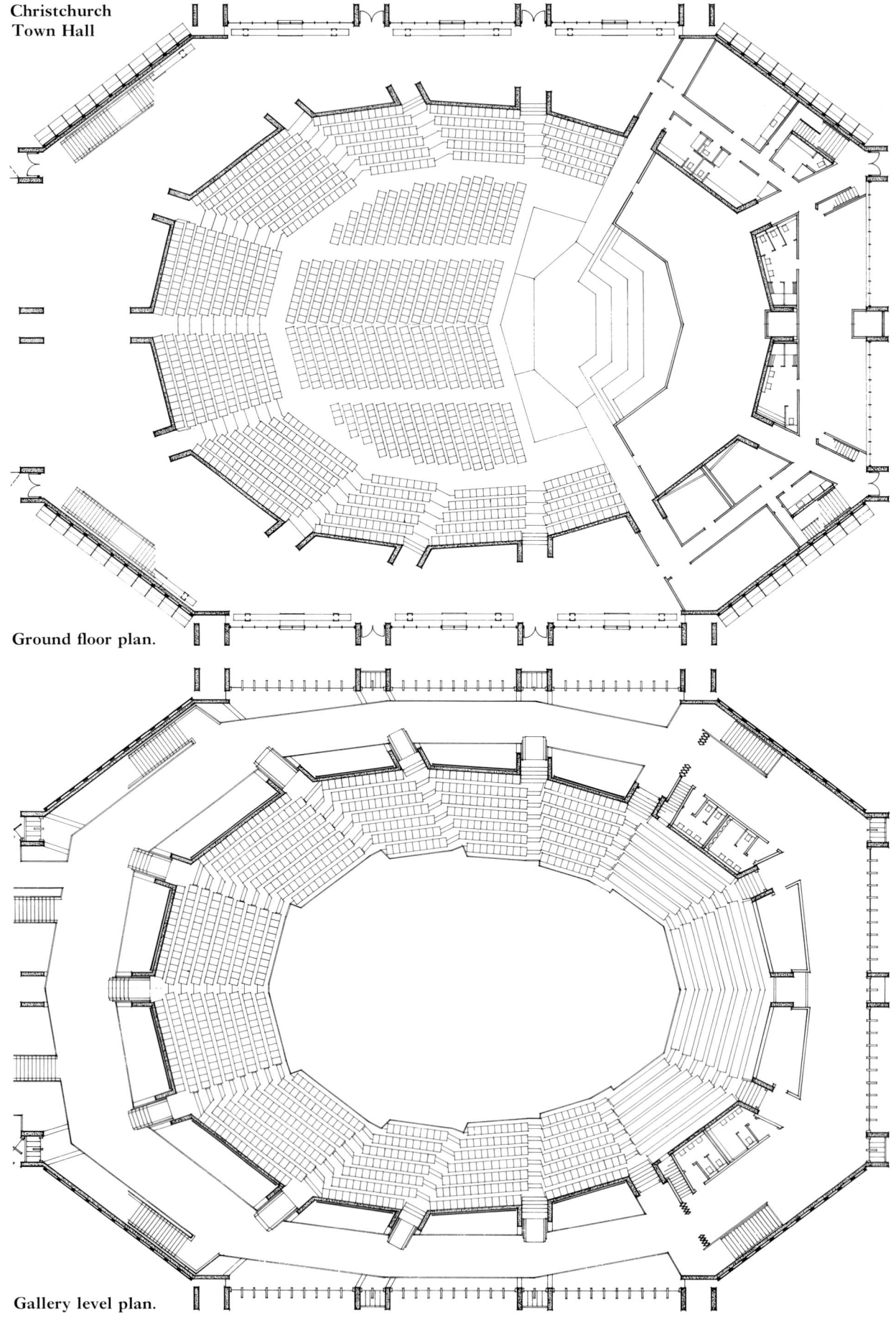

Ground floor plan.

Gallery level plan.

Longitudinal section.

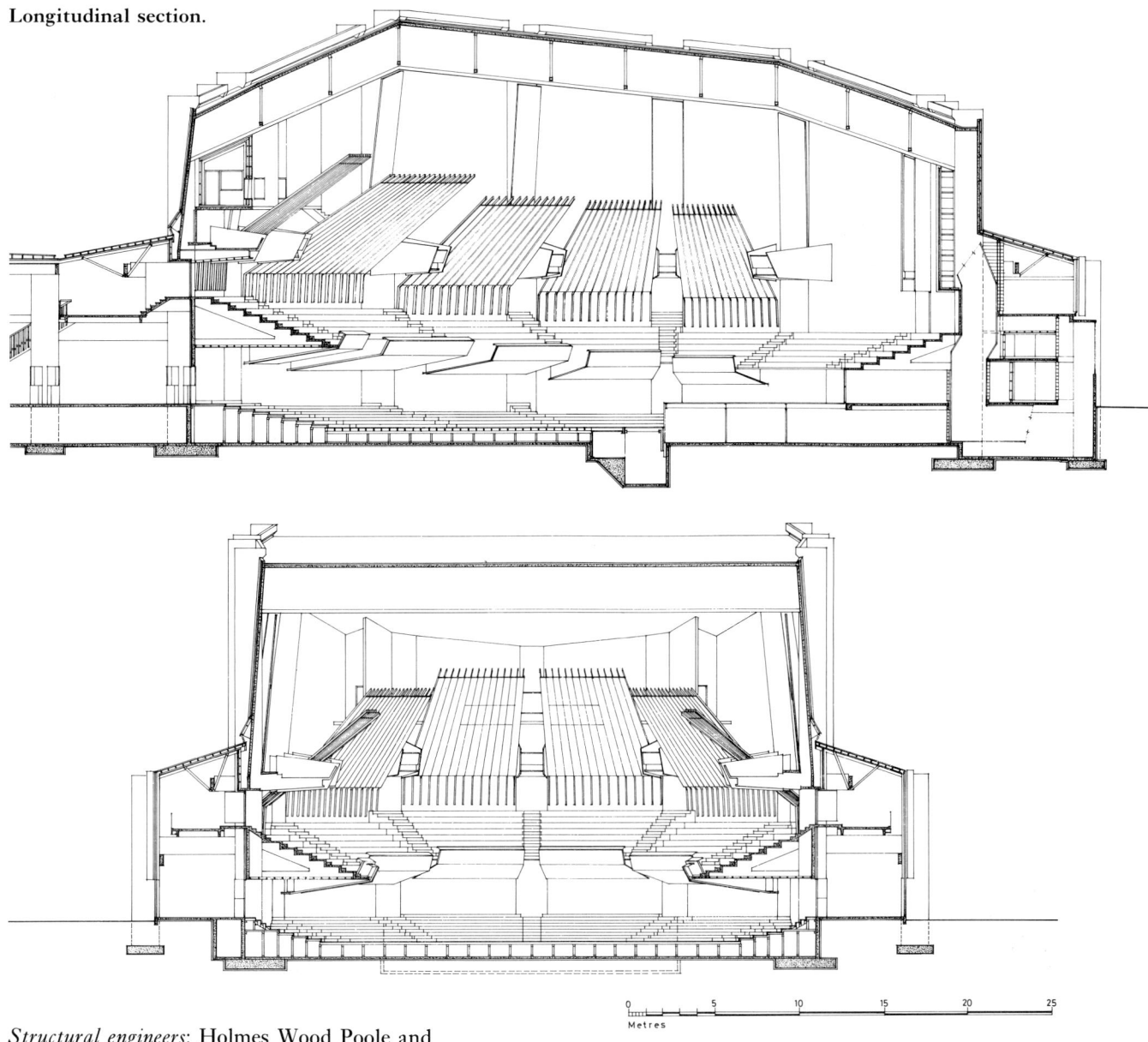

Metres
0 5 10 15 20 25

Cross section.

Structural engineers: Holmes Wood Poole and Johnstone

Mechanical and electrical engineers: Maindonald Miller and Associates

Quantity surveyors: Russell Drysdale and Thomas

Main contractor: Fletcher Development and Construction Ltd

Opened: 1983

Cost: NZ $17.9 million

Primary use: concerts, also conferences

Seats: total 2451, main floor 1459 (592 in conference desk configuration), gallery 992, and in addition choir seats 115 and 158 demountable seats

Furthest gallery seat from stage front: 30m (99.5ft)

Stage: 186 sq.m (2000 sq.ft)

Volume: 22,700 cub.m (800,000 cub.ft)

Reverberation time: 2.2 sec. at mid-frequencies with full audience (calculated)

These two similar elliptical concert halls, both in New Zealand, are designed fundamentally around the discovery described above, of the overriding importance of early arriving lateral sound reflections in concert halls. These provide a sense of 'spatial impression' and envelopment by the sound, because of the binaural hearing process, as well as increasing clarity and loudness. The two halls are an interesting case of a theoretical idea being translated into built form—and also of close co-operation between architects and an acoustical research team.

Although strong lateral reflections were known to be a major attribute of the narrow concert hall in the Leipzig tradition, the required seating capacities of both the New Zealand halls were roughly twice those of the venerable but smaller historical model. At Christchurch and Wellington the aim was to combine laterally reflected sound energy with a relatively broad arena plan where a

The auditorium arena with the suspended array of reflecting panels.

large number of seats could be close to the stage—hitherto something of a contradiction in terms. This was achieved by controlling lateral sound with a suspended array of large reflecting surfaces along each side of the hall, tilted inwards over the galleries. Projecting over the heads of the listeners, the reflectors in effect reduce the width of the hall acoustically. The panels are independent of the halls' acoustical boundaries which determine the air volume and therefore the reverberation time. The cubic volume could be adjusted at the design stage for the correct reverberation time without this affecting the relationship of the sound reflecting surfaces to the listener—as with halls that rely upon sound reflections from the ceiling and other enclosing surfaces.

The design for Christchurch Town Hall was won in competition in June 1966; construction commenced early in 1969, and the building was opened three and a half years later. The 2338 seats of the concert hall are divided between a main floor and a 'semi-surround' arena gallery which continues around the platform as choir seats which are sold when not in use by a choir. The tilted reflectors, which are separated to ensure that the reverberant upper volume of the hall is coupled with the seating areas, are built of laminated 50mm (2in) thick Pinus Radiata, with a clear varnish finish. Between the reflectors are projecting perches for television cameras and stage lighting and in their front ends are air supply outlets. Further supply-air is fed from the ceiling and gallery soffits and used air is extracted beneath the seating. Out of sight behind the reflectors is a continuous walkway linking the camera and lighting platforms with the light and sound control rooms. The main ceiling is made of 1.2m by 2.4m (4ft by 8ft) panels of 50mm (2in) mahogany-veneered particle board, with 240 spotlights set in 75mm (3in) recesses. Above the ceiling is a 2.1m (7ft) high walk-in roof space,

Michael Fowler Centre, Wellington

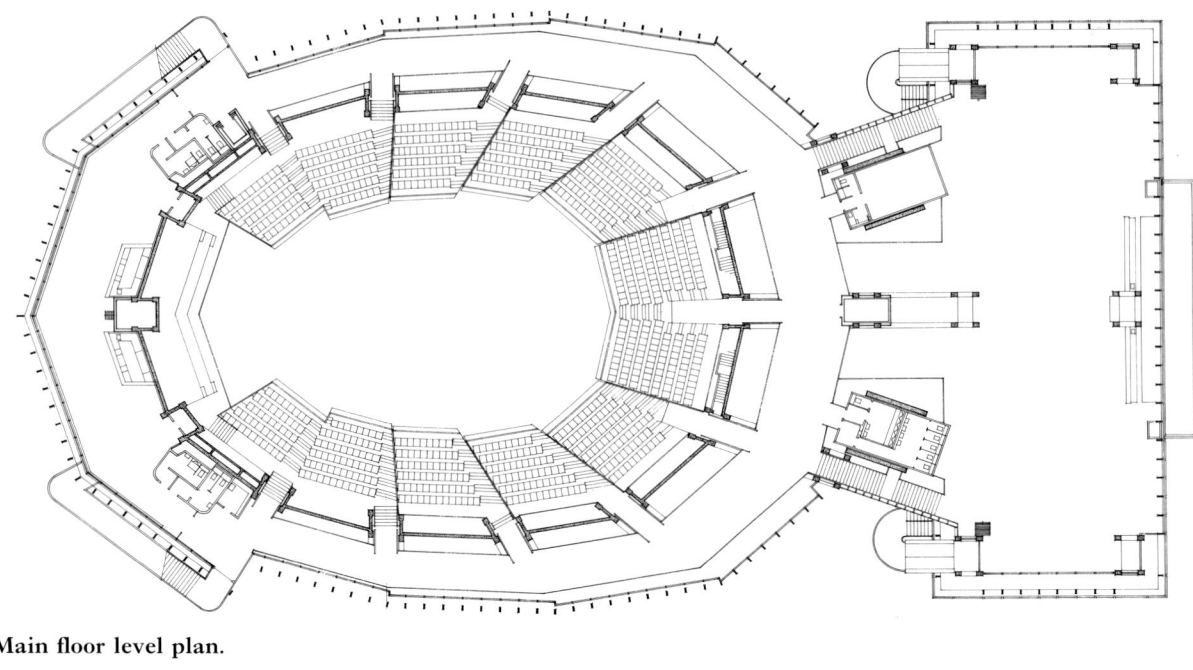

Main floor level plan.

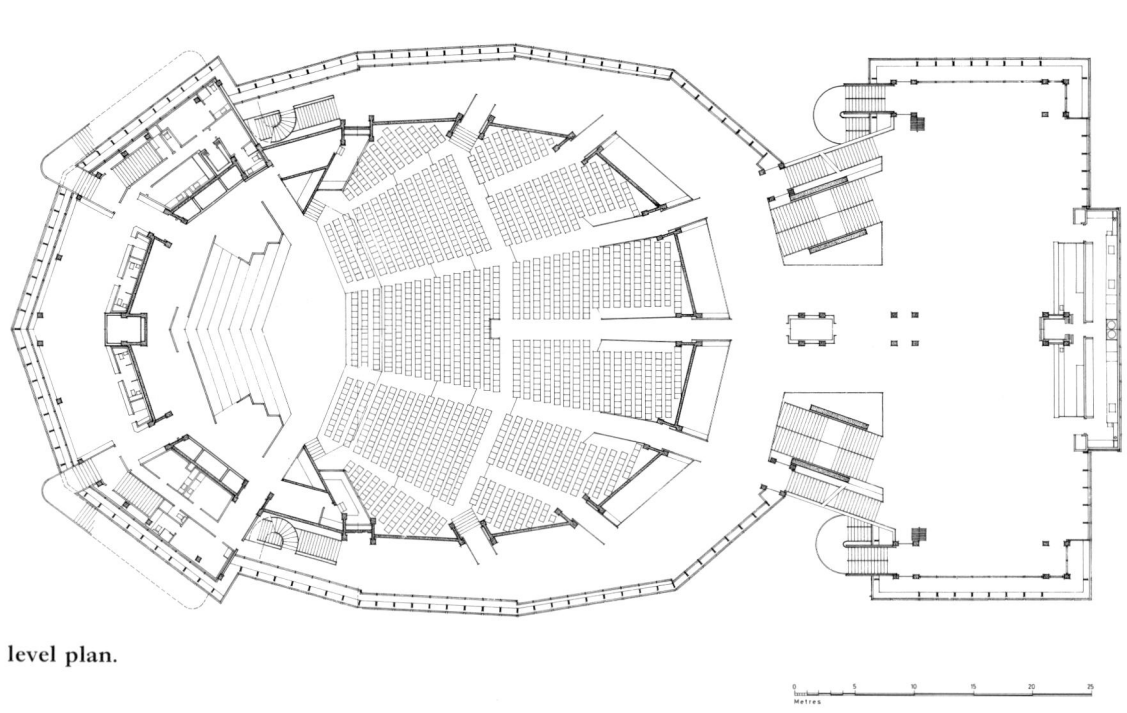

Gallery level plan.

with a pre-cast concrete outer skin supported by steel trusses.

The wooden floors of the auditorium and stage area are of 75mm by 25mm (3in by 1in) Australian 'Brush Box' laid over 12mm (0.5in) plywood, finished with polyurethane and wax polish. The front of the orchestra platform is divided into three movable sections mounted on stage elevators which can be raised or lowered to become part of the auditorium floor or an extension of the main platform. The middle platform can also descend to two basement levels—a piano store under the auditorium and a large store for the stalls seating when a clear

The design of the tilted reflecting panels was slightly modified with wooden strips to diffuse sound. This prevents 'false localization', the impression that the sound originates from the direction of the reflectors rather than the stage (*opposite and overleaf*).

Longitudinal section.

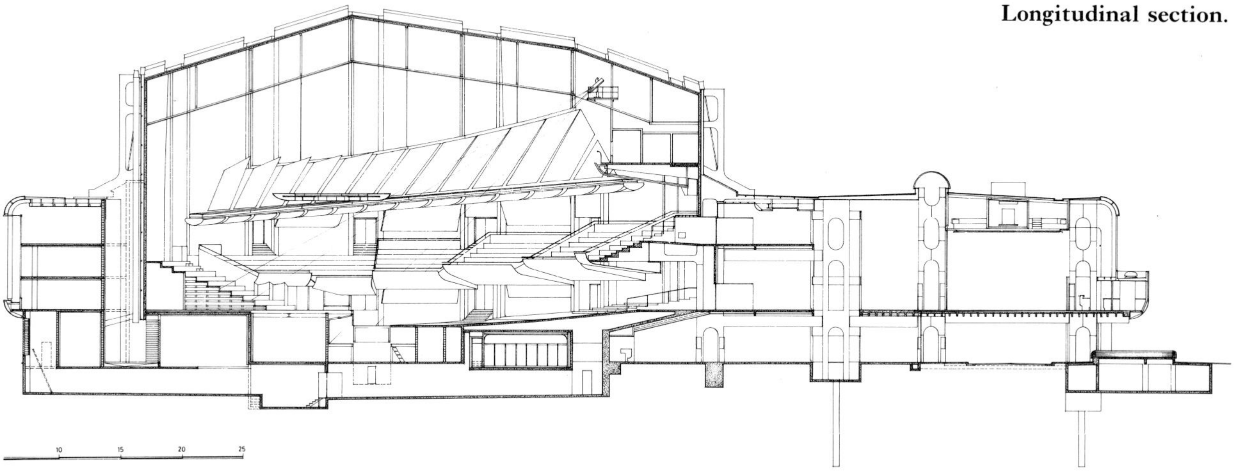

10   15   20   25

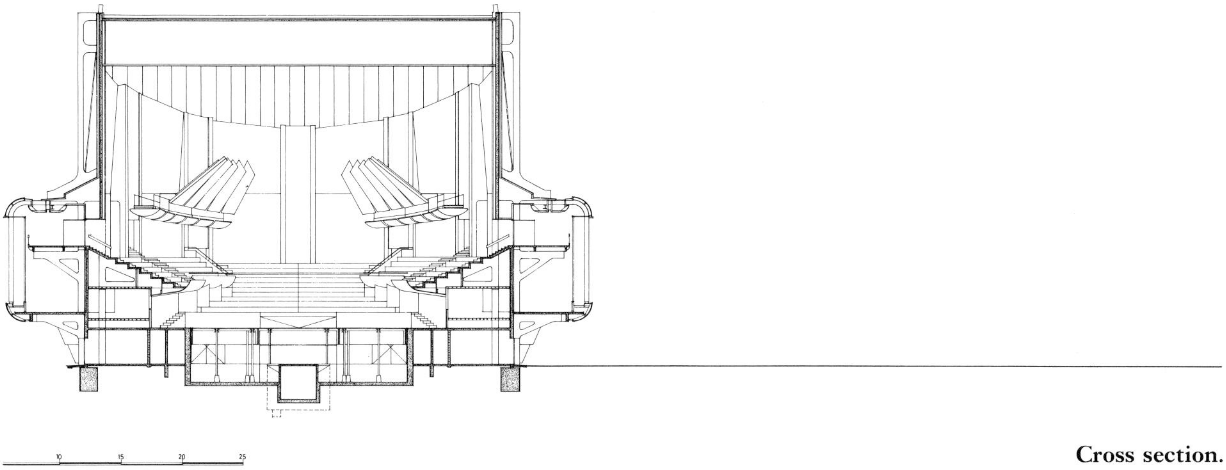

10   15   20   25

Cross section.

auditorium floor is required. Tiered rostra for further platform adjustment are stored at stage level below the choir seating.

When the same design team was commissioned in 1975 to build a concert hall for Wellington, a similar form was adopted because of the success of the Christchurch auditorium. The basic design could then be modified in the light of measurements taken in the completed hall. The reverberation time in Christchurch was found to be different to that originally predicted because, in reality, the reflectors tended to mask the sound-absorptive seating areas from the reverberant upper volume of the room. This effect was taken into account in the choice of the volume at Wellington to provide a reverberation time at just over 2.0 seconds. In the intervening ten years, too, a large body of research had been carried out into this

type of hall and the psycho-acoustic effects of lateral reflection. It had been discovered that reflections from the side of the listener which are too strong or too early relative to the direct sound can cause 'false localization'— the impression that the sound source is actually in the direction of the reflectors rather than the stage. This is avoided by providing an uneven reflecting surface, called a quadratic residue diffuser (QRD). These surfaces are mathematically determined stepped sequences which scatter the sound through the full 180 degrees, regardless of the angle of incidence. Consequently, the timber reflectors were this time divided into 300mm (1ft) strips with varying depths, interrupted by 20mm (.78in) thick fins. An acoustical study of this and other aspects was then carried out with a 1:10 scale model, and modifications made prior to construction. For instance, in certain areas, the fins returned some of the high frequency sound to the orchestra rather than to the listeners, and when the surfaces concerned were modified the effect disappeared. Also, another area was found to be deficient in early lateral energy, and extra reflectors were added to provide it.

On the site immediately adjacent is Wellington's old Town Hall, containing a traditional rectangular concert hall. The intention was to demolish this on completion of the Michael Fowler Centre. In the end, the existing facility was retained as overspill accommodation; this made Wellington probably the only city in the world to have a rectangular concert hall and an arena concert hall next door to one another for immediate comparison!

Boettcher Concert Hall, Denver, Colorado

Owner: The City and County of Denver

Architect: Hardy Holzman Pfeiffer Associates (Architect for planning the Denver Center for the Performing Arts: Kevin Roche, John Dinkeloo & Associates)

Acoustic consultant: Jaffe Acoustics, Inc.

Theatre consultant: Jules Fisher

Structural engineer: Ketchum Konkel Barrett Nickel Austin

Mechanical engineer: Cosentini Associates

Lighting consultant: Jules Fisher & Paul Marantz, Inc.

Construction manager: Turner Construction Company

Opened: 1978

Cost: $13 million

Principal use: orchestral concerts

Seats: 2750

Furthest balcony seat from stage front: 26m (85ft)

Stage: 223 sq.m (2400 sq.ft), with hydraulic platform lifts in the raised position 340 sq.m (3660 sq.ft)

Orchestra pit (hydraulic platform lift in lowered position): 80 musicians

Volume: 35,500 cub.m (1,250,000 cub.ft)

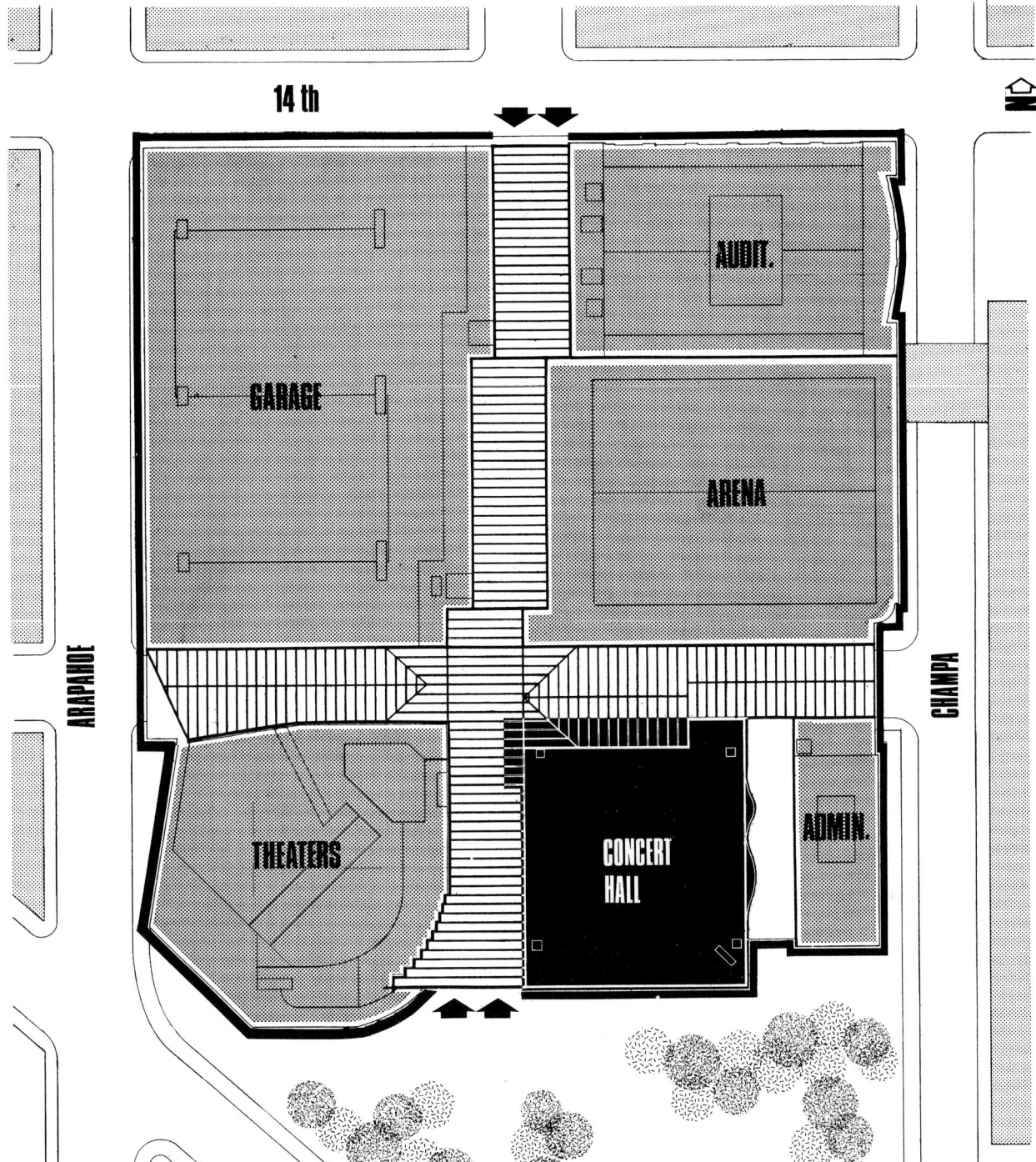

Site plan of Denver Center for the Performing Arts.

Maximum background noise level: PNC 15 (estimate)

Reverberation time: 2.0 sec. at middle frequencies with full audience

The hall forms part of the Denver Center for the Performing Arts, a complex of four square blocks in downtown Denver, an expanding city spectacularly sited against the Rocky Mountains. The performance facilities are linked by a great raised walkway which is partly enclosed by a glazed vault in the manner of Milan's Galleria. This is due to be extended over the remainder of the cruciform circulation spine by the end of 1989. The walkway is an extension of the city's street system and will eventually link with Denver's pedestrianization programme which has so far created Sixteenth Street mall a short distance away. The Center for the Performing Arts incorporates, among other facilities, the Denver Symphony Orchestra's former home, the elderly Auditorium Theatre and a theatre complex designed by the architects Roche Dinkeloo, who also designed the masterplan for the Center as a whole.

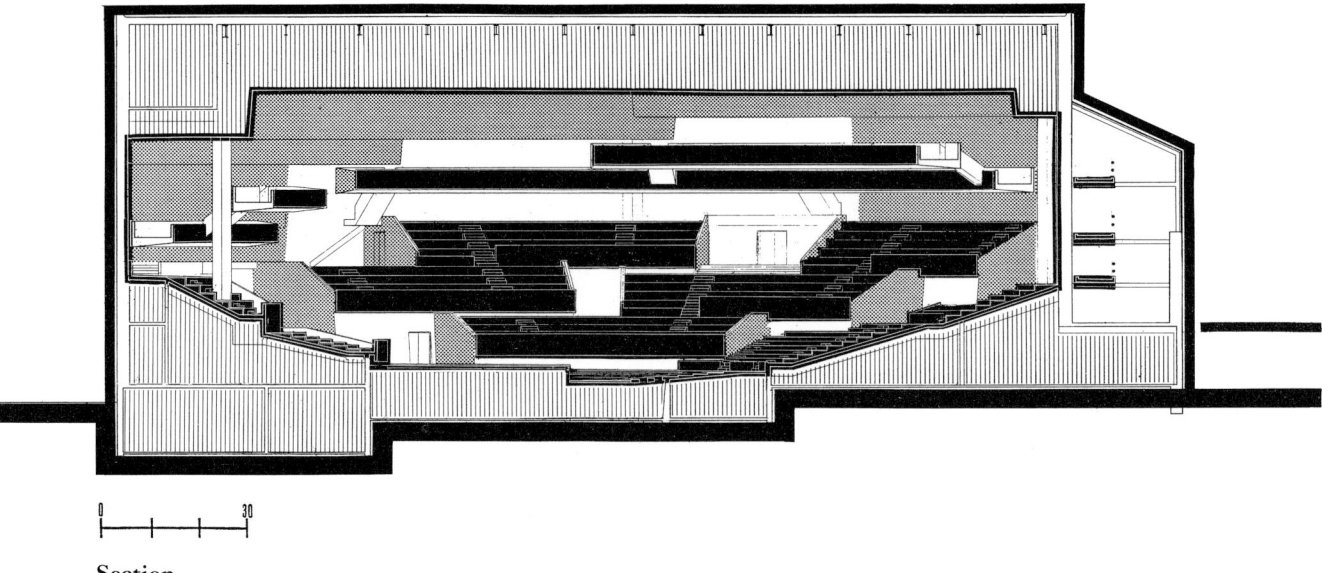

0   30

Section.

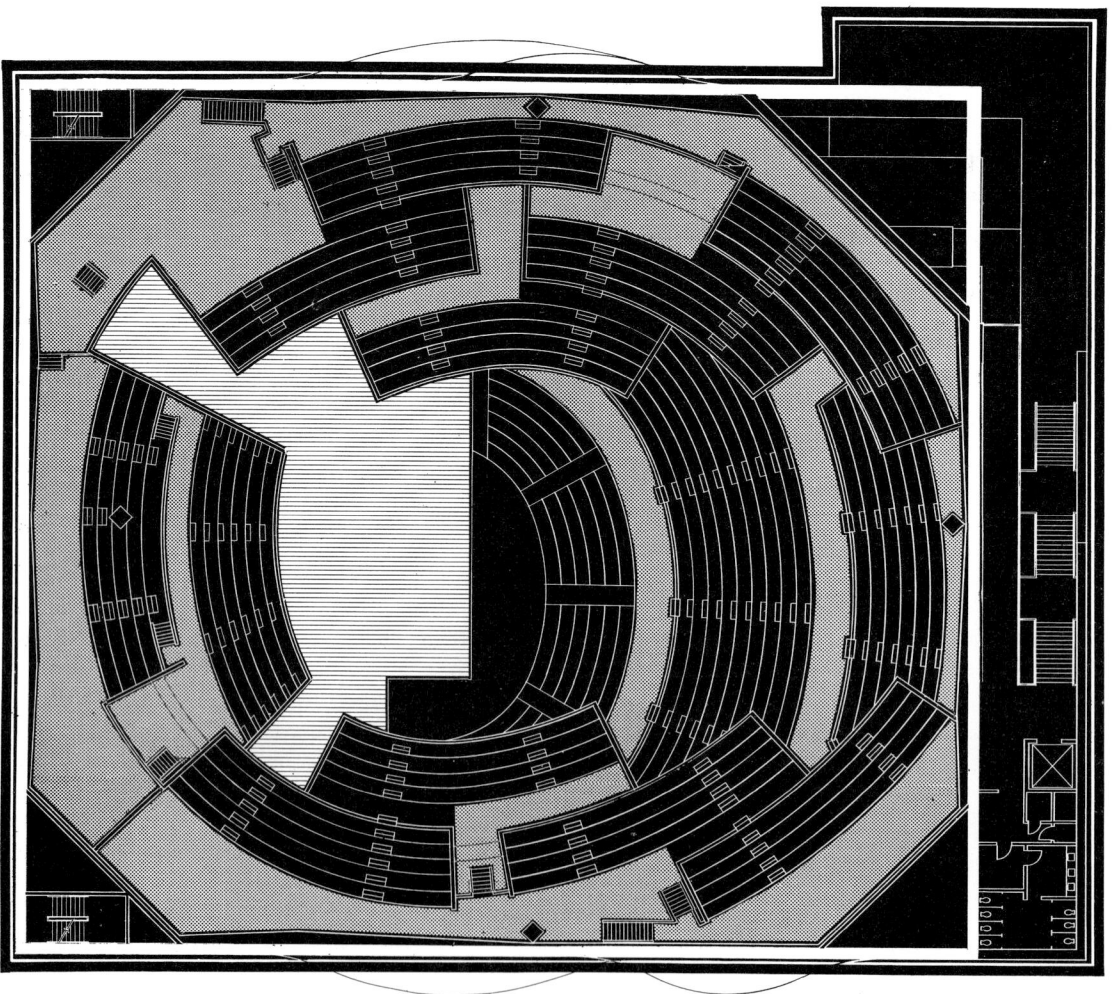

Concert hall plan.

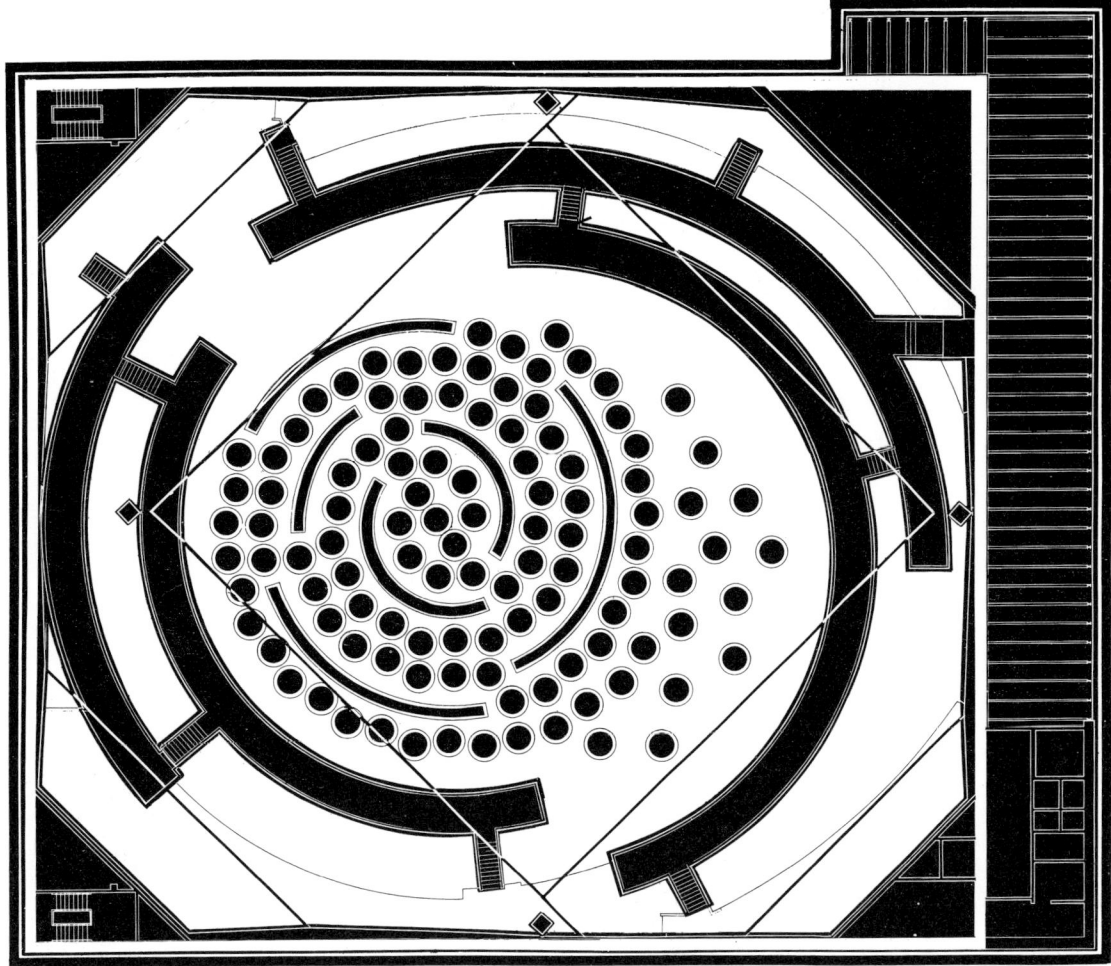

Reflected ceiling plan, indicating the suspended
acrylic discs, the four upper level seating rings and
diagonal ceiling structure.

This is the first American concert hall in which the
audience completely surrounds the orchestra like the
Berlin Philharmonie and Muziekcentrum Vredenburg,
Utrecht (page 19). Several 'semi-surround' halls have
since been opened, but to date Boettcher, as a fully
centralized plan, remains unique in North America. The
amphitheatre form was influenced by the orchestra's
experience of occasional performances at the outdoor
Red Rocks amphitheatre, a desert auditorium built
outside Denver in the 1930s. The aim was to recreate the
informal, relaxed atmosphere of music-listening 'under
the stars'. The audience is seated in tiered and
cantilevered arcs extending 360 degrees around the
orchestra. The curved seating banks are arranged
asymmetrically around the musicians, providing a sense
of informality as well as reflecting, according to the
architects, the directionality of musical instruments and
the asymmetry of orchestral sound. Also, the seating

curves have different foci, so as to concentrate not
entirely on the conductor but on the orchestra as a whole.
The stage is covered in red oak and is resiliently mounted
for dance. There are two lifts, one for pianos and another
to form an orchestra pit or a forestage extension as
required.

Here, as in all surround halls with their steeply raked
seating banks, is the inherent lack of a sound reflective
sidewall area close to the stage, which in traditional halls
provides the listener with the strong lateral sound energy
that is now considered vital in auditorium design for
'presence' and 'spatial impression'. To compensate, the
early reflected sound energy is increased by an array of
106 translucent acrylic discs which hang in a spiral over
the stage and the first few rows of seats. With these,
sound is reflected to all listeners within the acceptable 20
milliseconds time gap after the direct sound, for
maximum clarity (in fact within an average 16.5

Suspended reflectors, high wooden seat backs and
plaster fascias must be incorporated in surround halls
to compensate for lack of vertical sound-reflective
sidewalls. Adequate height is also required in the
upper part of the auditorium for a 'hard cap' to build
up reverberant sound energy.

The glass vaulted galleria will be completed along the entire mall within the Performing Arts Center, which will eventually link with the city's pedestrianization scheme.

milliseconds), while enabling the mid- to lower-frequency sound to reverberate in the upper ceiling zone. The central 30 discs can be raised or lowered to vary the proportional strength of the first-reflected to reverberant sound—and hence the acoustical definition and intimacy—for different types of music. There are also some sound reflective surfaces dispersed among the seating areas, including extended seat backs and the semicircular balcony fronts. These have undulating canted plaster fascias (with a horizontal decorative motif in gold leaf) to diffuse and reflect sound to the seating below.

Again because of the lack of vertical wall surfaces which in traditional halls prevent the sound from being absorbed too quickly, the centralized plan also results in a shorter reverberation time for a given audience capacity and cubic volume. To maintain fullness of tone, late-arriving lower-frequency sound energy is provided by extending the upper wall area—the so-called 'hard cap' of the hall as opposed to the 'soft bowl' of the audience area—to give a volume per person of 12.7 cub.m (450 cub.ft). To compensate further for this potential loss of reverberance, there is a void, or reverberation chamber, under the stage and the front rows of seats. Vibrations are transferred through the wooden stage floor into the chamber, which is coupled with the volume of the hall by a slot (the step between the main floor and the orchestra platform; the gap is concealed with thin curtains) so that sound energy is returned to the hall as late-arriving low-frequency reverberance. Some variability is provided by a curtain system on tracks within the chamber. The problem with such a feature is that the air volume of the chamber has to be large to be really effective—probably larger than at Boettcher—and the opening between the auditorium and the chamber also has to be substantial to make the coupling fairly effective. Additionally, the returning sound energy may be further reduced if the under stage space is used for storing sound-absorptive articles (as the room is connected with the stage by a stage lift).

This is an extraordinary and colourful room. The ceiling has a pattern of painted strips and squares like a blanket, in plum, pink and light green, juxtaposed across the curved geometry of the seating. The walls are dark green so that the seating appears to float in space when the lights are dimmed. The arena plan provides close contact with the orchestra and 80 per cent of seats are within just 20m (65ft) of the stage. Because of the large overall diameter, it is not a particularly intimate hall, and the further seating, in narrow suspended 'rings' that 'hover' above the other seating, feels somewhat remote looking *down* on the reflectors and lighting catwalks (though these are the cheaper seats). But many people can occupy front row dress circle and balcony seats, and there is also the advantage that listeners are socially aware of each other across the hall as well as being focused on the performers.

Manuel de Falla Centre, Granada

Owner: The Town Council of Granada

Architect: José Garcia de Paredes

Acoustic consultant: Lothar Cremer and Thomas Fütterer

Structural engineer: Otep Internacional

Mechanical and electrical engineers: Argu & Monroy

Main contractor: Pasto Peris & Co.

Opened: 1978

Cost: pts. 180 million

Uses: symphony, chamber music, recitals, chamber opera, also some drama and conferences

Seats: 1311, variable to two alternative halls of 897 or 414 seats; 96 additional chorus seats may be used

Furthest seat from the stage: 24m (78ft)

Stage: 181 sq.m (1950 sq.ft)

Volume: 10,100 cub.m (356,530 cub.ft)

Reverberation time: 1.8 sec. at middle frequencies with full audience

---

The building is exotically situated on a steep wooded hillside near the Alhambra—that most evocative name among architectural monuments—the famous ridge-top Mussulman fortress-palace of rich interiors, terraces, fountains and courtyards. The Spanish nationalist composer to whom the centre is dedicated, though not born in Granada, spent his most creative 20 years there. Working from his nearby *carmen*—or villa—his name became in the 1920s closely identified with the old university city, which for 30 years has hosted an International Music Festival and more recently an International Music Course based around this association.

The concert hall itself has a traditional rectangular form, but with the orchestra centrally placed and about one third of the seating behind the platform instead of the usual single-directional layout. The significance of this is that the hall combines the advantages of narrow width—for strong lateral sound reflections—with the intimacy of a centralized plan. The design almost entirely overcomes the major difficulty in 'surround' halls of providing adequate vertical sound-reflecting surfaces. The hall's acoustician was earlier consultant to the Berlin Philharmonic Hall, and in fact the longitudinal section through the De Falla hall, with its steeply raked seating and profiled ceiling, is not unlike a 'slice' through the Berlin Hall. The layout is also an extension of the traditional European practice of selling the seats behind the platform when these are not in use by a choir.

The auditorium is of modest size—with some 1300 seats—about that of the Konserthus, Gothenburg (1371 seats), and the Queen Elizabeth Hall, London (1106 seats). Because of being less used outside the International Music Festival, some adaptability of size and seating layout was desirable. With the two seating rakes and central stage, the hall is divisible with movable partitions into two alternative auditoria of some 400 and 900 seats respectively (not usable simultaneously). The elongated threefold space—of audience, performers and audience—has been given visual unity by four rows of huge, stylized, Andalusian hanging lanterns which decrease in size and light intensity towards both ends of the hall. The stage itself has several possible arrangements: for symphonic music, chamber music, recitals,

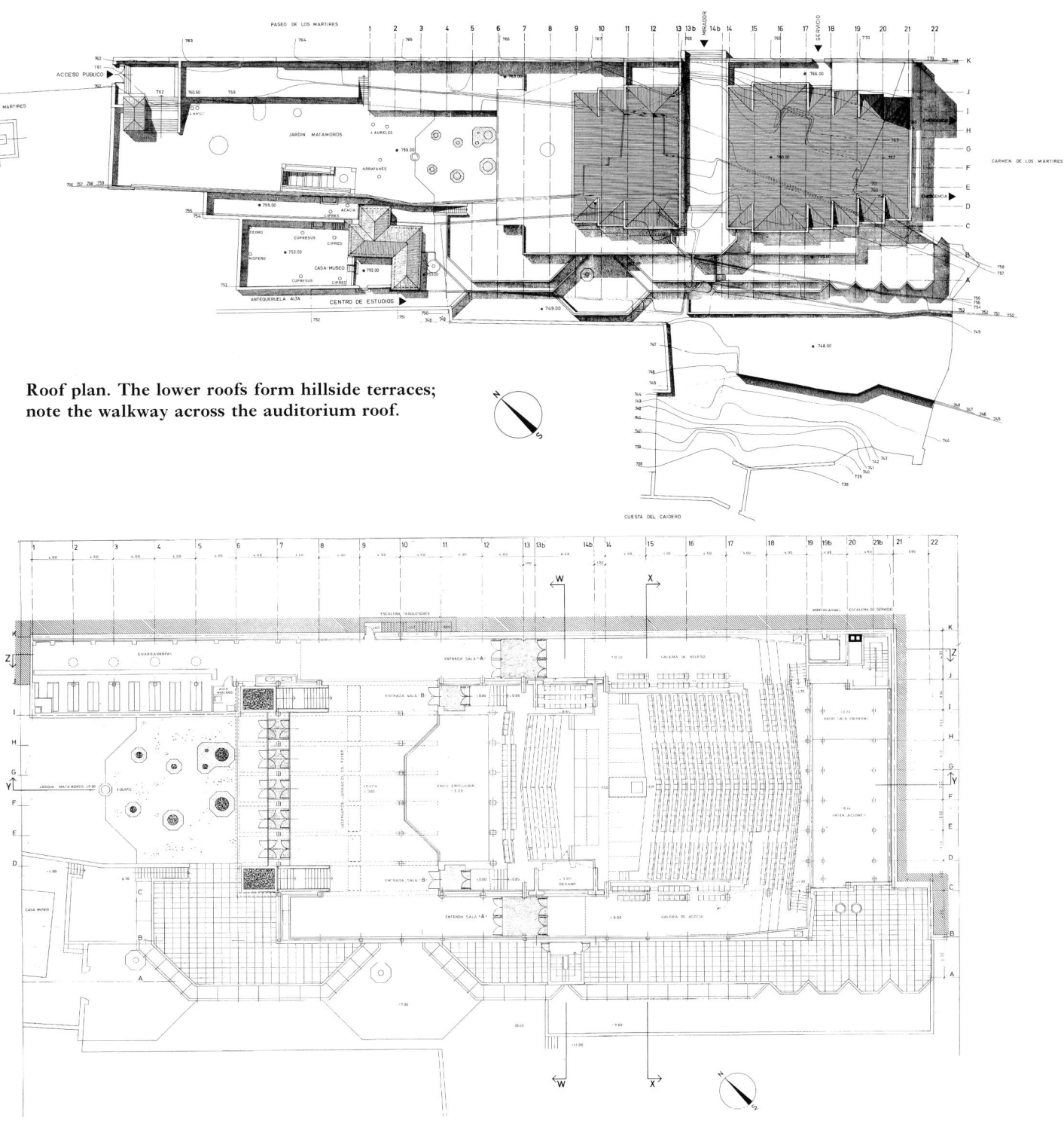

Roof plan. The lower roofs form hillside terraces; note the walkway across the auditorium roof.

Plan at the upper seating level. The stage is shown arranged for orchestra and choir but can be varied in size and layout. Full-height movable partitions to both sides of the stage can adapt the hall to a one-directional recital hall facing in either direction.

chamber opera, theatre or conference use. There is also a piano lift to storage below, and an organ to the left-hand side of the stage.

All public access is from the entrance foyer level through two central groups of doors to the seats behind

the stage and two entrances to the side for the main seating area. The performers' backstage areas are situated on the level below the foyer, segregated from the public, with direct access to the stage.

Acoustically, the large sound reflective sidewall area with small balconies either side of the stage enables the orchestra to hear itself and maintain 'ensemble'; it provides powerful lateral sound reflections for the listeners, important for gaining 'spatial impression', and the strong cross reflections also diminish the inherent disadvantage in surround halls of poor balance for those

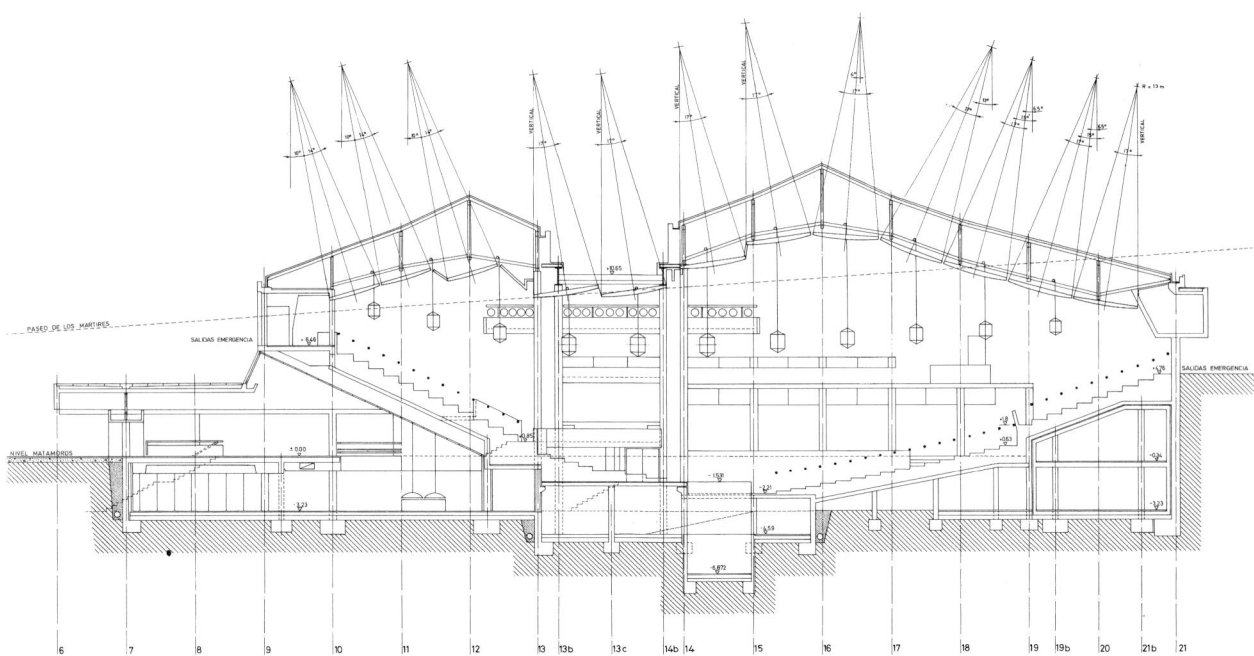

Longitudinal section through the auditorium.

The auditorium looking towards the stage front, with the bank of seating beyond.

Enormous Andalusian hanging lanterns give visual unity to the hall and also help to diffuse sound.

The exterior form sits unobtrusively against the hillside and is constructed entirely of traditional local materials.

listeners facing the conductor behind the orchestra. The De Falla hall in this respect is superior to the Berlin Philharmonic Hall. To ensure the dominance of early side wall reflections, an overhead canopy was considered undesirable, and the ceiling itself is formed into an efficient sound-diffusing profile with a continuous series of suspended convex wood panels. The large polyhedral lanterns also help to diffuse the sound.

Although the hall is principally for music, some conference and theatrical use was also planned. One concession to the hall's alternative congress use was that the seating was upholstered more comfortably than the acoustician would have preferred. There is a designed reverberation time of 1.85 seconds with full audience— less than the old European halls such as the Musikvereinssaal, Vienna, and the Concertgebouw, Amsterdam, but the same as Boston Symphony Hall, and slightly longer than the Konserthus, Gothenburg. To balance the mid- to high-frequencies absorbed by the audience, some of the wooden ceiling panels were made, within a uniform visual appearance, to absorb lower-frequency sound.

The division of the auditorium internally into two parts reflects on the exterior roof form. A public walkway leads across the roof of the stage to a terrace which provides panoramic views towards Sierra Nevada. Further balconies, terraces and gardens integrate the building and its roofscape with the surrounding landscape. The forms of the De Falla Centre grow, like those of the Alhambra, from the inside volumes, resulting in a long, low cluster of forms and large fortress-like walls with few openings, which barely rise above the tree line, for much of the building is built into the hillside. The concealed, understated technology employed in the building, combined with its frugal exterior construction in traditional materials—weathered brickwork and pale terracotta roofs—give the building a timeless quality. The architect says that 'the almost monastic austerity and utmost economy of means' employed in the building's construction is intended to be a reflection of the personality of De Falla himself. Giancarlo de Carlo has said of the building, 'The respect of the historical setting is just as strong as the desire to remain faithful to the present time; to the point that the result has the great merit of appearing obvious'.

On 11 August 1986 the building was completely destroyed by fire. A £2.5 million reconstruction programme commenced immediately, for a reopening in June 1987. Although the general design remains unchanged, technical improvements include platform lifts, better stage lighting and new translation booths, and also five new seating boxes along one side.

Berwald Hall, Stockholm

Owner: The National Swedish Board of Public Building

Architects: VBB (Erik Ahnborg, Sune Lindström)

Acoustic consultant: Vilhelm Lassen Jordan

Landscape architect: Walter Bauer AB

Structural engineers: Scandia Consult

Heating and ventilation engineers: AxRo Consult

Electrical engineers: Folke Johanson Ing.Byrå

Quantity surveyors: Bygganalys

Main contractor: Reinhold Gustafsson Byggnads AB

Opened: 1979

Cost: 58 million kr., of which 44 million for construction, and 14 million for interior decoration, fittings and technical equipment

Principal use: symphony concerts for live and recorded broadcasting; can also be rented by outside groups for other purposes

Seats: total 1306, of which 486 are in the stalls

Furthest balcony seat from front of stage: 23m (75.5ft)

Stage: 275 sq.m (2690 sq.ft)

Volume: 12,400 cub.m (440,000 cub.ft)

Reverberation time: 1.9 sec. at mid-frequencies with full audience

Maximum background noise level: NR 20

The hall is named after the Swedish composer Franz Berwald (1796–1868), and, being part of the Swedish Radio and Television Centre and built to house the 105 piece Swedish Radio Symphony Orchestra, it was officially classed in the designers' brief as a large music studio. The hall is situated in parkland just beyond Stockholm's built-up central area, and the informal natural siting led to the decision to sink two thirds of the building into the rock. This also provided direct street access for outside broadcasting trucks; it placed the auditorium on the same level as an existing tunnel system which links the other broadcasting buildings; and it helped protect the auditorium from outside traffic noise.

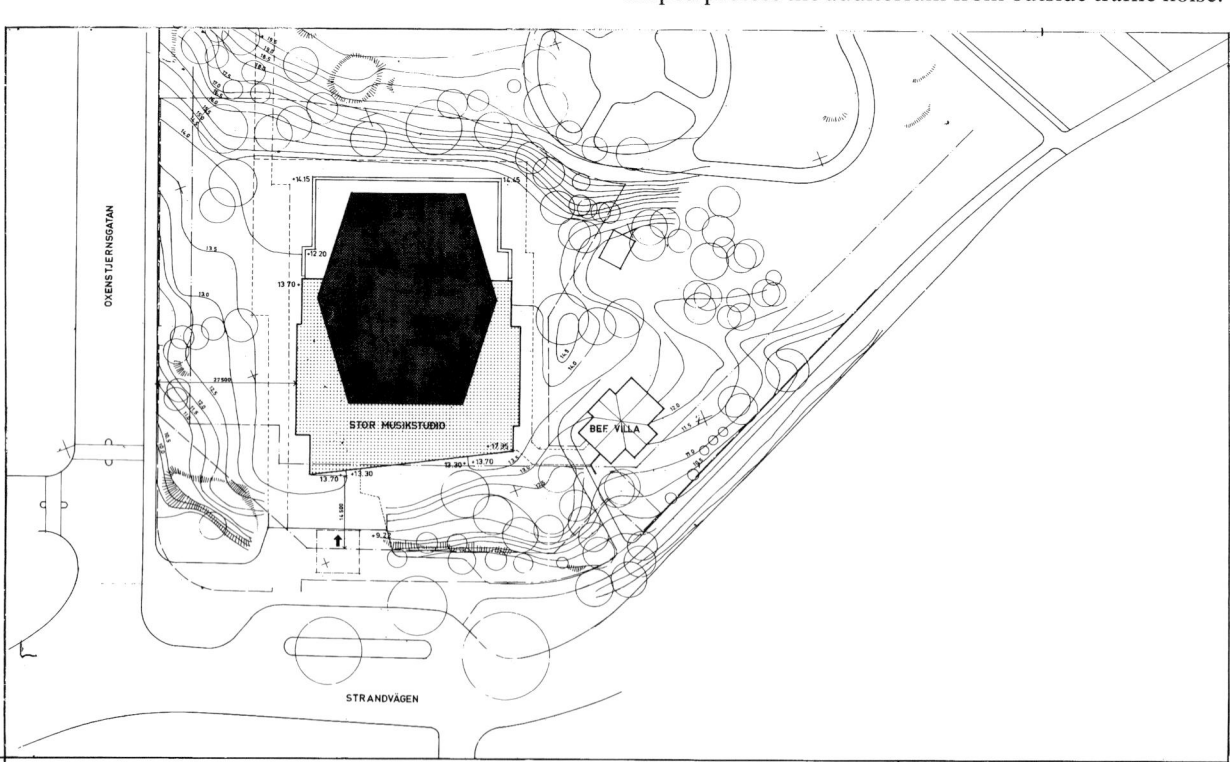

Site plan.

Upper level plan.

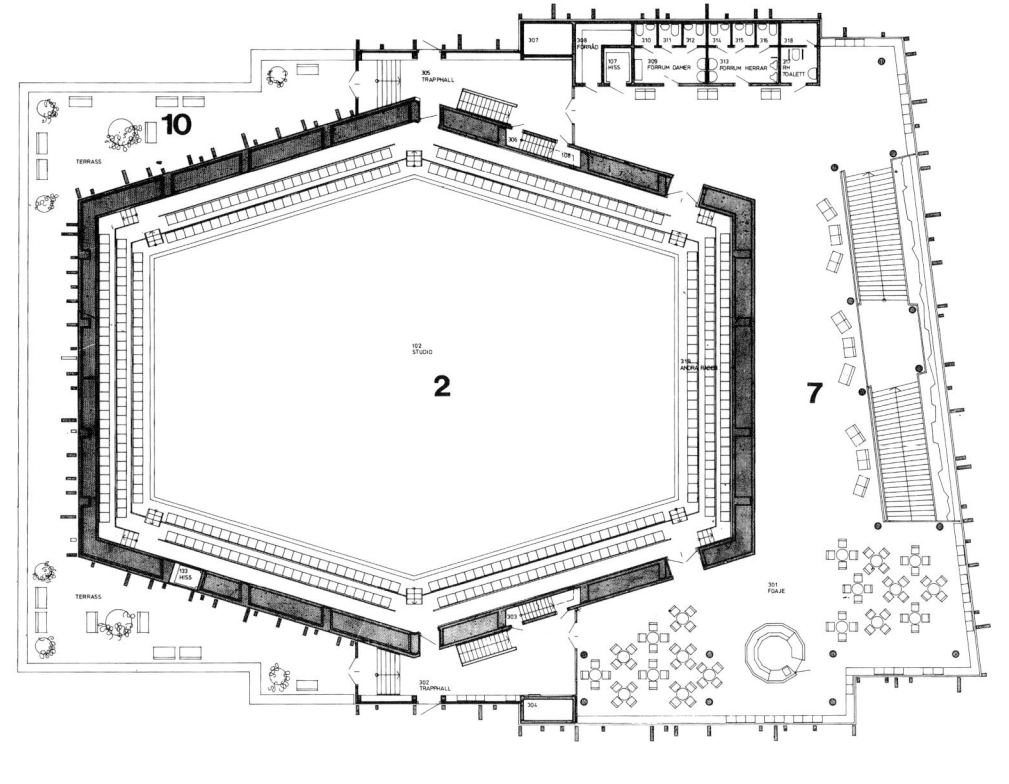

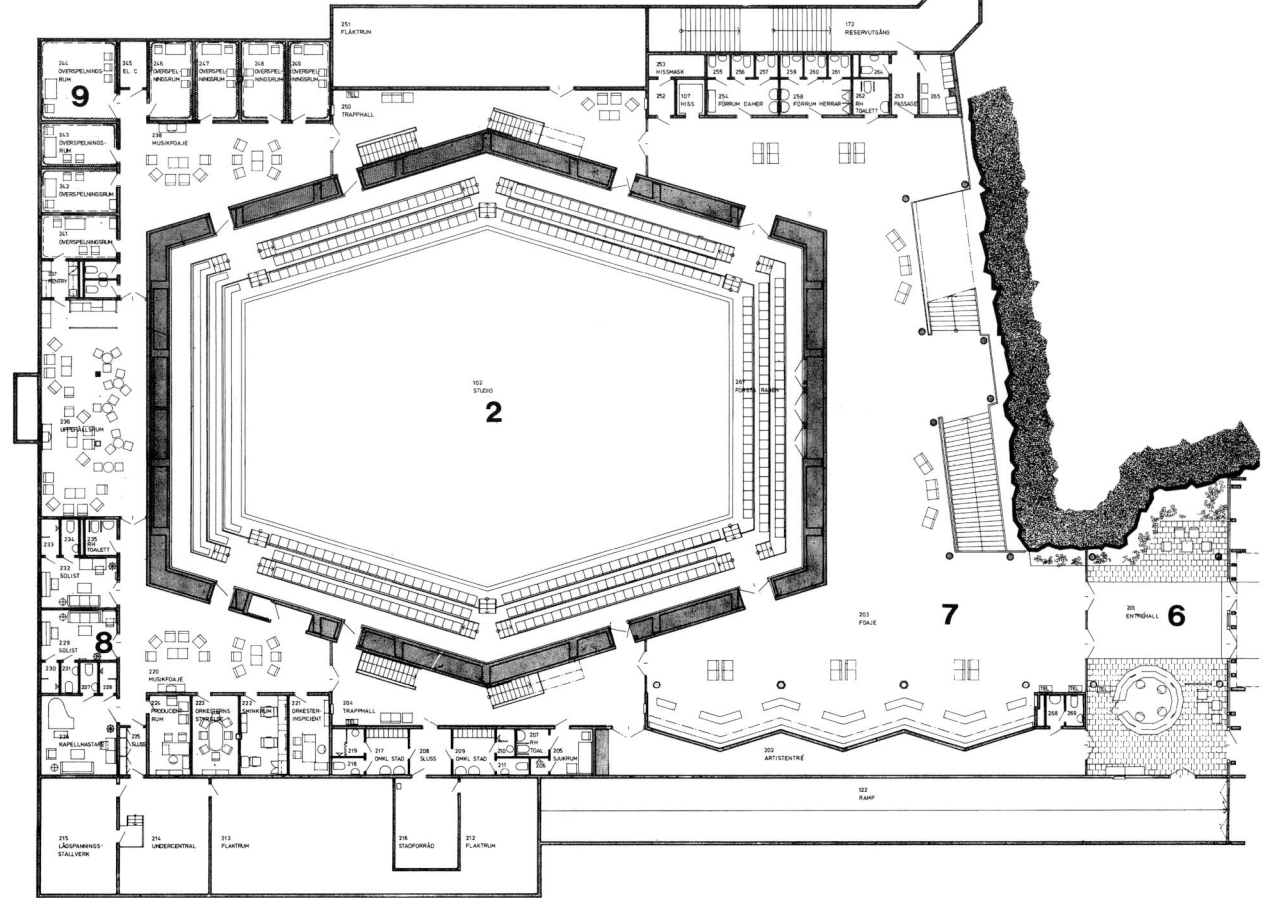

Entrance level plan.

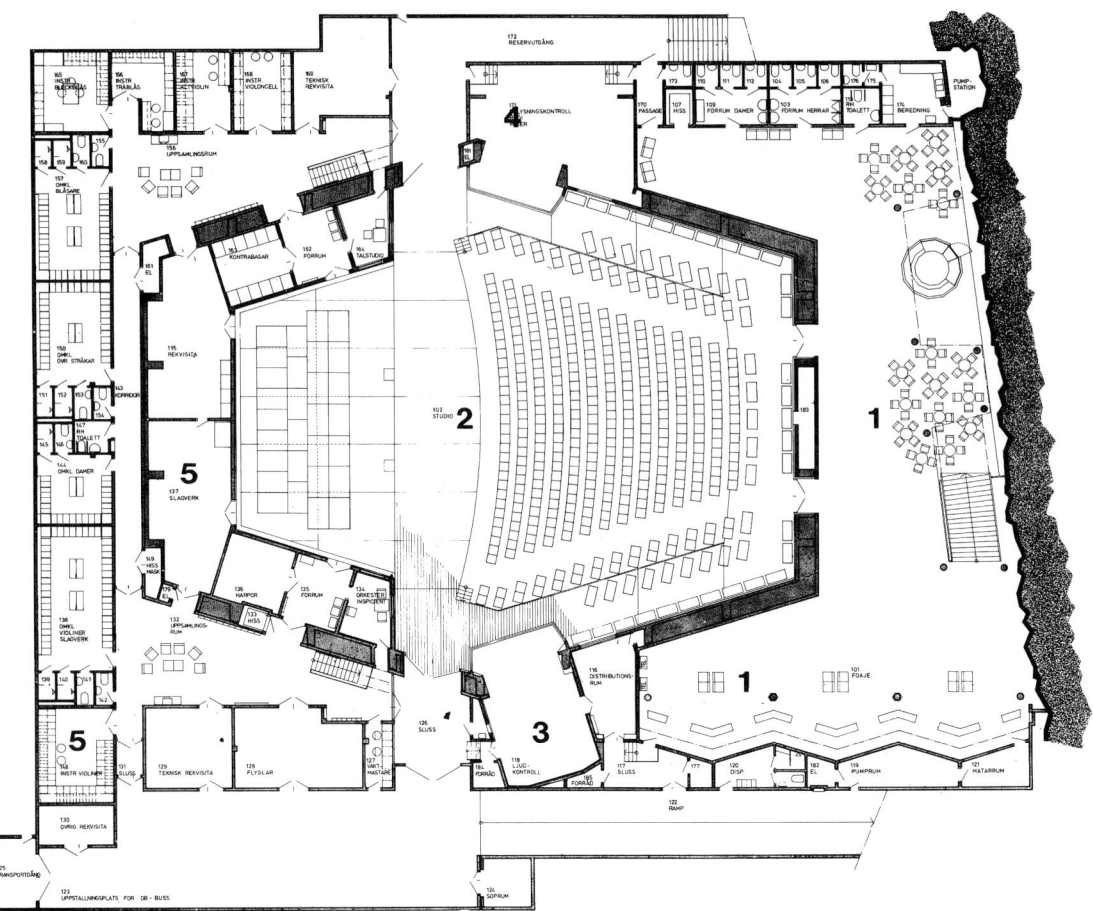

Lower level plan. Key: 1 lower foyer, 2 concert hall, 3 sound control, 4 light control, 5 instrument store, 6 entrance hall, 7 foyer, 8 soloists' rooms, 9 practice rooms, 10 terrace

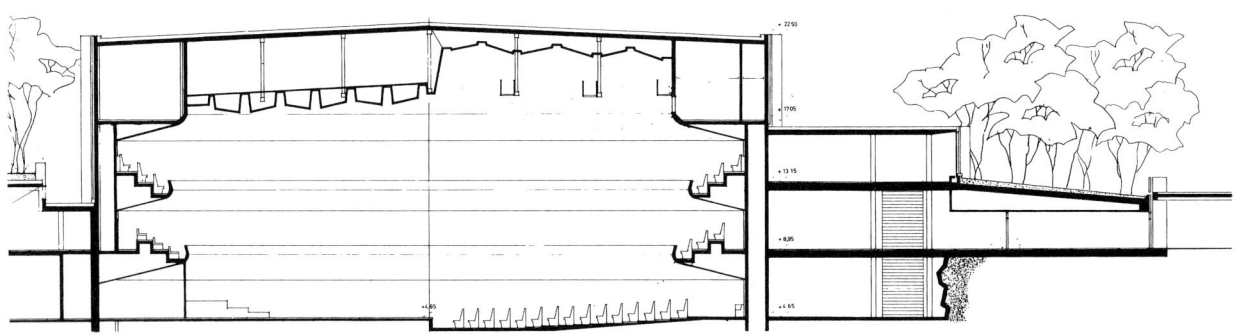

Section.

The auditorium itself is surrounded by three floors of support space. The main entrance and foyer are in the middle at the level of the auditorium first balcony. This foyer is interconnected with foyers at the other two levels by a single main staircase. This is built next to the exposed, rough-hewn rock of the hillside, which contrasts with the precise, manmade materials of the building itself—glass, concrete and extruded aluminium. Daylight filters through all three levels, creating a public space of considerable drama. Spacious backstage facilities wrap around the stage end of the auditorium at the middle and lower levels.

In contrast to the cool, light design of the foyers, the auditorium is warm and intimate, with red and brown colours and a birch veneered wall finish, with glowing incandescent lighting. The shape of the hall is derived from the traditional plan of narrow width, with galleries extending along the sidewalls—an arrangement that provides the audience with strong early reflected sound energy from the balcony soffits and wall-ceiling junction. In the Berwald Hall, the soffits are canted to increase their efficiency, and the traditional rectangular plan is modified into a hexagon. This provides walls close around the orchestra at the 'sending end', while forming a reverse fan shape at the audience end of the chamber—a shape which is ideal for directing reflected sound from the sidewalls and balcony soffits into the centre of the

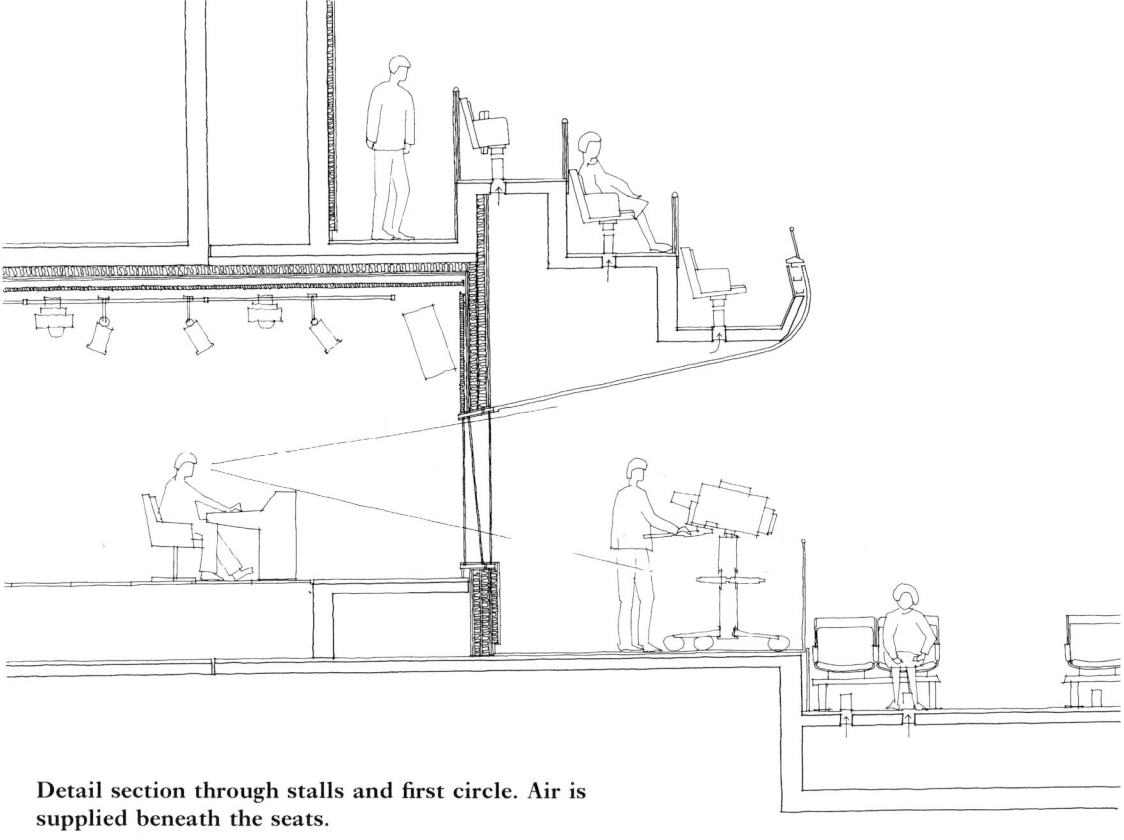

Detail section through stalls and first circle. Air is
supplied beneath the seats.

Two tiers of galleries extend around the auditorium, forming a 'semi-surround' plan.

The main entrance is at the middle of three foyer levels, interconnected by a staircase which contrasts dramatically with the rough hewn rock face.

The upper public level, which is fully glazed, has close contact to the natural parkland outside which extends up to the building.

The concert hall is two thirds sunk into the rock in order to be unobtrusive, to help service access and to help as a barrier to noise.

main floor. At the rear, the hall is only 18.6m (61ft) wide (with a maximum floor to ceiling height of 16.5m [54ft]). The other modification from the traditional concert hall plan is that, like De Doelen Hall, Rotterdam, this is a semi-surround arena hall. The orchestra platform extends across half the main floor area, and two tiers of galleries wrap equally around all sides of the hall. The pattern of reflected sound was studied in detail at the design stage with the aid of a 1:10 scale model.

The auditorium walls are of double leaf construction, with two layers of reinforced poured concrete walls around the junction with the foyer, which is structurally isolated from the hall. Elsewhere the acoustic barrier consists of a concrete outer wall with an inner leaf of multiple layers of plasterboard and sound-absorbent material. The hall inside is lined with timber panels backed with mineral wool, with continuous or perforated pressed metal inserts which allowed potential adjustment to the reverberation time. The heavily modelled ceiling is hung from lattice roof girders.

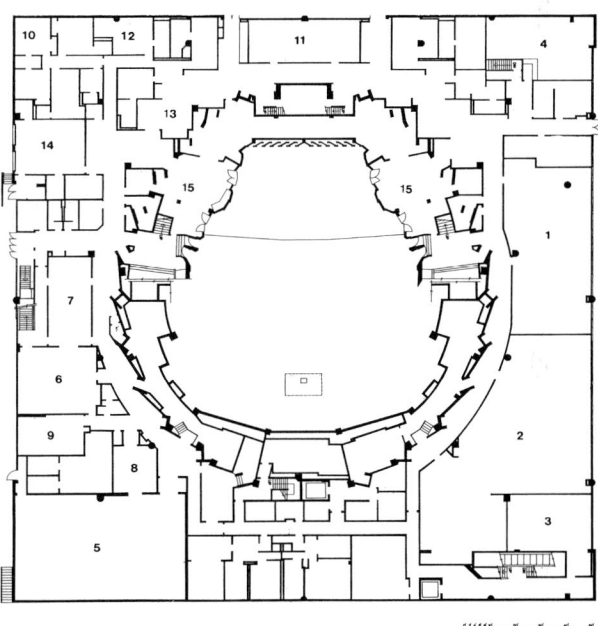

Plan at musicians' level. Key: 1 management, 2 Symphony offices, 3 Toronto Mendelssohn Choir offices, 4 library, 5 rehearsal hall, 6 boardroom, 7 green room, 8 recording, 9 catering, 10 artists' rooms, 11 lounge, 12 locker room, 13 warm-up area, 14 loading, 15 storage

Roy Thomson Hall, Toronto

Owner: Roy Thomson Hall

Architects: Arthur Erickson/Mathers & Haldenby Associated Architects

Acoustic consultants: Bolt, Beranek and Newman, Inc.—Theodore Schultz

Structural engineers: Carruthers & Wallace

Mechanical and electrical engineers: Crossey Engineering Ltd and Kalns Associates Ltd

Lighting consultant: Claude R. Engle

Landscape architects: EVM Ltd

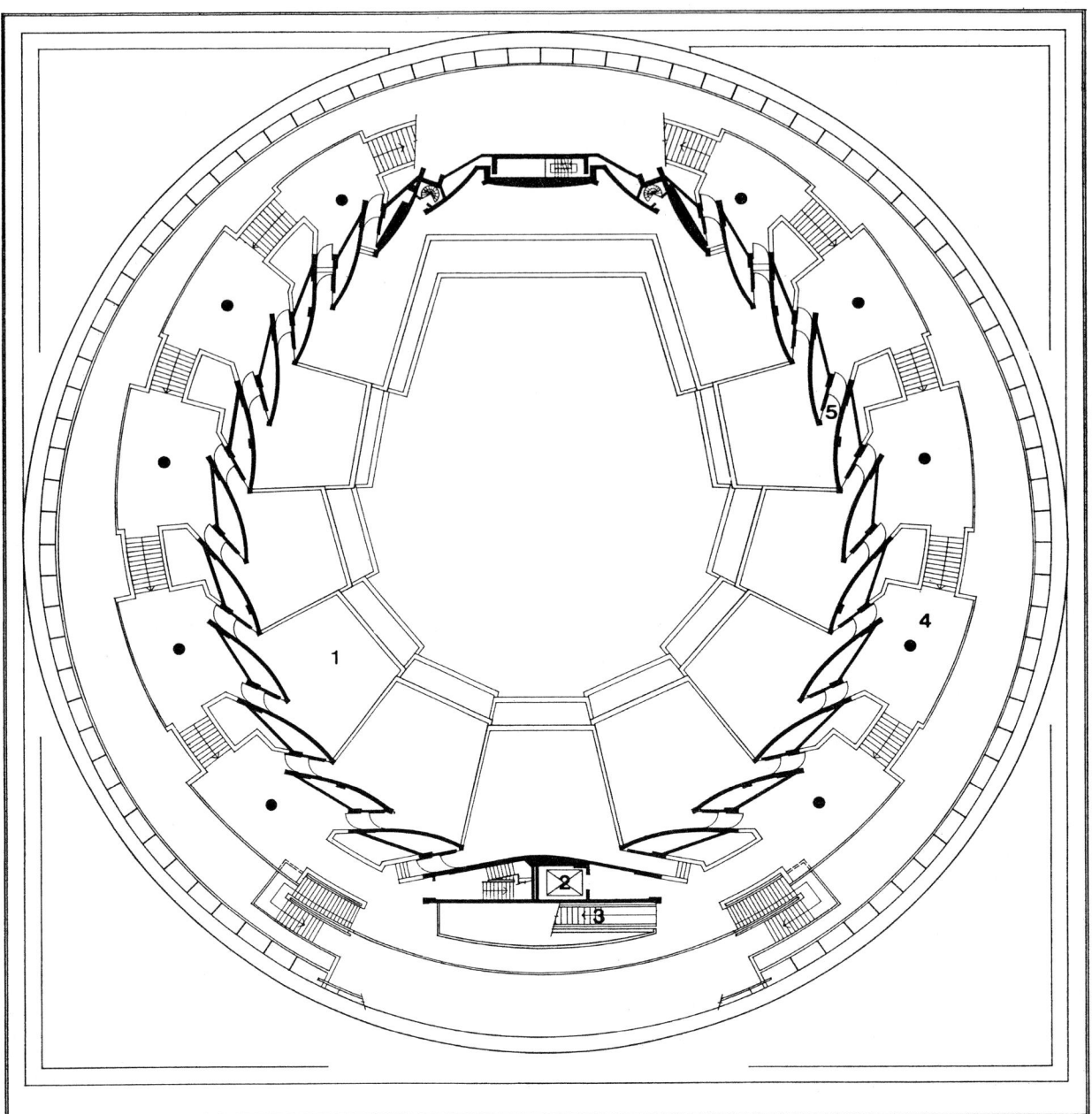

Plan at balcony level. Key: 1 seating section, 2 lift, 3 escalators, 4 access galleries, 5 sound locks

Main contractor: Eastern Construction Company Ltd

Opened: 1982

Cost: Can. $45 million

Principal use: orchestral and choral music

Seats: total 2812, main floor 1095, mezzanine 670 and 119 choir seats, balcony 928

Furthest balcony seat from front of stage: 32.6m (107ft)

Stage: 208.1 sq.m (2204 sq.ft)

Volume: 28,300 cub.m (1,000,000 cub.ft)

Reverberation time: variable between 1.5 sec. and 2.0 sec. at mid-frequencies with full audience

Maximum background noise level: NC 15

The designers' main aim was to create a hall which is as acoustically and visually intimate as possible for its relatively large seating capacity. In this they were influenced by the intimacy and excellent sound in the best seats of the old Massey Hall of 1894, the Toronto Symphony Orchestra's former home, where the audience is close to the stage and sightlines are good. (Massey Hall was also used by the acousticians as the initial model for Davies Hall, San Francisco, the Victoria Arts Centre, Melbourne, and the Joseph Meyerhoff Symphony Hall, Baltimore.) The result is a shorter, wider plan than the classic shoe box shape, which it was felt places a large part of the audience at a greater distance from the performers than that to which Toronto audiences were accustomed, as well as producing poor sightlines for those in the side balconies.

Longitudinal section.

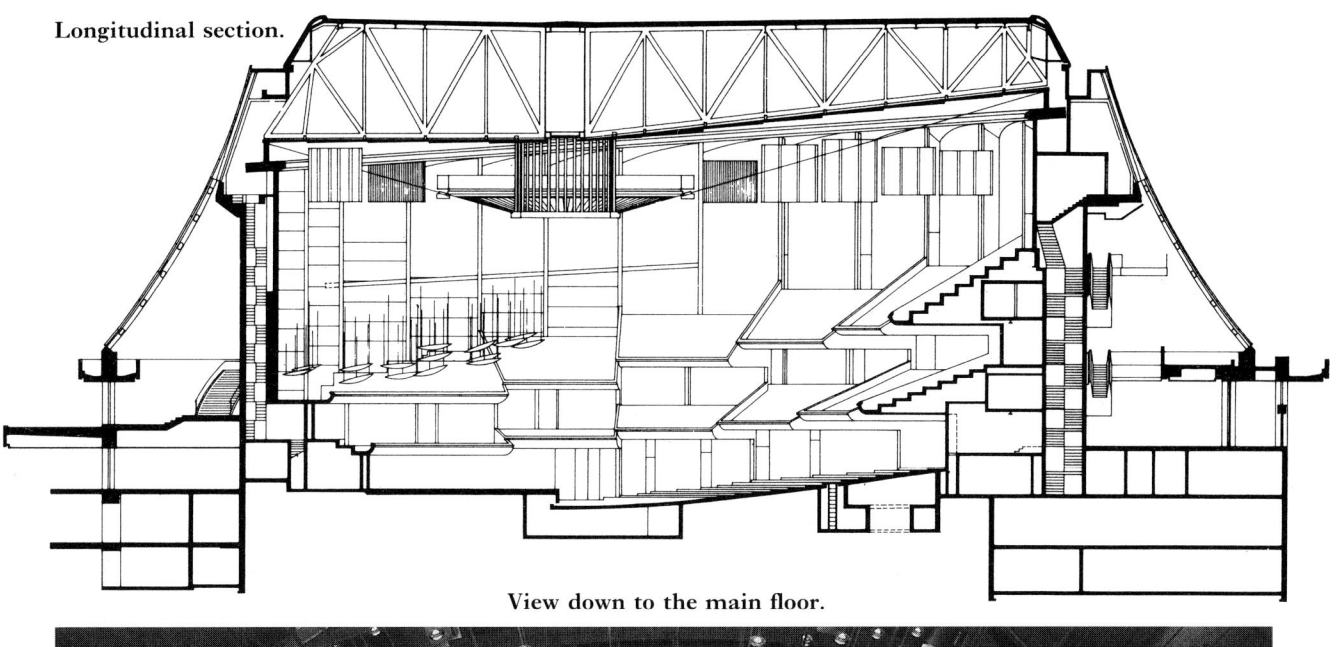

View down to the main floor.

The bicycle wheel ceiling integrates lighting, sound system, air outlets and acoustic banners.

The hall has a main floor of continuous rows of 'continental' seating and two balcony levels of conventional aisle seating in the form of petal-shape modules that fan around the auditorium. These continue behind the stage as an organ gallery and choir seats, which are sold when not used by the Toronto Mendelssohn choir. This 'semi-surround' arrangement is visually unified while avoiding the lack of orchestral balance experienced by a larger proportion of listeners in the 'surround' halls of Berlin and Denver. About 9m (29.5ft) above the stage is an array of 31 round clear acrylic sound reflecting panels, to aid onstage communication and to establish the balance and clarity of sound in the audience areas.

The form of the hall is echoed in a radial 'bicycle wheel' suspended below the ceiling, of mirror-finish stainless steel rods with a central 'hub', with two concentric rings of lighting fixtures like a gigantic chandelier. This also supports air diffusers and stage lighting, and the cylindrical hub also houses a large cluster of loudspeakers which are lowered to the level of the reflecting panels when the sound system is required. The reverberation time of the hall, of around 2 seconds at 500–1000 Hz with full audience, is suitable for large romantic orchestral works; this is reducible to 1.5 seconds for classical or smaller-scale modern works by means of sound-absorptive cylinders which can be lowered from slots in the ceiling between the radial spokes. The cylinders—designed by the Canadian fibre artist, Mariette Rouseau-Vermette—are covered in knitted wool and connected together with heavy wool membranes to provide 1100 sq.m (12,000 sq.ft) of sound-absorptive surface. The effect is of a three-dimensional tapestry with a variety of colours: red, purple, burgundy, whites, creams and shades of grey. As groups of the banners retract into the ceiling for different performance modes, the tapestry itself changes appearance with the acoustics of the hall. (Further non-acoustic decorative cylinders that were designed to complete the ceiling array have had to be replaced with ones of an alternative material as they proved not to be fully sound transparent and were inhibiting sound reflection from the ceiling.) As a neutral background to the orchestra, audience and ceiling display, all other materials and finishes in the hall are tones of silver grey: sandblasted concrete, grey carpet, polished silver-coloured metals, clear acrylic, sandblasted glass and silver grey upholstery.

For sound reflection, particularly in the bass frequencies, the auditorium walls are of 152mm (6in) in-situ concrete formed in convex sections, and the ceiling is made of convex precast concrete sections tilted up and down for sound diffusion. The entire concrete floor is carpeted and the seats are upholstered to compensate acoustically for lack of audience during rehearsals. Protection from outside noise is ensured by a concrete 'box within a box' construction, and the *pochés* between the inner and outer walls of the auditorium contain sound-and-light locks, air ducts, and other services.

The balcony seating sections extend around, and visually unify, the hall.

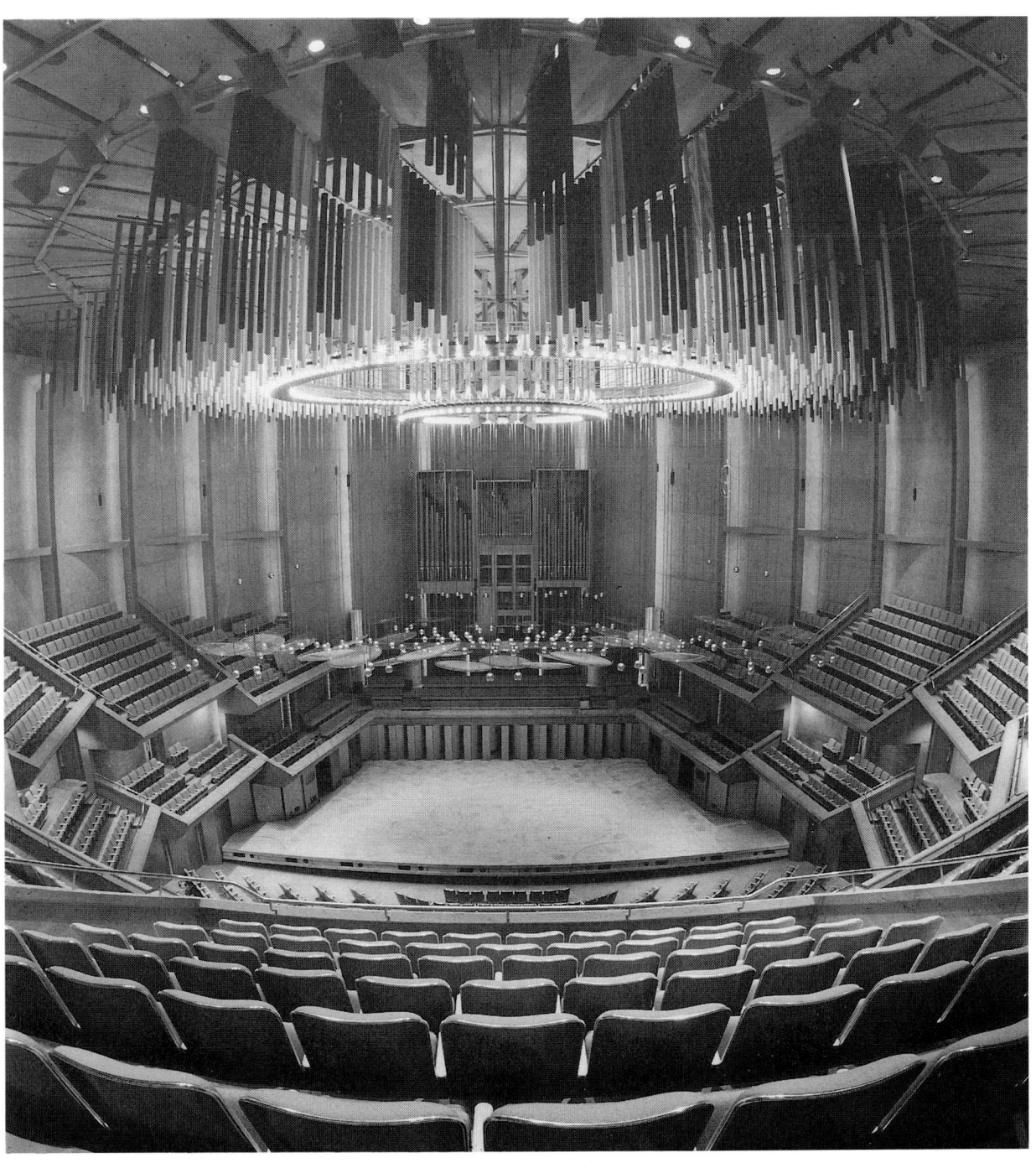

Access galleries in the foyer. The auditorium walls are mirrored, reflecting the lattice roof structure and glazing.

The hall is visually intimate for its size, all seats being relatively near the orchestra platform. However, to achieve this the auditorium had to be wider than is ideal for acoustical intimacy. Because of the relatively long travel path for laterally-reflected sound energy compared with that of the direct sound, the orchestra as a result sounds somewhat 'distant' and lacking in strength. The hall is, at the time of writing, being re-examined with a view to installing sound reflectors which could rectify this. Nonetheless, the basic design is a good example of the difficulty in auditorium design of combining attributes, both visual and acoustical, that are inherently contradictory.

The different levels of the auditorium are entered from tiered balcony foyers which step down to the main floor level. The elliptical enclosure of the auditorium is set within a square foyer area, which is enclosed by a net-like glazed structure which spans between the two. This ties

Externally, the building was conceived as a 'pavilion on a park', with ancillary support areas opening onto a sunken court.

the geometry of the hall to the rectilinear site, the streets and the buildings outside. The 3600 sq.m (39,000 sq.ft) glass canopy is supported on a structure of welded tubular steel diagonal members prefabricated into a series of diamond shaped modules and welded together on site to provide the circular and tapered configuration. By day from outside, the gem-like facets of glass reflect light differently according to the angle, weather and time of day; by night from the street the illuminated interior is visible, together with the movement of people on escalators and along the stepped access galleries—radiating the anticipation of the performance within. In the foyer, the walls enclosing the auditorium are mirror-clad, creating remarkable reflections of the glazing structure, lights and people. The lobbies continue the grey hues of the auditorium, with sandblasted concrete, two-tone grey carpet; the doors, handrails, bars, telephone booths, drinking fountains and signs are sandblasted on the reverse side of the mirrored and glass surfaces. The lobby seating is a series of custom-designed benches of cream-coloured leather with chrome bases and trim.

The hall forms part of a 1 ha (2.5 acre) projected commercial and cultural development on the site of the former Canadian National railway terminal just west of Toronto's business centre. A landscaped watergarden will form the centre of the development, focusing onto a cascade which will convert, when the water is turned off, into an amphitheatre for outdoor summer concerts. The auditorium was conceived as a 'pavilion on the park', with the bulk of the backstage support areas below ground level, opening onto a sunken court where daylight is required.

St David's Hall, Cardiff

Owner: City of Cardiff

Architects: The J. Seymour Harris Partnership

Theatre consultants: Carr and Angier

Acoustic consultants: Sandy Brown Associates

Structural engineers: Ove Arup and Partners

Mechanical, electrical and services engineers: Sandy Brown M.S.U.

Quantity surveyors: Cyril Sweett and Partners

Interior design: Read Ward Partnership

Organ consultant: Ralph Downes

Main contractor: John Laing Construction Ltd

Opened: 1982

Cost: £13 million

Principal use: concert hall

Seats: total (maximum) 1952, main floor and first tier 762, choir 354, tiers 836; total seating in front of seating line, i.e. without choir seating, 1598.

Furthest balcony seat from front of stage (standard orchestra platform): 32m (105ft)

Stage (not including two forestage lifts): 176 sq.m (1900 sq.ft)

Orchestra pit: large size (two lifts) 75 musicians, small size (one lift) 30–35 musicians

Volume: 22,000 cub.m (780,000 cub.ft)

Plan at stage level.

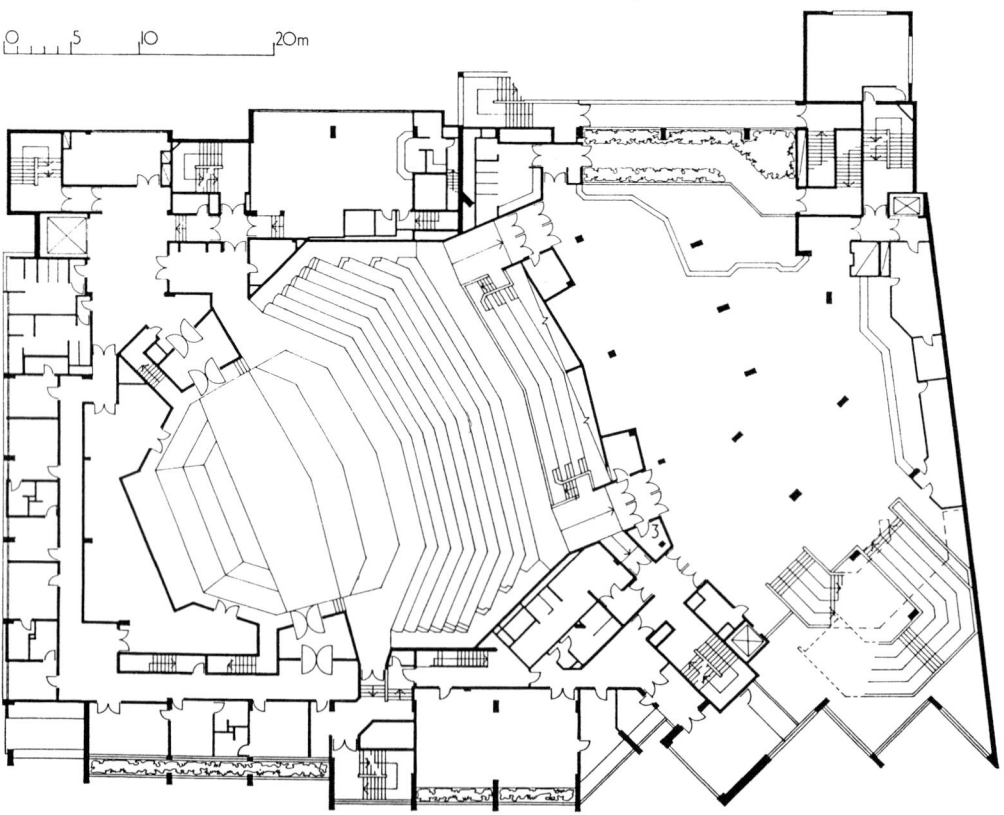

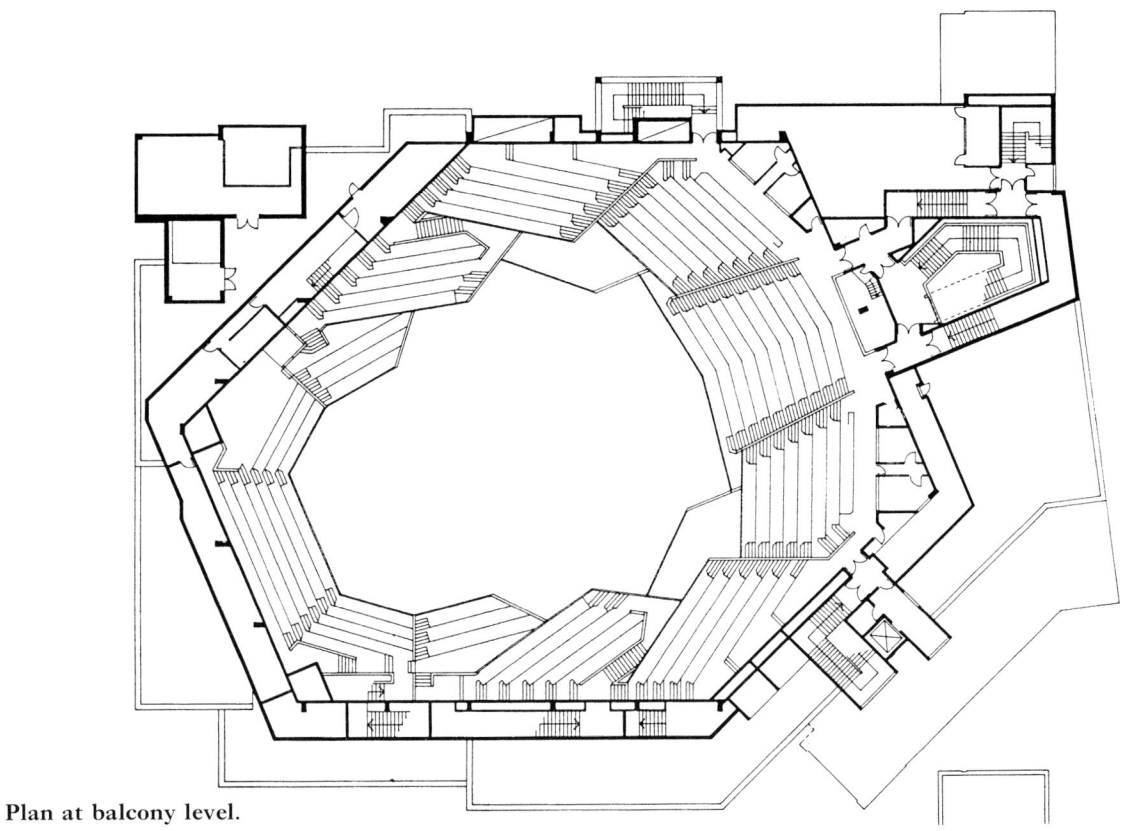

Plan at balcony level.

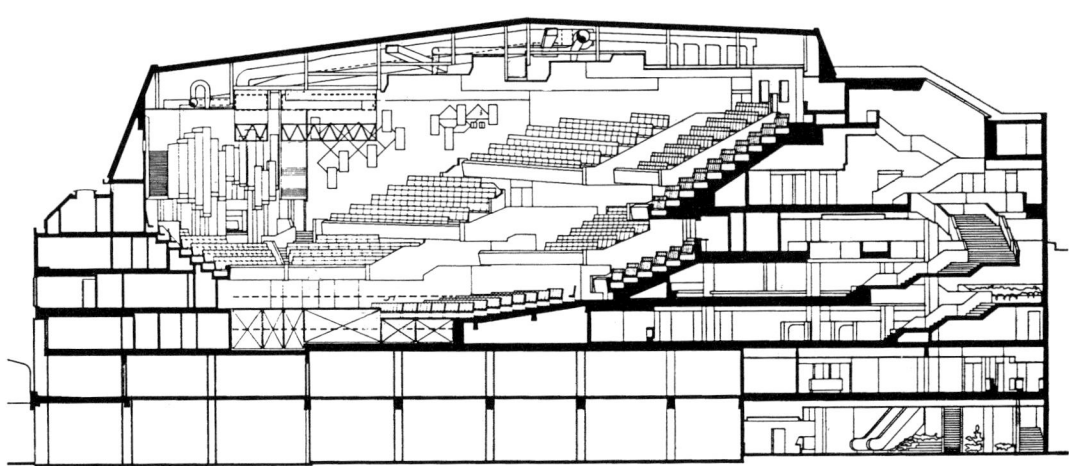

Longitudinal section. The acoustic boundary of the
hall is the roof, and below this is a visual,
acoustically transparent, ceiling.

Maximum floor to ceiling height: 19.6m (64ft)

Reverberation time: 1.9 sec. at mid-frequencies with
full audience

Maximum background noise level: NR 20

The auditorium is built at high level over St David's
Shopping Centre, on a rooftop site originally earmarked
for a county public library but later acquired by the City
of Cardiff for the concert hall. The Arts Council of Great
Britain had as long ago as 1959 'expressed concern that
there are no proper facilities for major concerts in
Cardiff, the capital of Wales, and that a large, suitably
designed concert hall is an amenity that should be
provided in Cardiff at the earliest possible date'. Cardiff

The semi-surround hall provides visual continuity without the problems of orchestral balance which affect a large number of seats in a truly centralized hall.

has several existing auditoria—the City Hall, the Sherman Theatre (part of University College), the New Theatre (a commercial theatre) and until 1982 the Sophia Gardens (an assembly hall) which unfortunately collapsed under an excess of winter snow. But their facilities and in some cases acoustics are far from ideal. Until the new site became available, one idea had been to convert the Capitol cinema into an opera house that could also put on concerts. However, with the new site the decision at the outset was to provide a concert hall first and foremost without a proscenium for theatre. During the later stages of design it was decided that with the aid of the public address system the hall could also double as a conference centre to tap the growing market for national and international touring conferences. Other expected uses included popular music, light entertain-

ment, some spectator sports and television recording performances.

The hall contains a series of seating tiers on two levels which step down around a raked main floor. The lower tiers extend behind the stage in a 'semi-surround' form as choir seats, which are sold when not in use by a choir. An important aspect of conference design which this layout permits is the movement of participants to the stage without the necessity to pass outside the auditorium. To create the feel of an arena and to reduce the longitudinal dimension, the hall is wider than ideal. To compensate for this, the aim was to provide vertical sound-reflective surfaces between the seating tiers, an idea similar to the stepped 'vineyard' seating at the Berlin Philharmonie. Despite this intention, however, the vertical steps in St David's Hall are not in fact generally useful in this regard as they do not direct the sound towards the seating. Interestingly, in practice there is not the shortage of laterally reflected sound that might be expected as a result, perhaps due to the reverse fan shape of the hall towards the rear, which again is similar to the Berlin hall.

The open-cell ceiling conceals ductwork, which is
within the acoustic boundary of the hall, as the roof
is a single skin construction.

For economy (the hall is good value for the
constructional standards and facilities provided) the roof
is very lightweight for a concert hall, and only single skin.
Although the walls are of heavy plastered reinforced
concrete and blockwork, the roof is of 200mm (8in)
aerated concrete supported on trusses over a maximum
span of 44m (144ft). This was permissible because the air
space above Cardiff is exceptionally quiet and because it
was decided not to allow the rise in reverberation time
usual in concert halls for fullness of tone because of the
compromise this would have imposed over speech
intelligibility for conference use. Because the hall is built
above two levels of shops, with restrictions on the total
height, it was not possible to provide the necessary cubic
volume and still leave room for the services in a void
above the acoustic boundary of the hall. The air
conditioning ductwork, lighting bridges and other
services were therefore included within the overall
volume, with the thermal insulation to the ducts fitted
inside to prevent sound absorption at the higher
frequencies. Again, some lower frequency absorption is

inevitable. To conceal the ductwork and structure there
is suspended below this an acoustically transparent open
cell ceiling. The slightly sound-absorptive effect of this
material is compensated for by a high cubic volume.

The stage, of oak strip, is highly adjustable,
comprising a series of platform lifts. There are two
forestage lifts, a major lift for the central part of the stage,
and three segmented rear lifts that can form risers for the
wind and brass sections of the orchestra. All the lifts can
drop to auditorium level to create a flat arena floor, and
the forestage lifts, which are normally at this level for
maximum seating, can also form an orchestra pit at
610mm (2ft) below auditorium level. Over the stage is a
platform suspension grid that can be lowered to stage
level, containing stage lanterns, acoustic baffles and
loudspeakers.

The hall is reached from the street level lobby and box office area via spatially interconnecting floor levels linked by stairs and escalators set at 45 degrees to the street. The catering facilities are extensively used during daytime by passers-by, though for the concertgoer the complexity of levels and escalators, the extreme detachment of the auditorium from the street and a complicated system of direction signs create a difficulty of access inherent in the building's site. The structural and constructional materials are everywhere essentially neutral in colour: white exposed concrete and stonework, and light coloured woods—ash, maple and, for the floor, oak. Furnishings, carpets and other decor use various shades of green—one of Wales' national colours.

Orange County Performing Arts Center Theater, Costa Mesa, California

Owner: The Orange County Performing Arts Center

Architects: The Blurock Partnership; Caudill-Rowlett-Scott (Associated Architects)

The brutalist style of the building is not very sympathetic to the old city of Cardiff, but the hall is built over a shopping centre, and the foyers are much used by passers-by (*opposite*)

All seats interconnect with the stage, for conference use.

Theatre consultant: John von Szeliski AIA

Theater operations consultant: Len Bedsow

Acoustic consultants: Joint Venture Acoustical Consultants: Paoletti-Lewitz Associates Inc.; Jerald R. Hyde; Marshall Day Associates

Stage lighting: Jules Fisher Associates

Rigging: Peter Feller Associates

Sound system and video: Paul Alan Magil

Architectural lighting: Jules Fisher-Paul Marantz

Landscape architect/site design: The SWA Group

Structural engineers: Martin and Tranbarger

Mechanical engineers: Nack and Sunderland

Electrical engineers: Frederick Brown Associates

Main contractor: C. L. Peck

Opened: 1986

Cost: Approximately $72 million

Main auditorium

Uses: multi-purpose including symphony, touring musical theatre, dance, opera, drama, film, and television events

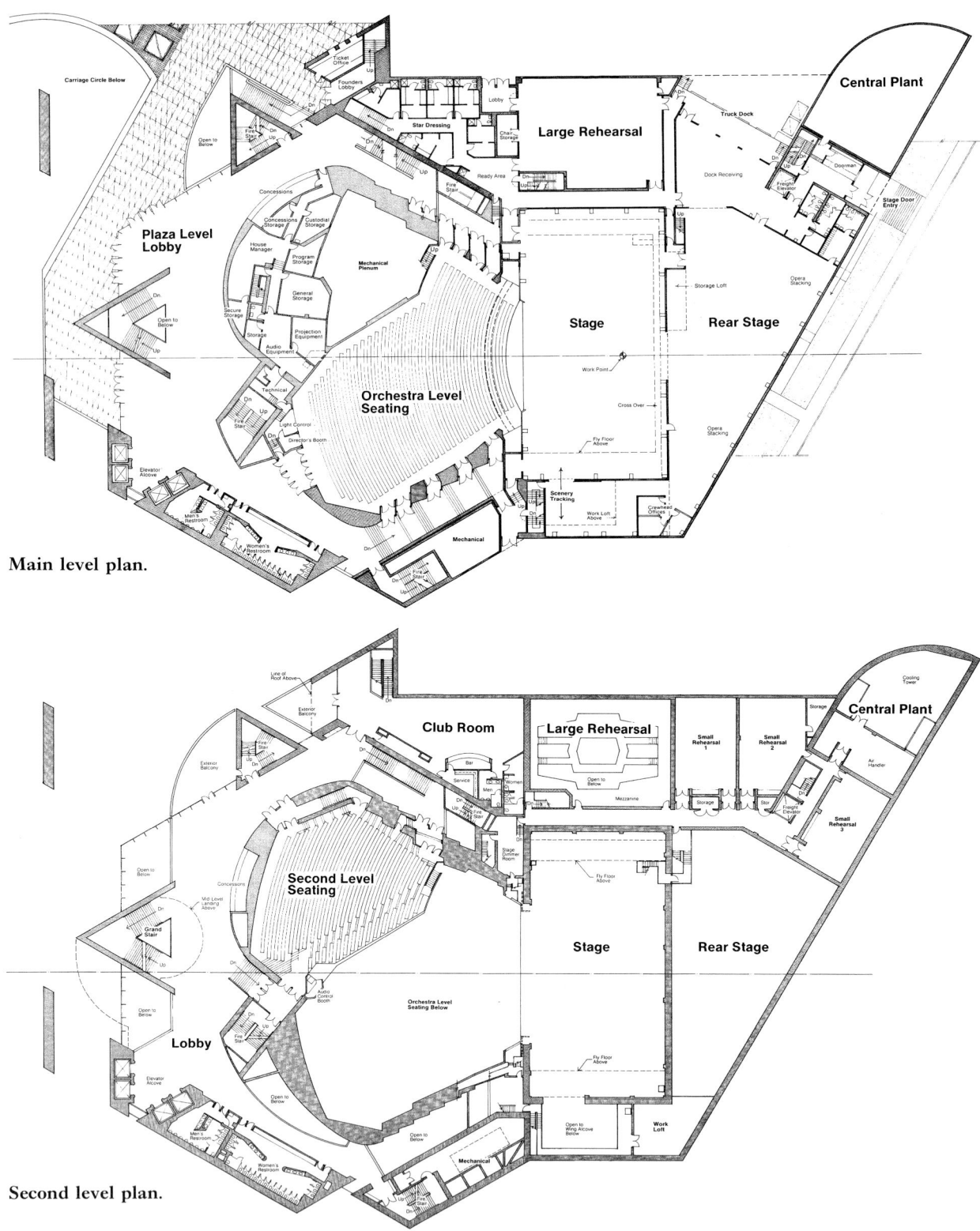

Main level plan.

Second level plan.

Seats: total 3000; orchestra level 1250, tier one 680, tier two 485, tier three 595; with symphony platform in place there are 1148 seats on the orchestra level

Furthest balcony seat from stage front: 42.7m (140ft)

Proscenium opening: variable with motorized panels from 15.8m (52ft) wide and 9.1m (30ft) high for musical theatre and drama, to 20.7m (68ft) wide and 12.8m high (42ft) for symphony mode

Stage: width 39.3m (129ft), 21m (69ft) from centreline to stage right wing, depth 19m (62.3ft) from proscenium wall to back wall, height to grid underside 33.5m (110ft), stage area in symphony mode, 185.8 sq.m (2000 sq.ft)

Flying system: 90 single purchase counterweight sets, plus special motor units

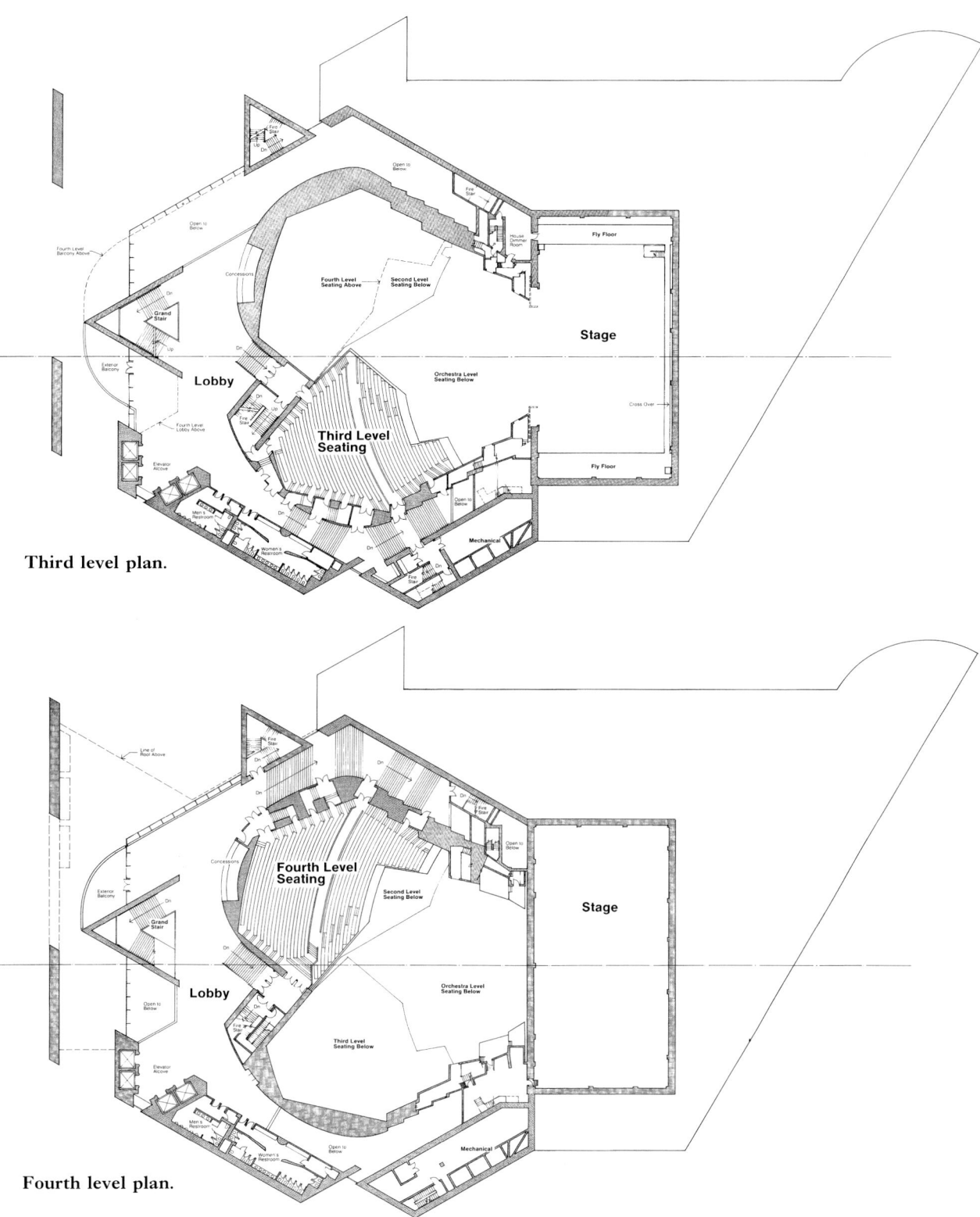

Third level plan.

Fourth level plan.

Orchestra pit: small pit (one lift) 35–40 musicians, large pit (two lifts) 120 musicians

Volume: 27,800 cub.m (982,000 cub.ft) (with orchestra shell in place)

Reverberation time: variable from 2.2 secs. to 1.4 secs. at mid-frequencies with full audience

Maximum background noise level: PNC 15

The attraction of the main auditorium in this new complex (there will also be a 300 seat 'black box'—actually dark red—and in the second phase a 1000 seat theatre) is, as the theatre consultant says, 'the organic bond between the acoustical concept and the resulting

Longitudinal section.

Model of the auditorium, seen from the stage area.

Model of the exterior. The geometry of the auditorium is expressed on the exterior of the building. The foyers are based on an angular grid pattern. The building is entered through a monumental granite-clad façade which frames the lobby levels like a giant proscenium, forming also the backdrop of a sculptured plaza.

architecture'. It is an ingeniously logical, if eccentric, translation into built form of criteria for acoustic excellence in concert halls, centering around the binaural hearing process and the concomitant need for lateral sound energy, as discovered in the 1960s and subsequently quantified by the acoustician, Dr A. Harold Marshall. Its form is an interesting development from his halls in New Zealand, discussed previously. The intention at Orange County was to combine the advantages of strong early lateral sound reflections, as provided in the traditional narrow shoe box concert hall, with the significantly larger seating capacity, comfortable seat-spacing and good sightlines generally required in most large present-day North American auditoria.

To achieve this the designers have notionally joined together two shoe box halls side by side, at an angle. A large 'prow' is left at the back near the middle, extending into the otherwise flat ceiling, to provide a large sound reflective side wall area for the rear seats. Where the side walls of the 'two halls' merge and disappear, the necessary lateral reflection to the central seats is provided

by segmenting the main floor into two areas with the second level seating rising to about 4m (13ft) above the first level seating. The step between the two levels forms a vertical sound reflecting surface which provides early lateral sound energy to the seats on the first level. Above these levels, two upper seating tiers on either side, like tilted trays, are correspondingly stepped in relation to each other, so that the soffits and balcony fronts provide lateral reflections to the seats of the respective tier below. The asymetrical solution has in fact the plan form of a conventional North American fan-shaped multi-use hall, but where the seating tiers are interrupted mid-house and are vertically displaced in relation to each other.

Another feature which the designers point out is that most orchestra level seats are placed on the primary axis of the violins. For other seats, large suspended reflecting panels near the sidewalls direct additional violin sound energy across the hall. Whereas in many halls the violins are easily overpowered by other instruments, the effect here is a more uniform early violin sound throughout the auditorium.

In common with most comparable North American auditoria, the hall is a multi-use facility as it was found to be impossible to obtain a site and budget for a complex of large single-purpose performance spaces. For theatre, opera and ballet there is a proscenium, flyloft and backstage. For symphony concerts, a shallow 5m (16ft) highly diffuse orchestra shell is brought into place to exclude the flyloft. The enclosure is visually and acoustically designed as an extension of the sidewalls of the auditorium, and because of the large proscenium opening, the performance area with the shell in place merges acoustically with the auditorium into a single volume. Using further reflecting panels, the shell can also expand to accommodate a choir with orchestra, and by removing reflectors, it can contract in width and depth for chamber music, smaller ensemble groups and soloists.

Certain architectural planning difficulties were created by the angled, interrupted and asymetrical seating tiers. These included problems of structural support, the provision of continuous ducts for mechanical services, and finding locations for low-angle stage lighting. A particular problem was the circulation to and from the seats, as the implied arrangement was effectively 'continental' on one side—with direct egress from the rows—and conventional seating using an aisle on the other. This was resolved by a special interpretation of the fire and safety codes, which actually combined the existing formulas for both seating types, in terms of aisle and door widths and back-to-back row spacing.

Motorized acoustic banners linked to a computerized control system can vary the effective room volume and reverberation for different performance modes. These are used to deaden the hall for certain types of music, or when the electroacoustic system is used. The curtains are located in the ceiling and upper sidewall areas, generally behind the large reflectors, and do not therefore interfere with the early reflection sequence.

The Morton H. Meyerson Symphony Center, Dallas

Owner: City of Dallas

Architect: I. M. Pei & Partners, New York

Acoustic and theatre consultant: Artec Consultants Inc., New York

Structural engineers: Robertson, Fowler & Associates, Inc.

Mechanical and electrical engineers: Edwards & Zuck, P.C.

Cost consultant: Hanscomb Consultants, Inc.

Life safety consultant: Rolf Jensen & Associates

Organ builder: C. B. Fisk, Inc.

Orchestra level plan.

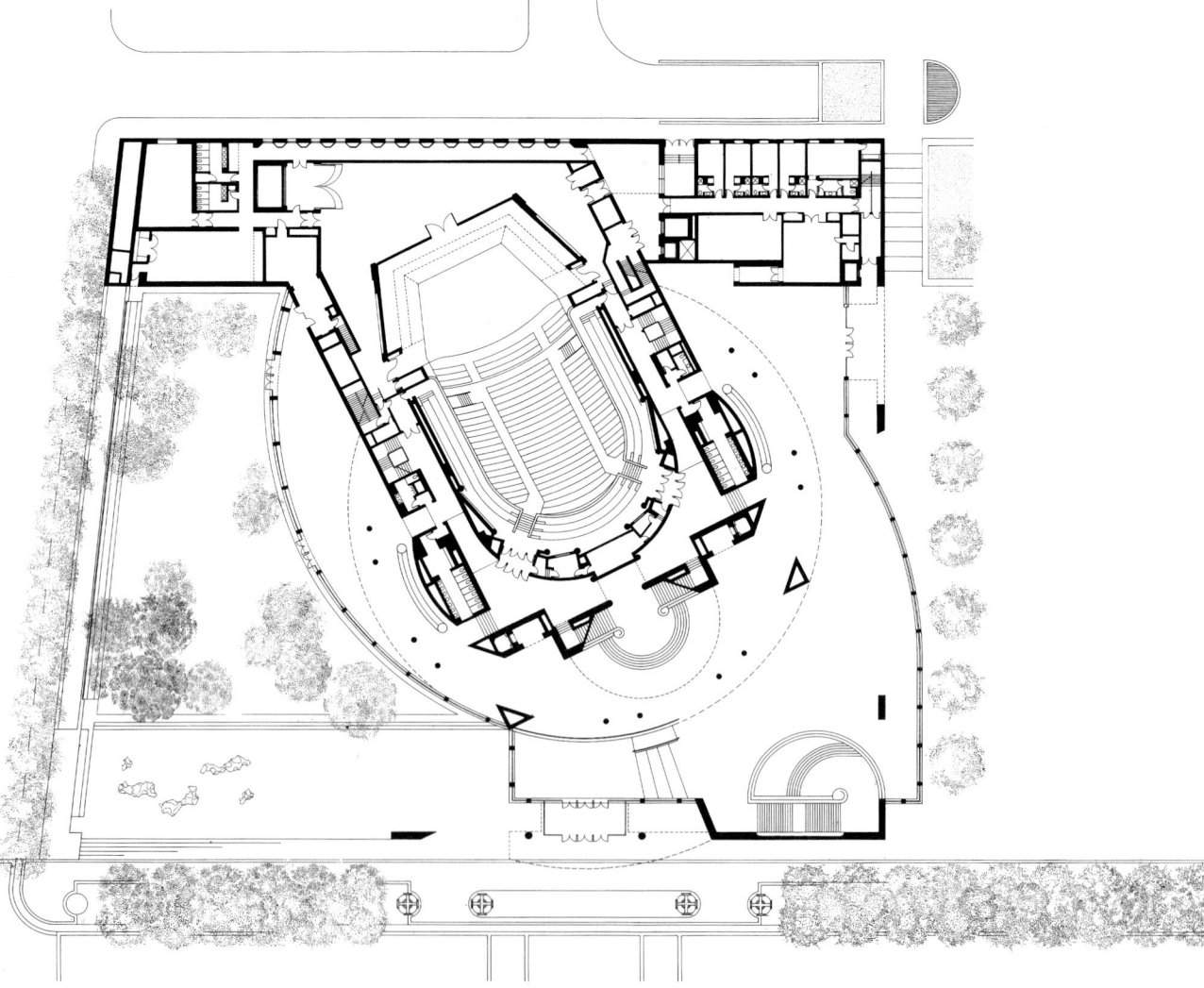

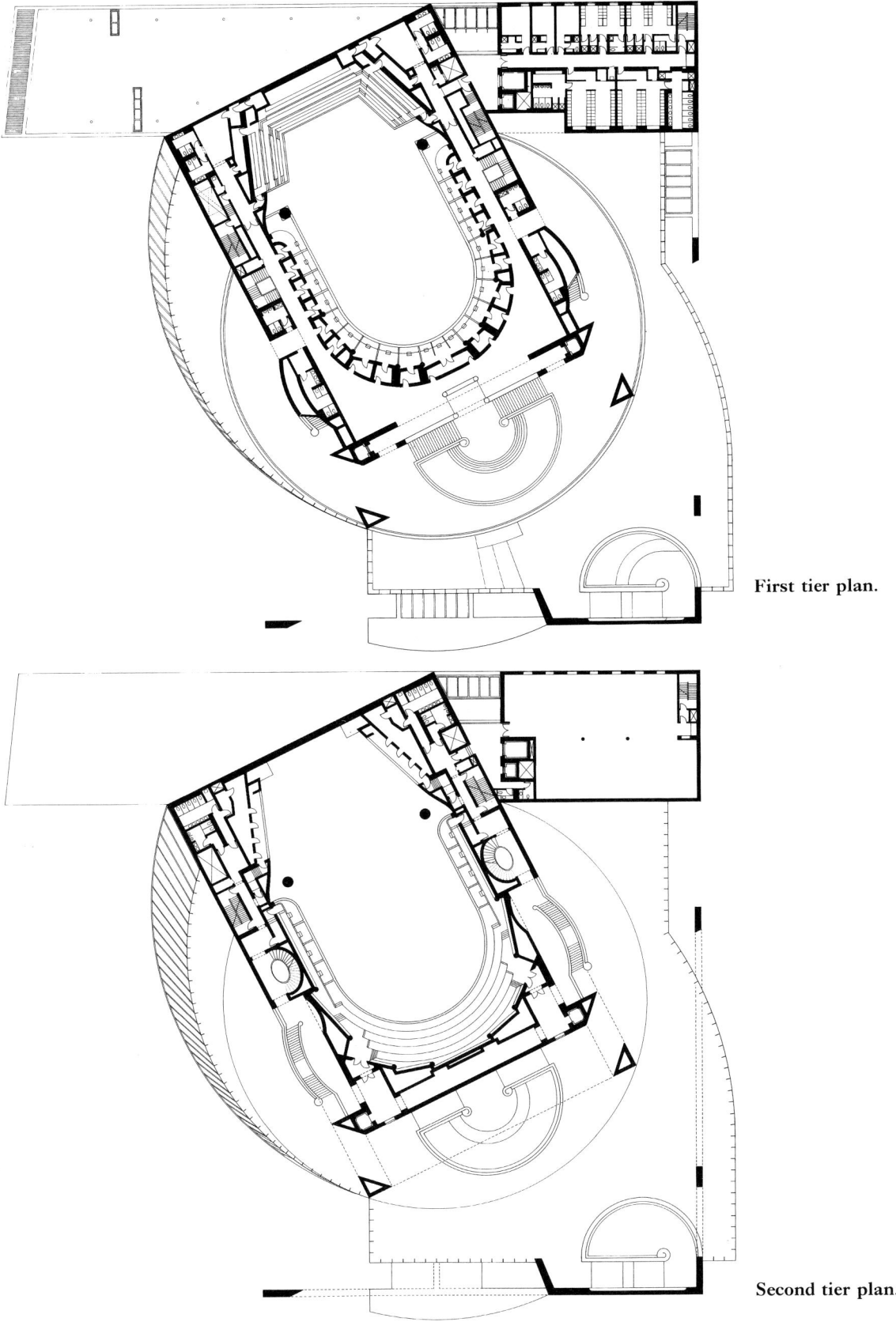

First tier plan.

Second tier plan.

Construction manager: J. W. Bateson Company, Inc.

Estimated opening date: 1989

Estimated building construction cost: $65,875,000
(including parking garage)

Principal use: symphony concerts

Seats: total 2200

Farthest balcony seat from stage front: 41m (134ft)

Main floor height: 25.9m (85ft) maximum

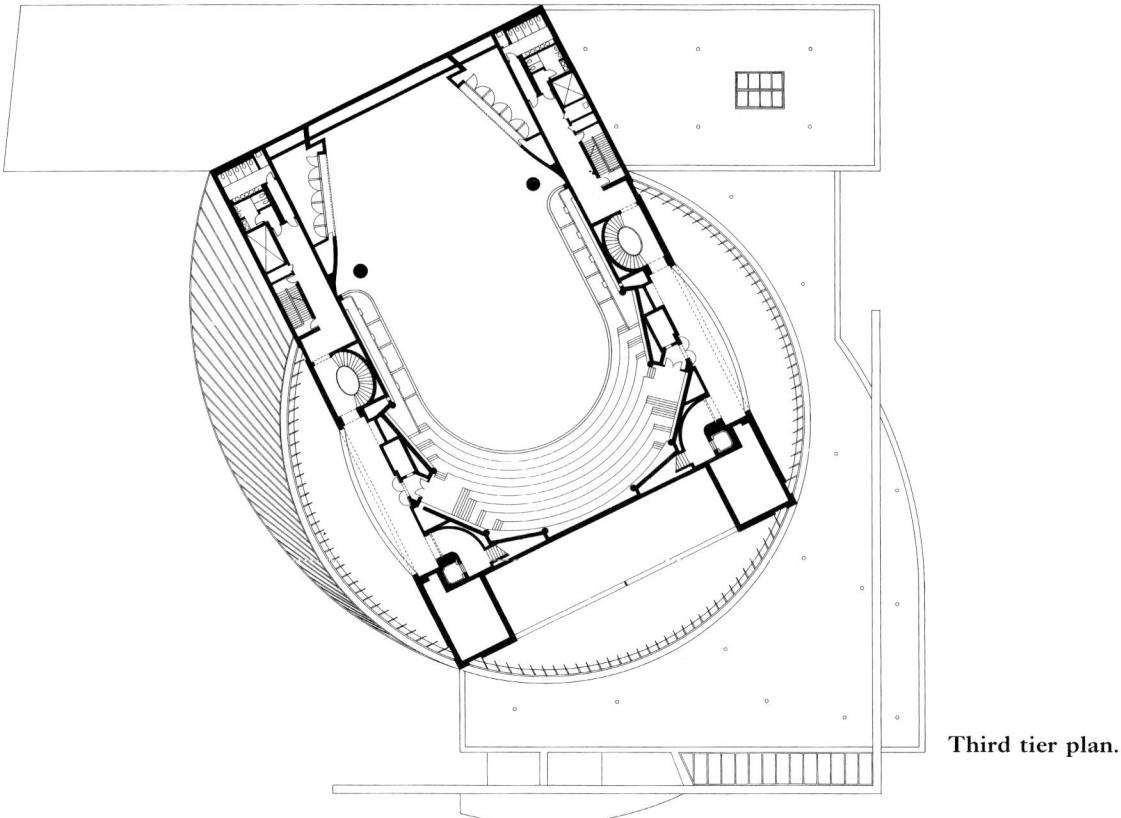

Third tier plan.

Main floor width: 25.6m (84ft) maximum (including terrace seating)

Stage: width 18.3m (60ft) downstage, 12.5m (41ft) upstage, depth from apron 11m (36ft)

(Acoustical data not available)

Maximum background noise level: threshold of hearing (continuous noise)

When completed, the Eugene McDermott Concert Hall, which forms part of the Morton H. Meyerson Symphony Center now under construction, could be one of the most significant and acoustically excellent twentieth-century concert halls, accurately modelling some of the features of historical precedents, while being an architectural refinement of the acoustically outstanding Pikes Peak Center at Colorado Springs, designed by the same acoustician (see page 102). The design is an intriguing combination of a hall with a traditional feel, while using the entirely contemporary architectural language for which its architect is famous.

The brief to the designers was 'to provide a sound environment which will, as closely as possible, duplicate the acoustical properties . . . (of) the Musikvereinssaal, Vienna, and the Concertgebouw, Amsterdam'. In terms of dimensions and seating distribution, the resultant plan in fact owes more to New York's Carnegie Hall. The auditorium is a simple rectangular shape, proportionally about 2:3, with parallel side walls for sustaining multiple reflections of sound energy, and a curved balcony front for visual uniformity and intimacy. The acoustical aim was to integrate the performers and audience into a single reverberant space—as in the traditional European halls—rather than incorporate an orchestra shell enclosure, as has been usual North American practice. Within the single room, the performing area is visually defined by a pair of giant columns either side of the stage front. On the main floor, the seating to the sides is raised to form a continuous bank of three rows parallel with the side walls, in order to decrease the apparent width of the hall. Above the side seating is a continuous shallow dress circle—like Carnegie Hall—and two tiers of balcony seats above this. The walls of the rear balconies narrow at the sides to a reverse fan shape in plan, to be effective reflectors of lateral sound.

The hall is conceived acoustically on the principle of the traditional shoe box concert hall, where the sound-absorptive audience area occupies the lower part of the auditorium, and is capped by a lofty sound-reflective ceiling crown where reverberant sound energy can be sustained. In this zone above the balconies, just below the ceiling itself, is a series of reverberant chambers with openable pneumatically-operated steel framed concrete doors that can couple or decouple the chambers with the auditorium. This device is an extension of the utilization of the stagehouse as a reverberant chamber as used in the halls at Kitchener and Colorado Springs (see page 107). The variation was necessary here because of the absence of a stage house, but also gives the advantage that the 'audible tail' surrounds the listener, rather than being

Model of the auditorium seen from the stage. The grills at the upper level conceal doors to reverberation chambers.

directional, from the front. The chambers cantilever forwards over the auditorium so that the effective width of the crown ceiling is reduced in the upper part of the hall. To maintain visual uniformity, the reverberation chamber doors (which may be half open or closed) are set behind a sound transparent grille. The trellis effect is continued onto the ceiling surround, creating the general impression of lightness and transparency. The acoustic 'scale' of the room can be adjusted by means of a variable height suspended canopy; this and the walls of the auditorium contain onyx sconces which glow softly, and the doors to the auditorium contain etched glass for the same lantern-like effect.

The hall will be the home of the Dallas Symphony Orchestra (which was founded in 1900) and will form the centrepiece, along with the Dallas Museum of Art, opened 1984, of a major 60 acre redevelopment area known as the Arts District, north east of the Dallas business core. The building is a combination of overlapping forms: a masonry rectangle enclosing the auditorium is set at an angle within a square glass and masonry block containing public and backstage areas. The rotation of the building acknowledges the overlaid street grids in Dallas, while having the practical advantage of creating more length for the auditorium on an otherwise tight site. The geometry of the forms is resolved by a 270 degree circular glass wall, a 'hub' which defines the audience circulation area. Entrance to the Symphony Center is via an underground parking garage. Street level vehicular traffic is to be limited in the Arts

Artist's rendering of the entrance staircase to the lobby.

Rendering of the exterior.

District and ground level parking will be prohibited. The rotated form allows a dramatic sequential entry to the hall along an 'eroded' symmetrical axis. A single grand staircase connects the entry point below ground with the lobby level, from where the audience, passing between a portico of two large triangular columns, is distributed via further stairs and elevators to the different parts of the auditorium.

CHAPTER 4

Adaptability and Multiple-use

Variability in auditoria is introduced below separately in terms of spatial organization and acoustics—aspects which in the building itself may be either more or less independent or integrally related. For example, a single-purpose concert hall may be designed with a variable reverberation time, or a single-purpose theatre with an adaptable stage, though in a larger multiple-use hall for speech and music the two become inseparable. The auditoria in this chapter illustrate different techniques for providing variability, and other chapters provide further applications. Chapter 5, in particular, discusses the use of the courtyard form for smaller adaptable theatres.

Fitting Form to Function

By the 1970s most large European and older-established North American cities had acquired a range of auditoria—concert halls, recital rooms, opera houses, theatres, conference centres, and so on. In provincial towns or the recently expanded cities in North America, however, where existing facilities may be outdated or non-existent, building a separate auditorium for each purpose is often out of the question in terms of cost and site-availability. Designers are frequently asked to provide in one hall a near-impossible range of activities, including symphony and choral concerts, ballet, recitals, professional and amateur drama and opera, rock concerts, musical revues, film, exhibitions, trade shows, conferences, ballroom dancing, spectator sports, and religious services. Even single-purpose halls with a principal tenant, such as a theatre company or an orchestra, usually require rental income from less specialized uses. In North America, where government funding of the arts is not traditional as it is in Europe, a large hall may have to be used some 300 nights a year to be economically viable. In practice, few of the auditoria in this book are truly single-purpose.

The use of theatres and concert halls for more than one purpose, and the adaptability that enables this, is as old as the building types themselves. European concert halls were often built with a flat floor for use as a ballroom, even though a raked floor would have improved vision and acoustics. Sometimes in theatres the raked parterre could be covered with a temporary floor for balls or banquets, as at the Opéra de Versailles by Jacques-Ange

Gabriel built in 1768–70. At the Residenz Theater, Munich, by François de Cuvilliés, built in 1751–53, the entire parterre could be raised to the horizontal by stage machinery. Nineteenth-century American theatres were regularly adapted, if only in a makeshift manner, from drama and vaudeville use to grand opera, as touring opera (many years before orchestras were established) was popular.

Multiple-use halls gained in the past a deservedly poor reputation. Referring to the common school and community hall with a flat floor and a stage with a proscenium at one end, the British theatre director Stephen Joseph said in 1963, 'If the adaptable theatre ends in compromise, the multi-purpose hall usually ends in inadequacy . . . Meanwhile, the multi-purpose hall proliferates all over the country, and is such a restriction on creative activity as to provide an efficient weapon for the destruction of the theatre.' On a more sophisticated level, large multiple-use auditoria in North America, and adaptable stage theatres in Germany, began to use computerized mechanical stage machinery from around 1960; several incorporated movable auditorium elements and orchestra shells which provided the possibility of a virtually demountable room-within-a-room. But the difficulty and cost of designing large moving elements without giving the hall a temporary, makeshift appearance meant in practice that the adaptability was usually confined to a couple of stage modes within a basic 'confrontational' layout. Many theatre directors found the complexity yet inflexibility of such systems theatrically inhibiting rather than liberating. Where there was a concert hall mode, the adaptability again tended to be limited, and the auditorium would retain some of the disadvantages of using a theatre for this purpose.

For drama, the principle of a fully adaptable stage, giving the possibility of a thrust, end or proscenium stage or theatre-in-the-round, became especially attractive during the 1950s and '60s when the future of the proscenium theatre seemed uncertain, as directors experimented with various forms of open stage. But because of the time and labour involved, full adaptability was usually considered uneconomic except in small experimental, so-called studio theatres built for schools and colleges. There, the adaptations would be made with their 'free' student labour. Typically, they would be equipped with rostrum units or retractable bleacher seating, perhaps a retractable stage or scaffold towers, 'shapes' for school use and scenery units or a white cyclorama cloth. A suspended grid over the entire auditorium or a continuous gallery would provide flexible lighting positions. The audience-performer relationship could be varied quite quickly. Such theatres are particularly useful in drama schools for presenting plays in an appropriate setting. The first of its kind in Great Britain was a studio theatre converted by Richard Southern from a former squash court at the University of Bristol's Drama Department. This was succeeded in the University by the Glynne Wickham (formerly Vandyck) Studio Theatre, a basically rectangular space regained from two floors of a former printing works. With a maximum capacity of 175 seats, it was designed to enable experimental forms of staging and any style of traditional theatre to be created within a few hours. This might be a fragment of a classical amphitheatre, a medieval booth theatre, an Elizabethan thrust stage, a candle-lit Restoration theatre, a proscenium theatre, a theatre-in-the-round, or a form of promenade theatre. The difficulty in creating a highly adaptable theatre is that each type of stage suggests its own floor plan—square or circular for an arena stage, a narrow rectangle for an end stage, a broader rectangle or fan for a thrust and proscenium. Any selected plan form, therefore, tends to be biased towards a particular seating arrangement.

The recent use of large hand-movable elements on air castors, as at the Derngate Centre, Northampton, has now introduced simpler and fuller adaptability and more adequate multiple-use to large-scale auditoria also. There, the entire stage end of the hall is demountable, together with large banks of seating in the stalls.

Mozart versus Mahler

A number of recent concert halls have incorporated the ability to change the acoustic character of the space according to the music to be performed. This is important because of the relationship that existed historically between the composer and the acoustics of the space for which he was writing music. The need for adjustable acoustics is even more acute in multiple-use auditoria where the conflicting requirements of speech, opera, amplified popular music, and so on, must be regarded on an equal footing. The most common variable is reverberation time, which may be designed to vary, say, between 1.5 and 2.2 seconds. This range will reveal on one hand the articulated detail of music by Mozart and other composers of the classical period, and provide a full-toned blended sound for liturgical music and for the late romantic music of Brahms, Strauss and Mahler on the other. Of course, matching the reverberation time of a modern hall to that of the original ambience of the music does nothing to vary the impression of the size of the room, which is possibly much more important. This has to do with the position of the sound-reflecting surfaces; chamber music may sound loud in a drawing room but

'quiet' in a 2000 seat hall. Devices that vary the position of reflecting surfaces may therefore be at least as effective as variable reverberation. The variability may be either mechanical, using retractable or movable elements, or electronic 'assisted resonance'. Both methods have been widely used for two decades or so, though an electronic system, however convincing acoustically, may be 'morally' unacceptable. Elaborate mechanical variability was particularly favoured by North American designers in the 1960s and early 70s to achieve 'several halls for the price of one', though the experience has been that the adjustability has to be simple to avoid being mis-used or simply under-used.

The reverberation time of a hall can be adjusted mechanically by varying either the amount of acoustic absorption or the cubic volume. The variable absorption is usually provided by retractable heavy woollen banners, which may be integrated with the architecture of the auditorium or perhaps concealed behind a grill. However, because of the enormous area of material necessary to alter the reverberation time significantly—roughly the same area as the audience—an alternative is to use retractable drapery simply to eliminate reflections from certain wall surfaces when a sound amplification system is used. This prevents the clarity of amplified speech from being obscured. For rock music also, which uses its own electronically generated acoustical effects, the hall should be acoustically 'dead'. Theoretically, the reduction of reverberation time by adding absorptive material has the disadvantage of reducing the sound level also. Although in practice this is not significant it is avoided by varying the volume instead, either with a movable ceiling or by coupling the auditorium with a 'reverberation chamber'.

Aside from adjusting reverberation time, the impact of the sound can be varied with movable sound-reflecting surfaces. These alter the arrival time of the first reflections in relation to the direct sound, a time gap to which the ear is highly sensitive. Removable panels in the stage surround can be used to balance the sections of the orchestra, and, together with other variable elements, give the capability for long-term adjustability according to the preferences of different music directors. A large, vertically movable reflecting canopy can even alter the impression of the size of a hall, quite independent of the reverberation time of the overall volume.

Electronic assisted resonance, the other method of varying reverberation time, was originally devised as a remedial measure for the Royal Festival Hall, London, which turned out to be less reverberant than intended by the designers, with a reverberation time of just 1.4 seconds at middle frequencies with a full audience. Raising the roof was considered, but this was thought to be too expensive and would have altered the appearance of the building. The electronic system comprises the installation of a large number of microphones, amplifiers and loudspeakers. The gain of the amplifiers is turned up almost to point of feedback, so that when sound is picked up by the microphones, the loudspeakers continue to 'ring' after the sound has stopped. Each channel is tuned to a particular frequency, though an alternative Swedish system does not involve this.

Hamilton Place, Ontario

Owner: City of Hamilton

Architect: Trevor P. Garwood-Jones

Acoustic consultant: Russell Johnson Associates

Theatre consultant: Bolt, Beranek and Newman

Structural engineers: Omen Lee & Associates Ltd., SNC Filer Ltd, Canaly Otter Ltd

Mechanical and electrical engineers: Quist & Associates Ltd, Keith Associates, Ltd.

Cost consultant: Hanscomb Roy Associates

Main contractor: Frid Construction Company

Opened: 1973

Cost: Can $9,675,000

Floor area: 20,088 sq.m (216,236 sq.ft)

Principal uses: concerts, opera, drama

Seats: total 2181, main floor 1193, first balcony 560, second balcony 428, total with orchestra pit 2091, total with forestage 1957

Furthest balcony seat from stage: 30.73m (101ft) from full thrust stage

Proscenium opening: width 15.2m (50ft), height 7m (23ft)

Stage: width 18.9m (62ft) left wing to right wing (23.5m [77ft] centreline to stage left wing), depth 11.3m (37ft) from fire curtain to structural columns (18.3m [60ft] from proscenium wall to rear wall), height to grid underside 21.3m (70ft)

Flying system: 64 rigging line sets (single purchase counterweight)

Orchestra area: (both stage lifts raised to form platform) width 21.9m (72ft) downstage, 14.6m (48ft) upstage, depth from apron 10m (33ft)

Orchestra pit: (stage lift no.1) 100 musicians

Cubic volume: 28,300 cub.m (1,000,000 cub.ft)

Reverberation time: variable

Maximum background noise level: PNC 15

The Canadian industrial city of Hamilton was in the situation of many provincial centres: wishing to upgrade

Orchestra floor plan. Key: 1 piano nobile, 2 controls, 3 main floor, 4 lift 2, 5 lift 1, 6 stage, 7 dressing rooms, 8 stage door, 9 guard, 10 stage manager, 11 lifts, 12 loading and unloading, 13 trucking, 14 meeting rooms, 15 upper studio theatre

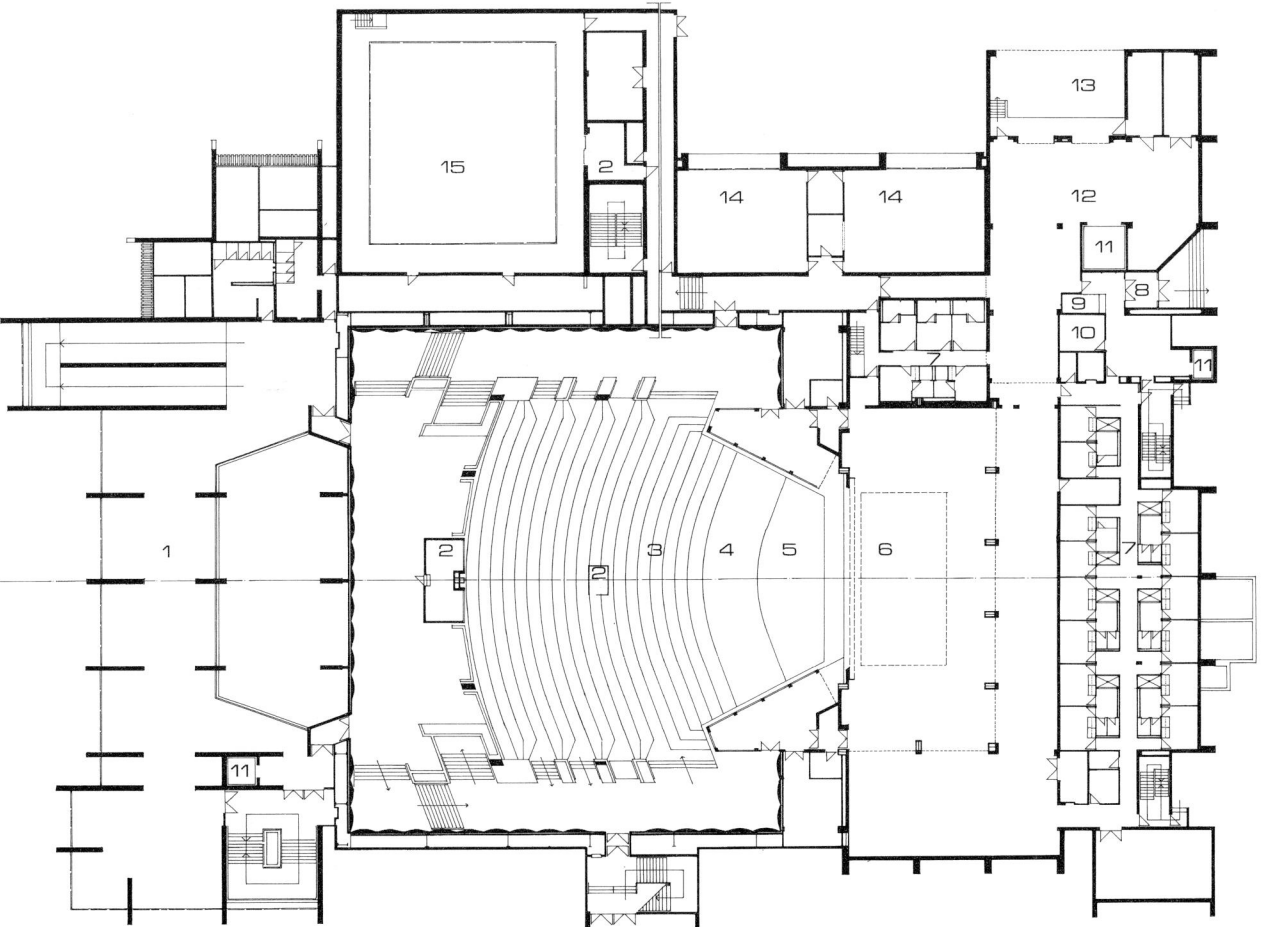

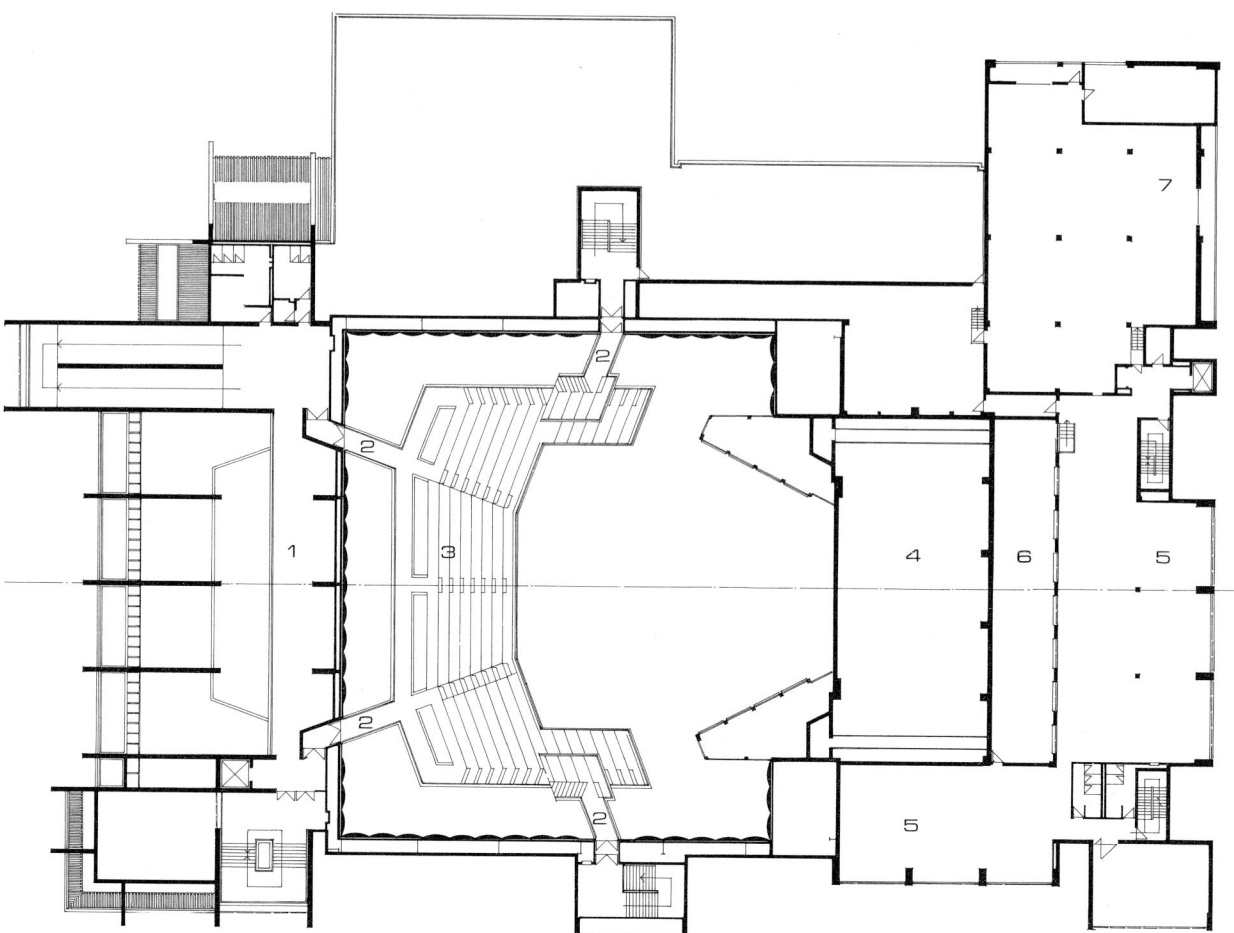

First balcony plan. Key: 1 lobby crossover, 2 bridges,
3 first balcony, 4 upper stage, 5 offices, 6 garden court,
7 mechanical room   Sectional perspective

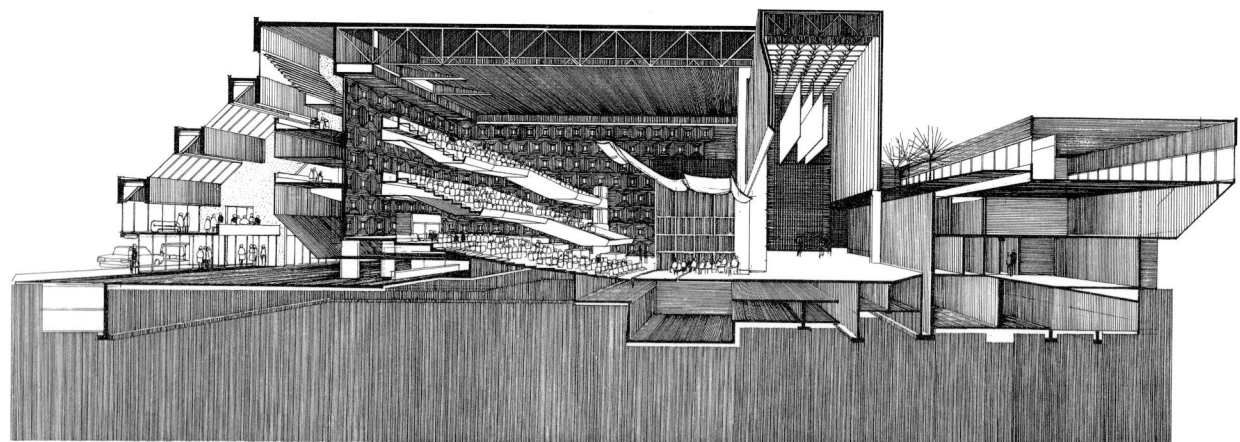

its cultural amenities, yet able to afford only one combination hall to house the whole of its community performing arts groups—the Hamilton Philharmonic Orchestra, Opera Hamilton, the Bach-Elgar Choir, Columbia Artists' Community Concerts, and MacMaster's University Symphony Orchestra—as well as needing to stage rock, country and western music, ballet, and a variety of touring shows.

Previous combination theatre-concert halls had normally placed the orchestra behind the proscenium on the main stage below the flytower (or, at most, had partially brought the orchestra forward). The main design problem had been to prevent loss of sound into the stagehouse by using portable shells and canopies and to cope with the fact that the orchestra was acoustically in a different 'room' to the audience. Hamilton's auditorium overcomes this difficulty for orchestral concerts simply by closing off the stagehouse at the proscenium with a 7.7 tonne (17,000lb) cedar 'guillotine' wall, and creating an orchestra platform in front—effectively a forestage to the

The auditorium with the acoustic banners fully
extended.

main stage—so that the orchestra is in the main body of
the hall. The first eight rows of seats are on two stage lifts
operated by hydraulic screw jacks. These descend so that
the seating can be stored below the main floor level; the
elevators are then raised to stage level, creating a platform
for 130 musicians forward of the motorized acoustic wall.
This leaves the main stage free for rehearsals, and sets can
be retained or built while the orchestra occupies the
forward stage. Alternatively, the first stage lift can form
either an orchestra pit, or a thrust to the main stage with
the second stage lift forming the pit.

With this arrangement, the reflecting surface above
the orchestra is no longer restricted by the height of the
proscenium arch. Here, there is a canopy at 11.6m (38ft)
to 14m (46ft) above the stage—though the subsequent
practice has been to place this somewhat higher. The
reflecting canopy is in three panels which were originally
to have been of variable angle, though in fact only the
centre panel is variable. Enclosing the orchestra platform
on either side are splayed walls to form a stage surround,
along with the motorized acoustic wall. The side walls
each contain twelve cedar panels on castors on three
levels, separated by concrete slabs, which are removable
for television cameras or lighting, or can be opened like
doors for acoustic adjustability. Hand-pivoted wings on
either side of the stage are moved into place to complete
the proscenium opening when the acoustic wall is raised.

The other innovative aspect of the hall is the acoustic
design of the audience area, to complete the conversion
from opera theatre to concert hall. To maximize
economically the volume of the hall for a reverberant
concert hall acoustic, the concept was, so to speak, to
remove the side walls so that the outer walls of the aisles
and lobbies became the acoustic boundary of the hall.
These outer areas are surfaced with hard, acoustically-
reflective finishes—quarry tile floors and brick walls (for
speed of erection the auditorium is steel framed, while
the surrounding structure is concrete). The brickwork is
divided into sculptured decorative panels. Inside this

The hall arranged for symphony concert, with the banners retracted and the stage elevators raised to form an orchestra platform.

structure, the balconies are free-standing, the top balconies being hung from the auditorium roof trusses and the lower balconies cantilevered in two directions from structural columns and tied back to the walls. For speech, or when the amplification system is used, the sound reflections from the sidewalls are controlled by heavy velour banners, 3.7m (12ft) wide and 19.8m (65ft) high. These are retractable for concert use, being operated by motorized cable drums in the ceiling. With the banners raised, the large square brick auditorium produces a strong and reverberant bass response—at some expense to the brilliance and strength of the upper string parts (the loss of the upper frequencies is possibly due to excessive sidewall diffusion). The dramatic architectural effect of the white-painted tilted balconies hovering inside the brick enclosure, with the orange-red banners suspended between the two, is that of a building within a building—notionally a new structure within a pre-existing shell. These elements, together with a dark-painted ceiling with nearly 150 quartz iodine lamps which simulate a starlight effect, and orange coloured seating, create a warm and intimate interior.

For events requiring amplification—such as rock concerts and musicals—there is a control booth in the centre of the main floor, and a floor-mounted loudspeaker beneath every two seats together with ceiling-mounted loudspeakers, with a delayed signal adjusted to 17 different zones within the auditorium. The hall is also designed with extensive television video facilities, and a significant aspect of its revenue is from the recording of stage productions such as opera and Broadway musicals.

Outside the main auditorium, which is acoustically isolated with a double wall construction, is the main foyer, which is conceived as a series of brightly furnished mezzanine lounges overlooking a quarry tiled entrance lobby below, divided by concrete buttress fins which form the building's outer structure. These public circulation areas have sloping clerestorey lights and large windows which relate to Hamilton's Main Street outside; part of the area has a dance floor which is used after theatre performances, and is also frequently used for television shows and interviews.

The exterior showing the glazed foyer.

Christ's Hospital Theatre, Horsham

Owner: Christ's Hospital

Architects: Howell, Killick, Partridge & Amis

Theatre consultant: Theatre Projects Ltd

Structural engineers: Harris & Sutherland

Mechanical and electrical engineers: Edwards & Blackie

Quantity surveyor: David Vevers

Main contractor: Bovis Construction (Southern) Ltd

Opened: 1974

Cost: £595,000

Principal uses: educational drama and concerts

Seats: arena layout 450 seats, proscenium layout 580 seats

Furthest balcony seat from stage front: 17m (56ft)

Proscenium opening: width 8.8m (29ft), height to header 5.7m (18.5ft)

Stage: width inside galleries 15.2m (50ft), depth from house curtain 11.6m (38ft), thrust stage width 6.6m (21.6ft), maximum thrust stage depth to front of orchestra pit 11m (36ft), flying height to roof void 10m (32.8ft)

Flying system: 6 winch operated line sets and 5 hemp sets over the stage area

This simple school theatre was the first and one of the most successful—partly because of its simplicity—of the recent generation of small adaptable theatres, relying for its adaptability on 'boy power', because a mechanical system for changing the interior form would have been prohibitively expensive.

Christ's Hospital was established by Edward VI in 1553, and the existing buildings date from 1896–1903 when the scholars—'Bluecoat boys'—were transferred from the City of London to rural Sussex. The buildings were a competition-winning design by Aston Webb—an enormous axial complex in Tudor-style polychromatic brickwork, like a large Cambridge college. The theatre is part of the Christ's Hospital Arts Centre, a facility where drama plays a major role, and which in practice serves the region as well as the school itself. The building is of bright red brick and surrounds the old music school to the south east of the main quadrangle, on the far side of a

fine avenue of lime trees to the south of the school. Besides the 450–500 seat theatre with ancillary accommodation, the school wanted nine classrooms, a small library and seminar rooms, 41 practice rooms, a band room, a library and a small recital room. The classrooms are planned at the foyer end of the theatre, so that they can be used as cloakrooms and even refreshment rooms.

The theatre itself is a simple elongated octagon, with one row deep timber galleries in three tiers extending around three sides of the rectangle. The fourth wall—the stage end—is highly adaptable, with four movable 3-storey stage towers, built with the same appearance as the fixed galleries. These can either complete the 'courtyard' for an extended thrust stage and seating on three sides, or they can be rolled away to form an end stage. The two parallelogram towers can be used to form a proscenium, while any of the towers can be used as scenic elements.

Plan of the music school and theatre, the auditorium arranged with an arena stage.

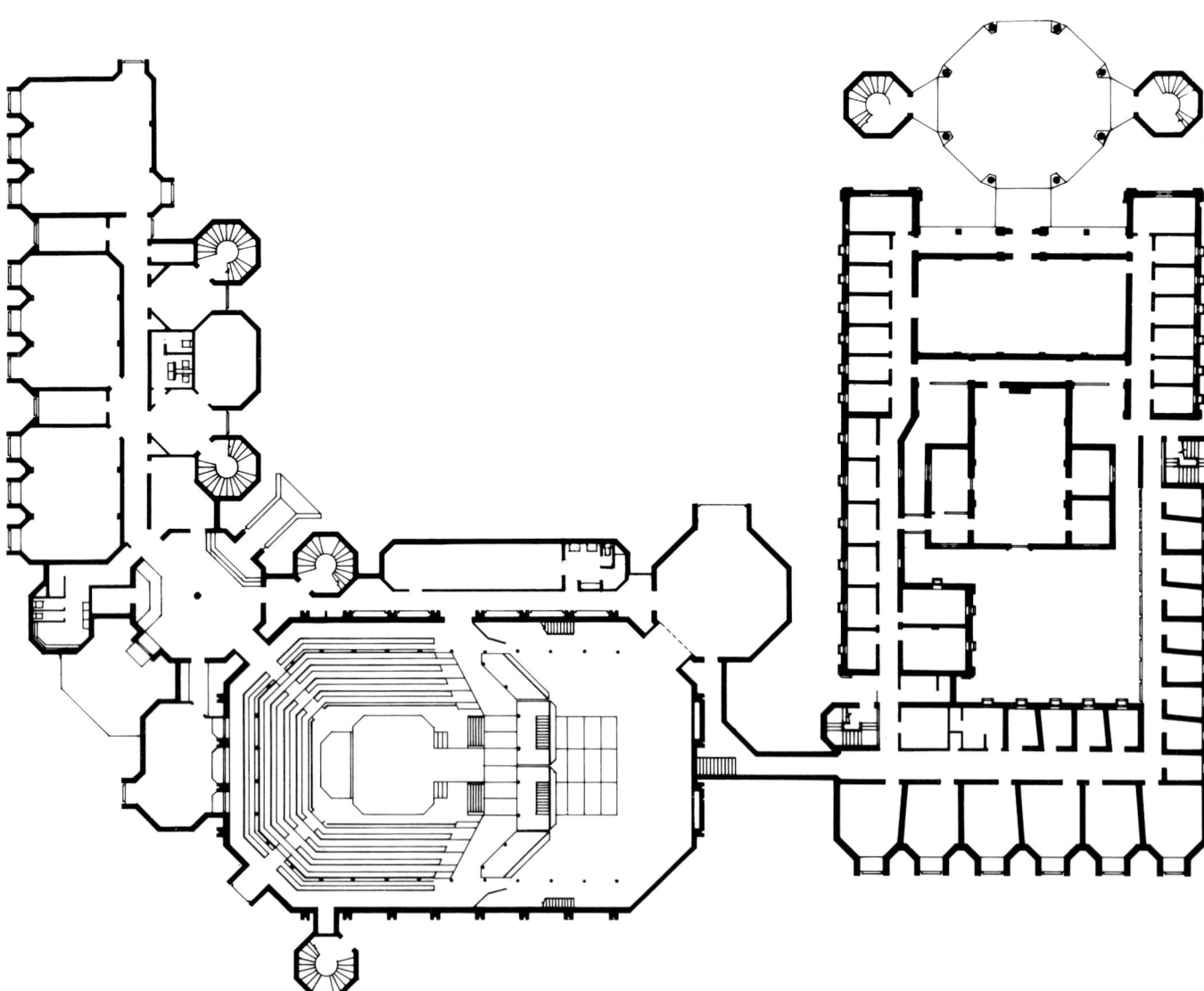

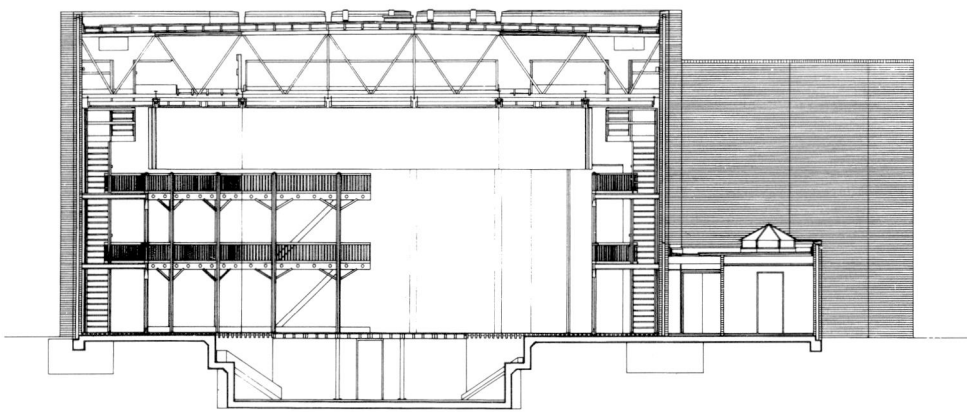

Lateral and longitudinal sections through the theatre.

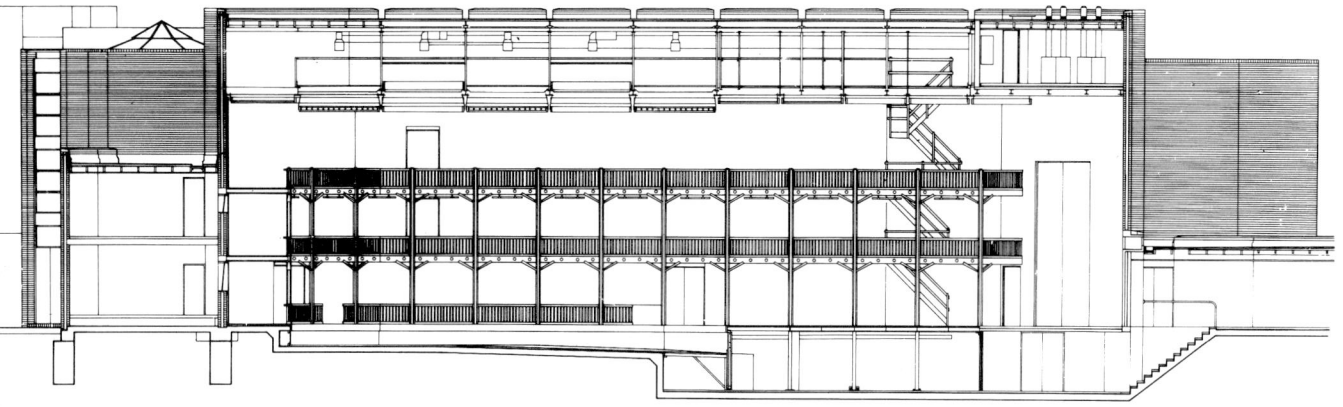

The theatre and music rooms from the south. The
theatre is steel-framed and clad in brickwork.

The entrance approach.

Arena stage layout, with the movable towers
completing the gallery along the end wall.

Cladding panels are attached to the towers giving them a solid appearance matching the fixed cladding to the brick walls of the auditorium, but these can be removed if open platforms are required. Removable floor and ceiling panels are provided in the towers to enable access staircases to be set up between the three levels of each tower when they are being used as individual elements. The towers are moved on large-diameter castors which are hydraulically jacked down onto the stage surface from within the tower base. A proscenium header can be tracked up and down stage to align with the towers in their proscenium positions, and the house curtain is rigged on a track mounted on the rear of the proscenium header. These are operated by winches mounted in the galleries. In addition to the simple flying facilities over the stage, spot lines can be rigged in the lighting boxes over the auditorium when in the thrust stage format.

The main floor has a raked concrete ground slab which steps down to form an orchestra pit and understage area. The stage is built up from the sub-floor on columns, and the seating and performing areas are arranged as required—again by the boys—with wooden rostra. The timber galleries and seating are all stained red and there is an eggcrate suspended ceiling, also in red. Rows of 'dressing room' tungsten bulbs set in the gallery and tower fronts provide houselighting. The effect is warm and cheerful, and the theatre, which has mellowed somewhat with use, remains popular with audiences. The extended thrust stage works particularly well, though the theatre is significantly wider in proportion, and consequently less intimate, than the subsequent small 'courtyard' theatres discussed in Chapter 5.

Music School: University of Cambridge

Owner: University of Cambridge
This building has been built in a series of stages. Stage I included the auditorium, Stage II teaching rooms, Stage III backstage accommodation, Stage IV the library and Stage V the public foyer and additional faculty rooms.

Architect: Sir Leslie Martin, with Colen Lumley for Stage I and Ivor Richards at later stages

The basic form of the floor plans evolved so that the building could be phased: Stage I the auditorium; Stage II teaching rooms and backstage accommodation (the south, bottom, and north portions respectively); Stage III completion of the surrounding band of accommodation including the library (Stage IV) and the entrance lobby (Stage V).

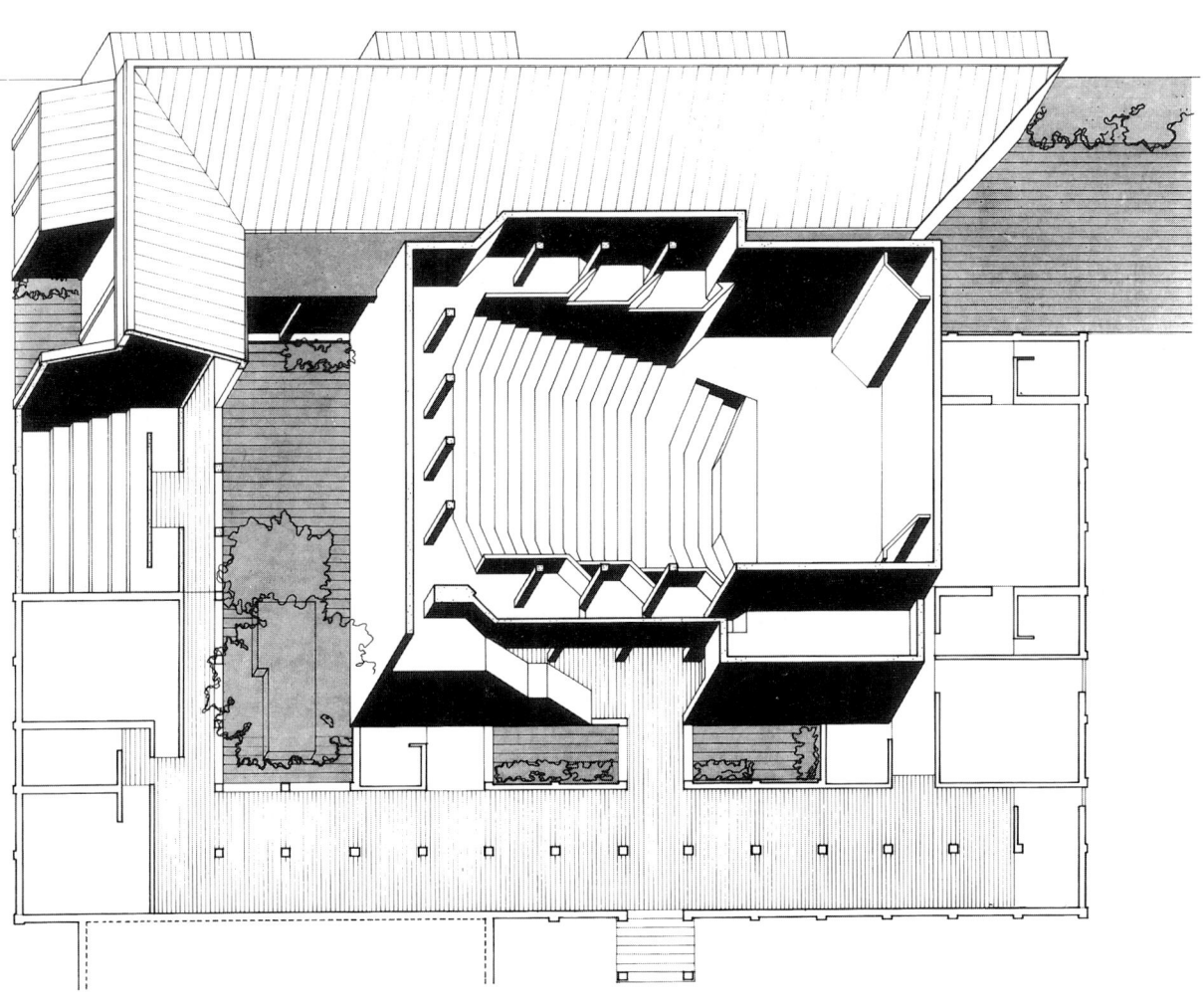

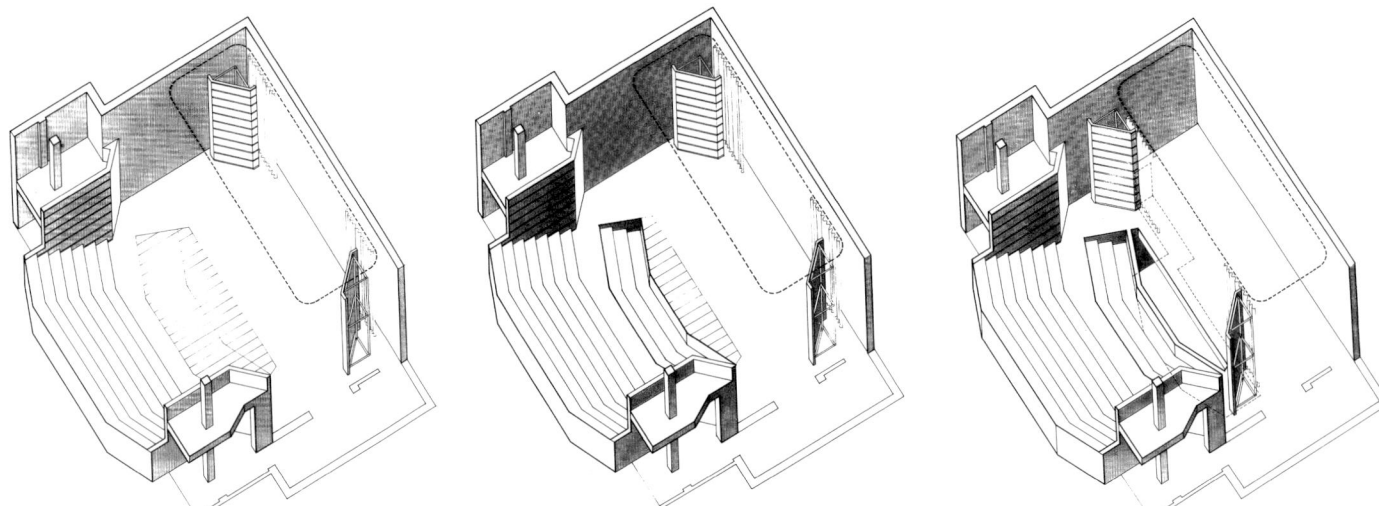

Three stage arrangements: (*left to right*) maximum flat floor, *periaktoi* in rear position, curtains retracted on rear wall; normal concert layout with some floor panels removed and loose seating added (the *periaktoi* can be moved to form a more intimate stage for chamber music); orchestra pit condition, *periaktoi* brought forward to form proscenium with stage curtain.

The auditorium looking towards the stage, showing the *periaktoi*, the movable ceiling reflecting panels and with some of the floor panels removed for extra seating.

The interior from the stage end. In the foreground part of the removable forestage can be seen, which forms an orchestra pit, together with the three rows of removable seating which create a flat floor condition. Note also the acoustically transparent ceiling and one of the adjustable ceiling reflectors.

Acoustic consultant: Hugh Creighton

Other consultants and contractors: these have changed for different stages of the work

Opened: 1977 (Auditorium only)

Cost: £380,000 (Stage I only)

Uses: teaching, orchestra, choir, recitals and other musical activities

Seats: 500

Furthest seat from front of stage: varies with different stage arrangements: stage with orchestra 18.75m (61.5ft); stage with orchestra pit filled in 16.75m (55ft); flat floor condition with orchestra pit and three rows of seats covered in 14m (46ft)

Stage dimensions: width 18m (59ft), depth varies as above: 6.8m (22.3ft); 8.8m (29ft); 11.55m (38ft)

Volume: 3965 cub.m (140,000 cub.ft)

Reverberation time: 1.9 sec. (curtain bunched), 1.6 sec. (curtain extended) at middle frequencies with full audience

---

The 500 seat auditorium for the University's Faculty of Music illustrates variability at its very simplest, for creating different performance modes within a fixed end-

Early model of the building, showing the isolation of the auditorium from the surrounding buildings.

stage layout. It was designed for a wide range of musical purposes including teaching, orchestra, choir and opera rehearsal and performance, and solo and chamber recitals.

The basic rectangular auditorium has a single steep rake of seating upholstered in bright red, with side galleries that step down towards the stage containing loose seating for flexibility. Both the galleries and the main body of the hall are naturally illuminated, because of its extensive use for teaching, with windows that admit light indirectly, reflecting off the buff-coloured brick-work. Various stage arrangements are possible. The first is a large flat floor surface extending from the front of the raked seating to the back of the stage. This provides a large platform, with a close integration of the platform area with the seating, for a variety of faculty uses. By removing a series of panels across the front of this area, three stepped rows of loose seating can be added, forming a conventional raised apron stage. By removing a further row of panels an orchestra pit is formed with a straight-fronted stage for opera. Two vertical free-standing 'periaktoi' on the stage are movable to alter further the scale of the performing area, or to suggest scenic flats for drama and background for recitals—and to provide an 'off-stage' area for chamber music players between applause. Pulled forwards, the panels suggest a proscenium opening.

Corresponding adjustments can be made to the ceiling area. For musical performances, three rows of plywood panels in the ceiling offer a 45 degree angle of sound reflection, lowering the effective height over the platform area. For opera, they can be manually rotated to a vertical position for hanging simple scenic flats or adding additional stage lighting. Some further acoustic control is provided by a curtain on a track above the rear wall, which continues around the front to give the potential of a stage curtain when the ceiling panels are in the vertical position and the 'periaktoi' are in the proscenium mode.

The plastered soffit of the pitched roof enclosure is sloped longitudinally to help diffuse the sound reflections. The volume of the hall was designed for a reverberation time of 1.4 to 1.5 seconds at mid-frequencies with a full audience, to 1.8 to 2.1 seconds when empty. The hall is made visually intimate by a suspended, acoustically transparent plywood eggcrate ceiling. This also partially screens the ventilation ducts, catwalks, exposed roof trusses and lighting, and in addition acts as a grid for potential extra stage lighting if necessary.

Associated with the auditorium are lecture, seminar, practice, administrative and common rooms, a display area for the historical musical instruments collection, foyers and a library. The auditorium was conceived as a central core surrounded by a broad band of supporting accommodation which has grown as funds have become available. The phasing of the project in this way added clarity to the original design by requiring the auditorium to be structurally and constructionally separated from the single loop of surrounding rooms. The separation also introduced the idea of small courts which increase the acoustic isolation of the auditorium from the related areas. The courts also allow the preservation of existing trees and provide a pleasant outlook from the interior spaces.

Plan, with the *espace de projection* **on the left-hand side, and the circulation spine along the top.**

Institute for Research and Co-ordination in Acoustics and Music, Centre Georges Pompidou, Paris

Owner: Ministère des Affaires Culturelles/Ministère de l'Education National

Architects: Piano and Rogers

Acoustic consultant: Victor Peutz and Associates

Scenography consultant: Guy Claud François

Structural engineers: Ove Arup and Partners

Services engineers: Ove Arup and Partners

Quantity surveyors: Ove Arup and Partners

Main contractor: Grands Travaux de Marseilles (GTM)

Opened: 1977

Cost: £10 million

Primary use: musical research

Seats: 400 maximum

Volume: variable from 6650 cub.m (234,000 cub.ft) to 1662 cub.m (58,500 cub.ft)

Reverberation time: variable from 4 secs to 0.8 secs

Maximum background noise level: NR 20 (in 'espace de projection'), NR 15 (in recording studio), NR 20 (in other studios)

The main studio of the subterranean Institut de Recherche et de Coordination Acoustique/Musique is the ultimate mechanically variable acoustic chamber. As the architect has said, 'the whole reason for its existence is to push the limits of acoustic variability as far as possible'. It is not a concert hall, but a workshop or research laboratory, born out of the need felt by the founders of the Centre Georges Pompidou to incorporate a centre for musical experiment and composition, 'directed by France's leading musician'. It is like a musical instrument in itself, the acoustical variations being written into the composer's score. Unlike most of the auditoria in this book, it must be viewed as a unique

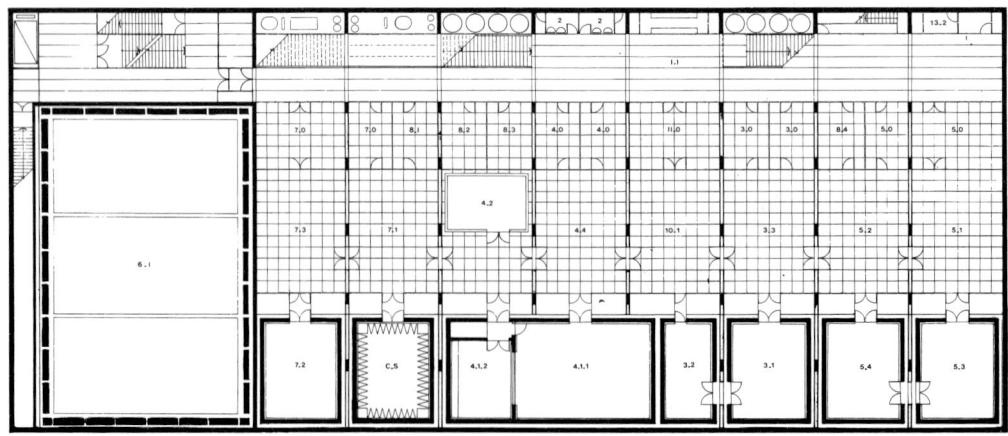

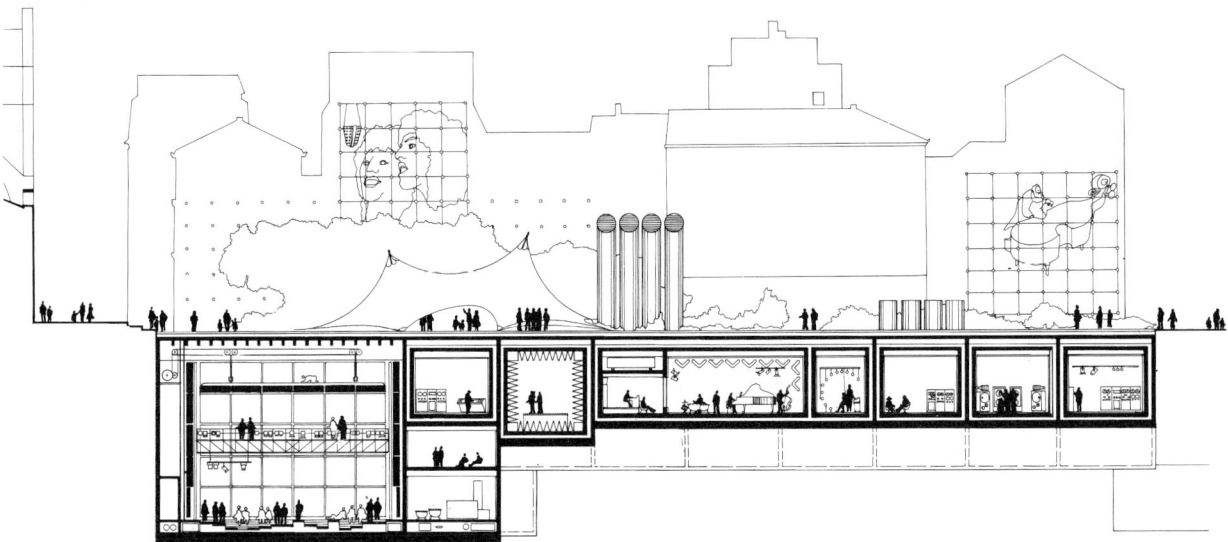

Longitudinal section.

Lateral section.

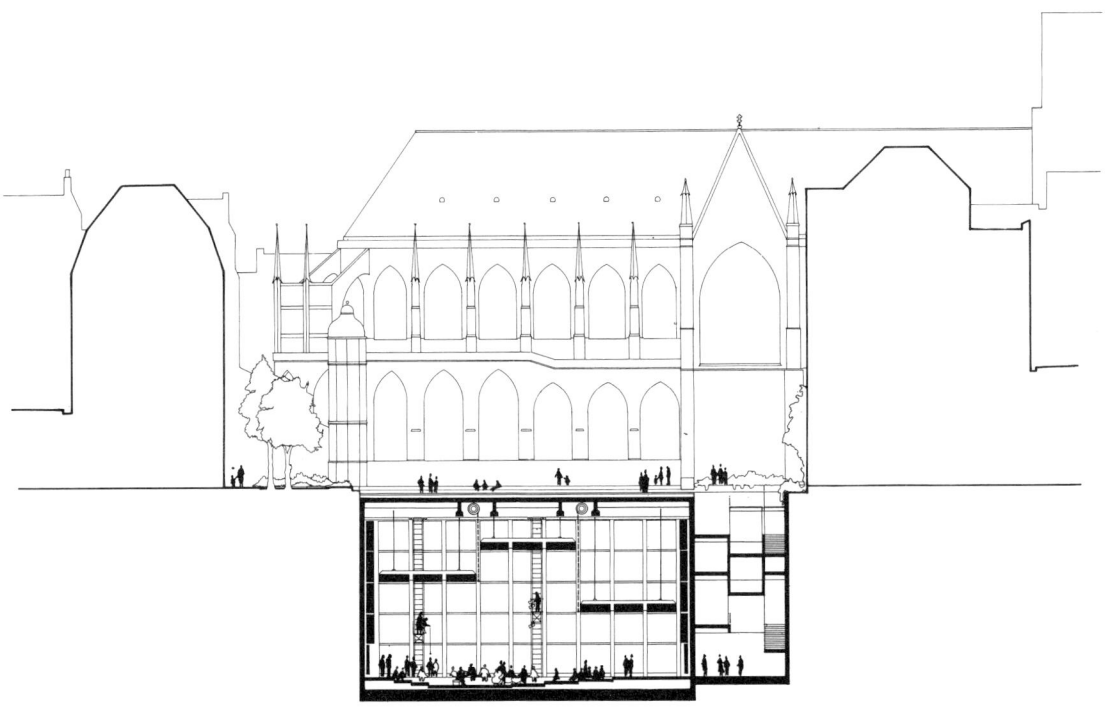

facility built at high cost around the approach of one composer, rather than as a prototype for broad application.

Pierre Boulez was attracted to return from New York—where he was musical director of the New York Philharmonic Orchestra—to become the *director générale* and catalyst of the new facility. He formed a core team, with Nicholas Snowman as artistic director and Pierre Armand as scientific coordinator. Boulez felt from the outset that IRCAM must be an essentially international centre for experimental music. To evolve a brief towards this goal, a seminar was organized at Senanque Abbey in southern France, to which a range of avant-garde musicians—including Ligeti and Luciano Berio—and related specialists were invited, to discuss the future of

music and the establishment of pedagogic departments for the new facility. These were related to computing and synthesis, electro-acoustics, instrumental and vocal music, and general acoustics. During the subsequent design period, IRCAM scientists, musicians and a scenographer worked closely with the architectural team.

IRCAM is sited underground adjacent to the main building of the Centre Pompidou, in the square between its brightly-coloured skeletal east façade and the church of Saint-Merri. The building is a series of studios and laboratories, built to very high acoustic performance requirements. The accommodation is contained within a reinforced concrete multi-level primary box sunk in the ground, the roof of which forms the piazza. It has a column and slab structure, forming eight structural

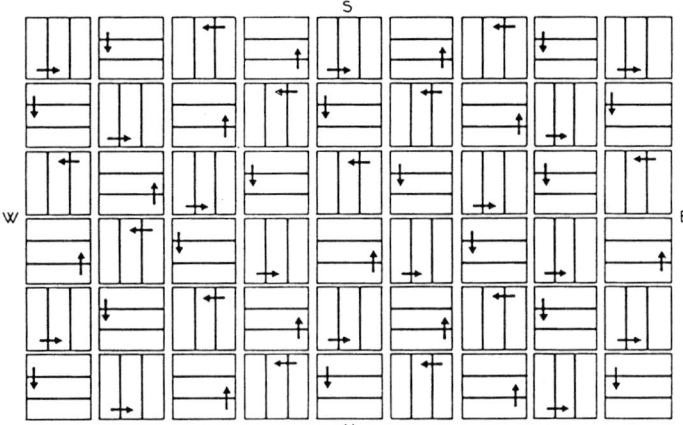

Ceiling plan of the *espace de projection*, viewed from below. Each square frame contains three revolving acoustic panels. An identical system is used for the walls.

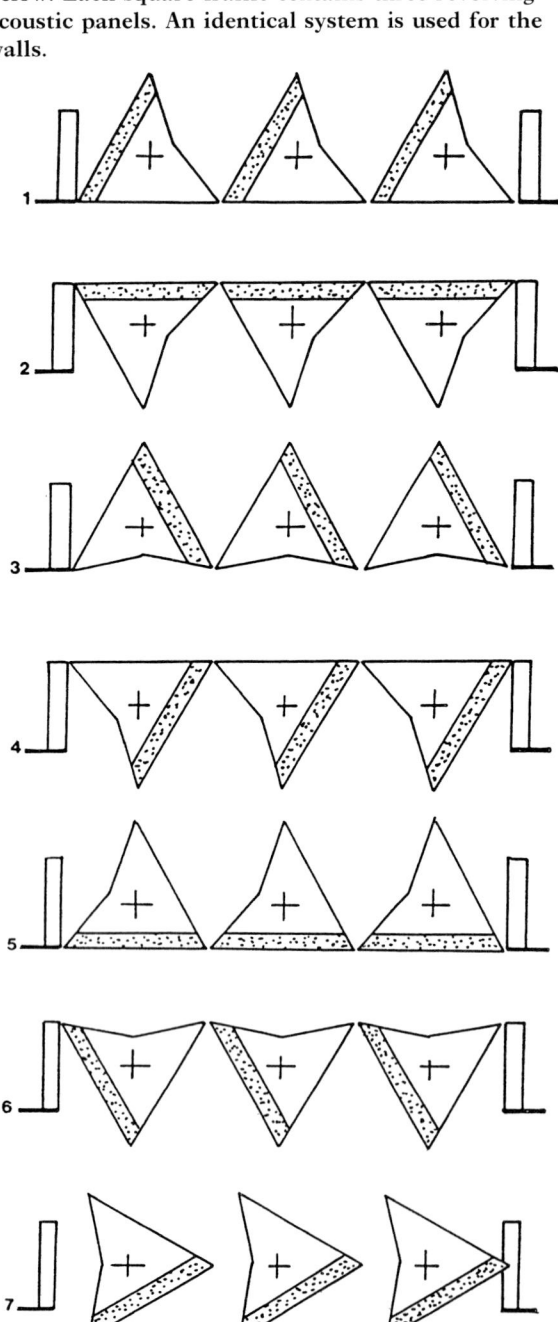

bays—two bays or about 1500 sq.m (16,000 sq.ft) to each department. The studios and other acoustically critical elements float independent of the structure as a 'box within a box', for acoustic isolation and flexibility. On the level below the research activities are mechanical plant rooms and other services, and on the lowest level, 16m (52.5ft) underground, at one end of the building is the main studio, an enormous 400 sq.m (4300 sq.ft) room known as the *espace de projection*. A broad circulation spine extends down one side of the building, with a glazed roof which floods the public areas underground with natural light. The research activities are zoned in relation to the circulation area according to the degree of acoustic control required. The offices overlook the daylit area, forming a buffer to the laboratories and the acoustically critical studios beyond.

The *espace de projection* is the meeting point between IRCAM and the public, where musical and dramatic events take place, which up to 400 people may attend and participate in. The room is 25m (82ft) long, 19m (62.3ft) wide, and 14m (46ft) high. Like the other studios it is a double box construction, but with variable inner elements. The reinforced concrete primary structure has walls of varying thickness, including one 800mm (2.6ft) thick on the two sides where the structure acts as a retaining wall. The roof is a 400mm (1.3ft) concrete slab with a floating screed on top, and a precast concrete paving slab finish on resilient rubber mountings, forming the surface of the piazza above.

The ceiling, wall and floor elements forming the inner box are all isolated from the main structure by soft rubber anti-vibration mounts. The ceiling is in three movable sections, each of which can be raised or lowered independently by means of electric motors. The ceiling is capable of a 10m (33ft) displacement, giving a 4:1 change in cubic volume. Between each ceiling section is a steel roller blind curtain system (with a single span of 19m [62.3ft], the largest of its type in Europe), which can fill the gaps created by the vertical displacement of the ceiling sections. Each curtain can also descend to floor level to divide the space into two or three separate rooms.

The ceiling sections and the walls, which are similar hung elements, together contain 172 panels. Each panel is made up of a frame containing three triangular panels which can rotate to expose three different acoustic surfaces; one side is sound-absorptive; another is sound-reflective; and the third is reflective and diffusing. This, combined with the adjustable volume, enables the reverberation time to be varied by 4:1. The panels have seven positions: three where the surfaces are flush with the wall; three where two faces are exposed; and one where the panel is turned to allow a gap for sound to pass through.

Section through the triangular revolving panels, illustrating the different acoustic conditions:
1 reflective, 2 reflective-diffusing, 3 diffusing, 4 diffusing-absorptive, 5 absorptive, 6 absorptive-reflecting, 7 joints open, in the event of fire

The *espace de projection*.   Top-lit circulation spine.

Entrance to IRCAM from Place Stravinsky. The only superstructure is the group of ship's ventilators. The church of Saint Merri is in the background.

For lighting and access to all parts of the volume, for scenic, performance and research purposes, there are three red-painted tubular steel transverse beam systems with ladders at either end, which can move both horizontally along the length of the room and vertically. All seating and theatrical equipment is also movable and has no determined position. The *espace de projection* is overlooked by a control room through a 5m (16.5ft) window, where the main console is housed, linked to the IRCAM central computer. All spatial and acoustic configurations can be pre-programmed, memorized and recalled and recreated at any time. Further consoles control a 32-track sound system and the lighting system,

which also has a memory control. Provision is also made for film and slide presentation. A further viewing window is situated on the west wall, with an electrically-operated shutter for public viewing when the research experiments may not be disturbed. All the elements can be changed during a performance, so that the acoustic and other variations can be incorporated into the work to be performed.

Stadthalle, Biberach an der Riss, and De Flint Cultural Centre, Amersfoort

Stadthalle, Biberach an der Riss

Owner: Municipality of Biberach an der Riss

Architect: Onno Greiner Martien van Goor Architekten B.V., Amsterdam

Theatre consultant: Wim Vesseur (died 1977)

Acoustic consultant: W. Tak (died 1985)

Structural engineer: Ingenieursgroep Van Rossum B.V., Amsterdam

Services engineer: Deerns Consulting Engineers B.V., Amsterdam

Landscape architect: Mien Ruys

General contractor: Arbeitsgemeinschaft Stadthalle Biberach

Design: competition held in 1970

Opened: 1978

Cost: DM 2.3 million

Area: 7600 sq.m (82,000 sq.ft)

Uses: children's theatre and many other community uses

Seats: main hall 1200 maximum, 830 for banquets, theatre 567 total (main floor 354, circle 213)

Proscenium opening: width 11.74m (38.5ft), height 6.5m (21.3ft)

Stage: width 28.77m (94.5ft) from right wing to left wing, depth 17.41m (57.1ft) from front of stage to rear wall, height to grid 18.15m (59.5ft)

Flying system: 40 rigging line sets

Volume: 3100 cub.m (109,460 cub.ft)

de Flint Cultural Centre, Amersfoort

Owner: Municipality of Amersfoort

Architect: Onno Greiner Martien van Goor Architekten B.V., Amsterdam

Theatre consultant: Wim Vesseur (died 1977)

Acoustic consultant: W. Tak (died 1985)

Structural engineer: Ingenieursgroep Van Rossum B.V., Amsterdam

Services engineer: Deerns Consulting Engineers B.V., Amsterdam

1

2

3

Calgary Centre for Performing Arts adopts the 'ideal' approach of separate auditoria for different functions. *1* Jack Singer Concert Hall is home of the Calgary Philharmonic Orchestra, *2* The Max Bell Theatre, of Theatre Calgary, *3* The Martha Cohen Theatre, of Theatre Projects Alberta. The auditoria are situated in the city centre like a theatre district, rather than isolated as a 'cultural campus.'

St David's Hall, Cardiff, is one of several recent 'semi-surround' halls after the general style of the Philharmonie, Berlin, where the audience seating continues around the stage. This provides visual coherence and avoids great distances from the stage for the furthermost seats, without compromising orchestral balance for too many seats, as in the case of the fully centralized orchestra platform.

The broad but visually intimate Roy Thomson Hall, Toronto, is based in plan on the proportions of the Toronto Symphony Orchestra's former home, Massey Hall of 1894. Retractable woollen banners descend from slots in the ceiling to vary the reverberation time, and adjustable acrylic sound reflectors can vary the strength of early sound reflections.

The concert hall of the Morton H. Meyerson Symphony Center, Dallas, is based on nineteenth-century models, and is dimensionally similar to Carnegie Hall, New York. *1* The grills at high level conceal openable 'reverberation chambers'. *2* The model illustrates how two giant columns visually define the platform, though acoustically the auditorium is a single space. The organ design is notional, for the purposes of the model.

Hamilton Place, Ontario, is a combined theatre-concert hall, and approaches the problem by creating, with stage elevators, an orchestra platform in front of the proscenium, bringing the musicians into the main body of the auditorium for concerts. *1* is set up for theatre use, *2* shows the orchestra platform in place. Note also the retractable acoustic banners.

1

Two community centres,
in West Germany and The Netherlands,
each provide multiple-use facilities in a
different way. *1* The Stadthalle,
Biberach an der Riss, contains a single
large space which can be subdivided by
mechanically movable walls and partitions
to form an intimate theatre, *2,* and other
small meeting areas. De Flint Cultural
Centre, Amersfoort, on the other hand,
has various permanent spaces connected
by internal streets, including a theatre,
3, and a concert hall, *4,* which is used
for many purposes like a town square,
including markets.

2

3

4

1

2

1, 2 Pikes Peak Center, Colorado Springs, converts from a theatre to a semi-surround concert hall by installing seating towers, which are moved into place on air castors. Alternatively, the towers can be reversed to form sound reflectors. *3, 4* At Thunder Bay Community Auditorium, sound reflectors are used in a similar way. The volume of the stage area behind becomes a reverberation chamber (the flytower is sealed off with a flown ceiling).

3

4

1

2

3

4

5   Various seating formats are possible at the Derngate Centre, Northampton, as the towers of boxes and seating rakes are mobile and can be rearranged: *1* 'lyric' format with a proscenium stage; *2* concert hall format; *3* arena stage format; *4* flat floor format; *5, 6* moving the seating wagons.   6

The Theatre Royal, Plymouth, is fundamentally a theatre for drama, but can be used as a concert hall with its assisted resonance system. It has a proscenium stage, but the geometry interlocks, giving the impression of a single space auditorium.

1

2

3

4

The Theatre Royal, Nottingham, *1,* uses a gigantic, vertically adjustable, suspended canopy to vary the acoustic and visual scale of the auditorium, *2, 3* For small-scale events, when the upper balcony may not be used, the canopy is lowered, giving the impression of a much smaller room. *4* Lighting effects can dramatically alter the 'mood,' as on opening night, for a concert by Elton John.

1

2

1 Standard scaffolding components within an existing building make up the Tricycle Theatre, Kilburn, creating an intimate space with the feeling of a Georgian playhouse. *2* A model of the structure.

1

3

1 The Barbican Theatre, London, is an entirely contemporary interpretation of an Italian opera house. *2, 3* The doors to each row of continuous 'continental' seats remain open with electro-magnets until the performance, then are released to close silently and simultaneously.

The simple 'courtyard' form of the eighteenth-century Georgian theatre was the precedent for the Wilde Theatre, Bracknell, where the actor has the feeling of 'being able to reach out and touch the audience'.

1 Ordway Music Theatre, St Paul, Minnesota, recreates the atmosphere of a traditional theatre, through the use of boxes with loose seating, bright colours, and eclectic motifs, ranging from Italian baroque to art deco. *2* An orchestra shell, usually stored at the stage rear, meets with the proscenium to convert the theatre for concert use.

1

1, 2 The Maltings Concert Hall, Snape, converted from a former industrial building, was built for Benjamin Britten's Aldburgh Festival, and is one of the most admired concert halls. Its acoustic excellence is helped by its small size, narrow shape, lofty volume, and possibly its ceiling shape.

2

1

2

3

1, 2, 3, Henry Wood Hall, London, was converted from a redundant church into a rehearsal hall and recording studio for London orchestras. Fine buildings such as this can be reused for such purposes at a fraction of the cost of new construction.

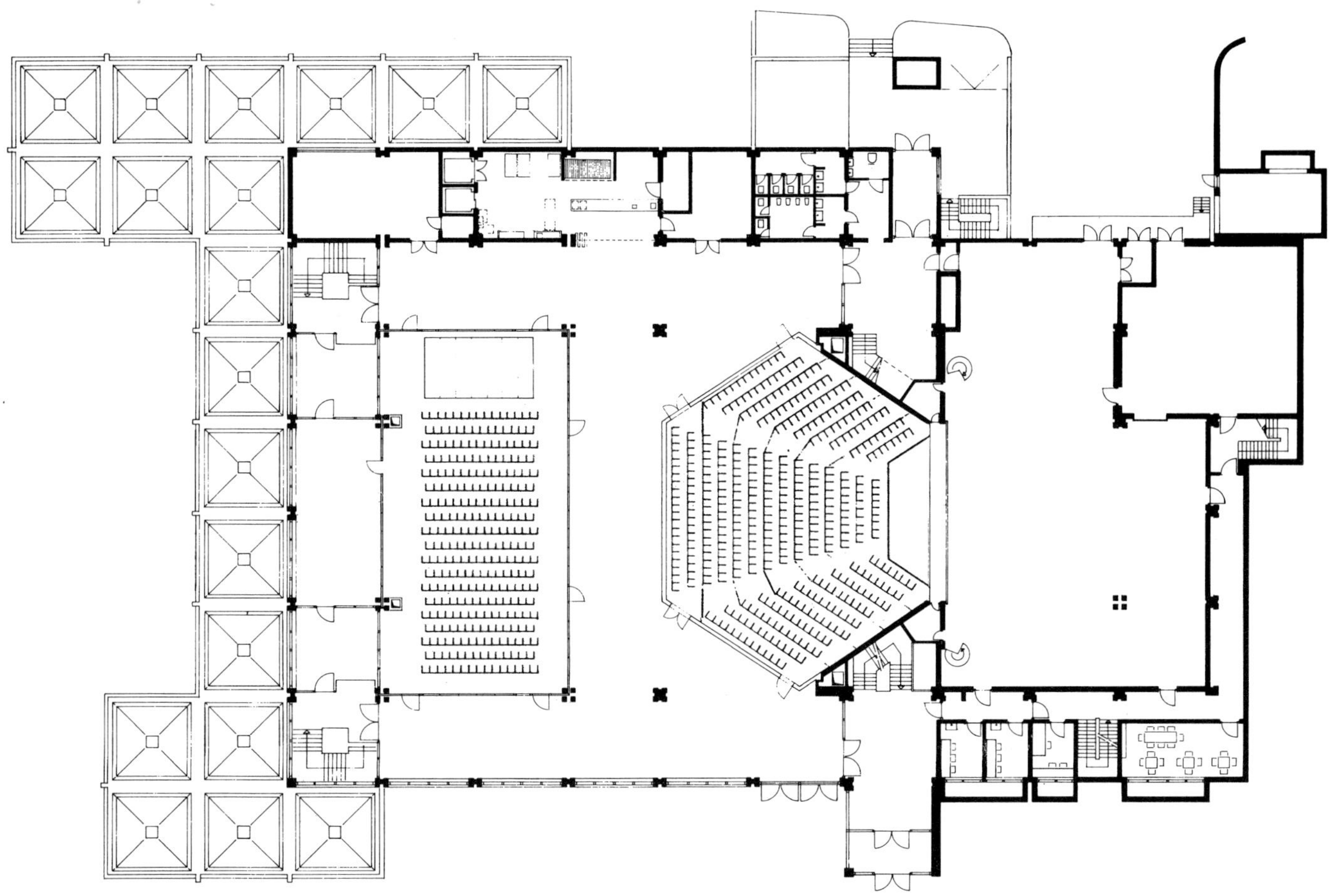

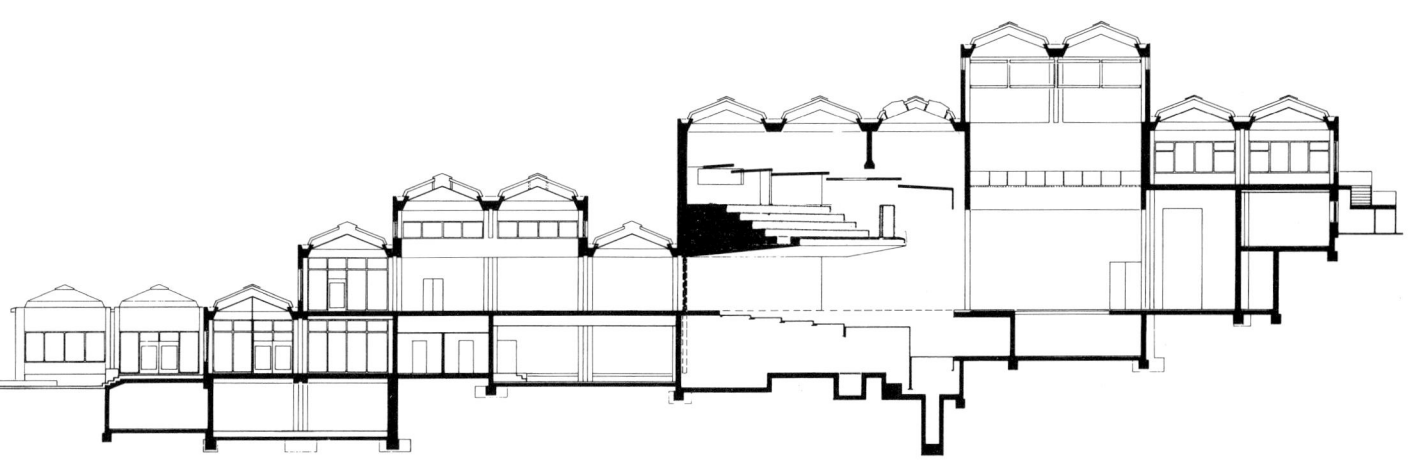

Stadthalle, Biberach an der Riss: main floor plan.

Stadthalle, Biberach an der Riss: section. Note the variable floor level inside the theatre.

General contractor: Heilijgers Bouw B.V., Amersfoort

Opened: 1977

Cost: Dfl. 11 million

Floor area: 7210 sq.m (77,600 sq.ft)

Uses: concerts, theatre, markets, and other community uses

Concert hall

Seats: 1000 maximum

Stage: width 19m (62.3ft), depth 13m (42.6ft)

Theatre

Seats: 500 on two tiers

Stage: width 31m (101.7ft) (20m [65.6ft] centreline to stage right wing), depth 22m (72.2ft)

Flying system: 30 rigging line sets

Volume: 2400 cub.m (84,750 cub.ft)

Variable plan arrangements in the Stadthalle:

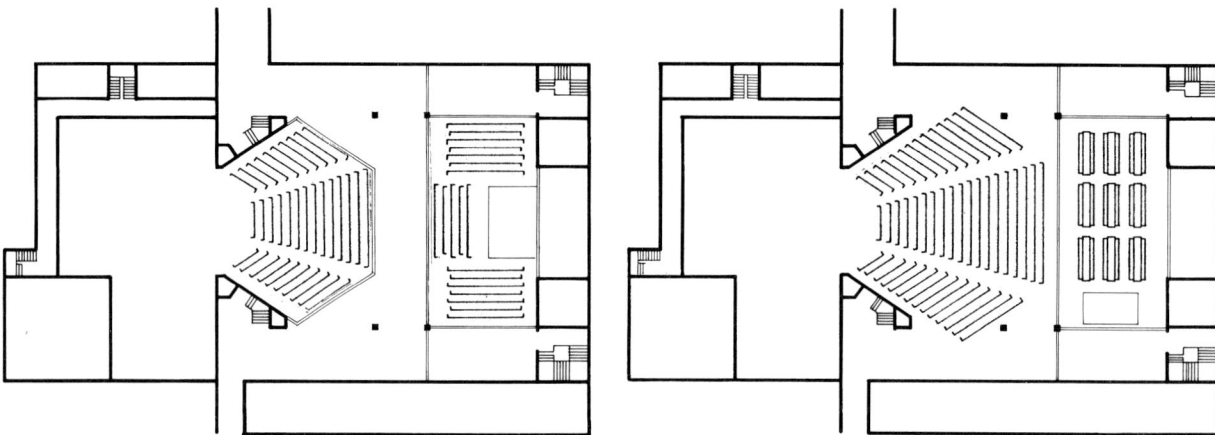

Theatre and small room with common foyers.

Small room with extended theatre.

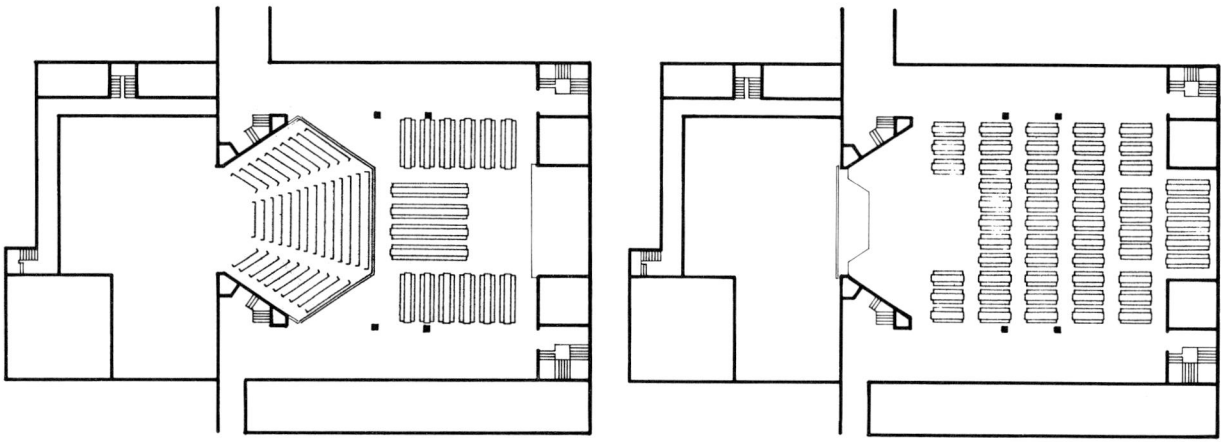

Intermediate size room, or theatre with large foyer.

Single large hall.

These two cultural centres in the Netherlands and southern West Germany have at first sight much in common. They are by the same Dutch architect; both are on the edge of provincial medieval towns with small-scale ancient buildings; they are designed to broadly similar briefs and with the same modular approach, typical of the Dutch modern architectural tradition. Yet they illustrate two quite different methods of providing for multi-use: at Biberach a variety of different functions are accommodated within a single, highly adaptable space; while at Amersfoort a range of activities can be carried out simultaneously at different points of the building in different types of room of relatively fixed configuration. Interestingly, because of different standards of finish and the cost of movable elements at the Biberach building, Amersfoort was built at well below half the unit cost of Biberach. At 1978 exchange rates, Biberach cost about £790 per square metre and Amersfoort just over £360.

The town of Biberach in the state of Baden Württemberg has for many years been noted for a lively interest in theatre, in particular a 150 year old tradition of children's drama, the so-called 'Schutzenfest' with around 60 performances a year by groups of 4–16 year

olds. The need to house this festival was the principal reason for the new building, which was required to house a theatre and a large multi-purpose community hall. A delegation from the town was organized to acquaint itself with developments in theatre architecture at home and abroad, and in 1970 a competition was launched, open to all architects in the Federal Republic of Germany and to four foreign invitees.

Greiner's winning scheme (somewhat modified subsequent to the competition) consists of a series of concrete frames on a 6m (20ft) column grid, each module having its own copper-clad pyramidal roof. This reduces the scale of the building, and enables it to step up the sloping wooded site, adjacent to the medieval rampart with towers and the old town centre beyond. The 'building block' arrangement also accommodates the varying internal heights within a unified overall form. To minimize the bulk of the flytower, the building is partly sunk into the hillside. In front of the flytower is the main hall of 24m by 30m (79ft by 98.5ft), holding 1200 people, which forms the central space of the building. This may alternatively be partitioned into a 600 seat theatre, foyer, small hall for 400 people, several conference rooms—or a

The main floor, with theatre seating in place on a stepped floor, and the theatre partition partially raised.

Large hall configuration, with floor sections raised to one level and the theatre partition retracted into the floor.

Stadthalle, Biberach an der Riss: the stepped, modular exterior is designed to reduce the bulk of the flytower. Unlike de Flint Cultural Centre, the building is in a parkland setting, detached from the town centre.

De Flint Cultural Centre, Amersfoort: ground floor plan. Key: 1 main entrance, 2 offices, 3 theatre, 4 stage, 5 backstage area, 6 dressing/conference room, 7 internal street, 8 concert hall, 9 stage, 10 conductor's room, 11 storage, 12 cafe-restaurant, 13 creativity centre

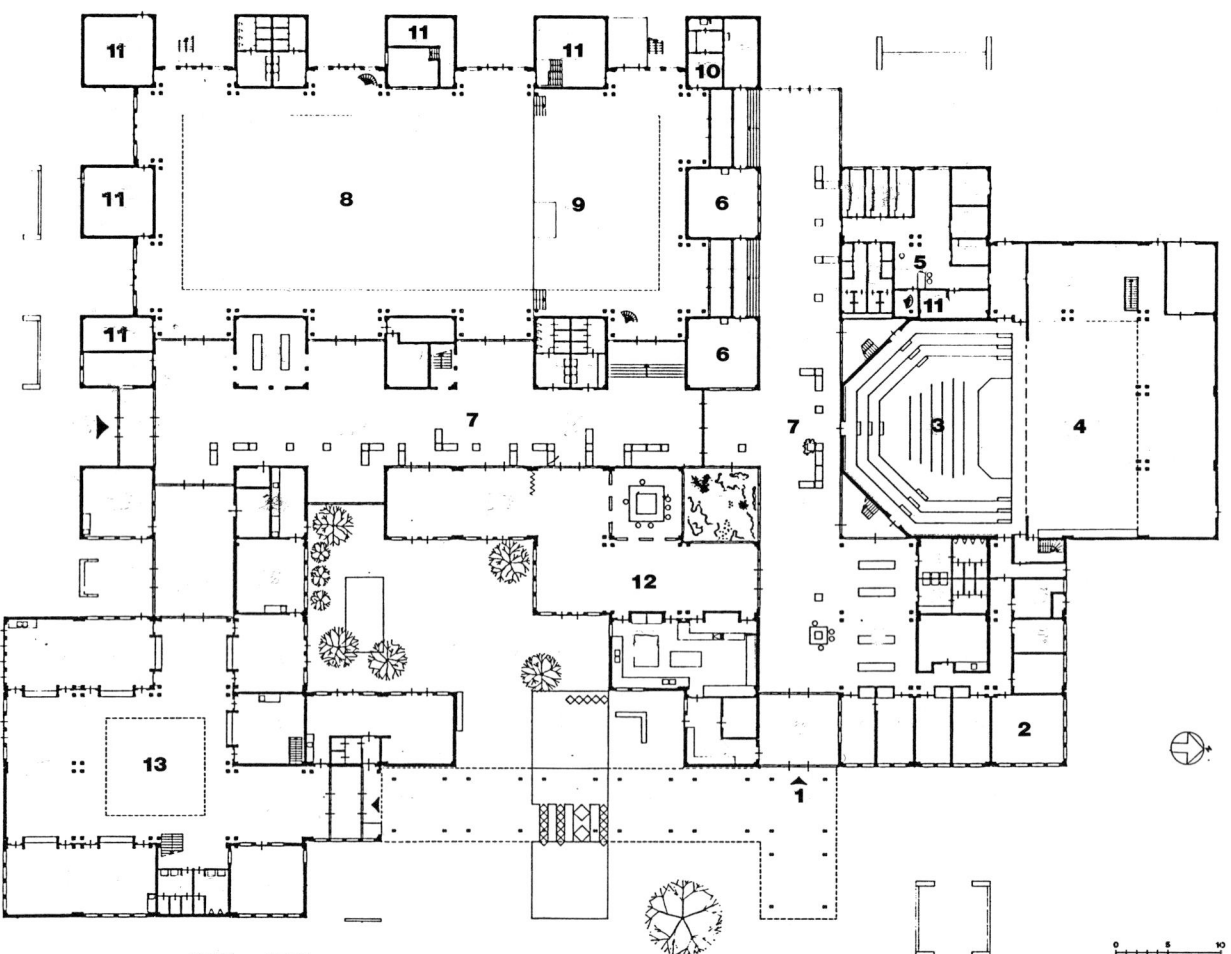

De Flint Cultural Centre: 500 seat theatre.

De Flint Cultural Centre: concert hall, here being used with stalls like a town square.

Constructed, like the old town, of brick, the complex is conceived less as an isolated building than as an extension of the town itself.

variety of further different-sized alternatives. Most of the partitions, which are centred on the structural gridlines, slide on tracks between the double beams and in the gap between the four-column clusters where the structural modules meet. The 800mm and 1200mm (2.6ft and 4ft) partition units are 85mm (3.3in) thick and give a sound attenuation of 35dB. The theatre is isolated by an enormous 36m (118ft) cranked wall 350mm (14in) thick, which retracts into the floor to form the main hall. The top, in the 'down' position, sits flush with the dance floor, and the wall rises to meet a compressible buffer. A stepped main floor for the theatre is created by movable floor sections on hydraulic jacks which descend to the required position, or the orchestra pit can be raised by its elevator to 1m (3.3ft) above the level of the floor to form a raised platform. Rows of seats clipped together are then

installed; only the circle seats are fixed. These moving elements, together with two removable proscenia, enable the theatre itself to adapt to a picture stage, theatre-in-the-round, congresses, musical performances, etc. The more permanent accommodation is on the other levels—dressing rooms for 120 children (doubling as practice rooms) above, and a bowling alley, meeting rooms, cafe-restaurant and cloakrooms on the entrance levels below.

Amersfoort's community centre was required to serve a similar range of functions, but here the multi-use is provided for by different, fixed types of accommodation: a 1000 seat concert hall, a two-tier theatre, meeting rooms, bars and a restaurant. Like Biberach, the building is modular, and is adaptable in the sense that the whole is conceived as a 'miniature town' which in the longer term can expand, alter or be infilled, depending on future needs; as the architect says, the formulation of a brief for a building of this type can never be more than a 'snapshot' of the community's needs at any one time. Within the 'town' each 6.4m (21ft) module is a 'building', with a self-sufficient structure and roof. The individual areas are linked by a T-shaped covered street which can become an extension of the different rooms if required. The main hall is like a town square, which besides symphony concerts is used for markets, fairs, meetings and sports. The finishes throughout, despite being very low budget, are robust, and the approach of providing different, more-or-less purpose-built rooms tends to be more successful than the variability of a single space as at Biberach.

Centre in the Square, Kitchener, Ontario; Pikes Peak Center, Colorado Springs; Thunder Bay Community Auditorium

Centre in the Square, Kitchener, Ontario

Owner: City of Kitchener

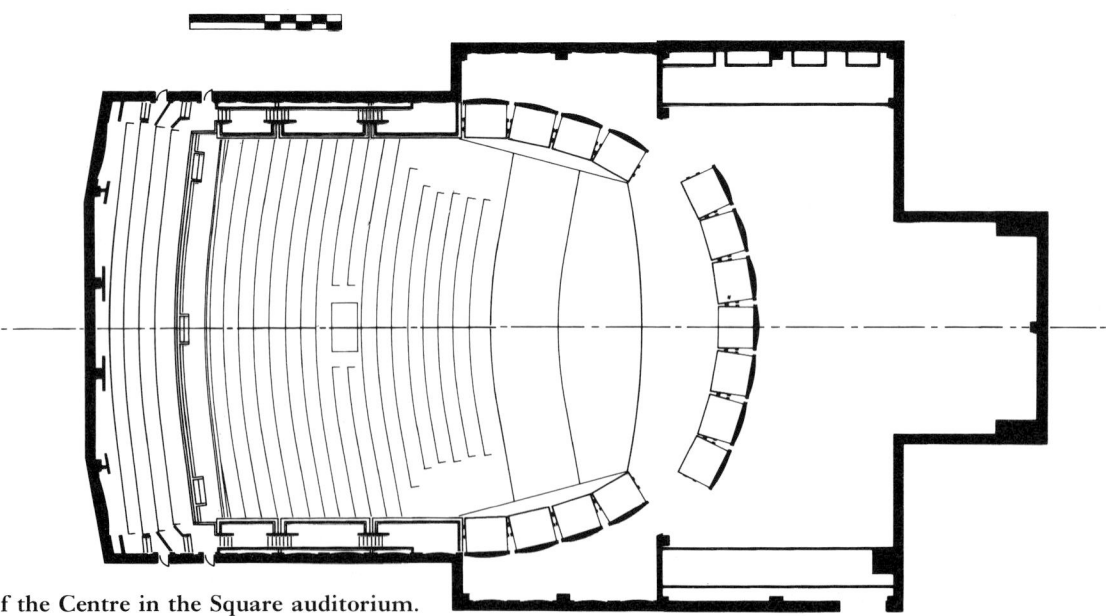

Plan of the Centre in the Square auditorium.

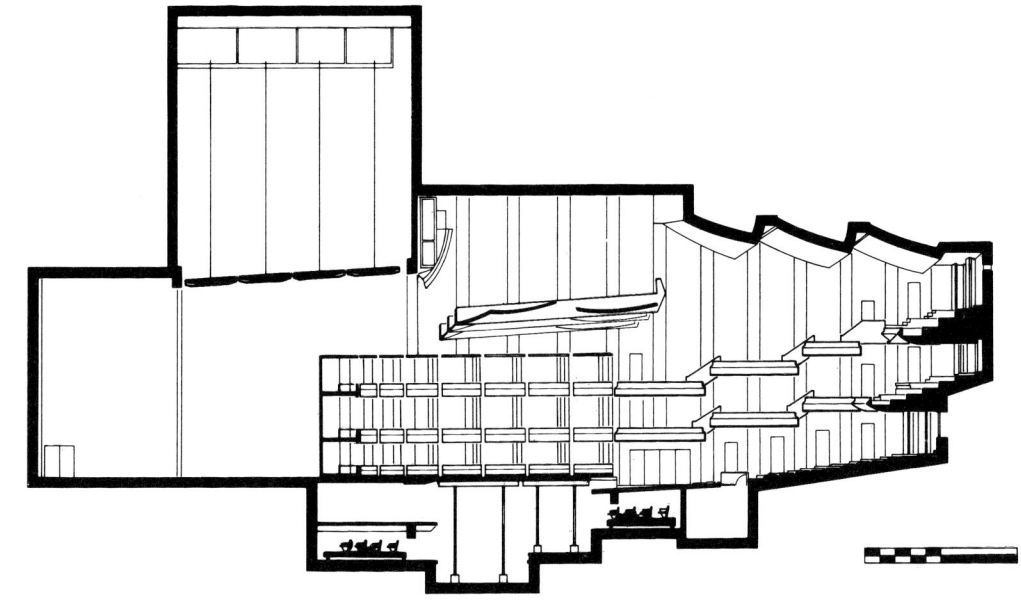

Longitudinal section through the Centre in the Square.

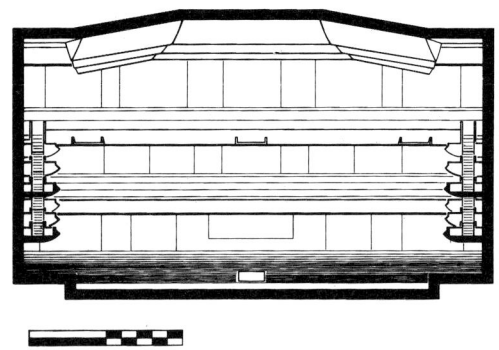

Lateral section through the Centre in the Square.

Architects: Rieder, Hymmen & Lobban

Theatre and acoustics consultant: Artec Consultants, Inc.

Structural, mechanical and electrical engineers: Walter, Fedy, McCarger, Hachborn

Main contractor: Ball Brothers, Ltd

Opened: 1980

Total cost: Can. $10.9 million

Principal uses: symphony, opera, drama and popular concerts

Seats: 1920

Furthest balcony seat from stage: 35m (115ft), 26m (85ft) from orchestra thrust stage

Proscenium opening: maximum width 26.8m (88ft), maximum height 13.7m (45ft)

Stage: width 35m (114.25ft), centreline to stage right wall 18m (59ft), depth from curtain line to rear wall 14.3m (46.75ft) height to underside of grid 27.5m (90ft)

Flying system: 46 counterweight sets, 1–36 single purchase (downstage), 37–54 double purchase (upstage) plus one motorized set

Orchestra area: variable; two orchestra pit lifts can be used as orchestra pit, seating or forestage extension of 200 sq.m (2100 sq.ft) (both lifts), 88 sq.m (950 sq.ft) (downstage lift)

Volume: 15,300 cub.m (540,250 cub.ft)

Reverberation time: variable

Maximum background noise level: NC 15

Pikes Peak Center, Colorado Springs

Owner: El Paso County

Architects: John James Wallace Associates, in association with Clifford S. Nakata & Associates

Acoustic and theatre design consultants: Artec Consultants Inc.—Russell Johnson, acoustician, and Robert W. Wolff, theatre consultant and project manager

Structural engineers: Howard C. Dutzi & Associates, Inc.

Mechanical engineers: Carrier & Day, Inc.

Electrical engineers: Consulting Engineers, Inc.

Main contractor: G. E, Johnson Construction Company, Inc.

Opened: 1982

Cost: $13,400,000

Principal uses: symphony, opera, drama, recitals

Seats: total 1955 (symphony), 1971 (opera), 2062 (drama), 2169 (recitals); main floor 957 to 1171 (with both lifts), mezzanine 290, balcony 528, stage towers 72 (six fixed towers) to 180 (all towers)

Furthest balcony seat from stage: 45m (147ft), 36.5m (120ft) from orchestra thrust stage

Example arrangements of the movable towers and stage lifts.

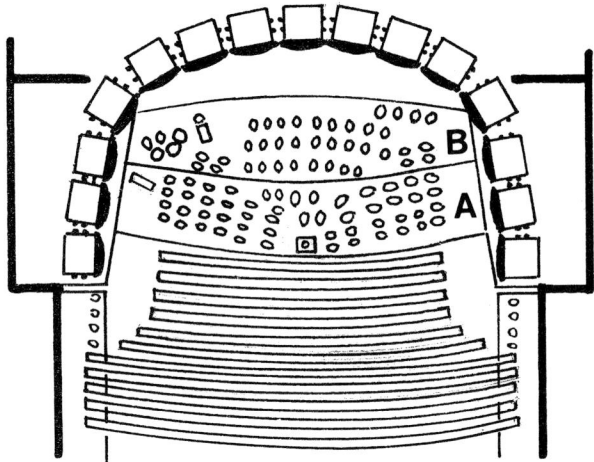

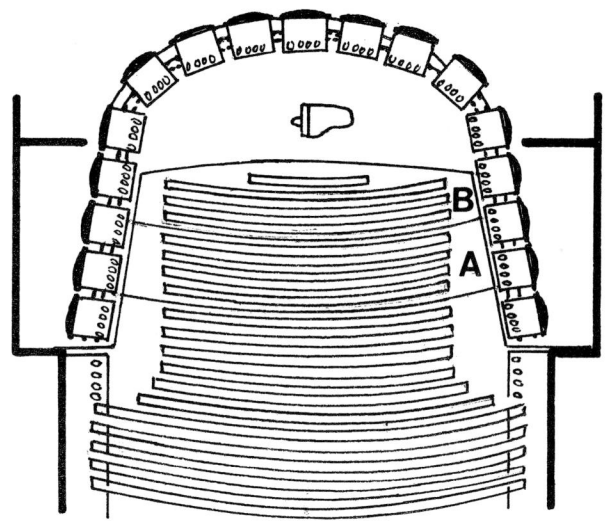

Both lifts at stage level to form concert platform, with towers behind for sound reflection.

Both lifts lowered for audience seating, with pianist on stage in front of towers.

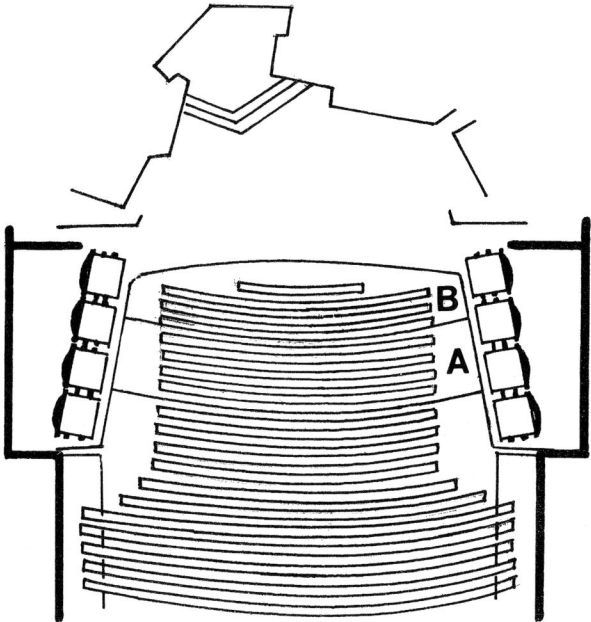

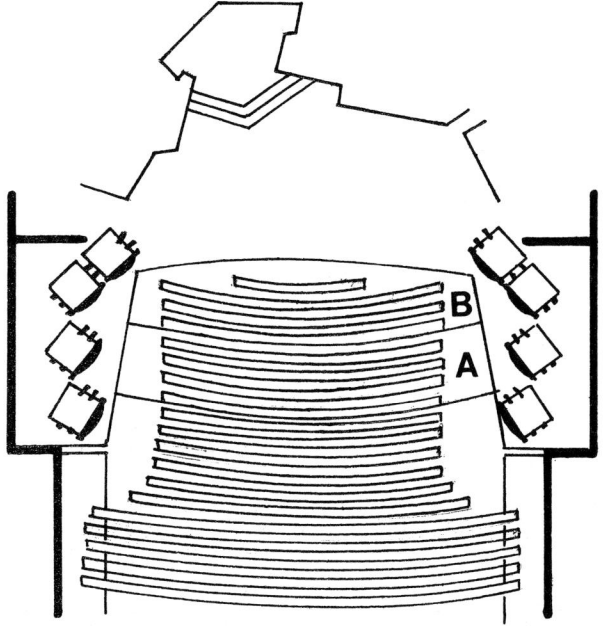

Masking creates a proscenium stage, and the towers form box seats at the sides.

Towers on side stages become light stanchions for dramatic productions on main stage.

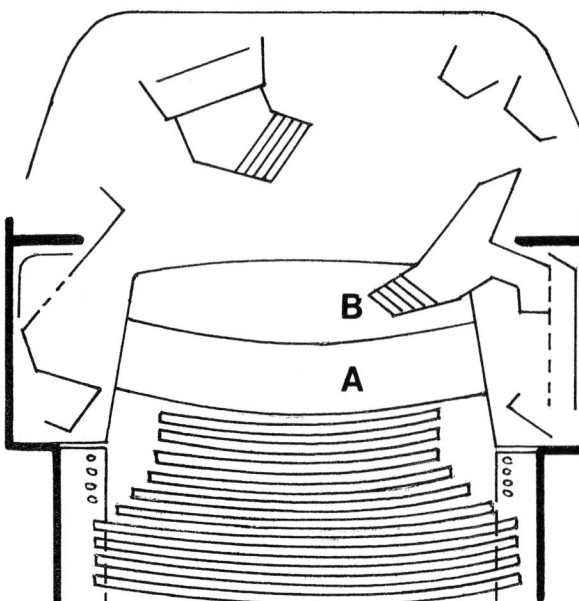

Proscenium opening: width 24.4m (80ft), height 12.2m (40ft)

Stage: width 35m (115ft), centreline to stage right wall 15.3m (52ft), depth 15.2m (50ft) from proscenium wall to rear wall in front of tower storage, gridiron height 24.4m (80ft)

Flying system: 42 rigging line sets

Orchestra area: approximately 353 sq.m (3800 sq.ft) with both lifts (variable)

Volume: 16,950 cub.m (598,500 cub.ft)

Front lift lowered for orchestra pit, back lift raised as forestage for opera productions.

Reverberation time: variable

Maximum background noise level: NC 15

Thunder Bay Community Auditorium

Owner: Thunder Bay Community Auditorium

Architects: Associated Architects for the Thunder Bay Community Auditorium

Theatre and acoustics consultant: Artec Consultants, Inc.

Structural engineers: C. E. Mickelson Associates Ltd

Mechanical engineers: Walter, Fedy, McCarger, Hachborn

Electrical engineers: Proctor and Redfern Group

Quantity surveyors: Hanscombe Inc.

Main contractor: Ball Brothers, Ltd

Opened: 1985

Cost: Can. $14.8 million

Principal uses: symphony, opera, drama and popular concerts

Seats: 1547 (maximum)

Furthest balcony seat from stage: 38m (125ft), 30m (98.5ft) from orchestra thrust stage

Proscenium opening: width 21.5m (70.5ft), height 12m (39.4ft)

Stage: width 26m (85.3ft), centreline to stage right wall 13.5m (44.3ft), depth 15m (49.3ft) from proscenium wall to rear wall, height to underside of grid 24m (78.7ft)

Flying system: 52 rigging line sets

Orchestra area: variable, with two stage lifts which can form an orchestra pit, seating or forestage extension: upstage lift 48 sq.m (516 sq.ft), downstage lift 54 sq.m (582 sq.ft)

Volume: 17,130 cub.m (605,000 cub.ft)

Reverberation time: variable

Maximum background noise level: NC 15

What these halls have in common is that they serve relatively modest communities which have developed a lively interest in the arts. They all support expanding symphony orchestras, professional or amateur drama groups and other organizations, each with its own performance requirements, though none of the towns could support more than one large auditorium. The problem in each case, therefore, was to provide a truly multiple-use auditorium of high standard, within an adequate, but not lavish, budget.

The basic difficulty in converting a multiple-use proscenium theatre into a concert hall is dealing with the acoustically separate volumes of the flytower and the auditorium, because, for concerts, it is desirable that the orchestra and audience occupy the same space. The solution in these halls has been to position the orchestra

Centre in the Square, the platform set for choir and orchestra.

View from the rear balcony in Pikes Peak Center,
with the stage set for orchestra.

forward of the proscenium on a raised forestage (at the
cost of a few rows of seats). This is similar to Hamilton
Place (see above), but here the volume of the stage area
below the flytower—which is sealed off—is utilized to
generate the reverberant energy, or 'audible tail', which
is desirable in a concert hall. In the concert format, an
orchestra surround is created using a series of stage tower
units or, at Thunder Bay, sound reflectors. One of the
most significant features is that these are moved into
place using technology which is very simple compared
with that of the previous generation of North American
multiple-use halls, built in the 1960s and early 70s.

The halls each incorporate five variable devices: the
movable stage towers; two forestage lifts; a reverberation
chamber; retractable acoustic banners; and a vertically
adjustable sound reflecting canopy.

The 'throat zone' forward of the main stage is capable
of various architectural transformations. Most unamplified music performances take place on one or both
of two screw jack lifts which rise to form a large forestage
level with the main stage. When not in use as a stage, one
or both lifts may be lowered to main floor level to provide
audience seating, or to low level to form either a 'Strauss'

orchestra pit or, by using the 'overhang' area beneath the
stage, a 'Wagner' pit. Combinations of these modes are
possible: lifts 1 and 2 may become respectively a forestage
and a smaller pit, a smaller pit and audience seating, or a
pit with a forestage 'runway'. The audience seating is
moved onto and off the lifts by motor-assisted wagons
which are housed in storage rooms at low level beneath
the main stage and beneath the fixed portion of the main
floor seating area.

The orchestra platform is completed by positioning a
series of stage towers, or at Thunder Bay 12 free-standing
panels, each some 9m (30ft) high by 3m (10ft) wide,
beside and behind the performers. These provide both a
visual and sound-reflective enclosure for the performers,
while enabling the stage depth and configuration to be
more or less infinitely variable. These simple elements
are movable from one position to another—like large
pieces of furniture—on air bearings (like a hovercraft,
rather than on wheel castors as at the earlier Christ's
Hospital Theatre, Horsham—see above). There are 15
towers at the Colorado Springs hall and 17 at Kitchener,
and, typically, three are placed each side of the stage at
Colorado Springs and four at Kitchener, with seven at
the rear. The tower units have three tiers of balcony
'shelves' which can be used for seating, giving a choice of
a one-directional or semi-surround layout to the
auditorium. Access to the side towers is from permanent

The auditorium, Pikes Peak Center, seen with the sound-absorptive banners extended.

galleries which extend around the sides of the hall, while those positioned to the rear are entered via a stair tower, also on air castors, which locates like the stair to an aircraft (though the rear boxes at Kitchener have not yet been used for people). The balcony fronts are detailed for theatre lighting instruments, and the side towers may be angled for good lighting positions and the boxes used for access by theatre technicians. Alternatively, the towers may be turned round to reveal the rearside face, which is built as a slightly convex timber sound reflector. This provides a more brilliant, less diffuse sound, suitable for choral concerts (Kitchener's community has several excellent amateur choirs) and recitals.

In the concert mode the cubic volume of the empty stagehouse, upstage of the mobile tower units, becomes a reverberation chamber. The upper part of the flytower, containing sound-absorptive scenery and masking, is closed off from the acoustically sound-reflective chamber below by means of rotating ceiling panels which are lowered from a vertical storage position at high level

The seating towers being moved at Pikes Peak Center. Note the compressed air connection for the air castors.

Thunder Bay Community Auditorium uses a series of sound reflectors behind the orchestra for concert use, instead of seating towers as at the other two halls.

within the flytower to a position at the top of the proscenium opening. They are then tilted horizontal to form an integral 'concert ceiling' between the hard reverberation chamber and the sound-absorptive flytower. Sound enters and leaves the reverberation chamber through openings between and above the tower units. Once sound has entered the chamber, it reverberates for a longer period than in the main auditorium (since the chamber contains no sound-absorbing audience), and the reverberant sound energy is returned to the auditorium adding liveness, tonal fulness and an 'audible tail' to music played in the main body of the hall.

Each auditorium is basically designed as a hard-surfaced room, with acoustically reflective finishes to maximize the duration and intensity of the sound for all unamplified music, such as symphony, opera, small ensembles and recitals. For amplified music and speech, sound reinforcement, tape playback, etc. (for which there is a loudspeaker array above the proscenium and a sound control cockpit in the middle of the main floor), velour banners are extended down the side walls to form a 'soft' surfaced room. These change the acoustics from 'live' to 'dead', preventing delayed sound reflections from obscuring the loudspeaker sound.

The acoustic scale can also be adjusted, to suit say an orchestra or a quartet, by means of a vertically movable canopy over the orchestra platform and front part of the auditorium. This raises or lowers the effective ceiling height of the front portion of the room, reproducing some of the characteristics of large or small spaces.

Like the rectangular halls of the nineteenth century, the overall plan shape of the auditoria is approximately a double square. They are of narrow width, and the upper sidewalls in the halls at Kitchener and Colorado are stepped into a reverse fan and tilted inwards. This is to develop strong laterally reflected sound energy directed towards the seating areas, and to shorten the travel distance of reflected sound in order to increase its impact and clarity.

Although the finishes in all three halls are necessarily modest, the Thunder Bay auditorium is architecturally the most refined. The other two are less developed, and have the quality of 'built acoustical sketches', for instance with an unresolved relationship between the tower boxes and the permanent balconies, and rudimentary detailing, even allowing for budgetary constraints. Acoustically, however, the halls are outstanding, and do much to eliminate the musical compromises inherent in the larger multiple-use auditoria of the past.

St Anselm's College Art Center, Theater-Recital Hall, Manchester, New Hampshire

Owner: St Anselm's College

Architect: Isaak & Isaak

Acoustic and theatre consultant: George C. Izenour

Opened: 1981

Cost: $2 million

Principal uses: music and drama

Seats: 700–350

Furthest seat from stage: 12.2m (40ft) for drama, 24.4m (80ft) for music

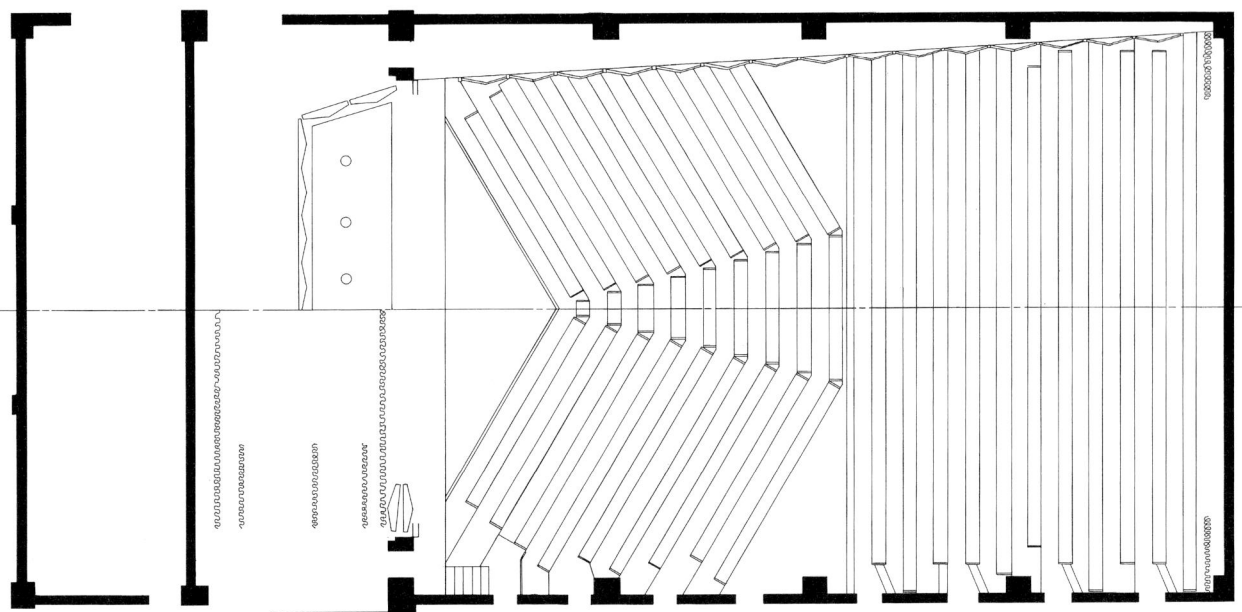

Plan.

Perspective section rendering of 700 seat large theatre mode with forestage.

Proscenium opening: 11m (36ft) for drama, 14.6m (48ft) for music

Flying system: manual counterweight

Reverberation time: variable, from 1.6 sec. with curtains retracted to 0.9 sec. with curtains extended at mid-frequencies with full audience

Maximum background noise level: NCA 25

This is the first of a series of prefabricated, low cost auditoria developed by George C. Izenour that fulfil a need in small colleges and other institutions of similar size, for public performance of all kinds, from speech to music, with a commensurate alteration of both acoustical environment and size of auditorium. The entire interior of the room, sidewalls, shell etc. are prefabricated from a standard design steel panel that is acoustically dampened on the back side and finished to the choice of the architect

350 seat small theatre mode.

700 seat recital hall mode.

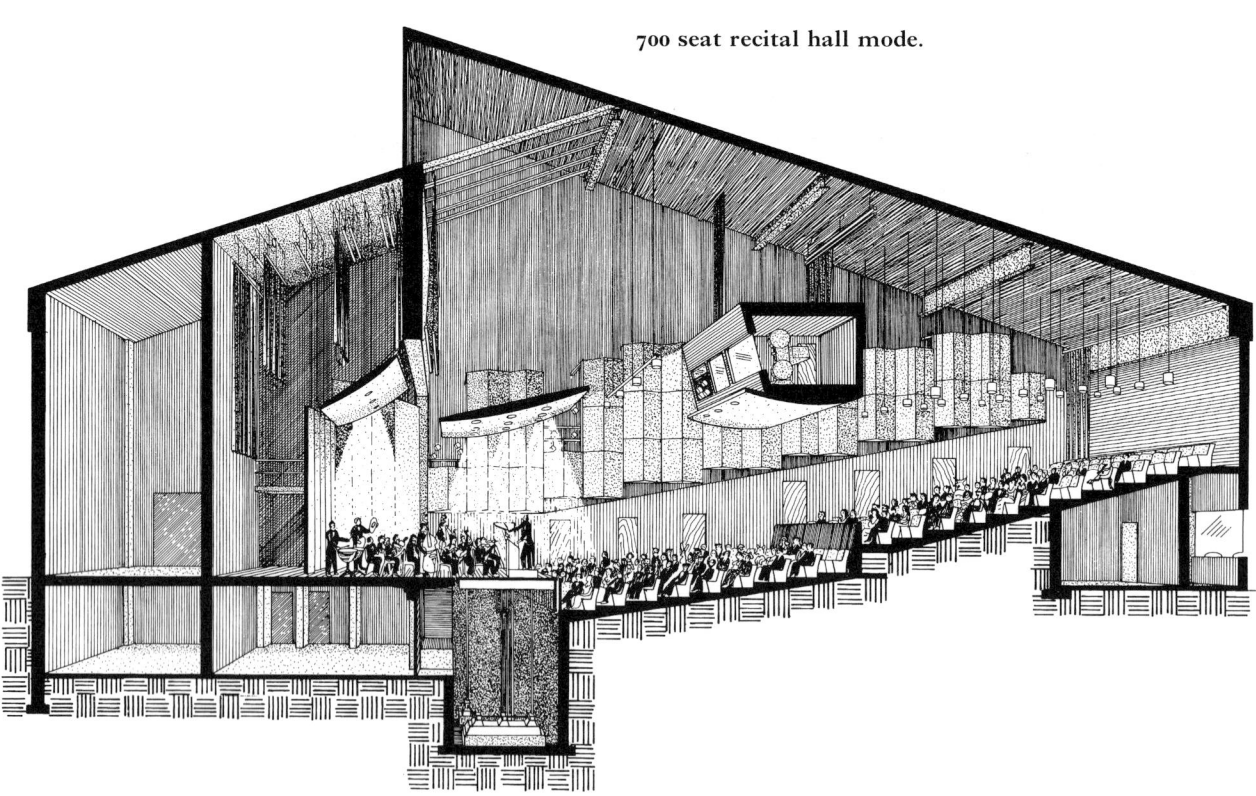

on the front side. The entire acoustical assembly is delivered to the job site 'knocked down' and assembled in 'Meccano set' fashion with nuts and bolts (with no welding) and fastened to the primary structure.

The auditorium volume is controlled above the visual plane (the upper void is coupled and/or decoupled as required) by absorptive means—with velour curtains—to achieve a live room for music at 1.6 sec. and, or alternatively, a suitably dampened one for stage speech at 0.9 sec. The control rooms for both light and sound, and a projection room, are contained within a structural hollow section beam spanning across the auditorium, which also

The stage from the auditorium.

The auditorium, viewed from a lighting position.

structurally stabilizes the sidewalls. The auditorium is rectangular and the seating is continental with access from aisles outside the hall on both sides. The seating in the front part is angled and tends towards a fan shape, reflecting the stage which has a pointed apron, and the rear part is in parallel rows. The auditorium can also be cut in half by lowering sound-absorptive drapery at the rear of the hollow beam to a fixed barrier in the seating plan. The system has been successful since its introduction, fulfilling the need for a simple non-mechanized auditorium where hitherto an unsatisfactory single-use hall would have been provided. At the time of writing there are six theatres of this type being designed or under construction.

Derngate Centre, Northampton

Building owner: Northampton Borough Council

Architects: Renton Howard Wood Levin Partnership

Theatre consultant: Theatre Projects Consultants Ltd

Acoustic consultant: Artec Consultants Inc.

Structural, mechanical and electrical engineers: Ove Arup & Partners

Quantity surveyors: Gardiner & Theobald

Opened: 1983

Cost: £6.2 million

Primary uses: concerts, drama, opera, spectator sports, banquets, exhibitions, trade shows

Seats: total, concert format 1400; arena format 1483; lyric format 1151

Furthest balcony seat from stage front: 30.5m (100ft)

Proscenium opening: width 14m (46ft), height 11.4m (37.5ft)

Stage (lyric format): width 28m (92ft), depth 12.6m (41.4ft), height to grid underside 22m (72.2ft) (orchestral format): 235 sq.m (2525 sq.ft)

Flying system: double purchase counterweight sets, 41 for the stage, 12 for the flown ceiling panels; total 53

Orchestra pit: 60 musicians

Volume: 15,500 cub.m (547,300 cub.ft)

Reverberation time: 1.7 secs at middle frequencies with full audience (estimate)

Maximum background noise level: NC 20

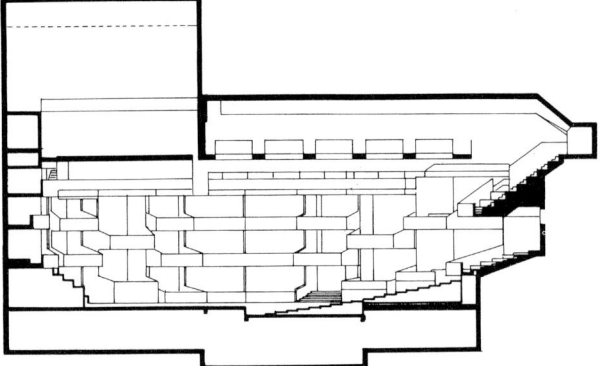

Longitudinal section through the auditorium, in concert format with the flytower sealed off.

Auditorium plans:

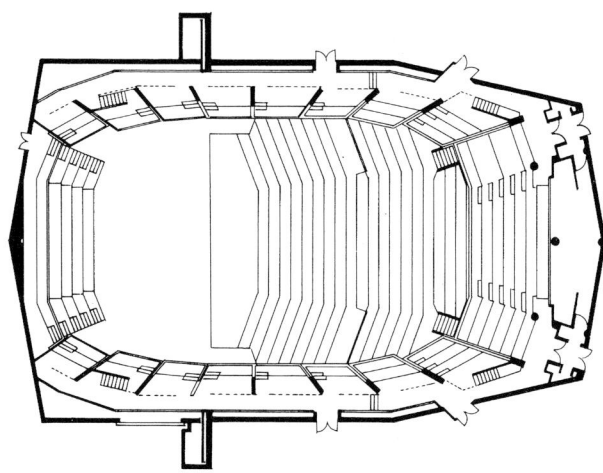

End stage concert format.

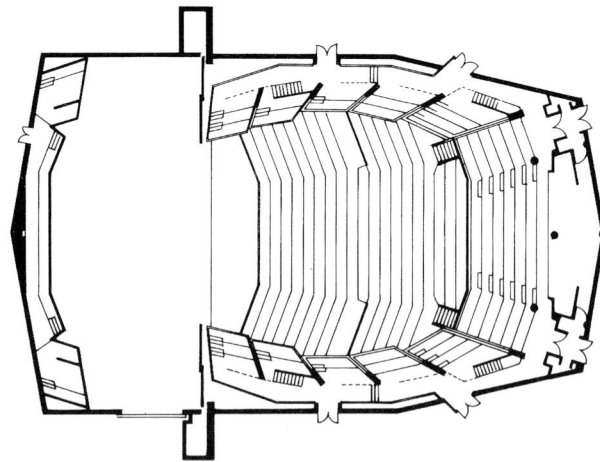

'Lyric' format, with the proscenium wall extended and two towers of boxes brought forward from the stage to close the proscenium opening.

If the seating towers and sound-reflecting screens in the halls at Kitchener, Colorado Springs and Thunder Bay (see above) are conceived like large pieces of furniture that can be moved around, the multiple-use auditorium at the Derngate Centre is like a three-dimensional jigsaw puzzle or kit of parts that comes apart and can be re-assembled in different configurations. Here, the movable elements—three tier seating towers around the front of the auditorium and beside the stage, and raked main floor seating wagons—are an integrated part of the architecture of the auditorium. Both are movable by hand on air castors, and the seating wagons can also move vertically on stage elevators.

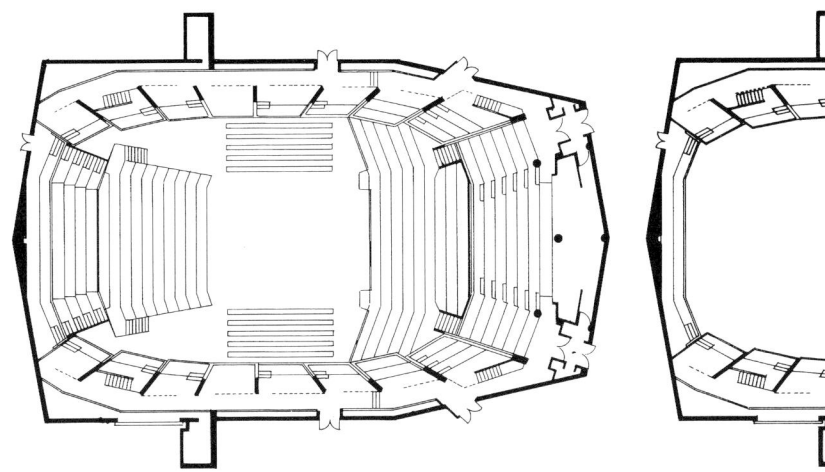

Arena format.

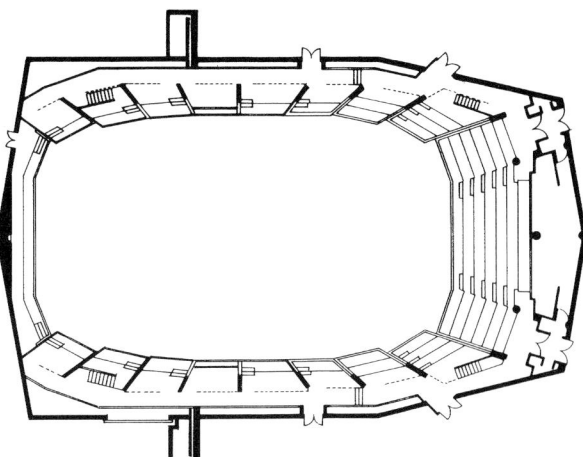

Flat floor format.

The auditorium in concert format. In the extreme top left the flown ceiling panels can be seen. These align with the catwalk system over the audience area.

The local authority client required a multiple-use auditorium, seating around 1500 people, on a site next to the nineteenth-century Theatre Royal. The latter has been renovated and linked with the main hall by foyers to create a single complex. The new hall is rectangular with parallel sides, which are slightly pulled in to a reverse fan shape at the rear. The roof is a double skin structure, the underside of which is a poured concrete slab, forming the ceiling to the hall, with a painted finish. Integral with the slab are deep, hollow beams that also create the air supply

Proscenium format with the fire safety wall extended
at either side and the forestage elevator forming an
orchestra pit.

Arena format, being used here for spectator sports.

ducts. The upper skin is a lightweight wood wool slab. Below the ceiling in the hall a series of lighting bridges span across the hall, which also act as structural tie rods to the roof structure. In addition, these form a visually lower ceiling to the auditorium.

The main floor of the hall is basically a single, flat level, the rear part of the stalls and the stage being concrete slabs and the middle section consisting of two stage elevators. With the raked seating wagons added, the elevators can be set at different levels to provide 'cut and fill' seating, with an orchestra pit if required. When not in use, the seating wagons are taken down by the elevators and stored at basement level beneath the rear stalls and the stage. To avoid potential dampness, the basement is used as a plenum for the return air, which is extracted through slots in the base of the seating towers. At the rear of the auditorium are two permanent balconies and three permanent seating towers on either side.

The building has two fundamental operating modes from the basic point of view of fire safety—a single room

Flat floor format, laid for a banquet.

The towers of seating boxes being moved on air castors. Note the hose connection for compressed air, and the mats laid over the floor joint to prevent loss of air.

format, and a proscenium stage layout where the stage can be separated from the main auditorium by a fire curtain. In the single space format, five movable, three-tier seating towers which visually match the permanent ones continue the boxes to the rear of the stage. These are linked across the stage wall by a double seating gallery. In front of this are four rows of retractable bleacher seating. The flytower above the stage is sealed off by flown ceiling panels at the level of the lighting bridges, forming a visually continuous ceiling. These are stored vertically in the flytower when not in use. The hall in this format can be used either as an end stage concert hall, or with an arena format, usually for spectator sports, or with a flat floor for civic receptions, banquets, dinner dances, exhibitions and trade shows. In the proscenium mode, a pair of horizontal-tracking fire walls extend from concealed pockets in the side walls to form a more narrow proscenium opening. These meet with a rigid, vertically-flown safety curtain in the centre. To create wing space, the three seating towers on either side of the stage are removed, and two of these replace the ones on either side of the stalls. When in place, they bring forward the line of boxes at an angle of 15 degrees to the sidewalls to meet

with the extended proscenium wall. Some acoustic variability is provided with retractable motorized wool banners in the ceiling. When extended, these prevent long-delayed sound reflections from obscuring speech clarity for events requiring electronic sound amplification. (Only about half the recommended banners could be afforded initially, but with provision for the remainder to be installed.)

The seating towers are free-standing within the acoustic boundary of the auditorium, and the rear of the tower units is enclosed with a visually and acoustically transparent metal screen. This is in order to utilize the full volume of the hall acoustically (and also incidentally provides opportunities for interesting concealed lighting from behind). However, because of the detachment of the boxes from the sidewalls, there is some lack of sound reflection normally provided at the junctions of wall and side gallery soffits, where the sound is 'turned back on itself' onto the main floor. Without strong, laterally reflected sound energy, there is some loss of acoustic strength on the main floor. However the moderate size of the hall is advantageous, coupled with its overall geometry, and the sound has considerable impact in the balcony seats which, as in many halls, benefit from ceiling reflections.

Theatre Royal, Plymouth

Owner: Council of the City of Plymouth

Architects: Peter Moro Partnership

Theatre Consultants: Carr & Angier

Acoustic Consultants: Sound Research Laboratories Ltd

Structural, mechanical and electrical engineers: Ove Arup & Partners

Quantity Surveyors: Davis Belfield & Everest

Main contractor: Costain Construction Ltd

Opened: 1982

Cost: £7.2 million

Uses: multi-purpose, principally drama but also opera, ballet, large-scale musicals and symphony

Seats (large auditorium): variable between 1271 and 768 without upper circle; stalls 400, dress circle 368, upper circle 503

Furthest balcony seat from front of stage: 20m (66ft) (large auditorium), 28m (92ft) (small auditorium)

Proscenium opening: width variable between 8m and 13m (26ft and 42.5ft), height variable between 6m and 8.5m (19.5ft and 28ft)

Stage: width 28.75m (94ft) (12.25m (40ft) centre-line to stage right wing), depth 15.3m (50ft) proscenium wall to back wall, depth with large pit 13.3m (43.5ft), height to grid underside 25m (82ft)

Flying system: 78 single purchase counterweight sets at 200mm (8in) centres. Between these, motor sets can

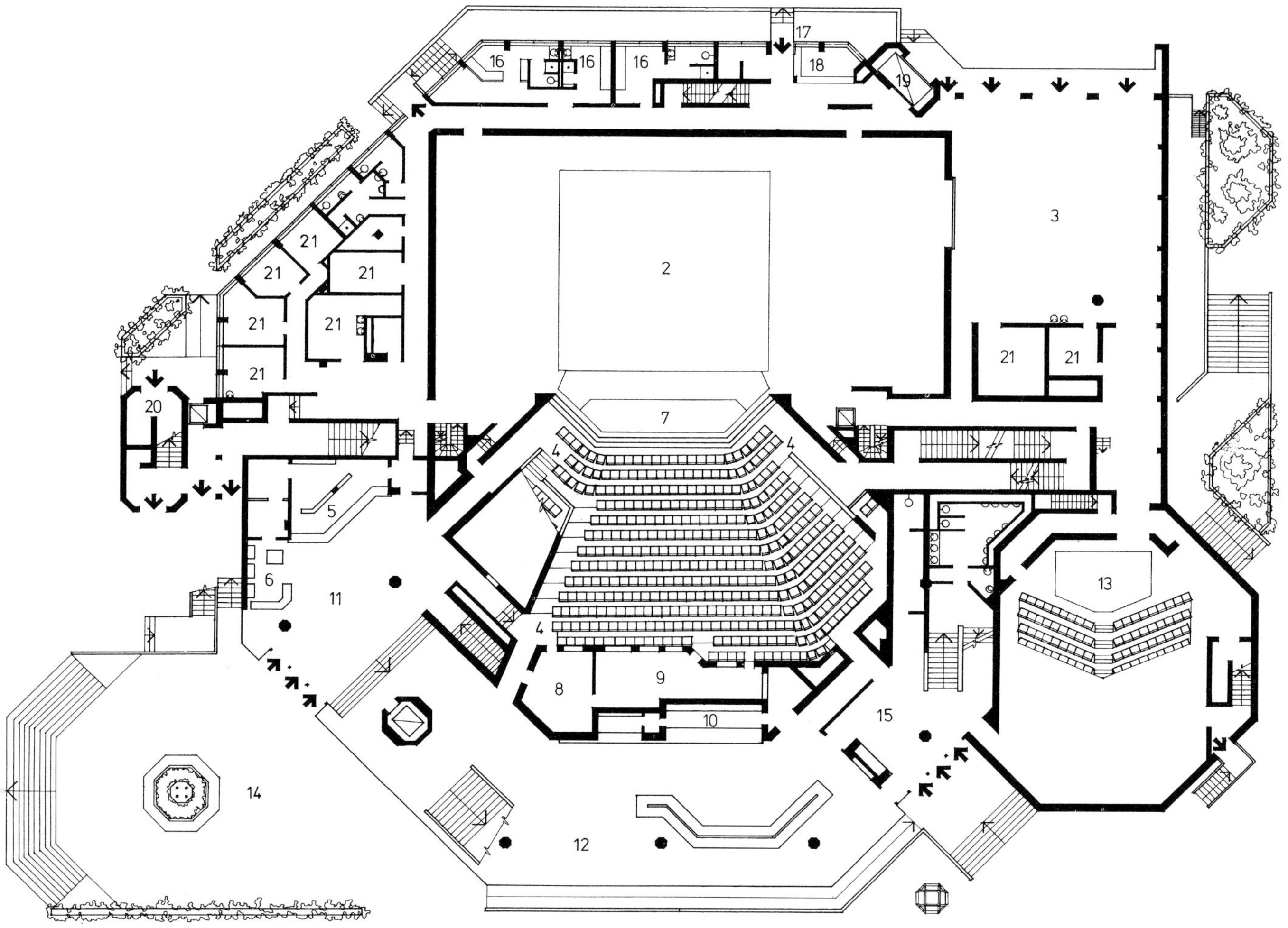

Plan at main floor level. Key: 1 clock tower, 2 stage, 3 scene dock, 4 stalls, 5 box office, 6 bookstall, 7 forestage, 8 sound control, 9 lighting control and projection, 10 bar, 11 entrance foyer, 12 stalls foyer, 13 studio theatre The Drum, 14 piazza, 15 Drum foyer, 16 dressing rooms, 17 stage door, 18 doorman, 19 goods lift, 20 refuse store, 21 technical spaces

be added to give a maximum suspension capability of alternate motor and hand sets at 100mm (4in) centres. The motor installation has been limited by cost initially to 12 sets

Orchestra pit: 75 musicians

Volume: varies

Reverberation time: 1 second at mid-frequencies with full audience

Maximum background noise level: NR 22

This is a 'recent generation', European version—the first of its kind in Great Britain—of a theatre type that has been extensively adopted in North America over two decades: a dual purpose auditorium for speech and music with a movable ceiling for large and small auditorium conditions. Besides refinements around the stage, the main difference from the majority of its predecessors is the use of electronic—as opposed to mechanical—acoustical variability to supplement the effect of the changes in cubic volume.

The intensive bombing of Plymouth during the Second World War left the city—and, apart from seaside entertainment, the region as a whole—almost devoid of live entertainment facilities; finally, in the 1970s a theatre was commissioned appropriate to the city's position as the main centre for the West Country. However, the two main political parties on the city council were divided between the option of an intimate repertory theatre seating around 700, suitable for the local theatre company, and a theatre of about 1500 seats (to be economically viable) for large-scale and popular touring productions, such as the Royal Ballet and the Royal Opera Company. Meanwhile, the theatre's architects, during an original competition for the building (which was initially to have been part of a large commercial complex), had independently concluded that the region actually needed not less than two theatres and a concert hall. The construction of three auditoria was out of the question, and the resolution was to commission a single auditorium that could expand or contract at the push of a

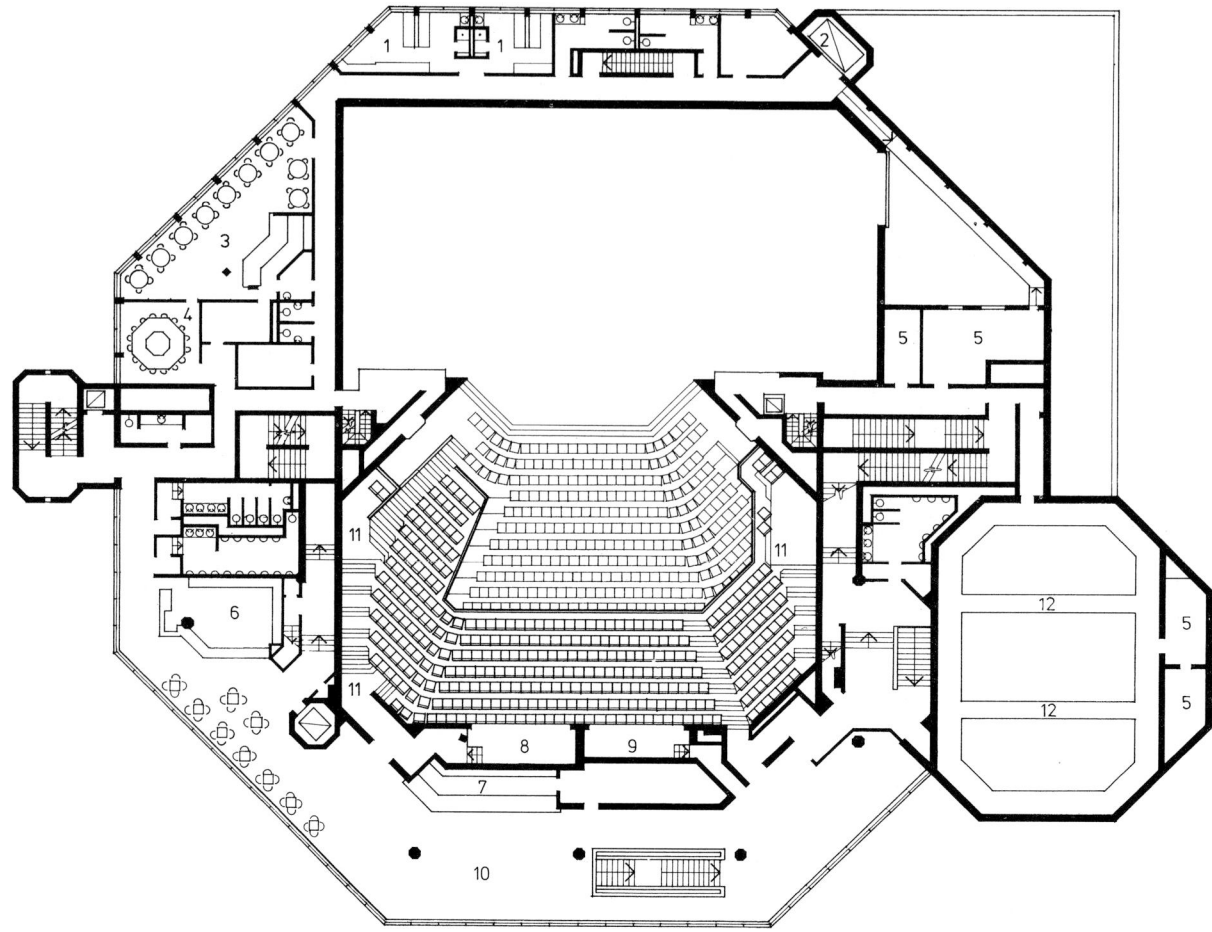

Plan at dress circle level. Key: 1 dressing rooms, 2 goods lift, 3 green room, 4 boardroom, 5 electrical plant, 6 snack bar, 7 bar, 8 technical area, 9 viewing area, 10 circle foyer and exhibition, 11 dress circle, 12 studio theatre lighting bridges

Section: large auditorium mode, ceiling raised.

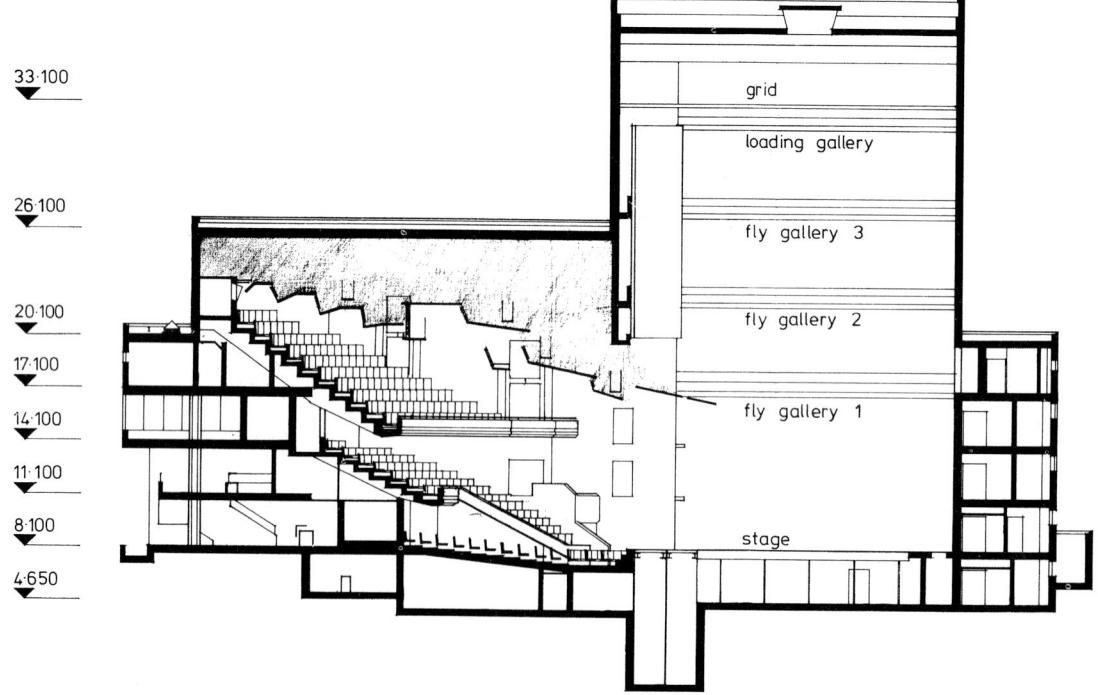

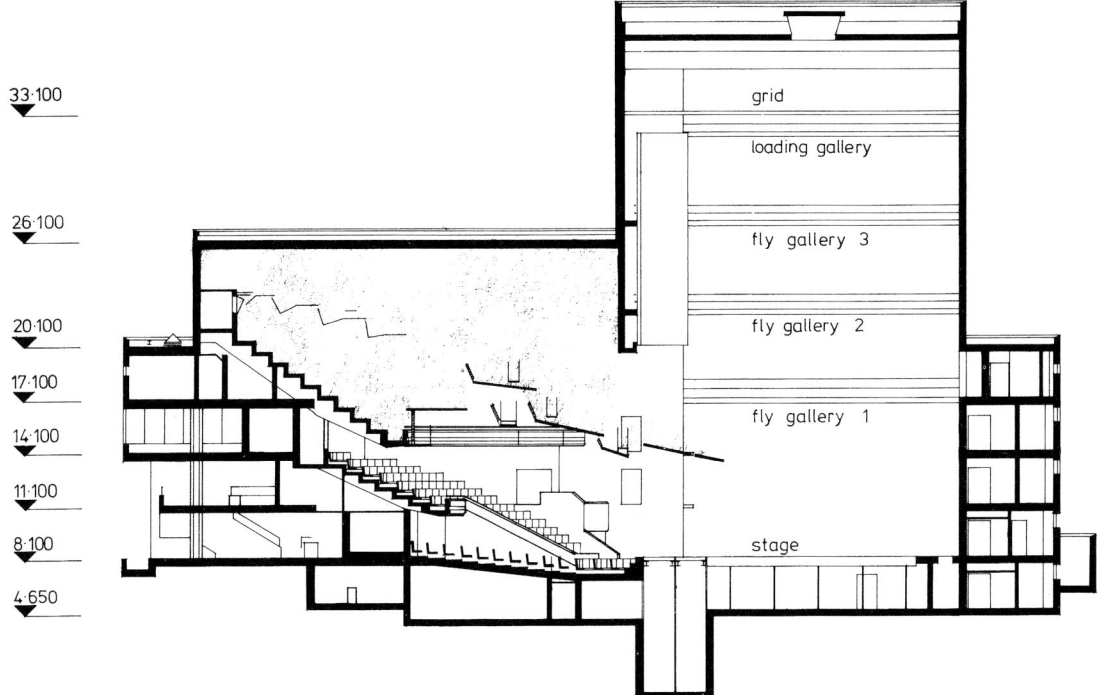

33·100

26·100

20·100

17·100

14·100

11·100

8·100

4·650

grid

loading gallery

fly gallery 3

fly gallery 2

fly gallery 1

stage

Section: small auditorium mode, ceiling lowered.

button, which would feel complete in either shape, and with a stage and backstage facilities that could accommodate a variety of production types.

The auditorium is fan-shaped, derivative of the amphitheatre, with angled rows of seats which generate the octagonal geometry of the overall building. There are three tiers, all with continental seats, the lower two being asymmetrical as the dress circle seats descend to the main floor on one side (a connection which can be useful at conferences). The movable ceiling is mounted on screw jacks and cables operated by electrically driven motors and is able to descend to close off the 500 seat upper circle, creating an intimate drama theatre. The ceiling is formed of three lighting bridges containing also air conditioning outlets connected to flexible ductwork. The ceiling sections reflect the seating angles and were profiled with the aid of model testing to encourage overhead sound reflections. The underside is faced with British chestnut wood veneer.

Even with the ceiling raised for the maximum seating capacity and reverberation time, the auditorium is still basically designed for drama: the cubic volume per seat is only a little over 3 cub.m (106 cub.ft) and acoustic treatment includes low-pile carpets and limited areas of timber panelling. For music, a 90-channel assisted resonance system is used, with tuned resonators in slots at the rear of the movable ceiling. These feed two rings of loudspeakers—one over the stalls and one over the front of the upper circle. Even when the system is not in use, there is also some further electro-acoustic treatment for the under-balcony seats which 'fills out' the sound, compensating for some loss in the upper frequencies.

The stage and backstage were required to meet the recommendations of the Arts Council for its proposed network of major regional touring theatres. This is because each theatre has to be compatible with other touring theatres and with the touring theatre's home. A proscenium stage with wing space and a flytower was necessary for the complex scenery almost always used by touring companies. The proscenium opening had to be about 12m (40ft) wide with a commensurate height, even though this is too large for normal repertory operations in the smaller auditorium format. Two proscenium towers were therefore provided, which track on and off stage, and are stored suspended at high level in the downstage corners when not in use.

For opera and ballet the Arts Council required provision for a 75-piece orchestra. However, Plymouth City Council stipulated that the orchestra pit must not spill out into the stalls seating in the conventional way, as the audience capacity had to be maximized for expensive productions of this kind. Any expansion of the pit, therefore, had to be taken out of the forestage. The solution adopted, instead of the usual moat between the stage riser and stalls, was to have the cranked safety curtain fall on the front orchestra rail, making the pit part of the stage area. The forestage is in two vertically movable sections, each with its own elevator, to give a choice of pit sizes. Another advantage of the whole forestage being behind the line of the safety curtain is that, when not in use as an orchestra pit, it can be used for scenery. The remainder of the stage floor over the acting area is removable, being divided into 45 modules, each 1.2m by 2.4m (4ft by 8ft) which can be taken out separately or in groups.

Within the proscenium form, which is traditionally associated with a 'two space' theatre, the architect has aimed to unify visually the stage and auditorium. Here,

Main auditorium: ceiling up.

Main auditorium: ceiling down.

Night view of theatre entrance.

the barrier is diminished by the absence of a proscenium header, as the auditorium ceiling forms the top of the proscenium. Also, the forestage, in the raised position, projects as a thrust into the auditorium, providing a closer link between the audience and performer than was possible in the old picture frame theatres. The splayed angle of the stage interlocks visually with the geometry of the seating, and also the stage riser is low and stepped to eliminate the sense of a barrier.

This spatial unity is especially important for symphony concerts. For this purpose, lightweight screens behind the orchestra and an overhead reflecting canopy help prevent loss of sound energy into the large flytower and provide visual enclosure. The screens are built of fabric stretched over aluminium frames and the canopy is inflatable, made of PVC-coated polyester, curved on the underside for sound diffusion. This is stored in the flytower when not in use.

The main variable elements—the proscenium, the forestage/pit, the ceiling panels over the stage—are all operable independently, giving several permutations.

Royal Concert Hall, Nottingham

Owner: City of Nottingham

Architects: Renton Howard Wood Levin Partnership

Theatre Consultant: Theatre Projects Consultants Ltd

Acoustic consultant: Artec Consultants Inc.

Services and structural engineers: Ove Arup & Partners

Quantity Surveyors: Gleeds

Main contractor: Bovis Construction Ltd

Opened: 1982

Cost: £10.1 million

Principal uses: multi-purpose, but excluding theatre

Seats: total 2510, stalls 856, first tier 639, second tier 820

Furthest balcony seat from front of stage: 39m (128ft)

Stage: 206 sq.m (2217 sq.ft)

Orchestra pit: 70 musicians

Volume: 15,740 cub.m (555,740 cub.ft)

Reverberation time: 1.45 sec. at middle frequencies with full audience

Maximum background noise level: PNC 15

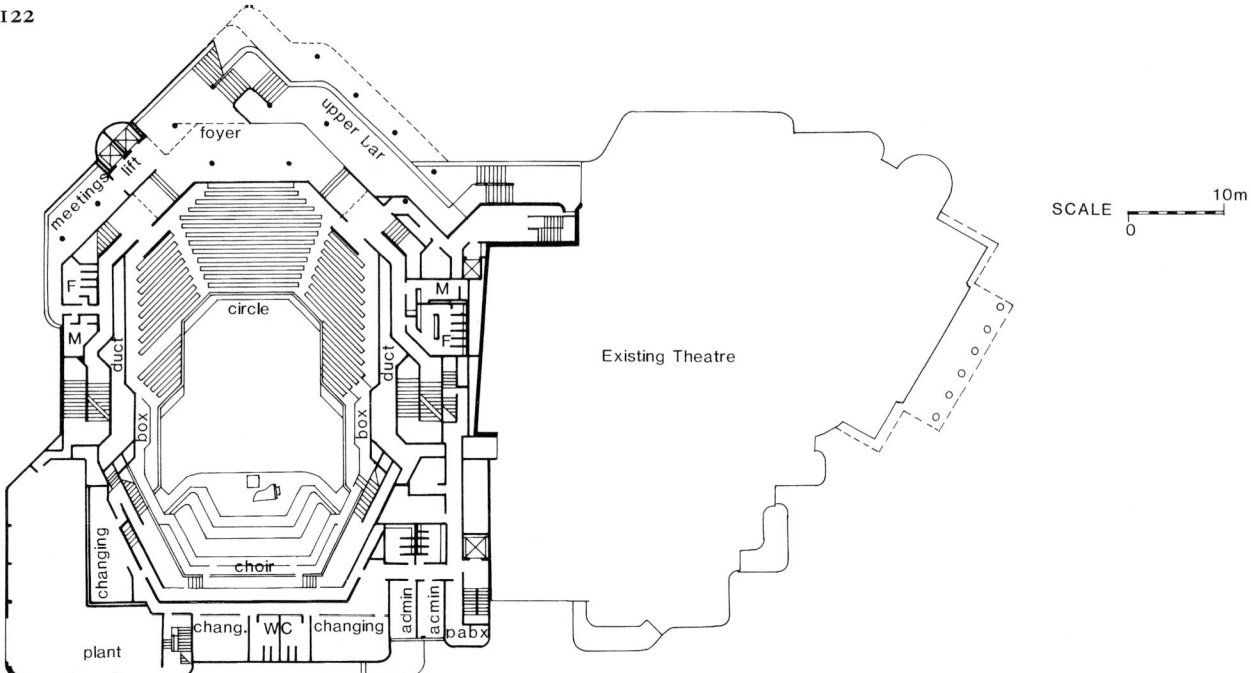

Plan at circle level.

Section through auditorium, showing the variable canopy.

SCALE

10m

0

Existing Theatre

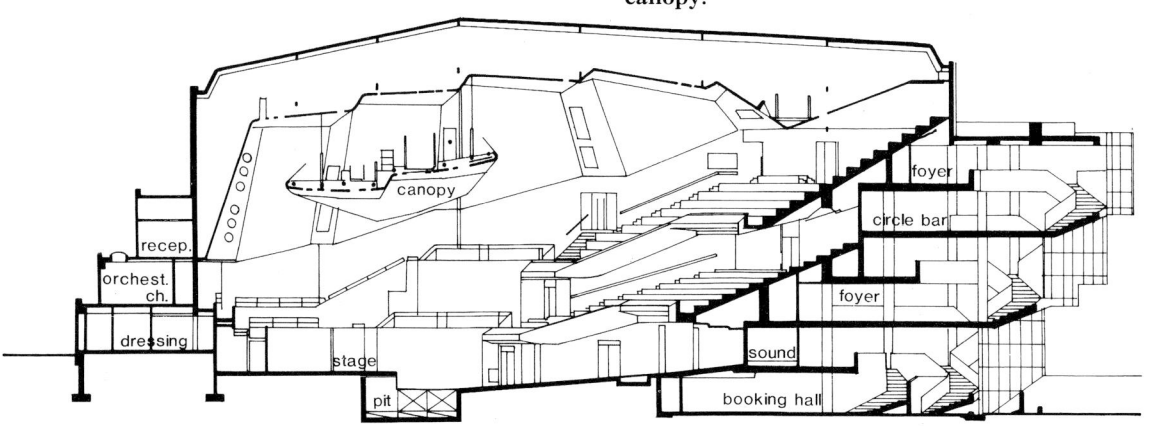

Although the auditorium is basically a concert hall, it actually has a variety of uses, both large- and small-scale. The giant sound-reflecting canopy can vary the acoustic and visual scale of the space, and the colour of the interior can be dramatically altered to suit different presentations.

Along with St David's Hall, Cardiff, which also opened in 1982, this was the first major auditorium intended primarily for music to be completed in the United Kingdom since 1951, the year which saw the opening of the Royal Festival Hall, London, and of the reconstructed Colston Hall, Bristol, and the Free Trade Hall, Manchester. As with nearly every new hall of its type outside the very largest cities, which usually have a range of facilities, the brief demanded accommodation not just for different types of music, including symphonic, choral, rock, jazz, chamber and brass band, but also for a range of events including conferences, big screen cinema, wrestling, international darts and product launches. However, there was no requirement for a proscenium stage, because the refurbished Victorian Theatre Royal next door (the work of the same design team) forms part of a single complex. The necessary adaptability was consequently to do with simple stage adjustability, acoustics (speech and amplified popular music versus classical music), scale (visual and again acoustical) and 'mood'. The acoustical environment can be changed from being 'live' to 'dry' for different types of event by adjustment to the acoustical 'scale' of the hall, where the strength of early reflected sound energy is varied relative to the reverberant sound rather than by adjustment to the overall reverberation time.

The principal feature is an enormous sound-reflecting canopy over the front part of the seating area and the platform. It can move vertically by 10m (33ft) down to just 4.2m (14ft) above the performing area, and it can also tilt by a maximum of 10 degrees. With the canopy raised, the reverberance of the room is suited to larger-scale orchestral concerts. When lowered, the canopy reduces the acoustical and visual scale of the hall for chamber groups or conferences, providing greater loudness and clarity as a consequence of the stronger and more immediate sound reflections. With a smaller audience occupying the main floor, the gallery can also be darkened to complete the impression of a smaller auditorium. The canopy is 16.6m (54.5ft) across, 14m (46ft) from front to rear, and weighs 32 tonnes. It is constructed from fibrous plaster 40mm (1.6in) thick attached directly to a tubular steel space frame above. Stage lighting is integrated into the canopy, together with a 'sound bridge' containing an array of loudspeakers— used in conjunction with stage tower loudspeakers, for example for amplified jazz bands—which can be lowered when in use, or retracted behind hinged panels concealed in the surface of the canopy. The canopy is suspended on wire ropes which pass onto two sets of winding drums located in the ceiling void above the auditorium. Each drum has three winches, each operating two cables; the equipment is controlled from the stage manager's position at the side of the concert platform.

For speech and amplified music, a series of 15 heavy fabric sound-absorbent banners descend from air-sealed slots in the ceiling along cables down the angled wall-ceiling surfaces. Their purpose is to reduce the apparent reverberation by reducing the intensity of time-delayed ceiling reflections which would otherwise obscure the clarity of the direct sound from the loudspeakers.

The form of the interior as a whole was developed with carved balsa wood models, and this is evident in the unusual sculptured and unified form. The chief feature of the hall is a massive ceiling hung inside the outer shell of the roof, shaped like a giant up-turned moulded hull and faceted to encourage lateral reflections. It is constructed of dense 125mm (5in) sprayed concrete, to reflect the bass frequencies; it weighs 400 tonnes and is suspended from steel roof trusses on 900 steel rod hangers. The void formed in the 3m (10ft) depth of the trusses between the ceiling and the roof contains, as well as the equipment for the canopy, motors for the acoustic banners, production lights with an access bridge, winches for point hoists above the stage, and the air supply ducts which connect to outlets in the ceiling. The ceiling as a whole is air-sealed around the edges and all light fittings and openings are also gasketed to maintain the acoustic isolation of the auditorium.

The client's brief required a one-directional layout; there is a main floor of continental seats (some of which are removable to reveal an orchestra pit) and two balcony tiers with traditional aisle seating. Economic necessity, particularly for rock concerts, demanded 2500 seats, which, although 500 less than the Royal Festival Hall, is around 1000 more than that of the acclaimed halls of the nineteenth century. The designers' approach with this dilemma has been to provide acoustically and visually optimal seating for around 2000 listeners, with the final few hundred seats being under a deep balcony overhang.

For a concert hall the stage is exceptionally adjustable to allow a wide range of events. The normally enclosed orchestral platform may be opened out both in depth and width to provide an open stage with 4.3m (14ft) high wing spaces on either side with suspension above. There is no proscenium and it is always an open stage. Two of the four rows of 186 choir seats are retractable to extend the orchestra area upstage and those at the sides may be removed to create access to the offstage wingspace. The front panels to the choir seating are acoustically adjustable. A rostra system can be set up in several permutations for an orchestra on stage. An orchestra pit may be formed by removing the front four rows of stall seating and the demountable structure beneath, or alternatively a forestage extension can be built for large-scale stage events.

CHAPTER 5

The New Antiquarians

Learning from the Past

Drama theatres, more than any other building type, must as a matter of functional necessity embody a range of intangible and relatively indefinable architectural qualities such as mood, intimacy, magic and memory. It was these qualities that the new theatres of the 1960s did least to encourage. Most have too broad a focus onto the stage for the actor to capture and hold the audience's attention, especially for comedy. Also, their often cold, uninviting interiors do little to put the audience at its ease and are counter to the idea that 'warm colours make people laugh more easily'. Actors consequently disliked them, and directors frequently sought alternative venues such as redundant railway sheds and warehouses. The return to traditional theatre forms during recent years has restored some of these qualities which were abundant in theatres of the past. This has coincided with the Post-modern movement in architecture which has made historical reference, colour and other popular qualities once again acceptable—qualities which to the puritanical Modernist would have been at the very least suspect if not downright kitsch. (Even so, the Ordway Music Theatre in St Paul, Minnesota—see below—has been called 'the luscious tart'!)

Most important of all, theatres should encourage actor-audience rapport. A theatre's success undoubtedly relates to its three-dimensional form, and a performance which is successful in one theatre will not necessarily be equally so in another. Traditional-style theatres with galleries or boxes tend to be more successful in 'raising the emotional temperature', for they give the actors the feeling of contact with their audience, of 'being able to reach out and touch' them. This sense is poorest in single rake theatres where, from the actor's viewpoint on stage, the audience appears to recede into darkness.

Theatres with side galleries or boxes also have the advantage of providing greater social rapport for the audience. The spectator is aware of other audience members across the auditorium at the same time as seeing the actors on stage (a quality also enjoyed by theatre-in-the-round). For one-directional theatres, however, this is only possible at some expense to good sightlines for the side gallery seats. (Before the age of gas lighting side gallery seats were desirable only because it was better to sit closest at the sides rather than centrally far away.)

Galleried theatres fall into two types. One is the 'courtyard', as inspired by the Elizabethan, Restoration and Georgian playhouses, and supposedly derived from medieval inn yards. This type lends itself to smaller community, school or experimental theatre buildings and gives the possibility of flat floor performances in the middle as an alternative to the end stage layout. Examples are Christ's Hospital Theatre, Horsham, the Tricycle Theatre, Kilburn, and the Swan Theatre, Stratford-upon-Avon. The other type recalls the Italian baroque opera house, where tiers of boxes 'line the walls with people'. The boxes are sometimes stepped, *en escalier*, for good sightlines (again an old Italian device) usually within a U-shape auditorium. Into this category fall the Ordway Music Theatre, St Paul, Minnesota, the Max Bell Theatre at the Centre for Performing Arts, Calgary (see Chapter 2) and, less overtly, the Barbican Theatre, London.

Another branch of the New Antiquarianism, which is interesting if rather aside from the aims of the present book, is the reconstruction of historical theatres with scholarly exactness. The principal project of its kind, as yet unrealized, is to recreate Shakespeare's first Globe Theatre at Southwark on London's South Bank, almost on its original site. The building is the idea of the American actor-producer Sam Wanamaker and has been designed by the architect Theo Crosby of Pentagram Design Limited with the help of Shakespearean scholars. Although based on the known evidence, the design had to be gently adapted to present-day fire and safety regulations (for instance thatched roofs have been forbidden in London since 1666). The idea is to incorporate the theatre into a tourist and study centre which would include a museum of the Elizabethan stage, an archive of Shakespearean performance, a public house, residential units and, eventually, a reconstruction of Inigo Jones's Phoenix Theatre, Drury Lane, of 1617, an enclosed 300 seat theatre which would hold evening performances throughout the year.

Another of the same kind is a North American replica of the Georgian Theatre, Richmond, North Yorkshire. The project, planned by Boston's Priscilla Beach Theatre Company, will cost £2 million and is due to open in 1988, coinciding with the theatre's 200th anniversary.

Teatro Regio, Turin

Owner: City of Turin

Architects: Carlo Mollino with Carlo Graffi; executive architects, Marcello Zavelani Rossi and Adolfo Zavelani Rossi

Acoustic consultants: Gino Sacerdote and Raffaele Pisani

Plan at street level. Below this level is a vast subterranean complex of backstage facilities on four levels. Key: 1 entrance atrium, 2 external covered gallery, 3 cloaks, 4 orchestra pit, 5 auditorium, 6 stage, 7 side stages, 8 rear stage, 9 dressing rooms, 10 stage door, 11 theatre entrances, 12 box office, 13 escalators

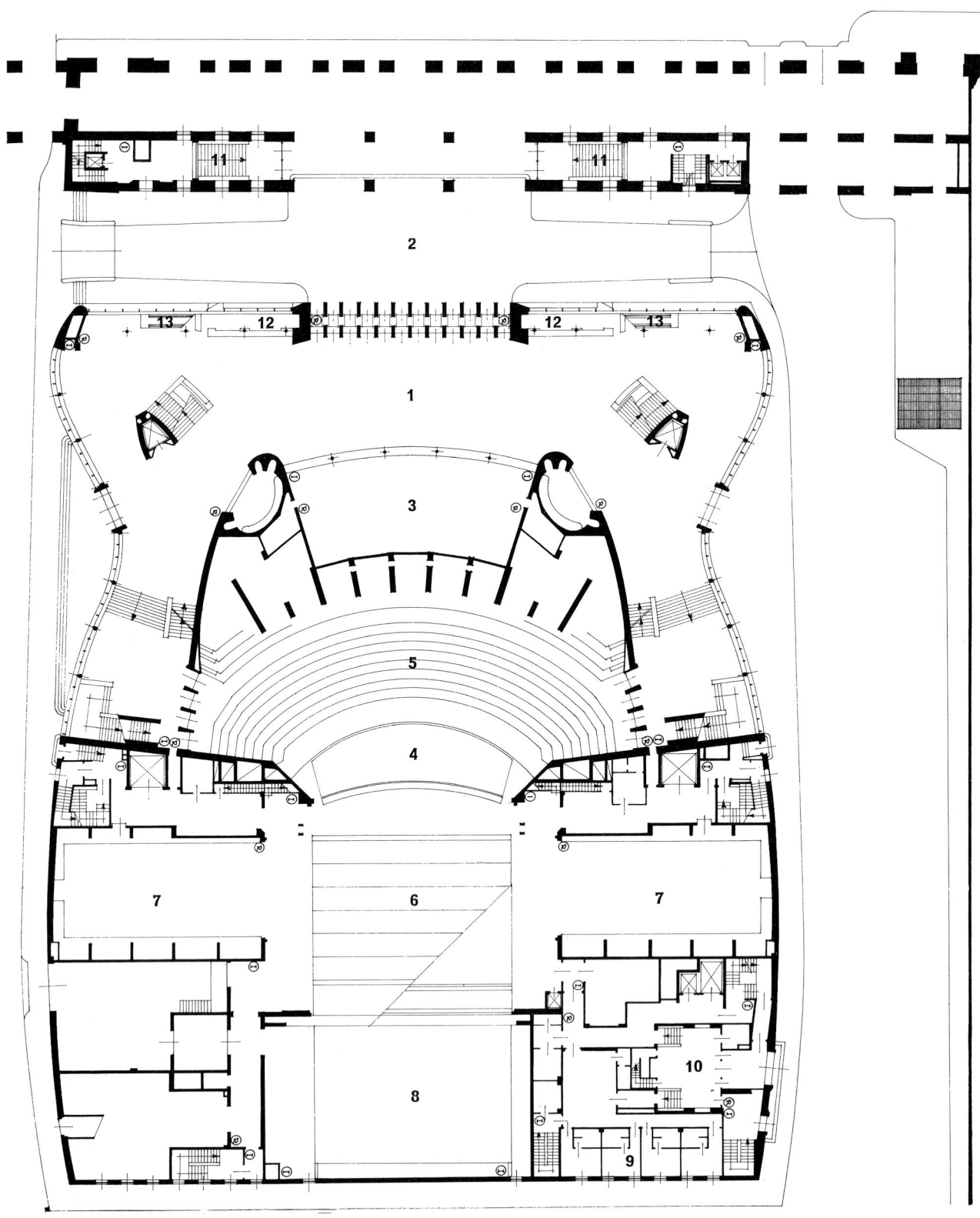

Structural engineers: Sergio Musmeci and Felice Bertone

Services engineers: Aurelio Vaccaneo and Mario Chiattone

Electrical engineer: Arturo Job

Contract management: Aldo Brizio

Opened: 1973

Primary use: opera

Seats: total 1788, main floor 1552, boxes 236

Plan at upper level. Key: 1 upper foyer, 2 president's box, 3 auditorium, 4 boxes, 5 dressing room: men's chorus, 6 administration

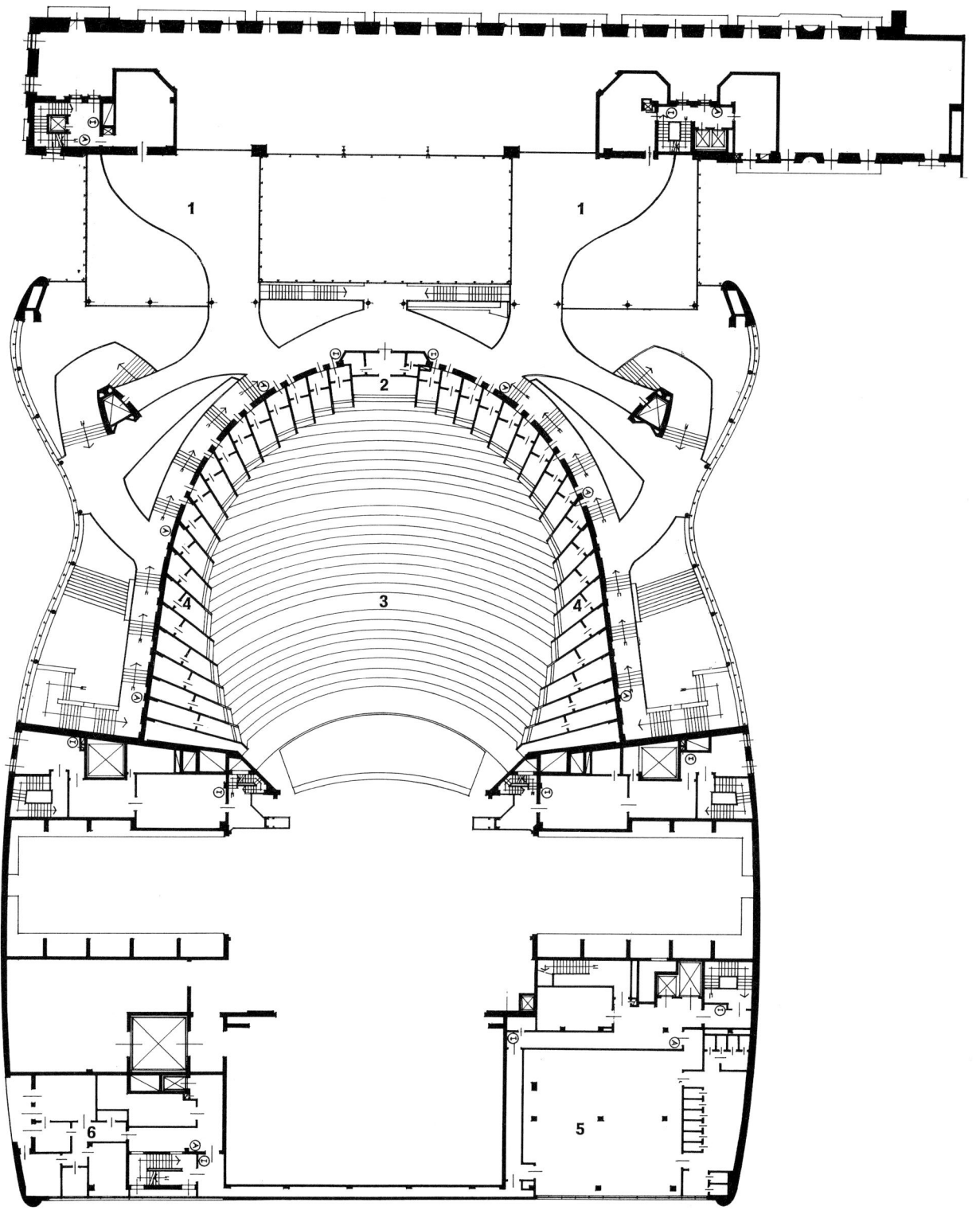

0   5   10 m

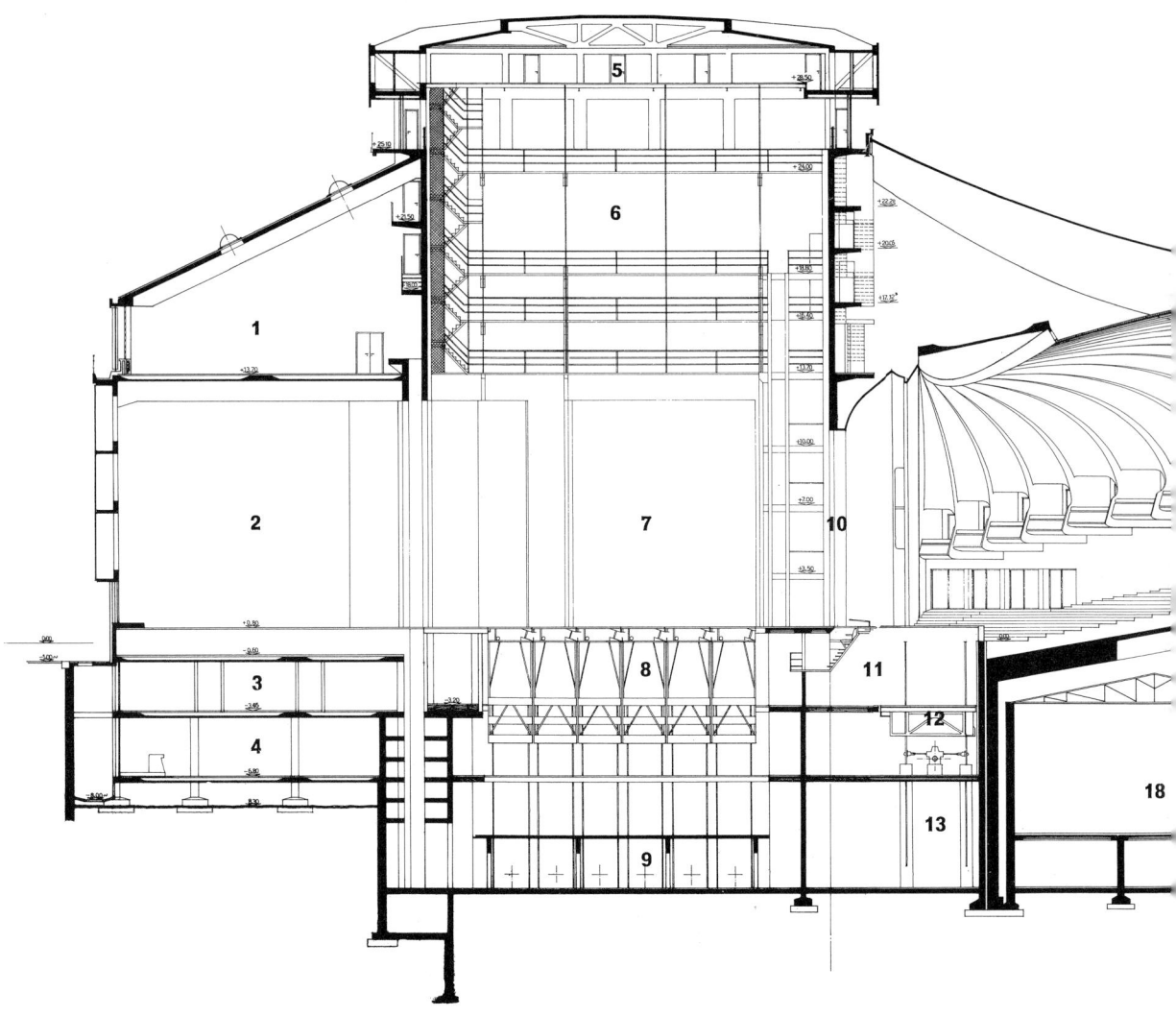

Longitudinal section through auditorium. Key: 1 scenery workshop, 2 rear stage, 3 backstage facilities, 4 plant room, 5 grid, 6 flytower, 7 stage, 8 hydraulic bridges, 9 motor room, 10 proscenium, 11 orchestra pit, 12 movable orchestra bridge, 13 orchestra bridge motor room, 14 roof space, 15 ceiling shell, 16 boxes, 17 auditorium, 18 rehearsal room (as built divided horizontally into two rehearsal spaces), 19 foyer, 20 cloaks, 21 offices, 22 choir room, 23 plant room, 24 covered gallery, 25 main entrance, 26 studio theatre, 27, 28 administration, 29 foyer, 30 portico, 31 electrical intake room, 32 transformer

Furthest box from stage front: 42m (138ft)

Proscenium opening: variable from a maximum width 17.1m (56ft) and height 10m (33ft)

Stage: width 74m (243ft) from stage right wing to stage left wing, depth 40m (132ft) from proscenium wall to back wall, height to underside of grid 31m (101.5ft)

Orchestra pit: 100 musicians

Volume: 15,500 cub.m (547,300 cub.ft)

Reverberation time: 1.3 sec. at middle frequencies with full audience

On the night of February 8, 1936, Benedetto Alfieri's renowned Teatro Regio of 1740, one of the most admired opera houses ever built, and the centre of Turin's artistic life, was totally destroyed by fire. After many years of alternative proposals a contemporary replacement for the same site was finally designed in 1966 and construction commenced in 1971. The result is theatre building at its most lavish. Aiming to recall through contemporary means the opulence of the traditional nineteenth-century Italian opera house architecture of boxes, chandeliers and regal red upholstery, the building is an extravagant mixture of advanced technology and of architectural forms that are simultaneously futurist-expressionist and neo-baroque. Stylistically the building stands outside modern movement conventions of good taste, and presents the question of whether the building is indeed the popular answer to the average operagoer's demands for an opera house that feels traditional—or whether it represents the ultimate in architectural kitsch. It is in any event an extreme example of a theatre that is wholly (and possibly over-) reliant on mechanical and electrical technology for its basic functioning.

Only the front façade of Alfieri's building remained standing after the fire, splendidly situated facing onto

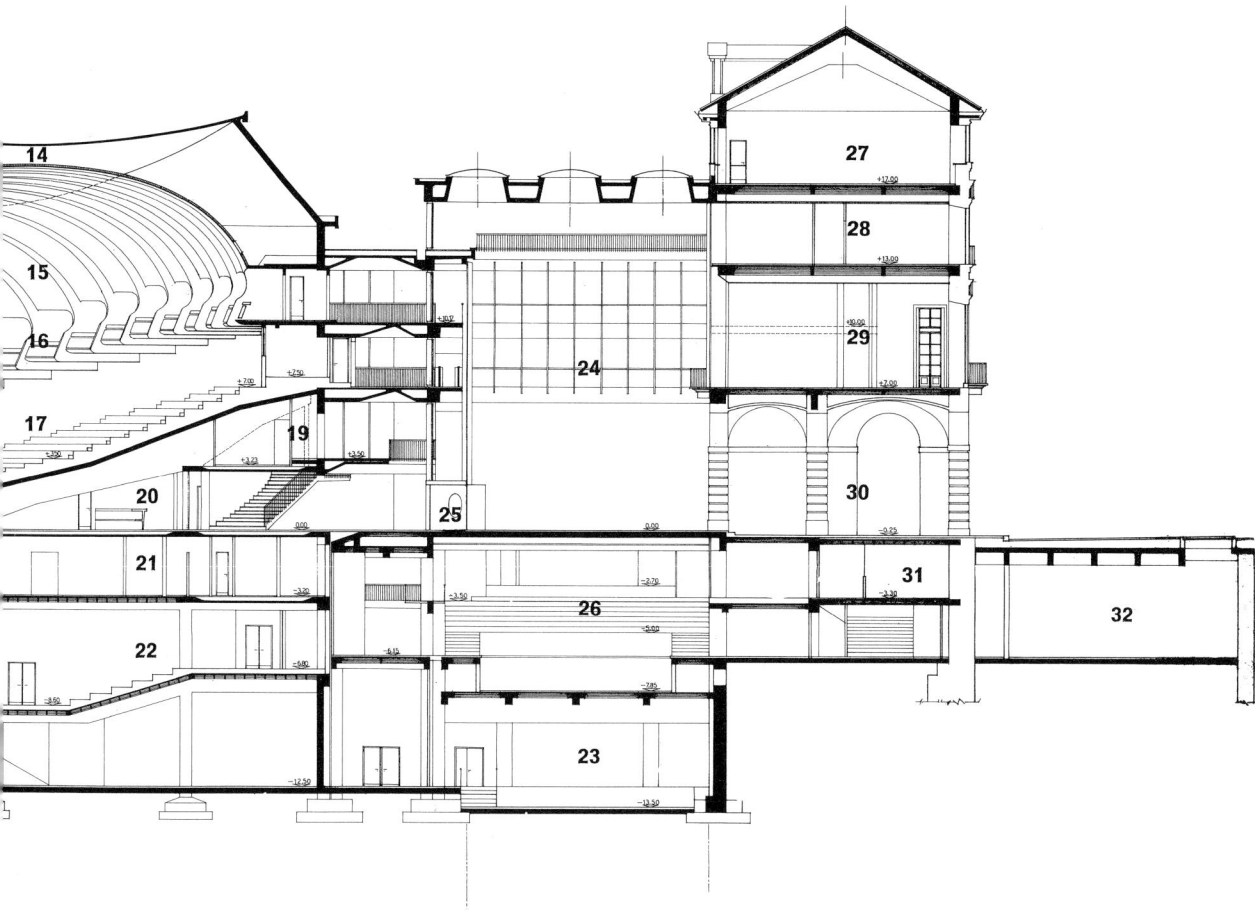

Turin's central Piazza Castello. The old theatre formed an extremity, with direct access from Amadeo di Castellamonte's Palazzo Reale, the former Piedmontese royal residence. The theatre's central axis used to be parallel with the centreline of the palace, but the axis of the new theatre, with its public access from the square, was rotated through 90 degrees, north-west/south-east, to face the Piazza Castello. Behind the old façade a *piano nobile* floor was built extending across its width, in the tradition of opera house grand foyers, with administration above and entrance arcades below. The auditorium with its support areas and immediate access foyers are set back from this, behind a bronze and glass curtain wall façade. The area between the two blocks forms a large open-air, but covered, vestibule or 'galleria' with roof lights, which is actively used for 'environmental' exhibitions and street displays. The two elements are linked by glazed bridges containing bar areas which connect the main foyer with the circulation areas.

These access areas for the auditorium comprise an extraordinary Piranesian system of walkway bridges, escalators, lifts, staircases and landings, curved, flowing and open to view, the form of which is derived from a literal transfer of audience movement flow-diagrams into

built form. The decor of the public areas is more like a 'boudoir' than a foyer, with crimson coloured carpets, matching wall coverings and padded seating upholstery, full-length wall mirrors, intimate low-level lighting, gold coloured satin finish metal wall cladding in the more open areas, and matching fluted column covers.

The auditorium is a raked, single-terrace truncated ellipse, extending 42m (137.8ft) from the proscenium to the rear with a 6.6m (21.7ft) change in level, with access from the sides, and surrounded by a crown of 37 boxes whose partitions are fanned to orientate towards the stage. This arrangement looks in plan entirely within the tradition of La Scala, Milan, La Fenice, Venice, and San Carlo, Naples. The effect in three dimensions, however, is very different, as there is only one tier of boxes, which step down towards the stage, thrusting forwards, cantilevered into the auditorium. While the boxes define the auditorium in plan, the dividing walls of the boxes in section also form the base of the ceiling. This is paraboloid in profile, shaped for optimal sound reflection (somewhat on the principle of the 'directed sound' halls of the 1930s) and is created from a series of arched facets. This elliptical three-dimensional unity is described by the architect as being like an egg, or a half-open oyster shell. The form and architectural treatment give rise to

The auditorium, looking towards the stage. The
extremities of the ceiling ribs form the box partitions.
The acrylic 'stalactites', like a vast chandelier,
provide general illumination.

further analogies, however, including 1930s auditoria like
New York's Radio City Music Hall and the art deco
cinemas of the period, and futurist (again perhaps 1930s)
space-age imagery—like the interior of a flying saucer.

The ceiling is formed of two layers of laminated 10mm
(0.4) plywood sections which form a ribbed structure like
a clinker-built wooden ship's hull, suspended inside an
outer concrete paraboloid roof shell. An oval section of
the ceiling over the orchestra pit is formed in concrete as a
sound reflector. The wooden ceiling is punctured by air
inlet diffusers, and the faceted form of the ceiling is
visually overlaid by a complex painted pattern of mauve
stripes. The traditional opera house chandelier is
transmuted here into a shimmering array of needle-like
crystal stalactites. These are made of suspended
cruciform-section rods of plexiglass interspersed with
hundreds of small light fixtures on stalks which diffuse a
magical glitter throughout the ceiling array.

Further lighting is provided in concealed troughs
above the boxes, while light bulbs in snowflake patterns
illuminate the boxes.

A deep, rounded proscenium arch which is shaped, as
the architect says, 'like a television set', resolves the
elliptical form of the auditorium, meeting the required
rectangular opening of the stage. The curved proscenium, according to the architect, is easier on the eye
than the traditional picture-frame stage, 'as it falls within

The undulating façade is influenced by the baroque
architecture of Guarini.

The rooftop and flytower of the opera behind the surviving façade of Alfieri.

the cone of vision'. A pair of green coloured proscenium curtains open asymmetrically, drawn diagonally upwards as if by an unseen hand. Within this fixed frame two mobile proscenium towers and a vertically movable architrave on the stage itself can vary the opening size according to each performance.

The stage has six 2.5m (8.2ft) by 18m (59ft) mobile bridges on hydraulic jacks which can extend or retract to a variety of levels. There are two wings and a rear stage area, each of which is equipped with a stage wagon, upon which sets can be built, then rolled onto the stage for rapid scene changing. The side wagons are each in four sections for versatility, corresponding to the front four bridges of the stage, while the rear wagon is exactly the size of the main stage. When special rails are laid to span across the orchestra pit, the rear wagon with its wheels located on the rails can roll forwards, powered by eight electric motors concealed within the wagon's 300mm (11.8in) depth, into the auditorium as far as the first aisle to form an enormous thrust for 'total theatre'. Seating banks for 400 people can be placed on the stage to form theatre-in-the-round; however, this capability has so far been used only once.

The orchestra pit also contains a bridge that can rise to extend the forestage for symphony concerts and also descend to an instrument store below. Apart from the loading bay, control booths and other support areas directly related to the stage at the same level or above, and

the scene-painting room—a lean-to against the flytower above the rear stage area—the substantial complex of backstage support is mainly underground. This includes dressing, practice and rehearsal rooms, a canteen (there are some 100 orchestra players, 90 chorus members, 110 technicians and 30 administrators employed in the building), and workshops for scenery and props. The latter are connected to stage level by an enormous elevator. The mechanical plant at the bottom of the building includes a standby generator for the entire building, a battery-operated uninterrupted power supply and water tanks for the sprinkler system, full air-conditioning and a master control room for mechanical and electrical services. This underground accommodation reduces the bulk of the building above ground, so that only the flytower protrudes at rooftop level, just above the parabolic shell roof over the auditorium, which is clad in diamond-shaped slates in the local tradition. The building in plan is 'waisted' to follow the lines of the auditorium, producing undulating side façades containing decorative masonry of baroque inspiration; the architect refers particularly to the influence of Guarini's swelling façade to the nearby Palazzo Carignano, with its decorated courtyard of brick and terracotta.

Tricycle Theatre, Kilburn, London

Owner: Wakefield Tricycle Company

Architect: Tim Foster

Theatre consultant: Theatre Projects Consultants Ltd

Structural and mechanical engineers: Edwards & Blackie (first phase only)

Quantity surveyors: Michael French Associates

Main contractor: J. T. Luton & Son Ltd

Scaffolding: Rapid Metal Developments Ltd

Opened: 1980

Cost: auditorium only, £38,000; upgrading existing building, £85,000

Principal use: drama

Seats: 200

Furthest balcony seat from stage front: 10m (33ft)

Stage: width 11m (36ft) right wing to left wing, depth 4m (13ft) front of stage to rear edge of scaffold structure

Volume: 2950 cub.m (104,170 cub.ft)

Reverberation time: 1.0 sec. (estimate)

Maximum background noise level: NR 30 (estimate)

The basic idea was to create out of contemporary materials a simple post-and-beam two-gallery theatre based on the form and dimensions of the Georgian Theatre at Richmond, Yorkshire of 1788. Steel scaffolding was chosen as the material, so as to be cheap and erectable by unskilled labour. The aim was that it

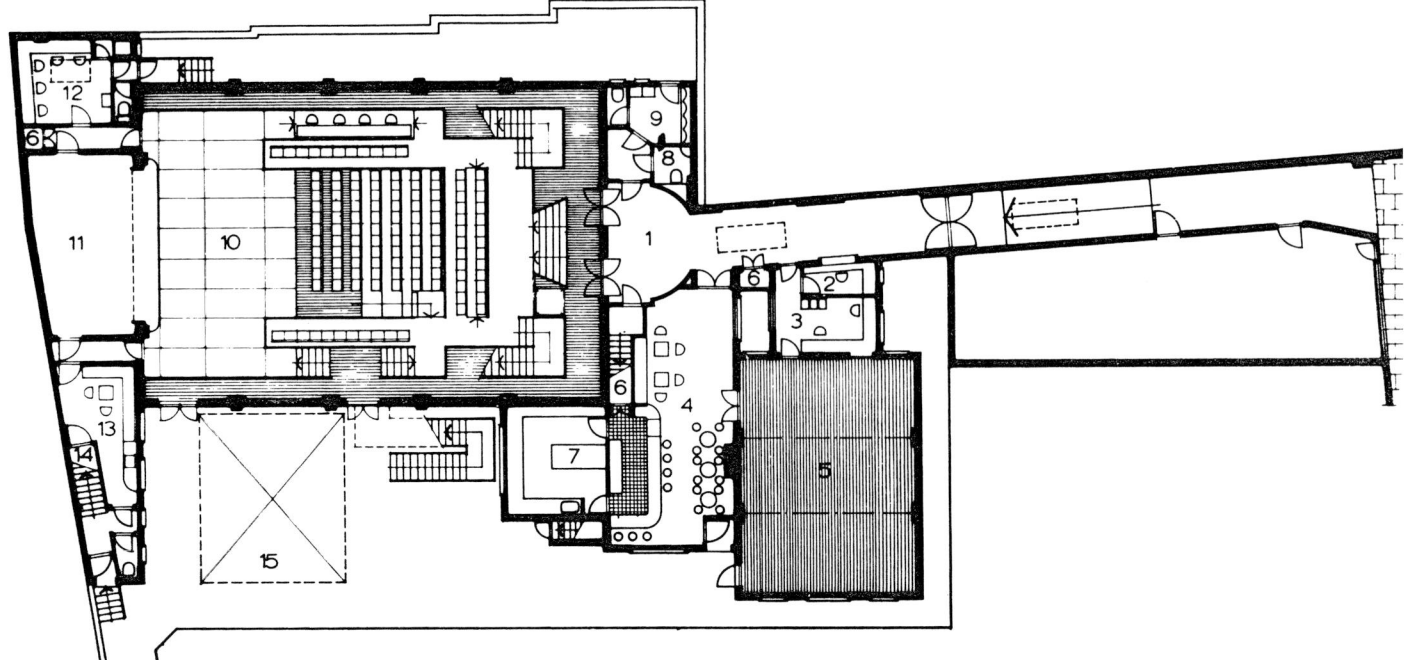

Ground floor plan. The existing building is set back from the street between other buildings, and is entered through a long entrance hall. Key: 1 entrance hall, 2 box office, 3 office, 4 bar, 5 rehearsal/meeting room, 6 store, 7 kitchen, 8 wc for disabled, 9 men's wc, 10 theatre, 11 rearstage storage, 12 dressing room, 13 actors' green room, 14 electrical intake, 15 future storage/workshop

could be altered or taken down altogether, just as Shakespeare moved the Globe and rebuilt it at Bankside.

It was built for the Wakefield Tricycle Company, which was founded in 1972 as a travelling alternative theatre group. The company initially performed in pubs, then from 1974 with Arts Council grants toured musical revues to colleges and community centres. By 1978 the Tricycle sought a permanent home, having now specialized in commissioning new works on social and political issues. The London Borough of Brent offered a former music and dance hall built in 1927 by a friendly society, the Ancient Order of Foresters, which had been subdivided and used for the previous 20 years as council offices.

Other 'fringe' theatres have been built of scaffolding, but this represents a considerable refinement and is the first scaffolding theatre to be granted a permanent licence even though it is theoretically demountable. Besides being buildable by the theatre company itself, another advantage of scaffolding was that the work could easily be phased, enabling conventional builders' work to the basic fabric to be completed before work on the theatre itself commenced. This enabled work to proceed rapidly on the basis of fixed grants and donations already available while funds were raised for completion of the theatre itself. The initial work included repairs to the building fabric, conversion of the ancillary areas to a bar, rehearsal space/cafe, foyer and dressing rooms, and the installation

of services to Greater London Council standards, including a heated mechanical ventilation system in the existing pitched roof space. The new theatre structure is built freestanding inside the existing main hall, which has a small proscenium stage that now serves as retiring space and storage or an occasional 'vista' stage. The two-gallery structure is built around three sides of a 'courtyard', containing raked seating and the stage at one end, in the manner of the Georgian Theatre at Richmond, to which the dimensions are very similar; the entire gallery and stage areas are contained within an area of approximately 10m (33ft) by 15m (49.5ft).

The structure took just two and a half months to build. A mass-produced contractors' scaffolding system was selected for its fail-safe, non-slip lug connections between the horizontal and vertical members, a type normally used for concreting form work. Also, the system offered a choice of bay sizes: 1.2m, 1.8m and 2.4m (4ft, 6ft and 8ft). The framework stands on timber bearers built off the existing wooden suspended floor and is braced against the existing walls. The only non-standard or modified components are the timber gallery floor structure, which is reinforced with steel beams because of the structural loads involved, and the access stairs and lighting trusses. All structural columns, balustrades, ties and lighting bars are made up of standard components. Seating, both in the central well and on the galleries, is fixed to removable steel-framed plywood rostra. The balustrade infill panels are made of bright blue flame-proofed canvas (which is soft on the knees) laced to the scaffolding framework, which is painted orange. The fire regulations normally require all structural steelwork to be fire-protected, but this was relaxed because the auditorium can be emptied in just one and a half minutes, following which the failure of the internal structure would not prejudice the structural integrity of the main building fabric.

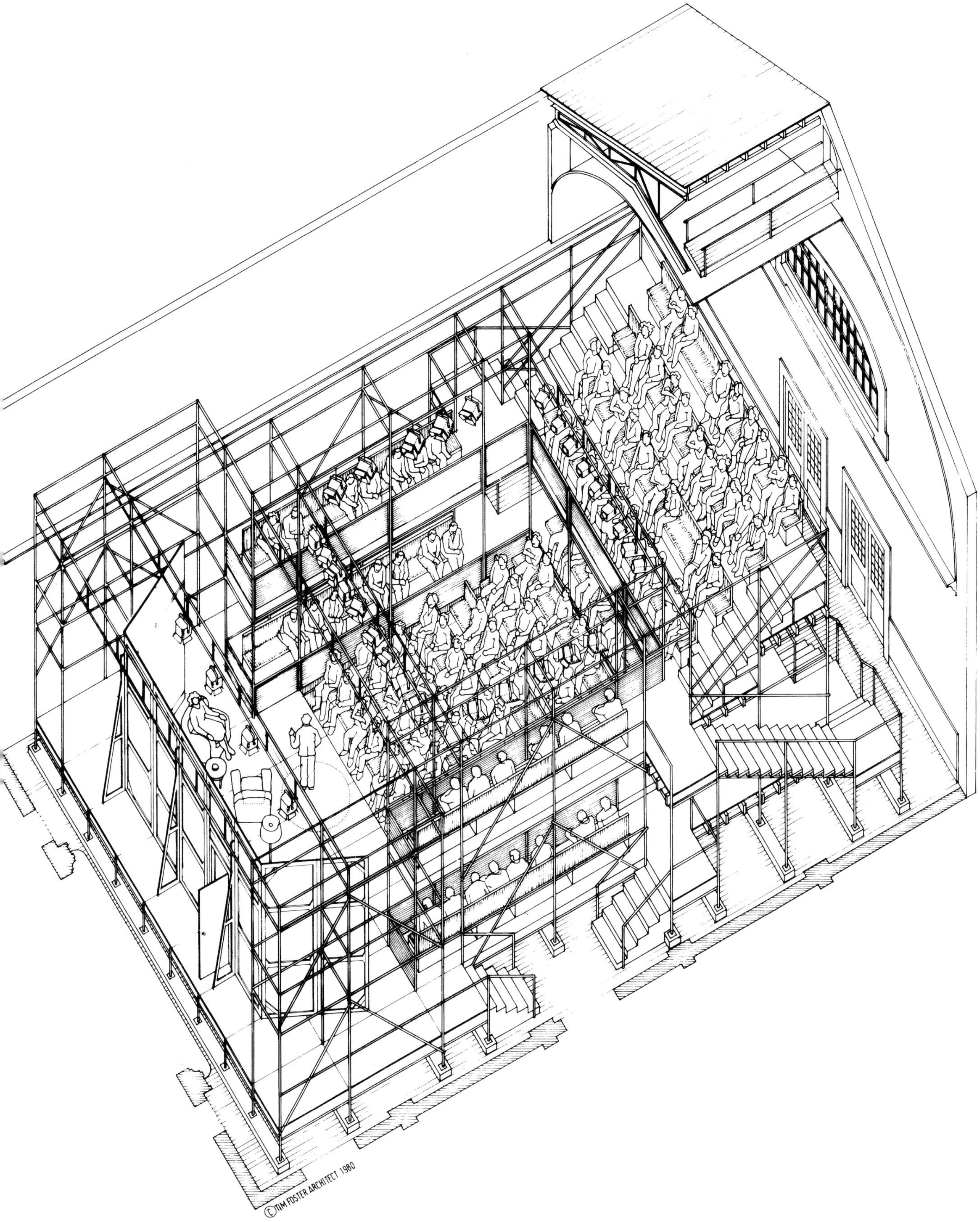

© TIM FOSTER ARCHITECT 1980

Axonometric drawing of theatre structure.

Theatre interior. The scaffolding is painted orange
and the canvas infill panels bright blue.

The Georgian Theatre, Richmond, Yorkshire, built
1788 and restored in 1962, on which the Tricycle
Theatre is modelled.

Although the end stage was the basic form required by the company, the scaffolding system is conceived as an adaptable architectural framework. The stage itself is raised on scaffolding, and the galleries can be extended on the same grid around the stage. The rostra on which the seating is mounted also correspond to the structural grid and can be lifted out or stored, or placed on the stage to create an acting area in the centre of the well. Alternatively, as the stage and lower gallery are at the same level, the seats can be removed and the pit filled in to form a flat floor for promenade performances. Although the company have not tried these configurations to date, this demountable Georgian-type courtyard theatre system could be adapted to the varying needs of the numerous low-budget alternative theatre companies that presently operate from inadequate redundant Victorian commercial buildings, churches and school halls.

Primary use: drama

Seats: total 1166, stalls 687, first balcony 195, second balcony 147, third balcony 137

Furthest balcony seat from stage front: 20m (65.6ft)

Proscenium opening: width 22.25m (73ft), height 9.1m (30ft)

Stage: width 35.4m (116ft) from right wing to left wing, depth 22.9m (75ft) from front of stage to rear wall, height to grid underside 22.9m (75ft)

Flying system: electric hoist, with bars spaced at 200mm (8in)

Volume: 4250 cub.m (150,000 cub.ft)

Reverberation time: 1.1 sec. at middle frequencies with full audience

Maximum background noise level: NR 15

Barbican Theatre, London

Owner: Corporation of London

Architects: Chamberlin, Powell and Bon (Barbican)

Acoustic consultant: Hugh Creighton

Theatre design consultant: John Bury (Royal Shakespeare Company)

Theatre technology consultants: Theatre Projects Consultants Ltd

Structural engineers: Ove Arup & Partners

Services engineers: Buckle & Partners

Quantity Surveyors: Davis, Belfield & Everest

Opened: 1982

Cost: (of Barbican Arts Centre including concert hall) £106 million

Although the original design, for opera rather than drama, was more like a traditional opera house with boxes, the theatre as finally built, with its shallow seating galleries, numerous doors and generally opulent, theatrical feel, is nonetheless a subtle and entirely contemporary interpretation of the Italian baroque theatre. It is especially significant and successful for the way in which the Royal Shakespeare Company's brief—which was precise, to the point (including dimensional criteria and a model of the stage), and never changed—was projected into built form, despite an unusually long and complex inception period.

The theatre was the final phase to be completed of the Barbican Arts Centre, the complex built to house a concert hall for the London Symphony Orchestra, the Guildhall School of Music and Drama, a public lending

Barbican Arts Centre: plan of the theatre in relation to the concert hall and the Guildhall School of Music and Drama.

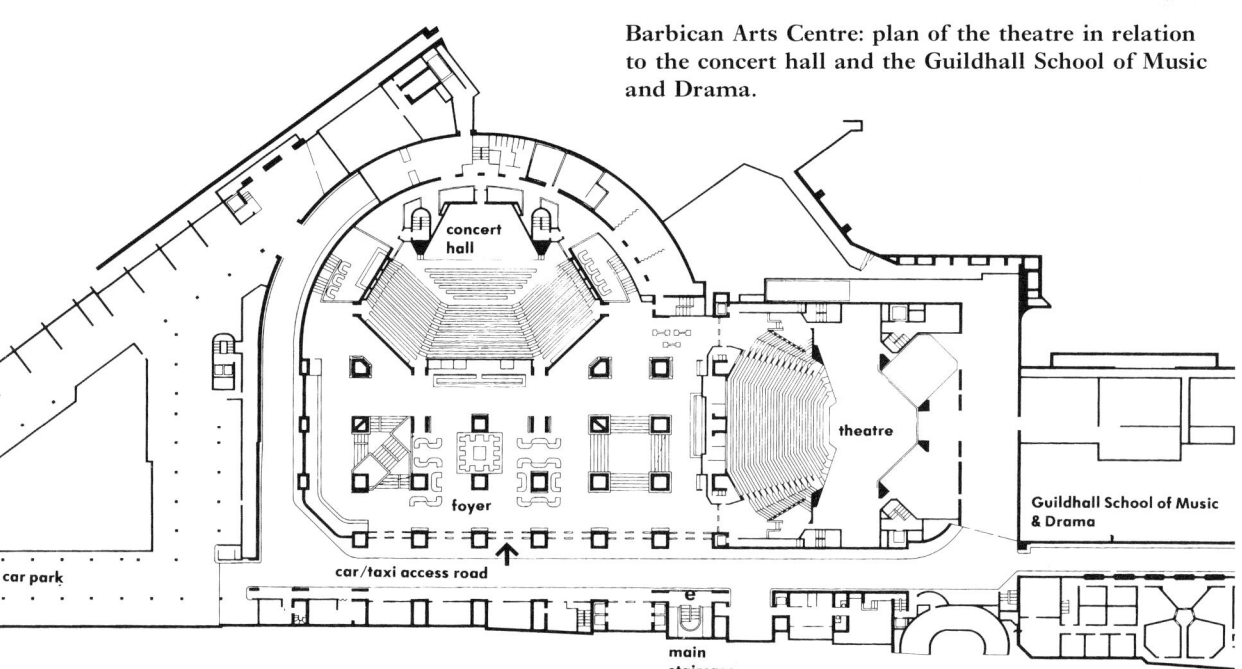

Barbican Arts Centre: sectional perspective through the theatre.

Section through the theatre. Below is a small studio theatre, The Pit. The jacks for varying the stage height are not installed.

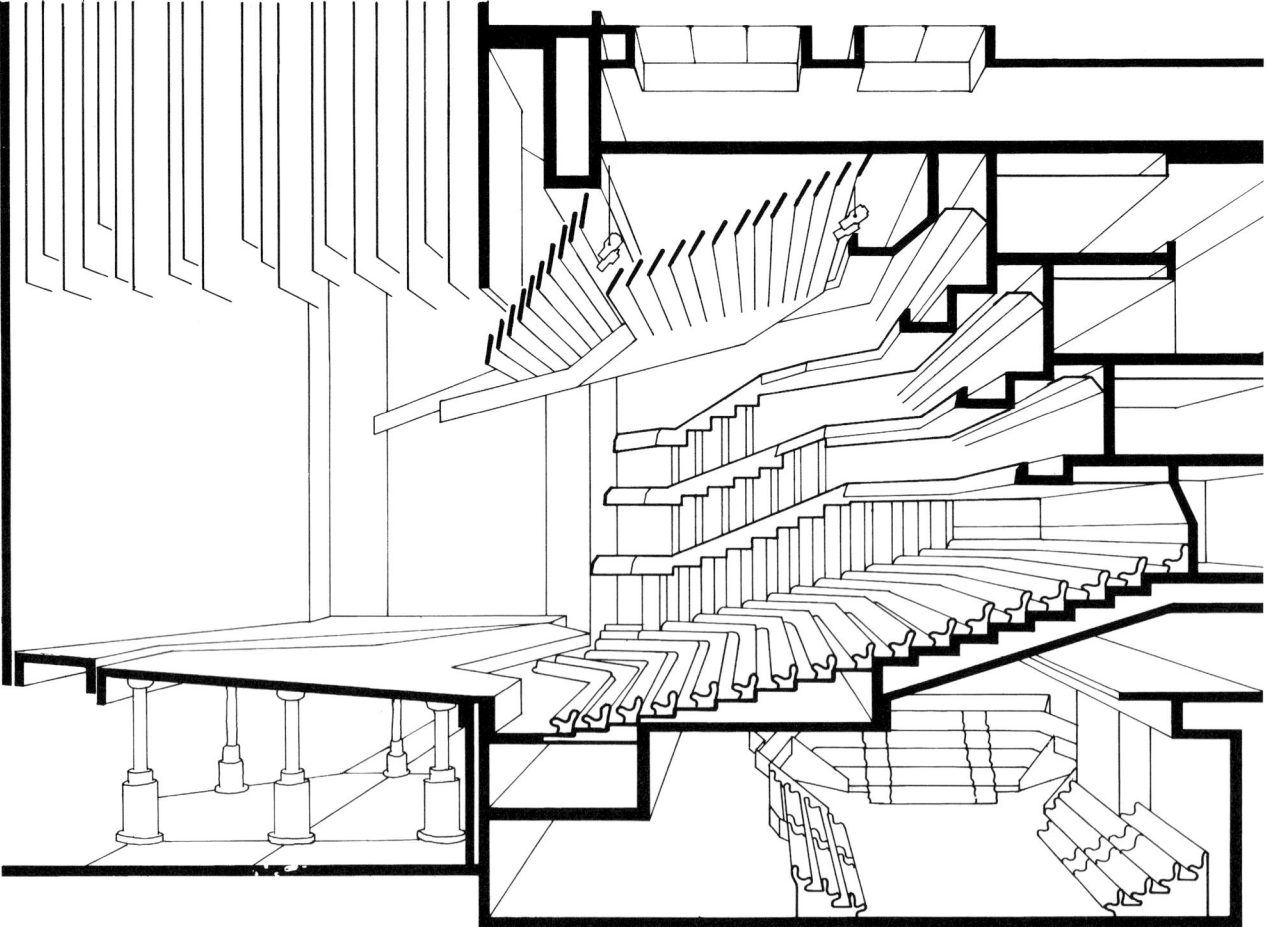

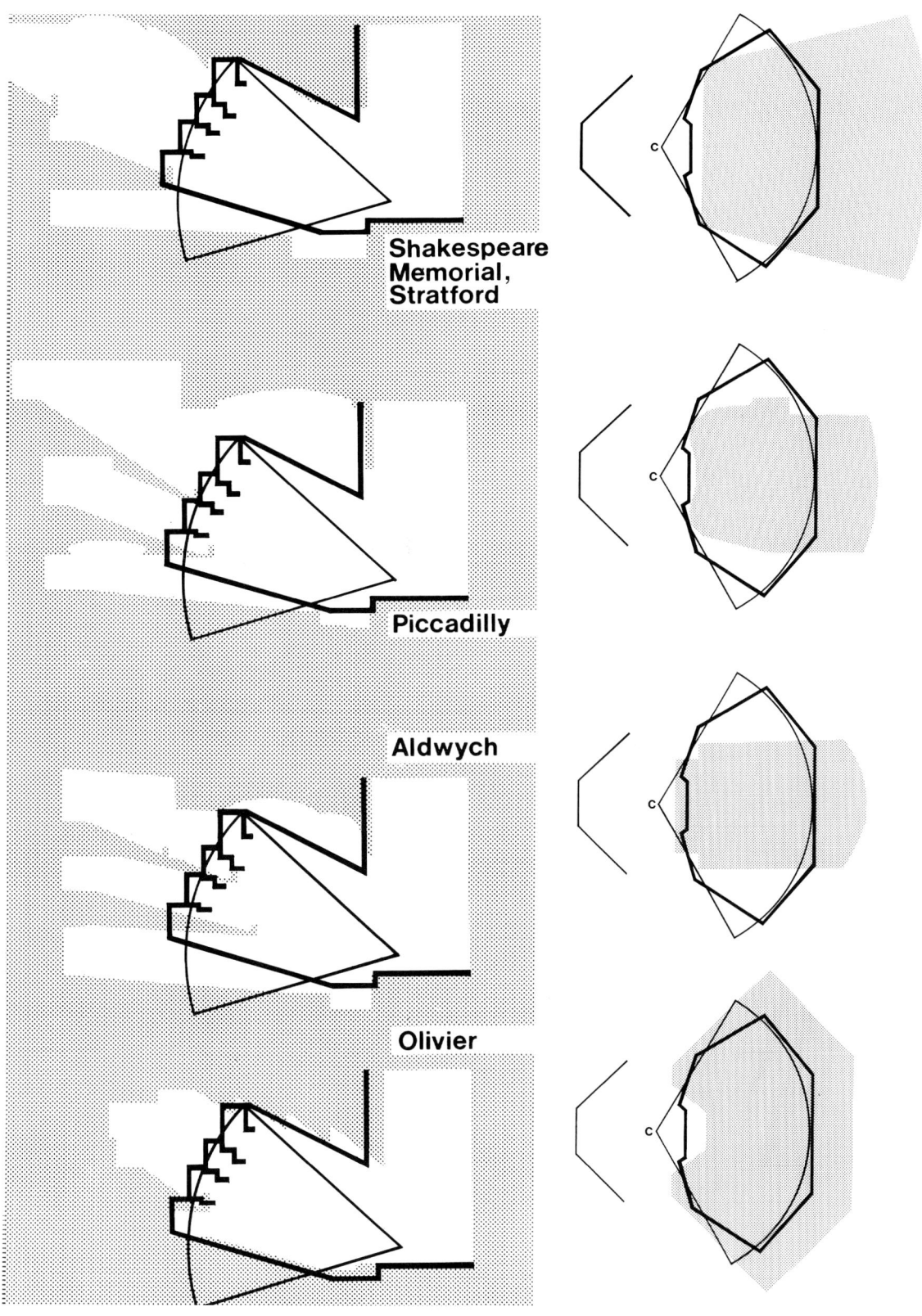

Shakespeare Memorial, Stratford

Piccadilly

Aldwych

Olivier

Plans and sections of four British theatres overlaid in black outline by the Barbican Theatre. The ingenious cross section of the Barbican results in an extremely intimate auditorium. The Barbican seats 1166, the Shakespeare Memorial 1500, the Piccadilly 1162, the Aldwych 994, and the Olivier 1215.

library, an art gallery and other facilities, all at the heart of the enormous Barbican Redevelopment in the area adjoining St Paul's Cathedral that was destroyed in wartime bombing. The Corporation of London began considering the project at least as long ago as 1952, with the aim of attracting people to reside in the 'square mile' of the City, where the resident population, mainly of

The stage from the balcony slip. The removable proscenium arch is being used here for *A Midsummer Night's Dream*.

small-business people living over their premises, had fallen from 100,000 to 5000 over the last 100 years. The architects first started work in 1954 and the major design study for the complex was submitted in 1959. The theatre element was originally intended to seat just 700, principally for opera, and was to be shared between the Guildhall School of Music and Drama and the public. In 1962 it was decided to build a separate music school and in 1964 the theatre became designated as the home of the Royal Shakespeare Company, whose London base was the Aldwych Theatre (its other base being the Royal Shakespeare Theatre, Stratford-on-Avon). Although the Aldwych is a good nineteenth-century commercial theatre, its seating, sightlines and backstage facilities— although adequate for West End commercial productions—were quite inadequate for the Royal Shakespeare Company. It was unsuitable first because the company wished to work in repertory, and second, because they introduced an apron stage for which the building was never designed.

The auditorium is a contemporary interpretation of the Italian opera house.

The Royal Shakespeare Company demanded of the new theatre that viewing distances should not exceed 20m (65ft). As Peter Hall, who was then director, said, 'You cannot act or communicate if you are more than 65 feet away from your audience. Even if you are in the fifth or sixth row and know there are people far behind you, it dilutes the experience for you, and . . . makes you fail to react to what's going on on stage.' Also, all seats were required to be within a 'cone' described by 130 degrees horizontally and 35 degrees vertically from the so-called 'point of command'. This a point on the stage approximately 3m (10ft) back from the front edge, from which the actor can address the entire audience without moving his head. In an auditorium with a wider splay than this, the actor has 'to chase round the stage, sharing himself out all over the place'. The brief also demanded that the auditorium should be filled with people from top to bottom and from side to side, or as somebody said, 'that the walls should be lined with people'. There should be as many seats as possible—certainly in excess of 1000—for financial viability, as the Arts Council did not undertake to increase the RSC's subsidy. Furthermore, sightlines should be excellent, with or without a proscenium, and the space of the stage and the auditorium should express the sharing between actor and audience—and within the audience—of the experience of theatre.

Auditorium from the stage.

The point of command theory, with its required maximum angle and the limitation on distance, suggested a fan-shape auditorium with about 14 rows of seats totalling about 800. Another 450 were accommodated on three galleries which thrust forwards over the main floor amphitheatre in an arc, this time in section, again set by the 19.8m (65ft) maximum allowable distance. This idea completely eliminates the problem of deep over-hangs, and is reminiscent of the tiers of boxes in old horseshoe-shaped theatres, adjusted for better sightlines. A fourth, top gallery, still in the same segment of a circle, is a lighting bridge. The original proposed capacity of 1250 seats included benches for about 120 'groundlings', very cheap seats at the front of the stalls where the young (and less pecunious) would sit closely packed together, in the tradition of the 'groundlings' in Elizabethan theatres. The RSC felt that the enthusiasm of such an audience close to the stage would help establish a good actor-audience relationship. The idea was eventually dropped and their substitution with ordinary seats reduced the capacity to the present 1162. The first three rows are removable to form an orchestra pit.

The main floor seating is entirely continental—without aisles, and with doors at either end of each row. The doors are held open by electro-magnets and released together when the house lights are dimmed and the performance is due to begin. The glimpses inside the auditorium from the stepped gangways outside recalls the access to traditional opera houses. The boxes *en*

escalier of the original scheme were changed to steeply raked side slips constructed, like the rear balconies, in bush hammered concrete, which continue the line of the rear balconies towards the stage. The walls are lined with dark Peruvian walnut.

To house 1162 seats so close to the stage, the auditorium had to be very wide in plan compared with other theatres of comparable size. This was made possible by the RSC not requiring a proscenium. The original design proposed a sliding 'false' proscenium for visiting companies. This would be stored in the wings when not in use, and brought out to reduce the 13.4m (44ft) stage width to a proscenium opening of 10.7m (35ft), when only the central seats totalling 900 would be sold, with the side galleries being closed off by heavy fabric louvres. This option was not taken up by the RSC. It is also of interest that in a theatre designed specifically for their use, the RSC did not request a thrust stage with side viewing, preferring good frontal viewing (in accordance with the point of command theory) combined with an ingenious stage arrangement. This appears to project and also combines the possibility of placing ramps for armies or crowds to enter the stage diagonally from the front on both sides, and was perceived from the beginning as 'a cross roads, a place of movement'.

The stage itself had to be large enough for the biggest productions and also to enable actors to appear isolated in space. The stage is backed by large panels which can be flown to enable the largest set pieces to be brought on stage. The company demanded a raked stage—which had hitherto gone out of fashion—and this is mounted on jacks which could be mechanized in the future to create an alternative flat stage for visiting ballet companies, etc. The flytower is double height and can fly more than two elaborate productions at once.

Despite the profile of the stage front and flytower, a safety curtain is provided to avoid all scenery having to be constructed in flameproof material, as UK regulations would otherwise require. This is impressively made in polished stainless steel, in two pieces, one of which descends and the other ascends as a rising barrier. This is for two reasons: first, because it is not permitted for a fire curtain to land on the *edge* of the stage because of the danger of people being guillotined by its descent; second, the variable height of the bottom section of the safety curtain allows the stage level to be changed—a useful feature should the mechanism be installed to motivate the stage jacks.

Wilde Theatre, Bracknell

Owner: South Hill Park Trust

Architects: Levitt Bernstein Associates

Theatre design and technology consultants: Theatre Projects Consultants Ltd

Acoustic consultant: Frank Fahy

Structural and building services engineers: Ove Arup & Partners

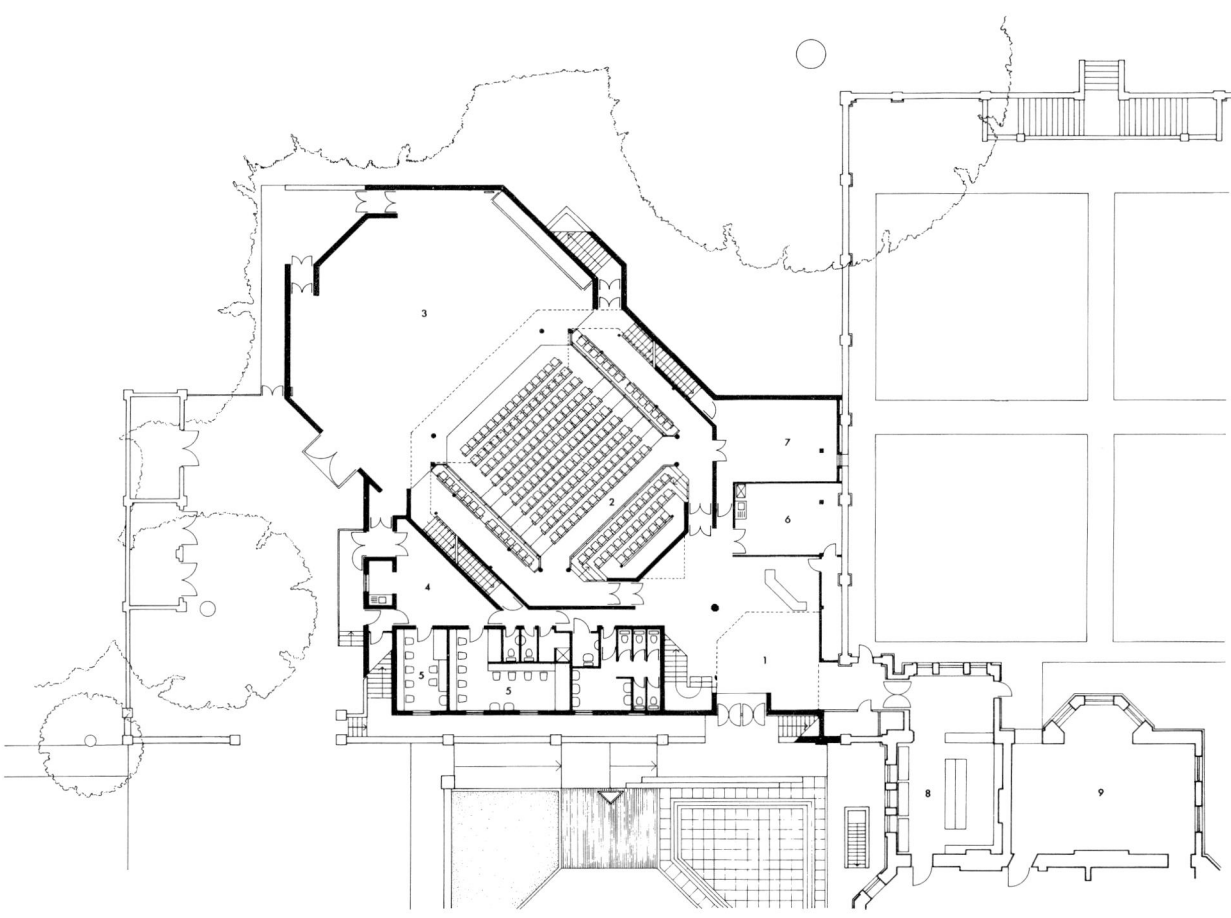

Ground floor plan. Key: 1 entrance foyer, 2 auditorium, 3 stage, 4 assembly area, 5 dressing room, 6 bar store, 7 seat store, 8 shop, 9 art gallery

First floor plan. Key: 1 foyer, 2 theatre bar, 3 first floor gallery, 4 control room, 5 plant room, 6 electrical room, 7 terrace

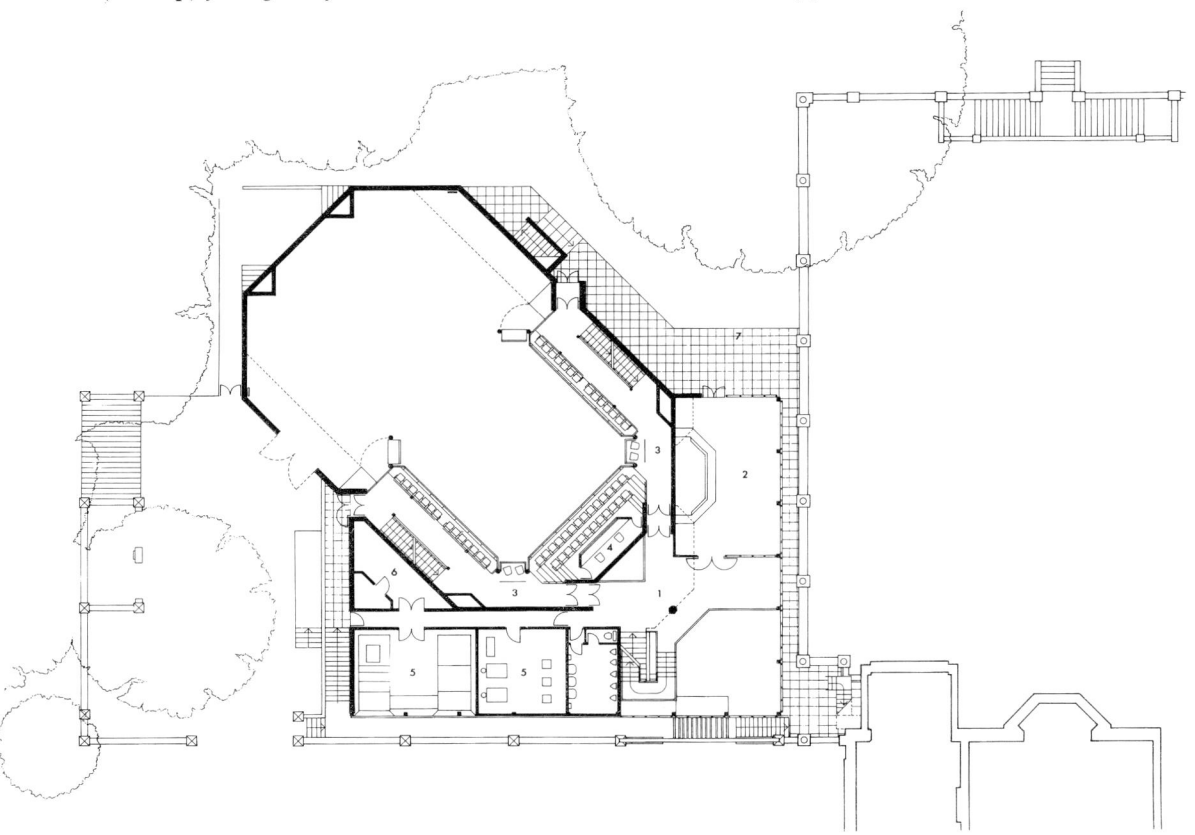

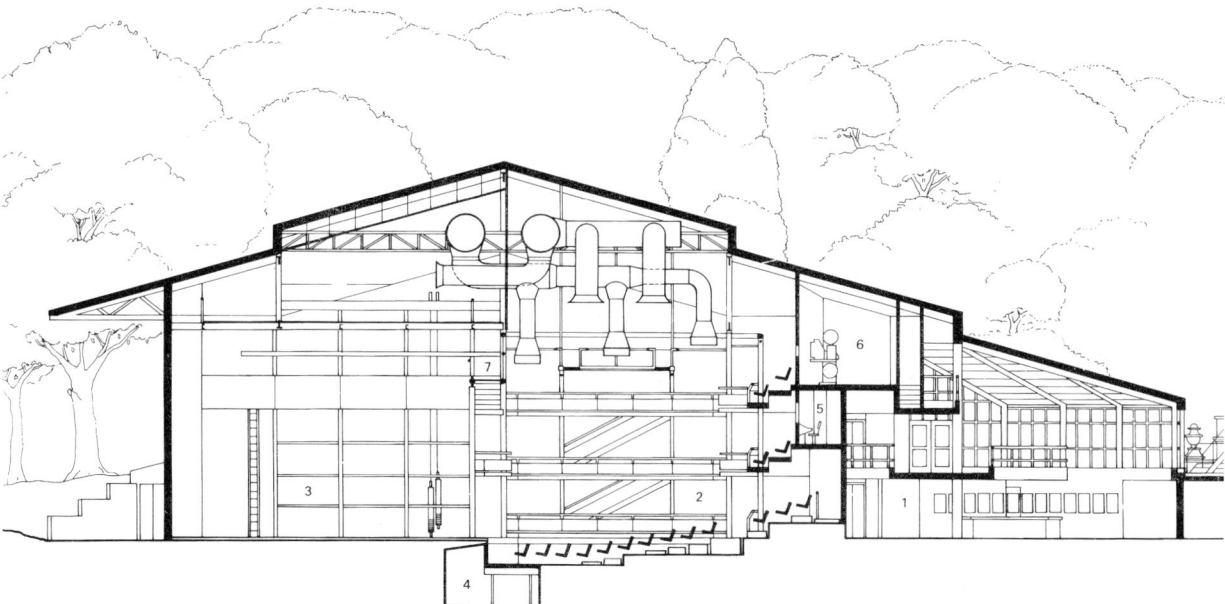

Longitudinal section. Key: 1 entrance foyer,
2 auditorium, 3 stage, 4 orchestra pit, 5 control room,
6 projection room, 7 lighting bridge

Quantity surveyors: Monk Dunstone Associates

Main contractor: Wickens & Sons Ltd

Opened: 1984

Cost: £1,157,330

Uses: multi-purpose including drama, baroque and
classical opera, dance, jazz and other concerts

Seats: 330, with standing room for 70, total capacity
400

*Furthest balcony seat from stage front (proscenium
layout)*: 12.5m (41ft)

Proscenium opening: width variable from 8.4m (27.6ft)
to 10.7m (35.1ft)

Stage: width 16m (52.5ft), depth on centreline
12.2m (40ft) (14.2m (46.5ft) with full forestage),
height to grid underside 8m (26.25ft)

Flying system: 10 single purchase counterweight sets,
10 hemp sets

Volume: 4950 cub.m (174,790 cub.ft)

Reverberation time: 1.3 secs. with a 20 per cent rise in
the bass

Maximum background noise level: NR 20

The site is part of South Hill Park, an active arts centre
established in 1973 in a splendid country house dating
from the eighteenth century with formal gardens, and
home of the Bracknell Jazz Festival and Bracknell Folk
Festival. The theatre was designed in 1981 to
accommodate these annual events, together with
frequent concerts, small-scale opera and every kind of
dramatic activity by small- to medium-size touring
companies and local societies.

Theatre interior in flat floor mode for dance or 'rug'
concerts

Conventional proscenium theatre format with the
hinged proscenium tower folded out

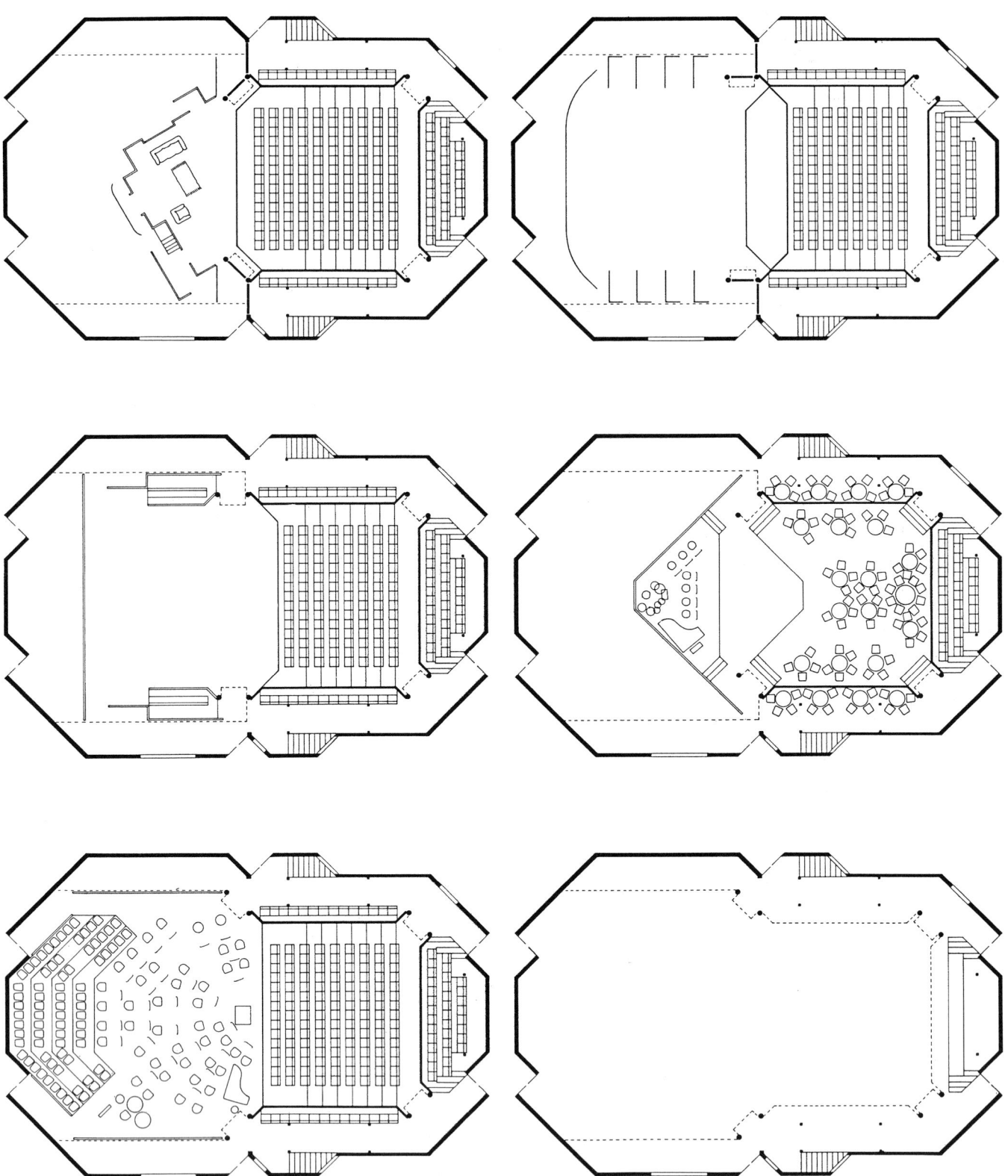

Plans showing alternative layouts: (*top*) proscenium, opera/dance (*middle*) end stage, cabaret (*bottom*) orchestra/chorus, promenade

The theatre was modelled on the rectangular courtyard form of the Georgian playhouse, in order to provide the necessary adaptability, particularly the possibility of raising the floor to stage level to provide a flat surface. The courtyard layout also had the advantage that the audience members would be aware of each other as well as of the performers. The theatre accommodates 330 to 400 people—just a quarter of the size of the Derngate Centre, Northampton—and provides intimate contact between the actors and spectators. Three gallery levels formed in brightly painted steelwork surround the

Exterior from inside the existing formal garden. The second stage of construction will complete the roofline.

stalls seating, with single rows of seats at the sides and two to three rows at the rear and standing room behind. Access to the galleries is by a staircase on each side within the auditorium. A hexagonal lighting bridge with bare bulbs is suspended in the centre, giving flexibility for stage lighting with the image of a large chandelier. The result is a delightful and colourful small theatre.

Its size and budget restraints resulted in a decision to make the adaptability entirely non-mechanical. However, despite the advantage of increased flexibility because of the absence of predetermined mechanically-driven elements, the time taken to change the layout manually means that the performance modes must be relatively long term, compared with larger theatres like the Derngate Centre which must respond almost nightly to different types of performance. Hinged proscenium towers with demountable balcony fronts at either side separate the stage and auditorium for a conventional

format with a curtain, and fold back when not in use to provide a single rectangular space with a full width stage. Although effective in principle, the towers are the least successful element visually, being simply a steel frame with a curtain, rather than of—albeit illusory—solid 'architectural' construction (though the intention is that the frame can be incorporated in a set design). The main floor seating is demountable and can be removed for promenade theatre or flat floor events, or rearranged to provide a thrust stage or theatre-in-the round. With simple demountable scaffolding and theatrical rostra, the stage can be varied to provide a large or small forestage, and there is an orchestra pit which extends under the stage. The main floor can be raised to a 'cabaret' position, or made flush with the stage for a continuous flat floor from the stage to the rear of the stalls, for activities such as exhibitions, informal jazz concerts, 'rug' concerts and dancing. There is no flytower, but there is a gridiron 8m (26.25ft) above the stage equipped with counterweight flying lines for rapid rigging of touring shows.

The theatre building is linked to the old house, the auditorium sitting at 45 degrees to the original building and to the support areas. These spaces, including the foyer, bar, dressing rooms, projection room, rostra storage and actors' assembly area, wrap partially around the theatre. It is hoped eventually to envelope the auditorium with further foyers and backstage facilities, the building of which in the first phase would have compromised the adequacy and size of the basic theatre; meanwhile, the scenery storage and wing space spill out into the garden!

Ordway Music Theatre, St Paul, Minnesota

Owner: Ordway Music Theatre Corporation

Architect: Benjamin Thompson and Associates, Inc.

Acoustic consultant: R. Lawrence Kirkegaard & Associates

Theatre consultant: S. Leonard Auerbach and Associates

Mechanical and electrical engineers: Ellerbe Associates, Inc.

Structural engineer: LeMessurier Associates/SCI

Lighting designers: Wheel-Gersztoff Associates

Main contractor: McGough Construction Company

Opened: 1985

Cost: $26 million including fixed equipment and furnishings

Principal uses: opera, orchestral and chamber music, ballet

Seats: 1815 (concert configuration), 1740 (opera with full width orchestra pit), 1690 (with thrust stage)

Furthest balcony seat from stage: 35m (115ft), 30m (95ft) from full thrust stage

Proscenium opening: variable between 14.6m (48ft) and 20.1m (66ft), 10.7m (35ft) high

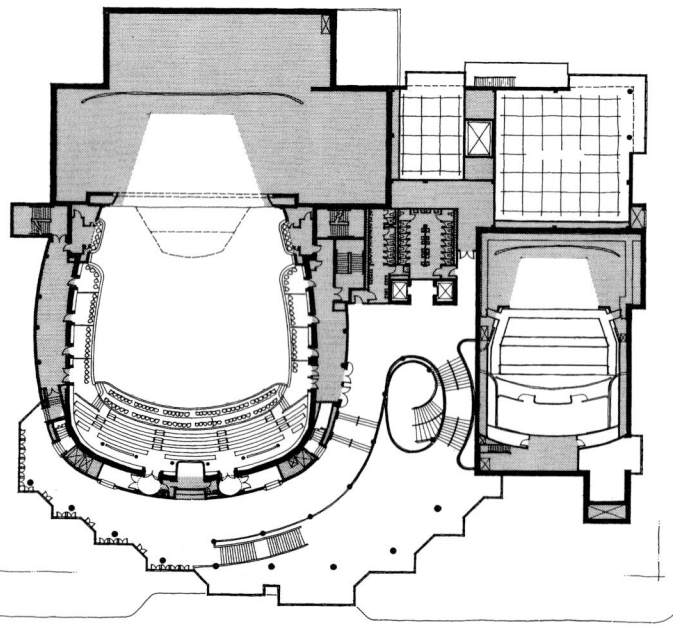

Stage: width 43m (141ft), 17.7m (58ft) centreline to the stage right locking rail, depth 13.4m (44ft) from proscenium wall to front of orchestra shell stored, height to gridiron 24.4m (80ft)

Flying system: 82 rigging line sets at 150mm (6in) centres

Orchestra area: 229 sq.m (2464 sq.ft) large shell, 164 sq.m (1768 sq.ft) small shell, 96.2 sq.m (1036 sq.ft) thrust stage (for chamber orchestra)

Orchestra pit: 110.5 sq.m (1189 sq.ft) large size, 80.3 sq.m (864 sq.ft) small size

Volume: house and orchestra enclosure 18,000 cub.m (636,000 cub.ft)

Reverberation time: variable between 1.4 sec. and 2.0 sec. at mid-frequencies with full audience

Maximum background noise level: NC 15

The theatre is situated in an American mid-west city on the Mississippi River, but is designed in the spirit of the traditional European opera house. It actually combines the functions of opera house and concert hall, but, unlike several recent halls that use the necessary acoustical variability to change the appearance of the hall for different performance settings, the aim at Ordway has been to conceal the movable acoustical elements and emphasize a richly elegant theatrical environment.

The theatre is horseshoe shape with three tiers of shallow sidewall boxes, ending in a double tier of boxes adjacent to the stage. The traditional proscenium is framed, like the boxes, in a gold and mahogany sunburst pattern, against the background of deep blue walls. Wrapping around the auditorium behind the balconies and side wall boxes are open lattice panels, with matching exit doors and surrounds, all in Honduran mahogany. Mounted light clusters illuminate the balcony fronts of sculptured plasterwork, which have red velour trim and brass handrails. The effect is warm, colourful and intimate, combining 'memories' from art deco (the sunburst pattern) to Italian baroque. The architect, Ben Thompson, stresses, however, that the design arose less from a conscious decision to build a traditional-style theatre than from the horseshoe form being a 'commonsense' solution to the particular problem at hand:

> We wanted a theatre with a spirit of celebration and festivity, whose technical perfection was obvious in performance but otherwise out of sight, with spaces that would enhance the feeling of sociability and excitement that is part of theatre attendance. If there is a 'model' in scale and feeling, it would be the Vienna State Opera; but it was not 'copied'—merely used as a reference point in making a design suited to these special conditions.

Plan at mezzanine level. Next to the main hall is a 317 seat studio theatre.

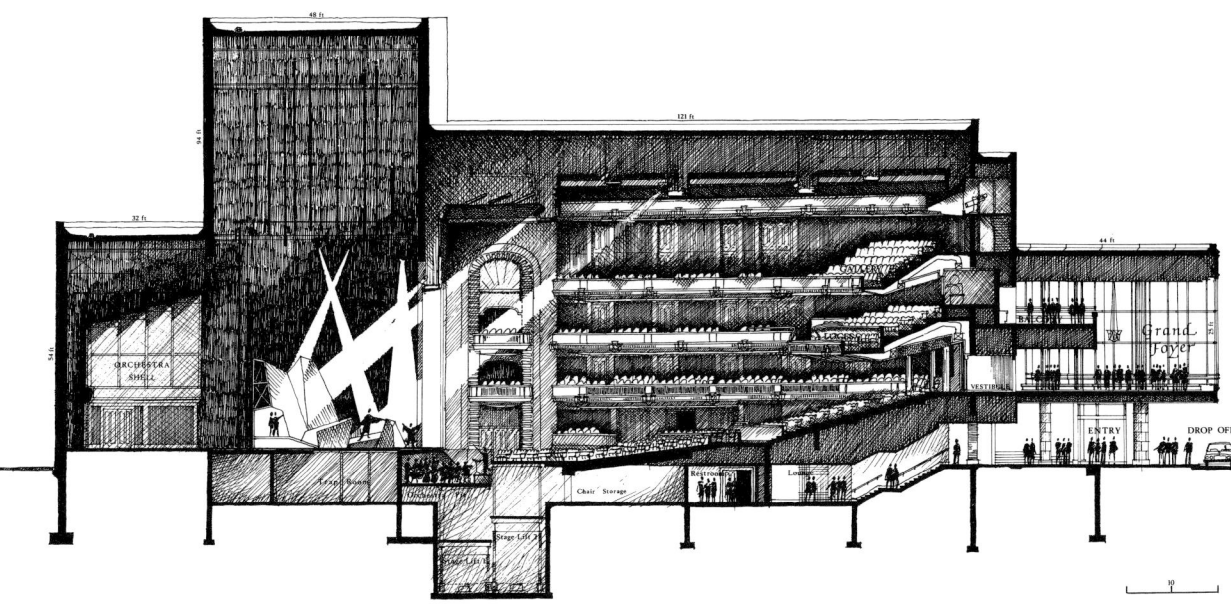

Section through auditorium, arranged for opera with thrust stage and orchestra pit.

Theatre interior with movable shell positioned for concert use. Side panels (tormentors) are partly retracted for extra width beneath proscenium arch.

Stage configuration for an opera production, with full proscenium arch and with both movable platforms recessed for an orchestra pit.

Despite having the appearance of an opera house, the hall had to serve several musical functions more or less equally, being the new permanent home of three groups: the Minnesota Opera Company, the St Paul Chamber Orchestra, and the Schubert Club (a non-profit sponsor of major recitals). The design of both function and capacity had to answer the dissimilar demands of these resident companies, all requiring natural, unamplified sound. The Opera Company's seating goal was about 1300 while the Chamber Orchestra desired about 2000 seats. Both users agreed with the architect that the demand for seating capacities between 2000 and 3000 that are usual in North America has helped to destroy the audience-stage relationship and person-to-person eye contact that is characteristic in traditional opera houses, as well as natural acoustic quality. So, early in the planning, the owners and users accepted 1815 seats as a typical capacity, with the potential for 200 additional onstage seats for chamber orchestra performances.

To convert the auditorium from an opera house to a concert hall, a 10.4m (34ft) high mobile orchestra shell, weighing 38.1 tonnes (84,000lb) is brought forward on air castors from a storage bay located at the rear of the stage, to fit into the full stage opening. This creates a sound-reflective 'room', suitable in its basic format for a chamber orchestra or choir; alternatively, the shell can be extended with the addition of towers at either side and 'flown' ceiling elements to create a deeper stage for a full symphony orchestra. To unify the orchestra platform with the auditorium, the steel frame of the shell has been clad with materials and details similar to the hall—mahogany doors and panelling, plaster walls and sconce lights. Because the shell is a permanently assembled unit, it can be used in its stored position—with the backdrop curtain removed—as a stage set for opera, ballet or drama, or the shell may be used as a rehearsal room when the stage is set up for another production. The movement of the shell from its stored position to its concert position takes about 45 minutes, including preparation time.

One design problem with the orchestra shell was its support on the stage floor. This is 'wood-sprung' for dance, and separated from the concrete subfloor by neoprene pads, which would be destroyed by the great weight of the shell. This was overcome by incorporating between the pads steel blocks on which the wooden floor would rest when the pads are heavily compressed.

Other stage variations are formed with a two-section elevator forward of the stage. There are four optional settings: with both sections raised a thrust stage is formed, suitable for a chamber orchestra which in this position plays against the sound-reflective backdrop of a mahogany panelled fire curtain; with the forestage

The foyers overlook adjacent civic buildings; the copper fascia will weather green like the turrets of the adjacent Landmark Center (right).

sections flush with the main floor, a further 90 seats are installed; with the elevators depressed a 3.7m (12ft) deep orchestra pit is created for grand opera; and with only the section adjacent to the stage raised or lowered, a smaller pit or thrust stage is formed. To adjust the acoustics to different types of performance, there are concealed, adjustable acoustic panels in three zones. The mahogany lattice wall panels below the sidewall boxes (referred to above) are in fact open grilles which conceal a 'plenum' containing sound-absorptive panels which may be raised or lowered. The visual ceiling to the auditorium is also acoustically transparent and conceals heavy curtains along the upper sidewalls. Variable sound-reflective panels located in the attic volume—what the acoustician calls 'clam shells'—reflect long-delayed sound energy to the main floor when horizontal, or alternately, for greater sound clarity, they can be turned to direct sound energy to the sound-absorptive rear balcony as useful amplification (where the time delay gap for ceiling reflections is less). The panels and curtains may be exposed—for a reverberation time of about 1.4 seconds—during drama productions, music recitals, popular music and other presentations where clarity is important, and retracted—for the maximum reverberation time of 2.0 seconds—during orchestral concerts.

Axonometric drawing of the development. The street entrance to the new courtyard is adjacent to the façade of the existing theatre in the former chapel. The main theatre building is behind, and in the garden (*top right*) is the Young People's Theatre Club.

Half Moon Theatre, London

Owner: Half Moon Theatre Company

Architects: Architecture Bureau: Florian Beigel, Jon Broome, Suresh A'Raj, Peter Rich, Mon Lee, Philip Christou

Theatre consultants: Carr and Angier

Acoustic consultants: Bickerdike Allen and Partners

Structural engineers: Ove Arup and Partners

Services engineers: Robert Matthew, Johnson Marshall and Partners

Quantity Surveyors: Davis, Belfield and Everest

Main contractor: C. J. Sims Ltd

Opened: 1985 (phase one, i.e. the main theatre and Young People's Theatre Club)

Cost: £653,000

Uses: drama, and many varied community uses

Seats: maximum 450, including Young Persons' Theatre

Furthest seat from front of stage: 15m (49ft) for end stage layout

Stage: no fixed size or position

Floor area of main theatre: 266 sq.m (2809 sq.ft)

Height of main theatre: 9.3m (31ft) (no grid)

Volume: 2474 cub.m (103,933 cub.ft)

Reverberation time: 1 sec. at mid-frequencies with full audience

Maximum noise level: NC 30

This is one of the more radical of recent theatres, aiming to recreate more literally than others images of the roots of popular theatre, in street and courtyard. Here, the auditorium is an actual extension of the street, with the aim of becoming a much used community focus.

The Half Moon Theatre Company's previous home was a former Edwardian chapel on Mile End Road in London's East End. The new theatre is immediately adjacent, and the existing building will be converted to provide front of house facilities—a 'withdrawing room' for the community and theatre company, acting both as a foyer and community centre. The artistic director's brief to the architects was as follows:

We are a radical theatre and welcome radical solutions. We seek to entertain in the traditional forms of theatre such as music hall and in plays demanding new ways of staging and new relationships with our audiences. We seek to reclaim the classical repertoire for a popular audience, and must be able to stage plays in the traditional forms such as in the round, thrust, traverse, proscenium and in forms as yet untried. Our specific aim is to draw new audiences into the theatre to give it a broad popular base. It should be a place where meetings can take place and newspapers bought and read, where to sit and have a beer or have a discussion is as legitimate as it is to watch a play. It should be a place where

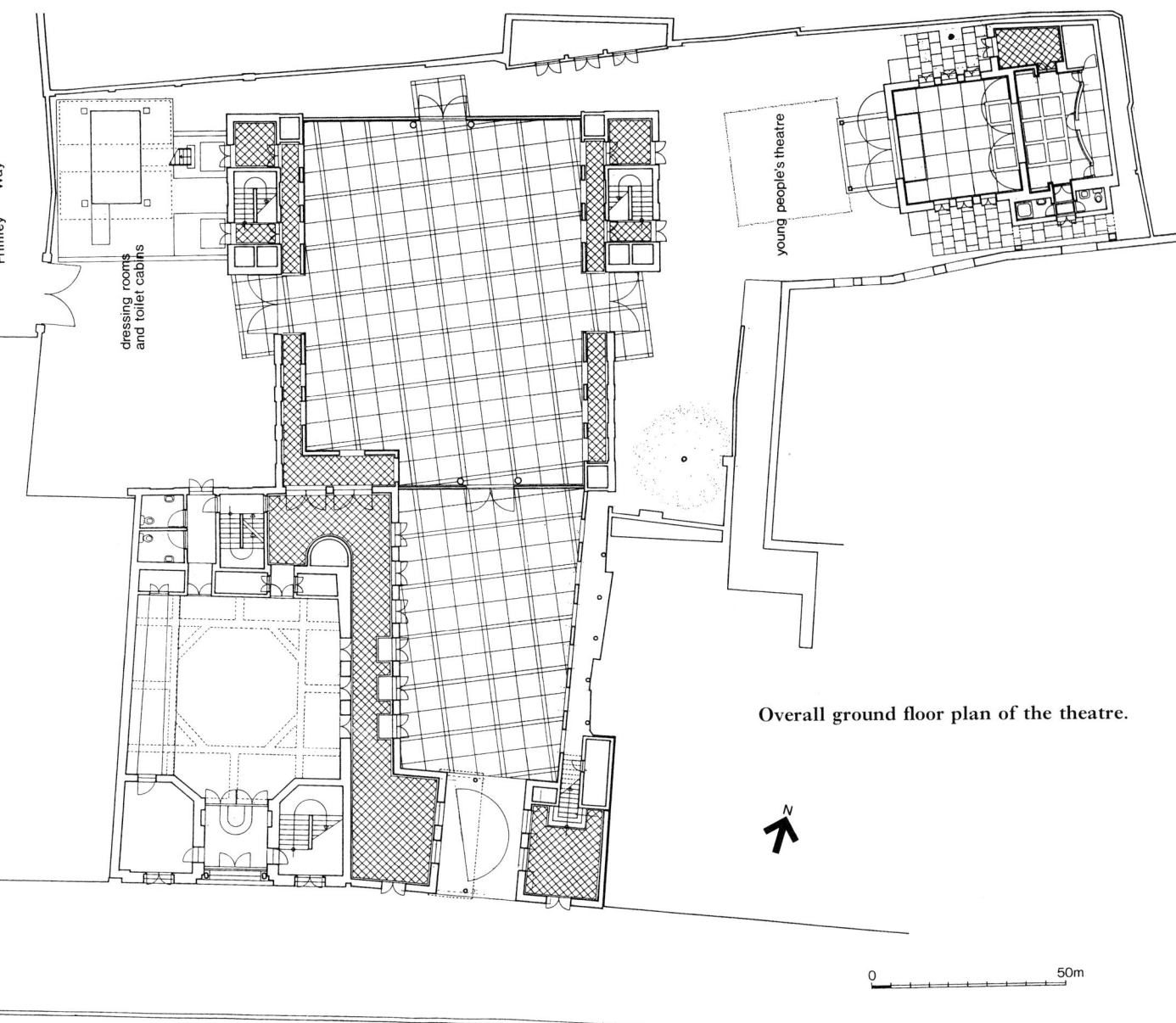

Frimley Way

dressing rooms
and toilet cabins

young people's theatre

Overall ground floor plan of the theatre.

N

0   50m

Mile End Road

you can have a good meal and see good entertainment, where you can bring an office party, your girlfriend, boyfriend, your colleague or your comrade. It should be a free flowing space from pavement to auditorium.

It should be rich. I mean corners where five pensioners' pictures could be exhibited or a mural by a whole class of a local primary school; where information about local events is easily accessible; where musicians could try out songs or poets, poems; where outdoor events could happen. Where a procession from the street could flood the building and coalesce into an event in the auditorium. ... The materials ... should not be tatty fringe, art house board, sturdy oak provincial, polished steel Swedish, wine bar smoked pine nor faded plush and gilt.

To inspire this basic social direction, the new theatre and its associated facilities are conceived as a series of external and internal spaces which are publicly accessible and contain easily recognizable architectural elements. The building takes the form of a 'street' leading off Mile End

Road between two gate lodges. The 'street' is lined with 'façades' which enclose an open public court with a cafe, where the general community can meet each other as well as the theatre company. Beyond, the 'street' is covered to become the auditorium; this serves as a community centre during the daytime.

Beyond the auditorium through large double doors, the scenic street terminates in a disused cemetery which is now a garden. To one side of the auditorium is another enclosed garden court, containing a young people's theatre, built as a separate pavilion, or 'temple'.

Access from the entrance court to the theatre and from the theatre to the garden beyond is through very large double doors which have both a technical function, for bringing in scenery, and a celebratory one for processions and as a thoroughfare for actors. The axis of the doors, the roof structure of the auditorium and the floor pattern are all skewed in relation to the façades. The screen walls in which the doors are set are built of corrugated steel

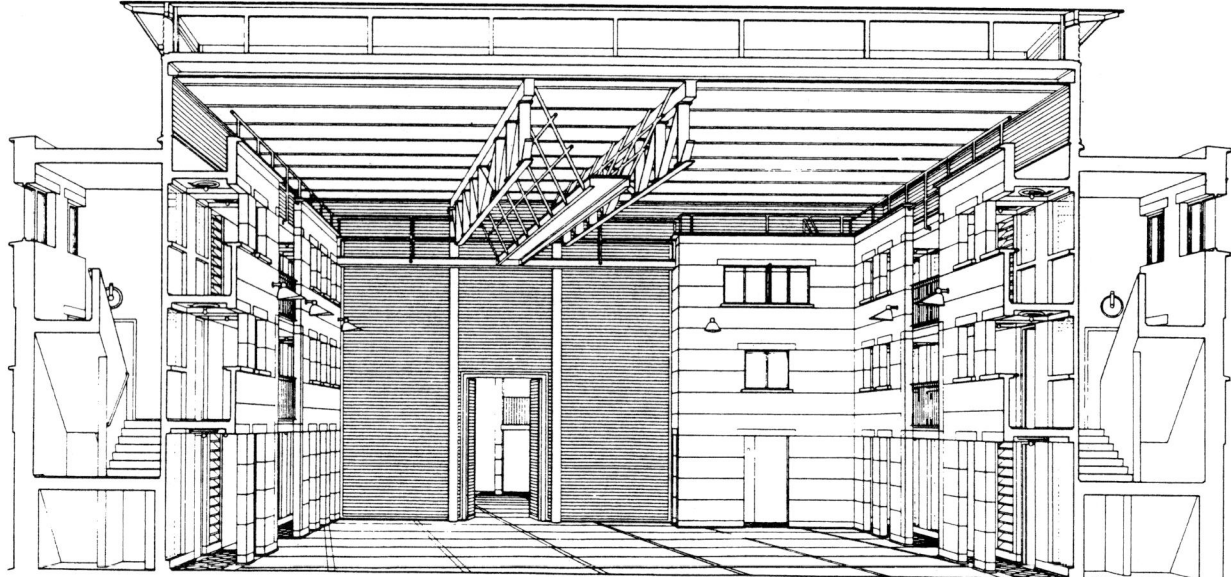

Perspective drawing of the main auditorium, the 'covered scenic street'.

Perspective drawing of the first floor gallery in the main theatre.

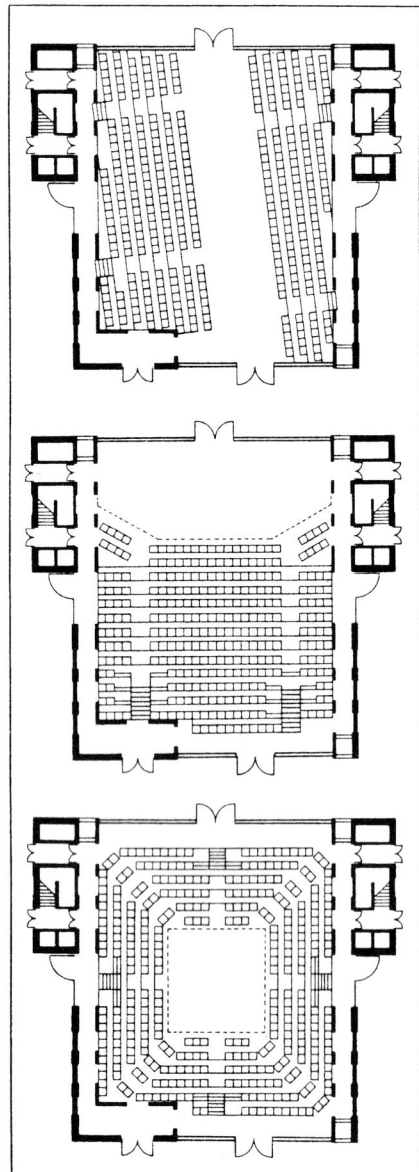

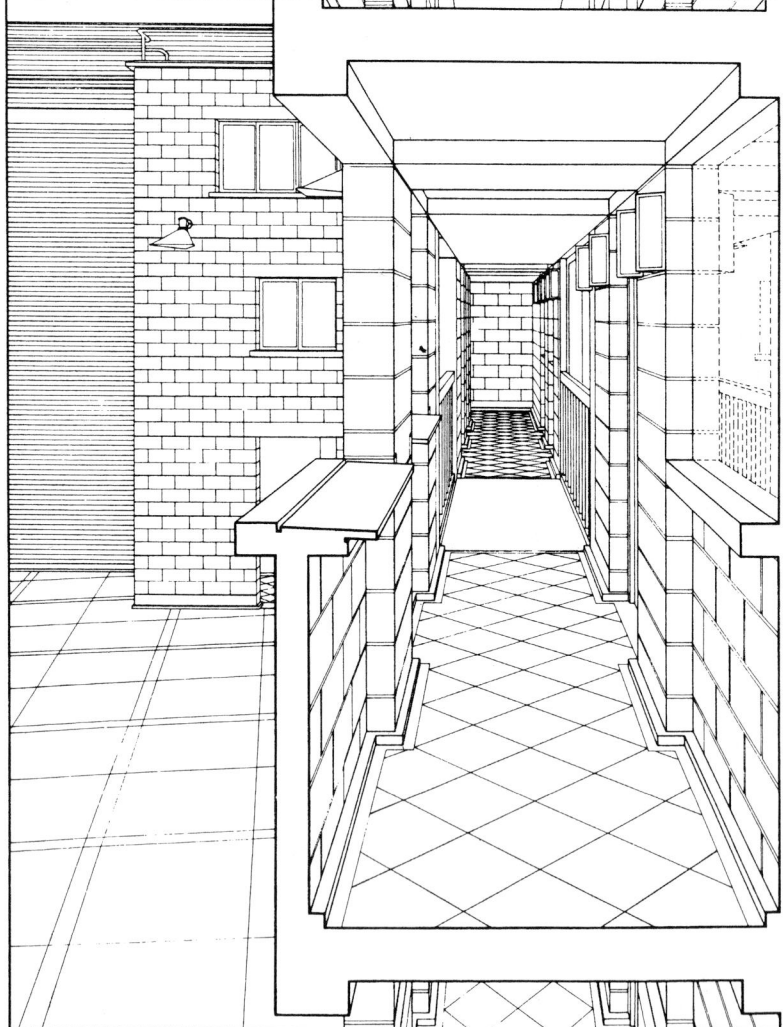

Some of the possible seating layouts. However, there is no predetermined arrangement and there are almost infinite seating possibilities.

View of the auditorium without seating, showing the arcade at ground level.

View from inside the main auditorium of the metal curtain walling with staggered lighting screens.

Performance of *Sweeney Todd*, set designed by E.
Cairns, the first production in the theatre.

The Young People's Theatre Club.

siding, perforated on the inside and backed by sound-
reflective boarding which doubles as fire protection. On
the entrance side, the wall is punctured by lighting
screens in a staggered arrangement intended to represent
patterned fabric curtains. The same perforated panels are
used on the ceiling, but this time are backed by sound-
absorptive wood wool slabs to prevent undesirable late
sound reflections to some parts of the auditorium. The
acoustics are thus like an outdoor street, with sound-
reflective buildings and a sound-absorptive 'sky'.

Because of the skewed axis of the floor and roof, the
floor pattern appears to continue underneath the façades
(or 'houses' as the architect calls them) giving a theatrical
dimension to the building. At the design stage there was
some debate as to the architectural style in which these
should be; they were eventually abstracted into an
'archetypal' façade—like a child would draw, with
openings composed from squares and double squares
with cills and lintels and an arcade at ground level, with
mirrors set in recesses behind the openings. Behind are
galleries with staircase access, where the audience sits, a
maximum of three to a window. The main material is
concrete blockwork, raked every three courses. The
general auditorium lighting is from wall-mounted street-
lamps, augmented by lighting in the galleries and star-
like lights in the ceiling, which is painted dark blue to
represent a night sky.

Two large steel trusses span between cylindrical
concrete columns to support the ceiling. The façades stop
short of the roof, making them appear free-standing, and
the gap which this creates forms a lighting gallery which
extends around the other two sides as a catwalk. The
auditorium roof is protected by a second pitched weather
enclosure to avoid condensation on the metal panels. The
floor is of hardboard panels, articulated into squares by

200mm (8in) black rubber strips, on a plywood base which is mounted on rubber-backed timber bearers. The floor is intended to be renewable and scenery can be nailed into it. There are many possible seating layouts, while in daytime the floor area can be used for flea markets, coffee mornings and the like.

The temple-like children's theatre ('allowably more idealized, being for young people') sits in the garden on a hypothetical extension of the main auditorium floor grid. It is basically a 6m (2oft) cube (a full-size mock-up was made by students as an open-air stage for the city of Bremen), overlapped on each side by other cubes which form 'aediculae' for performing in, although acting can take place anywhere in the building.

The Swan Theatre, Stratford-upon-Avon

Owner: Royal Shakespeare Company

Architect: Michael Reardon & Associates

Theatre consultants: Royal Shakespeare Theatre

Acoustic consultant: David Walters

Structural engineers: Gifford & Partners

Mechanical and electrical engineers: Peter Jay & Partners

Quantity surveyor: Gordon Cain

Main contractor: William Weaver Ltd

Total project cost: undisclosed

Primary use: drama of the period 1570 to 1750

Seats: total 461; stalls 261, first gallery 98, second gallery 102

Distance of furthest seat from stage: 10m (33ft)

Stage: 10.5m (34.5ft) by 6m (2oft), height to underside of lighting galleries 8.5m (28ft)

Flying system: manually operated variable height lighting bars; provision for suspension of individual scenic items

Volume: 3250 cub.m (114,780 cub.ft)

Reverberation time: 1.1 sec. at middle frequencies with full audience

Maximum background noise level: NR 25

The new theatre is constructed within the Gothic Revival, almost Wagnerian, shell of the 800-seat

Plan at ground level. Key: 1 main entrance, 2 Royal Shakespeare Company collection and bars, 3 foyer, 4, 5 washrooms, 6 stage door, 7 auditorium, 8 rear scene dock, 9 lift, 10 green room, 11 main house stage

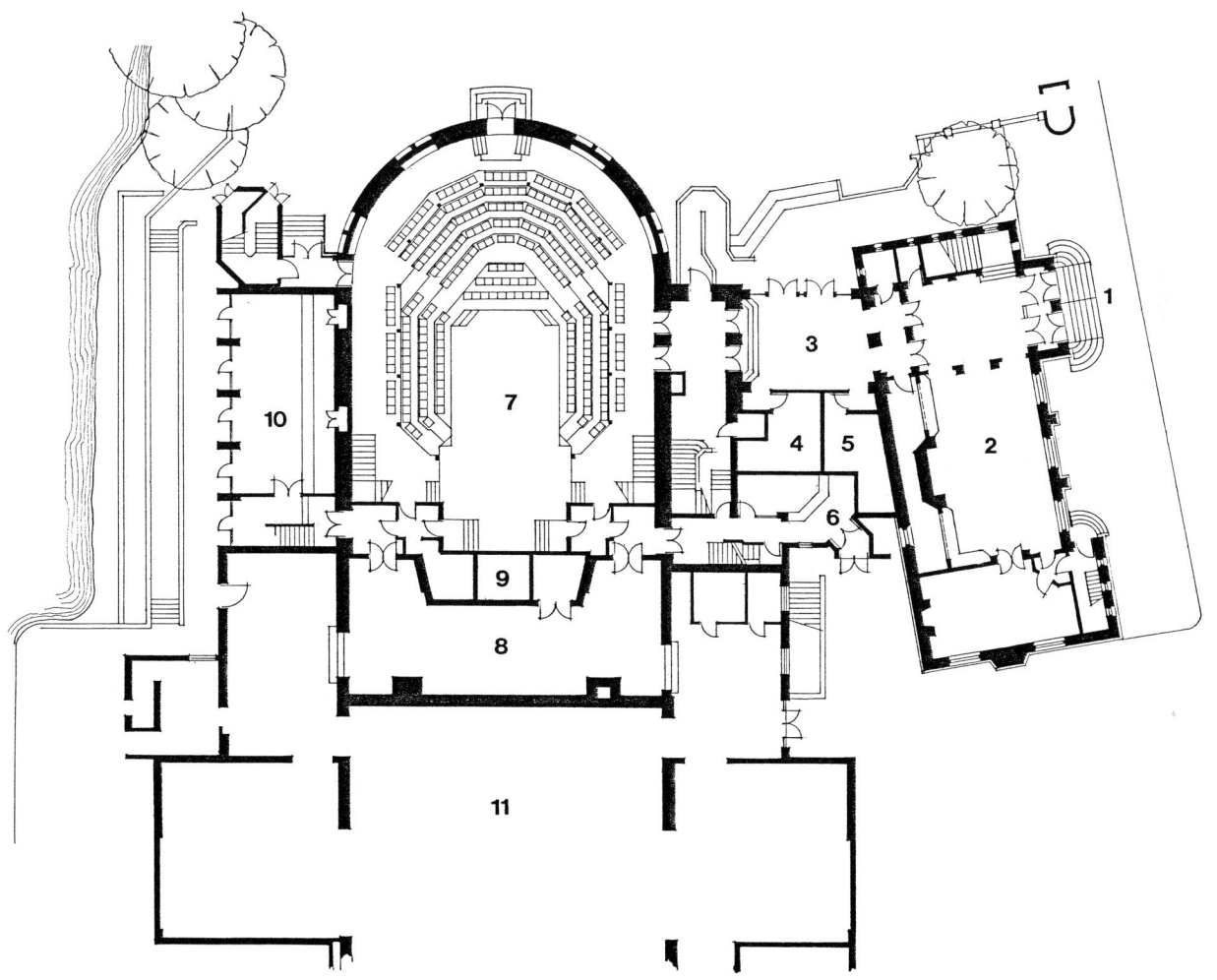

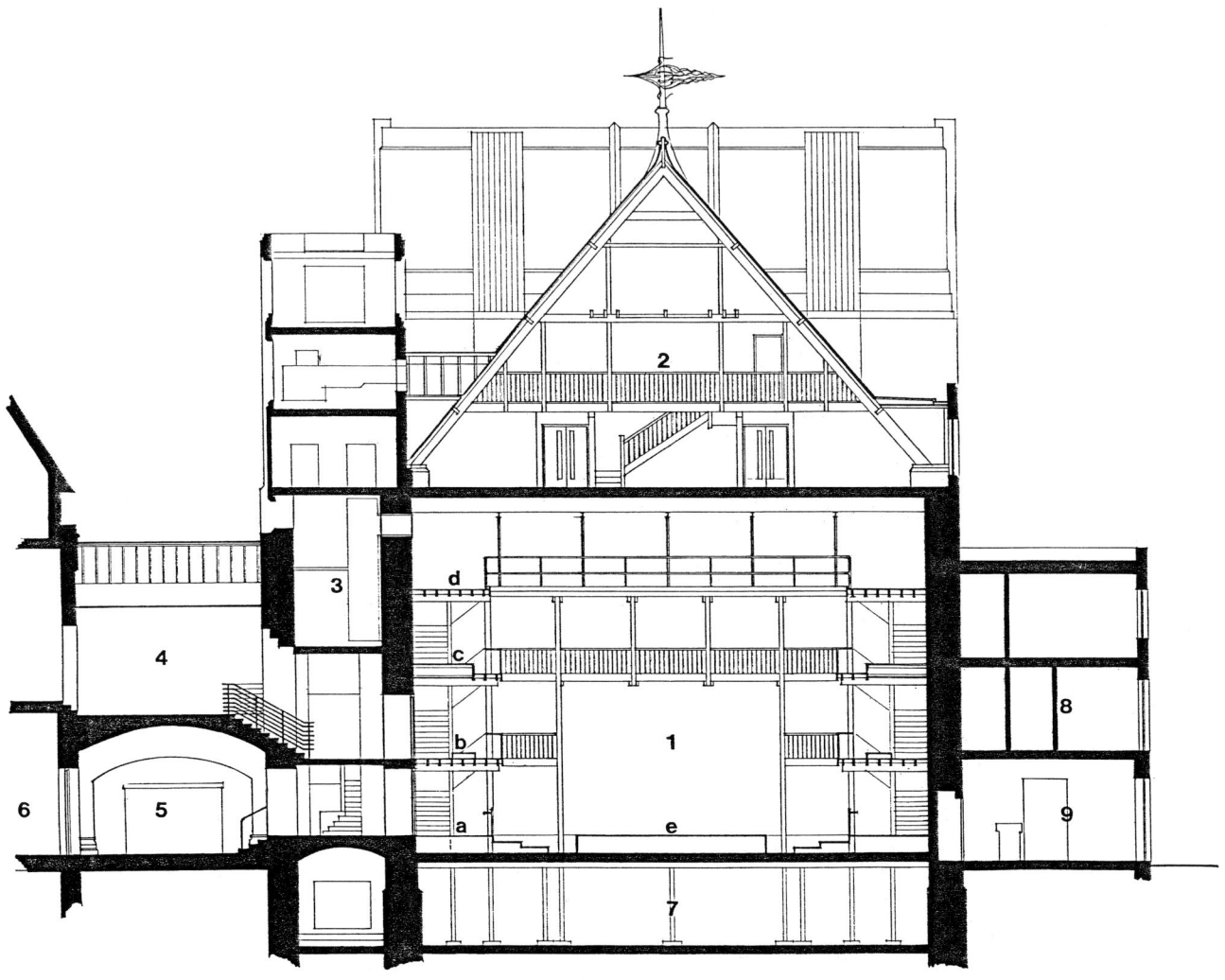

Lateral section through the theatre. Key:
1 auditorium, (a) ground, (b) gallery 1,
(c) gallery 2, (d) technical gallery, (e) stage, 2 rehearsal
studio, 3 service tower, 4 bridge link, 5 foyer,
6 Royal Shakespeare Company collection,
7 basement, 8 dressing rooms, 9 green room

Stratford Memorial Theatre of 1879, which was
destroyed by fire in 1926 just a year after the granting of
its royal charter. Productions had then moved to a local
cinema until the new theatre, designed by Elisabeth
Scott, opened in 1932. During the 1960s and 70s, the re-
named Royal Shakespeare Company, in addition to
opening a London base at the Aldwych Theatre, widened
its repertoire to include experimental work, including
new plays, in small performing spaces. This led to the
opening of The Other Place, Stratford-upon-Avon, in
1974, The Warehouse, London, in 1977, and The Pit, a
small theatre in the RSC's new London headquarters at
the Barbican (see above).

The Swan, which was also the name of the old rival
theatre to the Globe, is quite different to these other
theatres, being specifically designed to stage plays that
are 'contextual' to those of Shakespeare. This includes
those which might have influenced Shakespeare, the

plays which he might have influenced, and the plays
which give greater insight into sixteenth- and
seventeenth-century England. For this purpose, the
architect's brief was to design a space that would
recapture the spirit of a small Jacobean theatre. In the
theatres of the sixteenth and seventeenth centuries,
where performances took place in daylight and without
elaborate scenery, the building itself formed the
permanent framework for the performance, so that the
world created by the carpenter contained both the actor
and the spectator. The new theatre, too, provides a
'permanent set', and, within the existing brick shell, is
also entirely carpenters' work.

The existing auditorium surround, backing onto the
1932 theatre, is U-shape, and the new interior, which is
constructed within, centres around a raised promontory
stage. This extends into the middle of the space, and is
surrounded on three sides by seating on the main floor
and on two tiers of shallow one- and two-row galleries.
These are reached by staircases within the auditorium. A
gallery at the second level continues across the back wall
of the stage to provide a musicians' gallery, and to create
the impression of an inner stage. A third gallery at high
level, from which two lighting bridges span across the
auditorium, contains the sound and lighting control and a

The promontory stage is surrounded on three sides by seating, which provides for close engagement between actors and audience.

The theatre is in the spirit of Jacobean galleried playhouses, but also has the character of a small baroque opera house.

The roof void creates a rehearsal space for the company above the theatre.

follow spot position. There is no flytower or flying grid, but suspension points provide for descents and a limited flying capacity. Acoustically, the space is somewhat more 'live' than is ideal for speech, but this does not matter because, as at Manchester's Royal Exchange Theatre (see Chapter 6), every spectator is close to the stage.

The result is by no means a historical reconstruction. The form is actually conditioned by the constraint of the existing dimensions, and also by the most straightforward use of timber, with regard to joints and junctions, and small, optimal spans. A combination of relatively small ground plan dimensions with ceiling heights that are greater than those in many historical theatres, creates a vertical emphasis to the space. The three-dimensional character is in fact reminiscent of small baroque opera houses (where, with lower headroom heights, there may be several tiers of boxes). This makes it necessary for the actors to project upwards as well as outwards. But the extreme intimacy of the space—most seats are well within a maximum 10m (33ft)—and the sense the actor gains of being surrounded by spectators, enables a very close engagement between actor and audience. Trevor Nunn, chief executive and artistic director of the RSC, says of the theatre, 'It is the simplest possible structure on which we can present the pre-proscenium plays of our dramatic tradition. It is a theatre for texts and actors, for the work of analysis, structure, insight and performance. Clearly, design will have a vital significance in what we do

The theatre, with its new, steeply pitched roof,
adjoining the 1932 theatre, seen from across the River
Avon.

there, but it cannot be design involving the configuration
of the stage, or even of "set building" in the sense that we
currently understand it.'

The old library and art gallery to the original
Memorial Theatre, all in Victorian gothic, provide the
foyers and bars to the new theatre, and they also house
the Royal Shakespeare Theatre collection, to which the
audience has access in the intervals. On the outside of the
building, a metal-clad, steeply-pitched roof has been
constructed in the character of the original, to replace the
flat roof which was built after the fire. Inside the roof
space, above the theatre, is a rehearsal room. This is an
impressive space enclosed by a massive timber roof
structure, like the loft of some grand Italian palazzo.

CHAPTER 6

New Theatres in Old Buildings

The Conversion Option

The practice of converting theatres and concert halls from, and building them into, existing buildings is as old as the building types themselves. The tradition of converting tennis courts into theatres was mentioned in Chapter 1, a relatively late example of which can be seen today in the recently restored Globe Theatre, at Devonport, Plymouth, which was converted in 1864 from a racquets court of 1788. The Ballhof Theater, Hanover, discussed below, is a unique modern example of this tradition; but many other building types throughout history have lent themselves equally well to such a role. The grand Teatro Farnese, Parma, of 1617–28 is just one theatre among many that were built within existing family palaces. The famous Altes Gewandhaus concert hall, Leipzig, of 1780–81 was so-called because it was built into the Gewandhaus, or Drapers' Hall. The old Philharmonie, Berlin, of 1888 was converted from a former roller skating rink, while the Grosses Schauspielhaus, Berlin, of 1919 was remodelled by the architect Hans Poelzig from a former circus building.

For the present-day owner, a conversion may provide the necessary accommodation at a fraction of the cost of a new building, often in a central area where sites may not otherwise be available. For instance in Toronto, Arcop Associates completed in 1985 the first phase of a conversion of a former gas-works and knitting mill into a 'back of house' facility for the Canadian Opera Company. This provided many times the floor area than would otherwise have been possible. The enormous central space of the gas-works has become a rehearsal hall, with sandblasted brickwork and massive timber roof trusses. The hall is designed to stage full sets for final rehearsals and, with a hydraulic stage platform and raked seating for about 400 people, will also function as an experimental performing space.

The most obvious buildings for conversion to auditorium use are, of course, redundant churches. Notable concert hall conversions in Great Britain include St John's, Smith Square, London, St George's, Brandon Hill, Bristol, and the Queen's Hall, Edinburgh. The latter is a former church built in 1823, which re-opened in 1979 as the home of the Scottish Philharmonic Singers, the Scottish Chamber Orchestra and the Scottish Baroque Ensemble. In East Germany, the answer to the problem of redundant churches—at Rostock University and Halle, and at former monasteries

in Frankfurt an der Oder and Magdeburg—has been to convert them into specialized concert halls for oratorios, organ recitals, and other suitable musical forms. Among the more unusual buildings to have been converted into auditoria are the Round House, Camden Town, London, a Victorian railway engine shed converted by Bickerdike Allen Rich and Partners in 1967, and the Tonhalle, Düsseldorf, a former planetarium which re-opened in 1978, having been excellently converted into a concert hall by the architects Hentrich-Petschnigg and Partner.

Because of their frequently central location, conversion projects for the arts may form an integral part of larger-scale urban conservation and revitalization programmes. One of the most interesting of its kind is the urban renewal programme along the 1.6km (1 mile) central waterfront in Toronto, where a variety of performing arts facilities are mixed with residential and commercial functions. In 1850 Toronto's Front Street used to hug the shore, but a policy of land reclamation detached it from the lake, and new shipping quays to the east and a traffic flyover created a no-man's land of railway tracks and redundant buildings. The Harbourfront Corporation, set up in 1976, produced a mixed-use development plan, unified by a network of waterfront promenades, quays and inlets busy with ferry boats and pleasure craft. Harbourfront was defined as a 'community centre for the city', and for the arts the goal was accessibility. Events—professional and non-professional—range from Sunday lunchtime concerts to ethnic festivals. The largest development is a converted warehouse known as Queen's Quay Terminal containing, among many facilities off a spectacular eight-storey atrium, the 450 seat Premier Dance Theatre, the only specialist facility of its kind in Canada. On an adjacent site is a 400 seat recital hall, converted from a former Ice House of 1923, a steel-frame brick 'shoe box' building of narrow width and roughly a double cube in proportion. A new steel frame has been inserted for two tiers of galleries, and a retractable seating rake and an optional orchestra pit/lower seating area can alternatively form a flat floor for summer events with refreshments or cabaret.

Although auditorium refurbishment is outside our present scope, this option can be mentioned at this point. An important such project is the renovation of William B. Tuthill's 2816 seat Carnegie Hall, New York. This fine hall of 1891, now regarded as an outstanding part of the city's heritage, was nearly demolished in the 1960s to make way for a notably uninspired skyscraper. It was reprieved at the eleventh hour after a campaign led by the violinist Isaac Stern. The renovation, due for completion in 1990, is being phased to allow for the continuous operation of the main hall and the other public and private facilities housed within the building. In 1983 the recital hall lobby and entrance were renovated, then the electrical and mechanical systems throughout the building were renewed. Next, a rehearsal and recording room known as the Kaplan Space was created within a former masonic meeting room; then the exterior shell was restored. The main hall itself was renovated and re-opened in December 1986, including renovations to the stage area, and new seating. The improvement most visible to the public will be a new street-level lobby to reduce over-crowding. Much of Carnegie Hall's charm is that gradual, informal additions have been made somewhat casually over the years, to provide additional office and studio space. The high quality work of the present architects, James Stewart Polshek and Partners, has respected this character, without attempting to reproduce exactly the style of William Tuthill, while avoiding a starkly ill-fitting contemporary interior. The renovation is part of a master plan which will also ensure the financial security of the hall. The intention is to build an office tower on the adjacent site to the east of the hall, which will also contain additional backstage space.

Many auditorium refurbishment projects also involve some change of use. For example, the splendid Orpheum, Vancouver, a former vaudeville house-turned-motion picture theatre built in 1928, re-opened in 1977 as a concert hall for the Vancouver Symphony Orchestra (see also Playhouse Square, Cleveland, Chapter 2). Although attention has been focused on historical theatres, a new field of refurbishment is that of remodelling the auditoria of the 1960s. The first to undergo this treatment was the St Lawrence Centre, again in Toronto (a city with a particularly active, workaday approach to the performing arts). Since opening in 1970, its main theatre had suffered from dwindling audiences in the cold, concrete interior, with its single rake of amphitheatre seating which was too broad for many types of production, especially comedy. The remodelling (by The Thom Partnership and Theatre Projects Consultants Limited) has created a traditional theatre with a Victorian flavour. New walls and a shallow-raked floor have been inserted within the existing structure, forming a narrower focus, with sidewall boxes and a dress circle. Within a reduced cubic volume, there are now 890 seats instead of 830, and capacity audiences have increased from 30 per cent to 80 per cent.

Maltings Concert Hall, Snape: site plan.

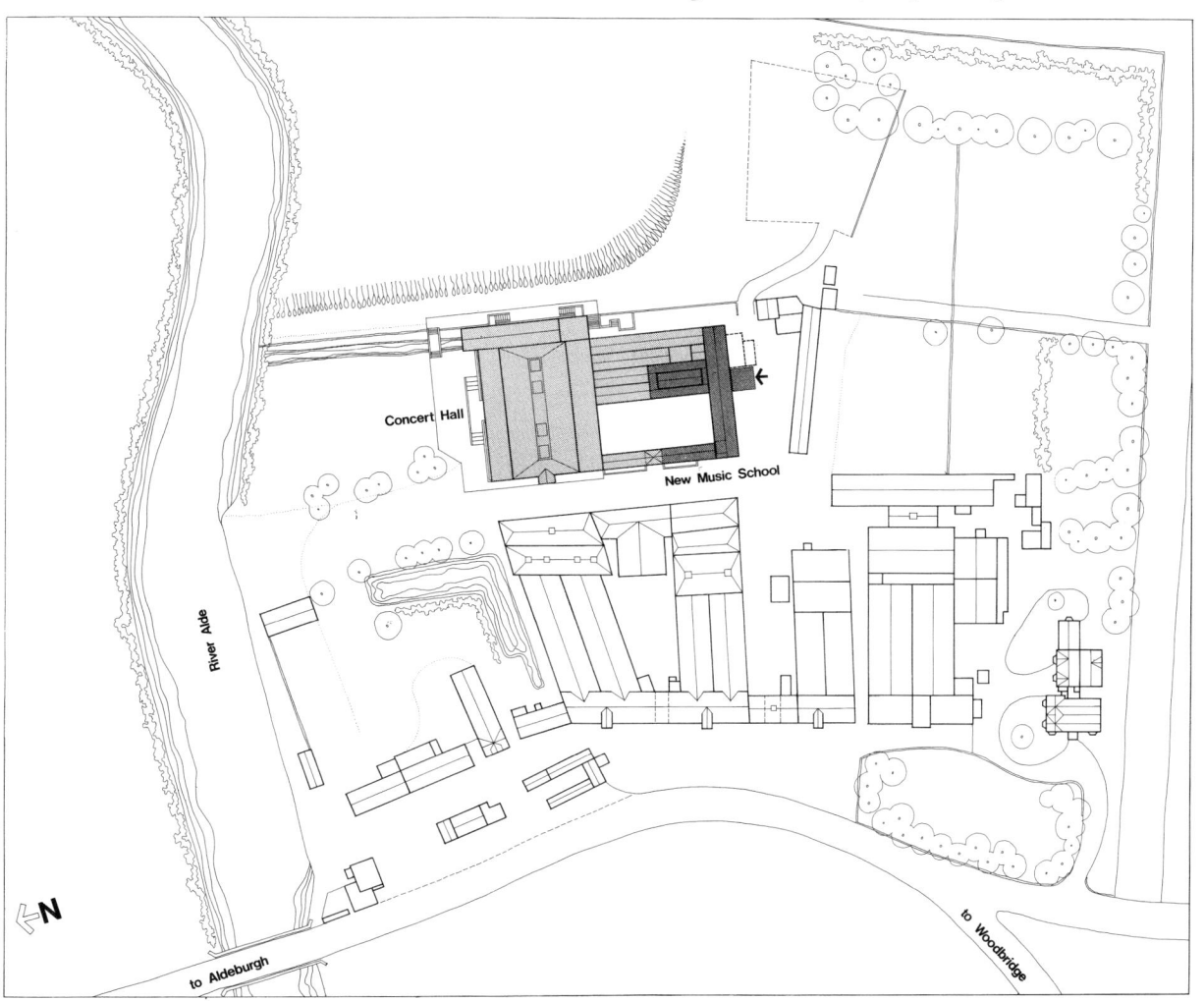

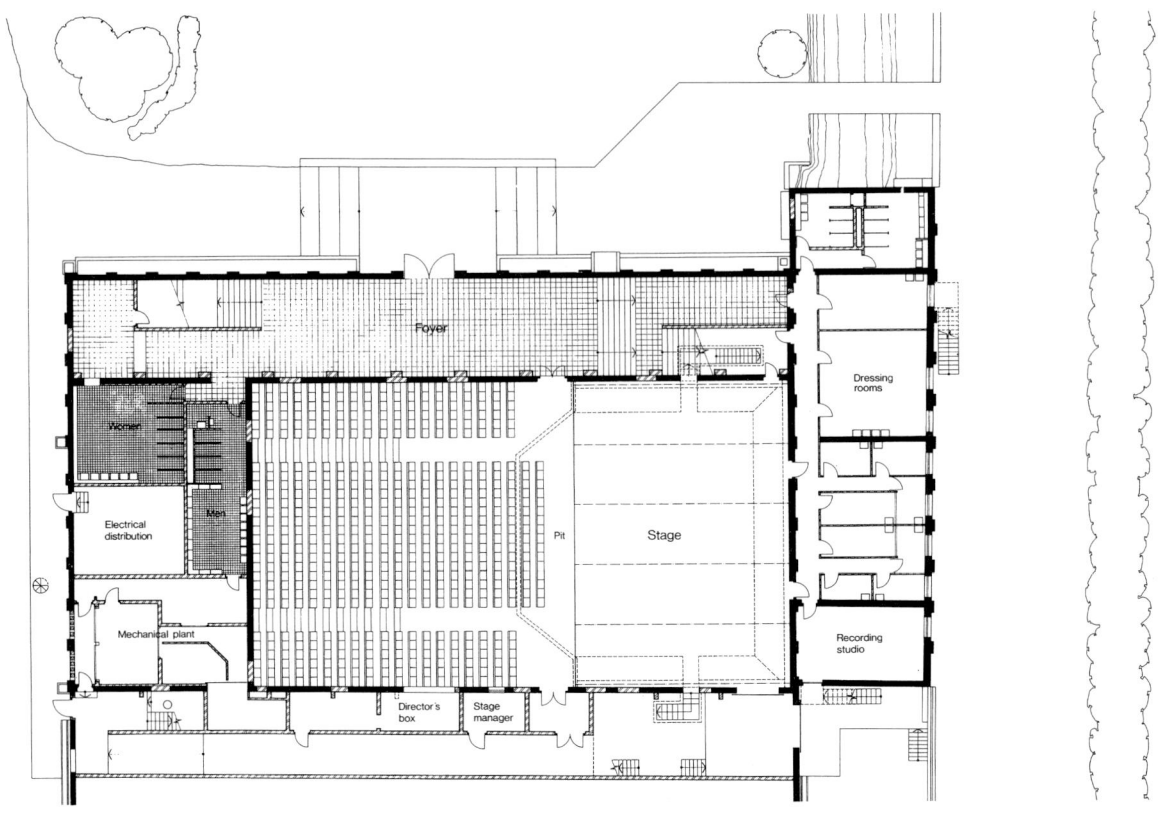

Entrance level plan.

Upper level plan.

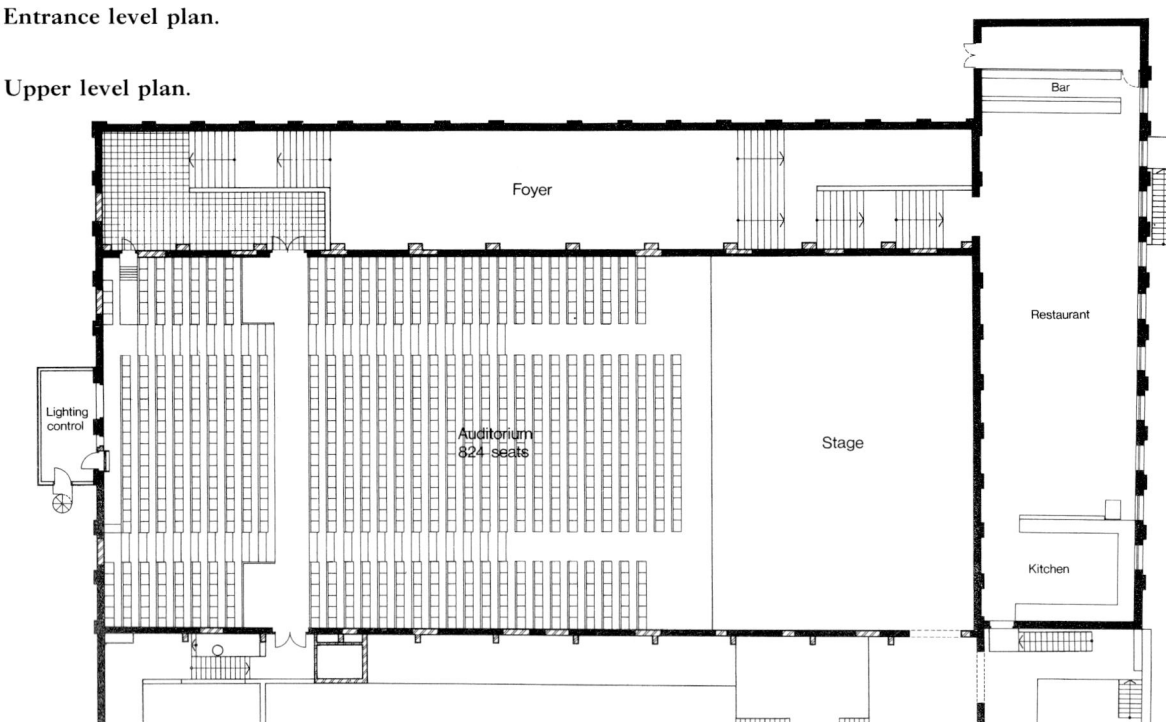

Maltings Concert Hall, Snape

Owner: Aldeburgh Festival of Music and the Arts

Architects and engineers: Arup Associates

Main contractor: Wm C. Reade of Aldeburgh Ltd

Opened: June 1967, destroyed by fire and re-opened June 1969

Cost: £127,000 (excluding opera house lighting and control) 1967 prices

Uses: concerts, also opera

Seats: 824

Furthest seat from stage front: 28m (92ft)

Stage: width 17.7m (58ft), depth 12m (39.4ft)

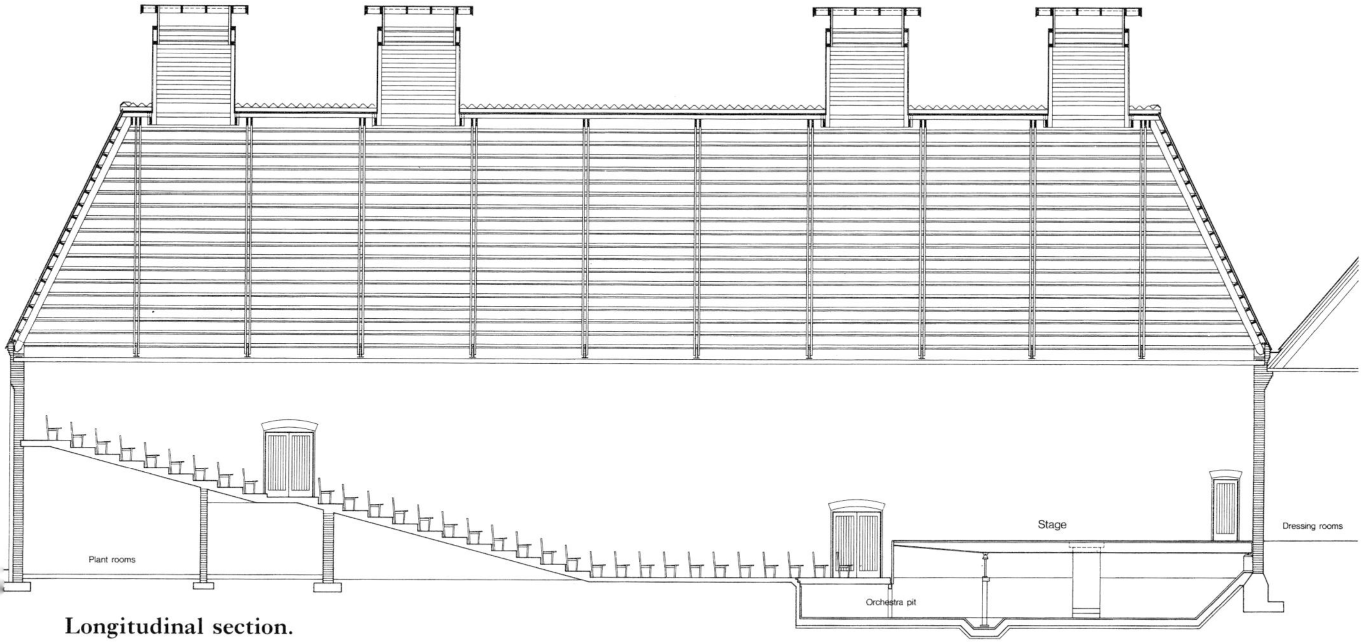

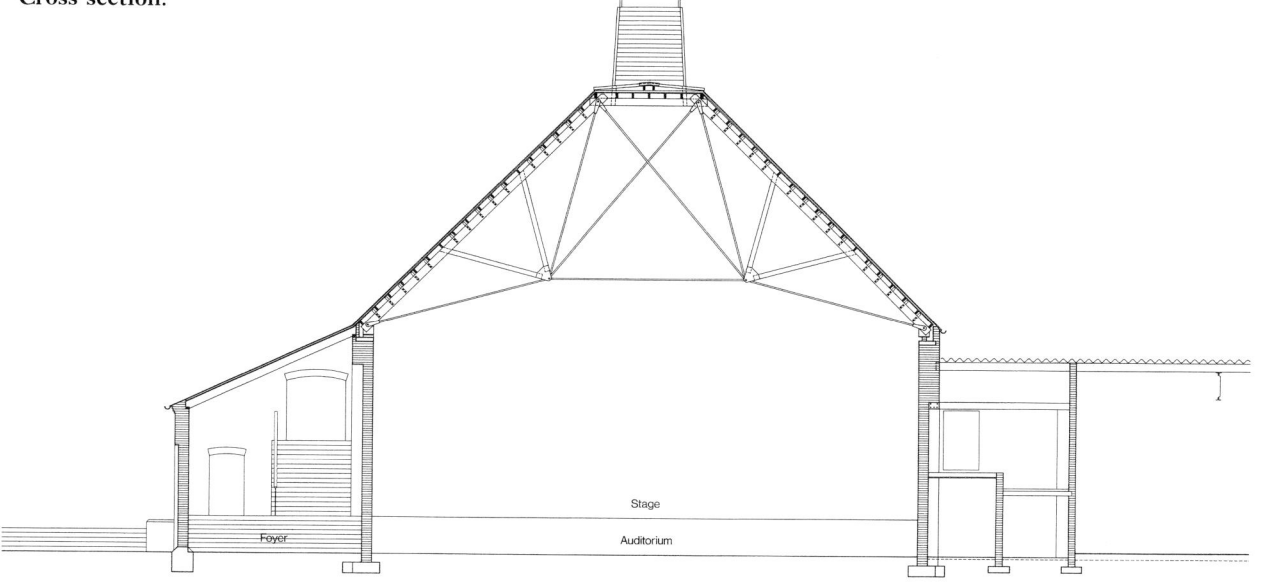

Longitudinal section.

Cross section.

Orchestra pit: open pit which extends under stage with adjustable screens. 30–60 musicians

Volume: 8150 cub.m (288,800 cub.ft)

Reverberation time: 2.0 sec. at mid-frequencies with full audience, 3.0 sec. at 125 Hz

Maximum background noise level: NC 20

This hall was the first conversion of its type in the United Kingdom—completed in the same year as London's Queen Elizabeth Hall. Yet it remains greatly interesting for its acoustic warmth, presence and clarity—perhaps unsurpassed in modern halls—together with visual charm and intimacy; in addition, it has the rare distinction, along with Wagner's Festspielhaus, Bay-

reuth and Boulez's IRCAM at the Centre Georges Pompidou, Paris, of having been commissioned by a distinguished composer for his own use. Benjamin Britten required the building to house the Aldeburgh Festival, which had begun in 1948 as 'a few concerts given by friends' but had grown by 1965, the year the hall was commissioned, to include an impressive array of visiting artists.

The building is a disused malthouse, which had, reputedly, the largest kiln in Britain. It is part of a group of traditional mid-nineteenth-century industrial structures situated amid the marshes and water channels of the remote Suffolk landscape—the region from which Benjamin Britten's music sprang. Indeed, it was Britten himself who saw the possibilities of the great shed, whose silhouette he had known since moving to the mill in Snape before the Second World War. The buildings are

The opera lighting control box, the only addition outside the original walls, is weatherboard-clad like a traditional hoist.

constructed of local red brick, with timber floors and deep timber roofs in the local shipwright tradition. Although required to house opera as well as concerts, both client and designers agreed at the outset for the auditorium to be fundamentally a concert hall with facilities for opera, rather than being a true multi-use hall, and with no compromise of the 'concert hall acoustic'. However, due to its small size, it is quite successful for opera. For this purpose, the brief required stage lighting facilities, an orchestra pit and a removable proscenium.

The conversion aimed at enclosing the auditorium and stage within a single volume. An existing internal wall running the length of the malthouse was removed to create a rectangular hall, while a second existing wall provided an adjacent foyer. The auditorium floor is raked, except for the first few rows of seats, as the Decca Recording Company required a partly flat floor. Beneath the rake, which is a suspended concrete floor slab, are plant rooms and washrooms. The only addition outside the original walls of the malthouse is the opera lighting control box, the design of which is based on the characteristic weatherboard-clad hoists of such build-ings, and this is supported on steel brackets. The auditorium seating is constructed of cane on a wooden frame for minimal sound absorption, and is based on the seating in the Festspielhaus at Bayreuth. A foyer runs along the entire length of one side of the auditorium, with a half landing at the east end giving access to the hall. A staircase at the west end leads to a restaurant housed in the upper floor of a two storey annex with fine views over the marshes to the east. Beneath the ground floor are changing rooms which have direct access onto the stage.

The dominant element in the conversion design was the roof. The existing roof was demolished and replaced with an entirely new design, and given a 45 degree slope centred over the auditorium, with large triangulated trusses exposed internally. The prominent smoke hoods to the original malthouse on the old roof were replaced, to house natural ventilators with the exhaust rate controlled by motorized dampers, and coupled with an air intake through honeycomb brickwork on the west gable.

The key to the hall's success is the combination of a small audience capacity and narrow width with an almost church-like volume, which was achieved by raising the existing brick walls by 1m (3.3ft). The dimensions in plan happen to be almost exactly those of Britten's favoured nearby Blythburgh parish church. From the outset Britten himself asked for a long reverberation time; he preferred his *War Requiem* in Ely Cathedral 'where you can't hear the words, to the Royal Festival Hall where you can' (to which Peter Pears added that 'you can't really hear all the words anyway unless you know them!'). The soft red brick walls received no treatment except sandblasting, and the control of the reverberation time was carried out in the construction and thickness of the timber roof, which presented a very large surface area. This was constructed of two layers of 25mm (1in) thick tongued and grooved pine, the first layer laid normal to the purlins and the second layer at 45 degrees. Together these create a very stiff membrane with low sound absorption in the lower frequencies. There is a reverberation time of 3 seconds at 62.5 Hz with a full audience and 2.0 seconds at mid-frequencies.

The plan is rectangular, almost a double square with a width of only 18m (59ft), like a smaller version of the famous old halls at Vienna, Basel, Glasgow, Leipzig and Boston. The narrow width provides strong early lateral sound reflections with a short initial time delay gap of around 20 milliseconds between the direct and first reflected sound and between subsequent reflections. The unusual feature of the interior is the exposed underside of the gabled roof, which possibly diffuses the sound better than a flat ceiling (though more investigation needs to be done to establish how significant this feature is). It is the combination of acoustical attributes that the hall possesses that is usually difficult to achieve: reverberance and fullness of tone, provided by the high cubic volume; clarity due to the hall's intimacy, and strong cross-reflections because of narrow width and the ceiling shape, so that the sound 'fills the hall'.

On the first night of the third Aldeburgh Festival to be held in the hall, in June 1969, when the English Opera Group was setting up the stage for *Idomeneo*, a fire started under the stage. It quickly spread to the auditorium with the result that the entire building burned down. It was rebuilt at once with some improvements to access and dressing rooms, and reopened one year later in June 1970. Interestingly, the reverberation time was within 0.1 second of that in the original building, throughout the frequency range from 63 Hz to 125 Hz.

Adjoining the concert hall, the southern building of the Maltings' central block now houses the Britten-Pears Music School, opened in April 1979. This contains a recital room, cafe, practice and seminar rooms.

The interior of the hall.

Henry Wood Hall, London

Owner: Southwark Rehearsal Hall Ltd, a charitable trust set up by the sponsors—the London Symphony Orchestra and the London Philharmonic Orchestra and their trustees

Architects, engineers and quantity surveyors: Arup Associates

Main contractor: J. W. Falkner and Sons Ltd

Opened: 1975

Cost: £410,000

Uses: orchestral rehearsals and recording

Usable floor area: 350 sq.m (3770 sq.ft)

Volume: 5460 cub.m (195,000 cub.ft)

Reverberation time: 1.7 sec. (curtains fully drawn) to 2.2 sec. (curtains fully open) at 1000 Hz

Maximum background noise level: NR 17

Named after the famous originator of the Promenade Concerts, this is the only example to date of an entire building—in this case a conversion—designed principally for orchestra rehearsal purposes. The facility was initiated by the London Symphony and London Philharmonic Orchestras principally for their own use, but the building is available to all other orchestras as well. The search for a suitable building centred on six redundant churches—three Victorian Gothic Revival and three Classical style—all within easy reach of London's musical centres, the Royal Festival Hall and the Barbican. Holy Trinity Church, Southwark, was selected because its dimensions closely matched the brief which had been drawn up at the same time. The former church, redundant under the Pastoral Measure of 1968, was designed by Francis Bedford and built in 1824. It is the centrepiece of the quiet and beautiful nineteenth-century Trinity Church Square, which had become part of a conservation area in 1968.

The church is an austere Classical revival ashlar-faced building with a Corinthian portico and a two stage tower

Ground floor plan.

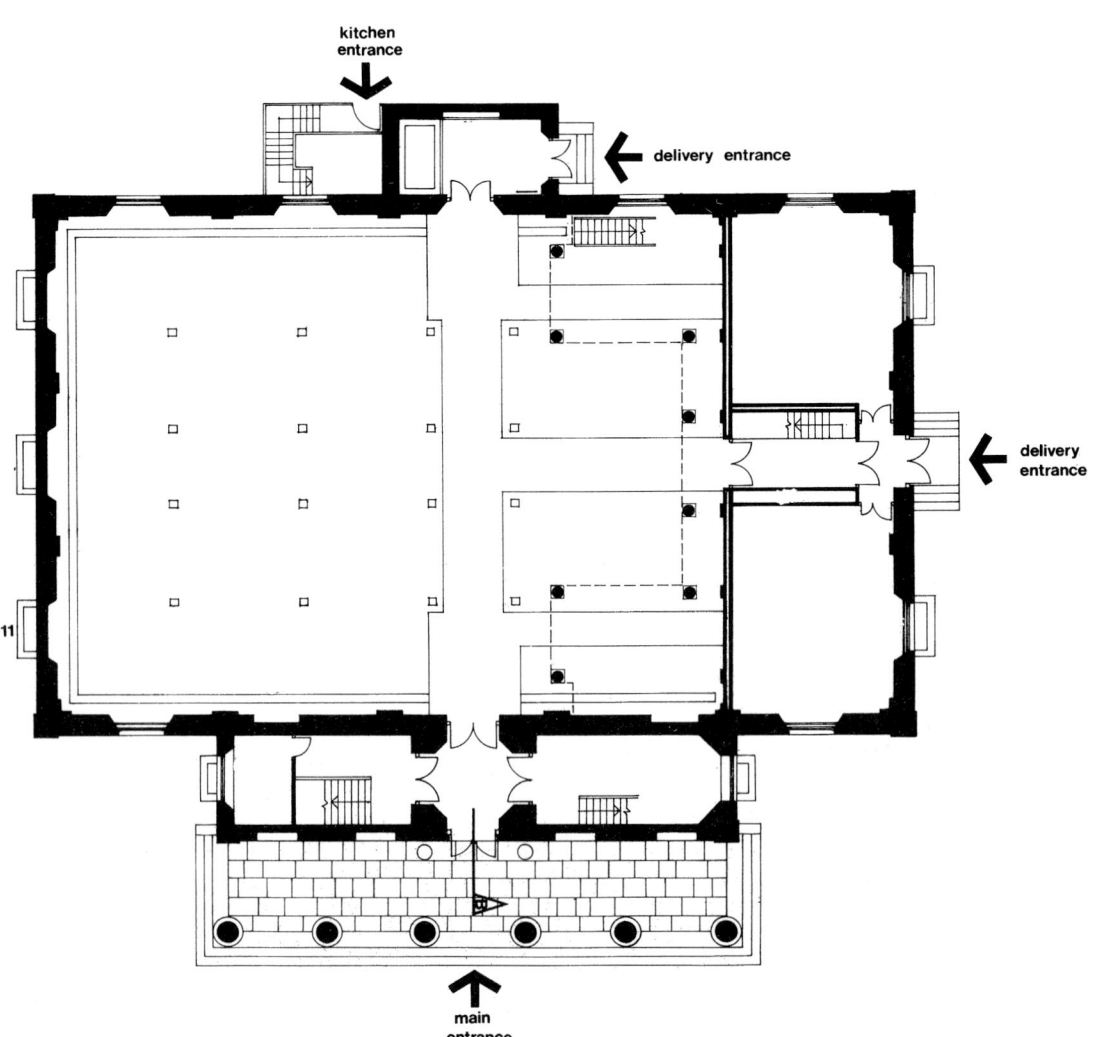

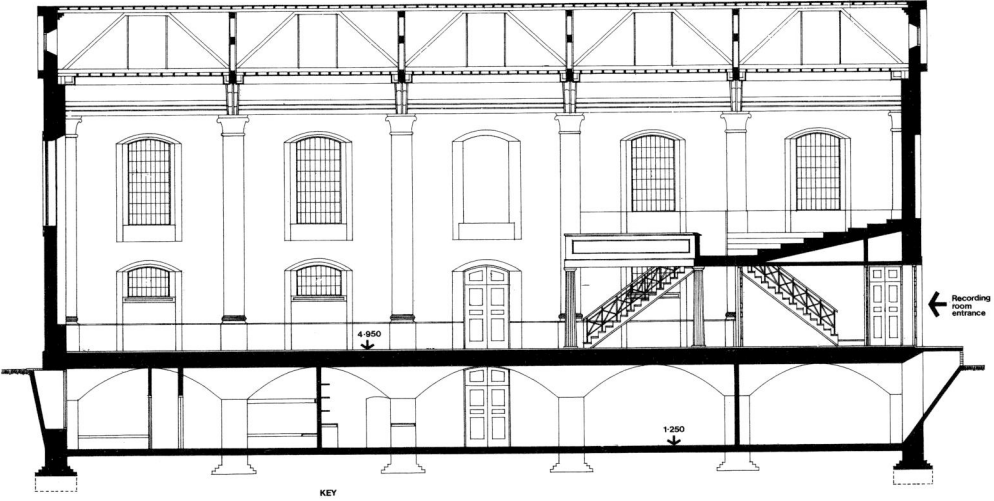

Longitudinal section through the hall.

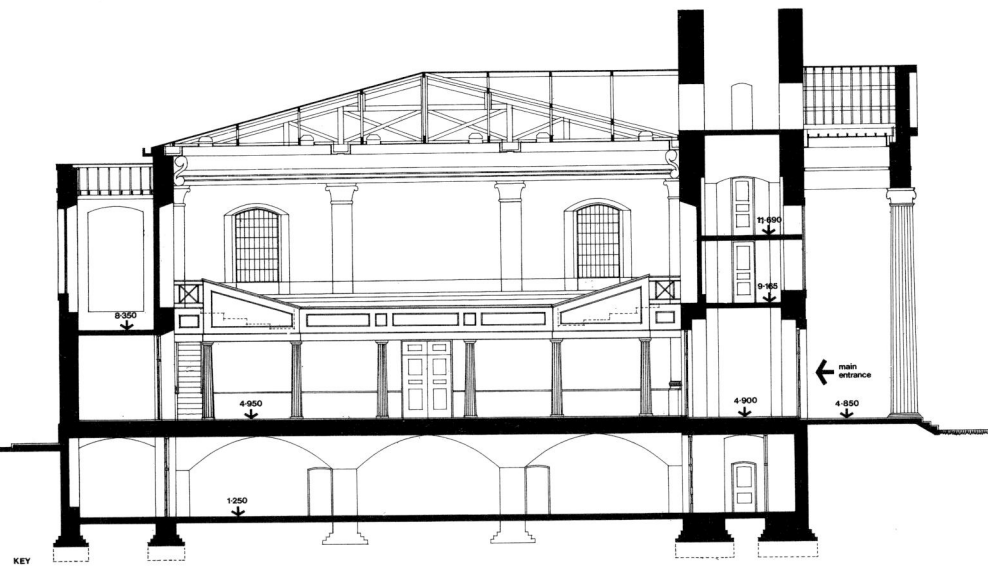

Cross section.

Rehearsal hall. The curtains provide some acoustical variability.

Detail of the plasterwork and balustrade, recreated after fire gutted the building.

topped by an octagonal lantern. The plan is a simple rectangle with a main gallery supported by Doric columns on the north-east wall and two short galleries (cut back in 1898) on the two adjacent sides. The plastered ceiling is divided by beams into fifteen 6m by 6m (19.7ft by 19.7ft) square coffered bays. The brief required a flat rehearsal space to accommodate a large symphony orchestra, with a reverberation time of 2.2 seconds at mid-frequencies with a 120 piece orchestra, with a slight increase in the bass reverberation time.

Back-up areas include two fully-equipped recording rooms under the rear balcony and, in the crypt, a cafeteria and kitchen, separate music libraries for each orchestra, a ventilation plant room, a conductor's room and other support spaces.

Before conversion work began, and despite the ceiling plaster being in a dangerous condition after heavy rainfalls, a test rehearsal took place in December 1972—with the orchestra in hard hats and with increased insurance for the instruments. On September 30, 1973, the night before the contractor was due to start, a fire gutted the building. Undeterred, work proceeded to underpin the foundations, rebuild the roof with steel trusses and to reconstruct the balconies, this time in concrete. The fine plasterwork was also reproduced, from photographic records that had luckily been made. Careful attention was paid to the detailing and installation of double glazing, doors and roof seals. To integrate a heating system unobtrusively within the classical interior the entire nave floor was raised on sleeper walls. This accommodated large low-velocity air ducts supplying warm, filtered air to the perimeter. Air is extracted through the light fittings in the ceiling into the roof void via a fan located in the church tower. To meet the required reverberation time for rehearsal, carpets were introduced onto the balconies together with an extensive curtaining system to provide variable acoustics for recording and rehearsals.

The musicians' cafeteria in the crypt.

Ballhof Theater, Hanover

Owner: Niedersächsische Staatstheater Hanover GmbH

Architects: Hochbauamt der Landeshauptstadt Hannover (design architect: Dipl.-Ing. Thilo Mucke)

Theatre consultants: Rudolf Schulz, Jochen Rissmann, Wolf-Dietrich Grube (Staatstheater Hanover)

Acoustic consultants: H. Keilholtz; Müller BBM

Structural engineer: Dipl.-Ing. G. Demuss

Site architect: Dipl.-Ing. R. Herzog

Mechanical engineer: V. Grabe

Opened: 1975

(*Top to bottom*) Section through auditorium and foyer, plan at balcony level, plan at main floor level showing arena layout, and plan of total building at main floor level, showing end stage layout.

Key: 1 bar, 2 upper foyer, 3 entrance, 4 box office, 5 foyer, 6 stairs to cloaks and washroom, 7 seats for disabled, 8 normal end stage layout, 9 rear stage area, 10 movable proscenium, 11 storage and side stage, 12 wc for disabled, 13 stage manager, 14 dressing rooms, 15 doorman, 16 green room, 17 artists' washrooms, 18 yard, 19 storage, 20 variable central stage, 21 balcony, 22 lighting control room, 23 sound control room, 24 lighting bridge, 25 lighting gallery 1, 26 lighting gallery 2, 27 archives, 28 rehearsal room, 29 studio, 30 lighting rigs, 31 attic, 32 grid, 33 counterweights, 34 under-stage area, 35 orchestra pit/forestage, 36 plant rooms for heating and ventilation

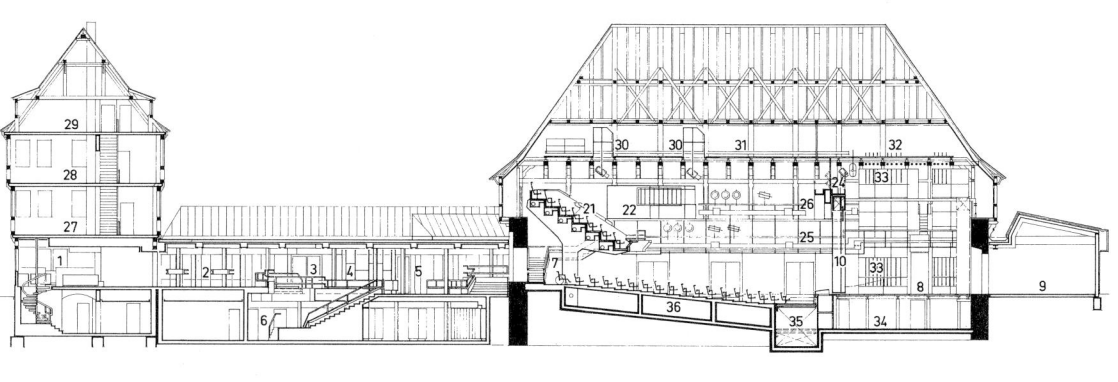

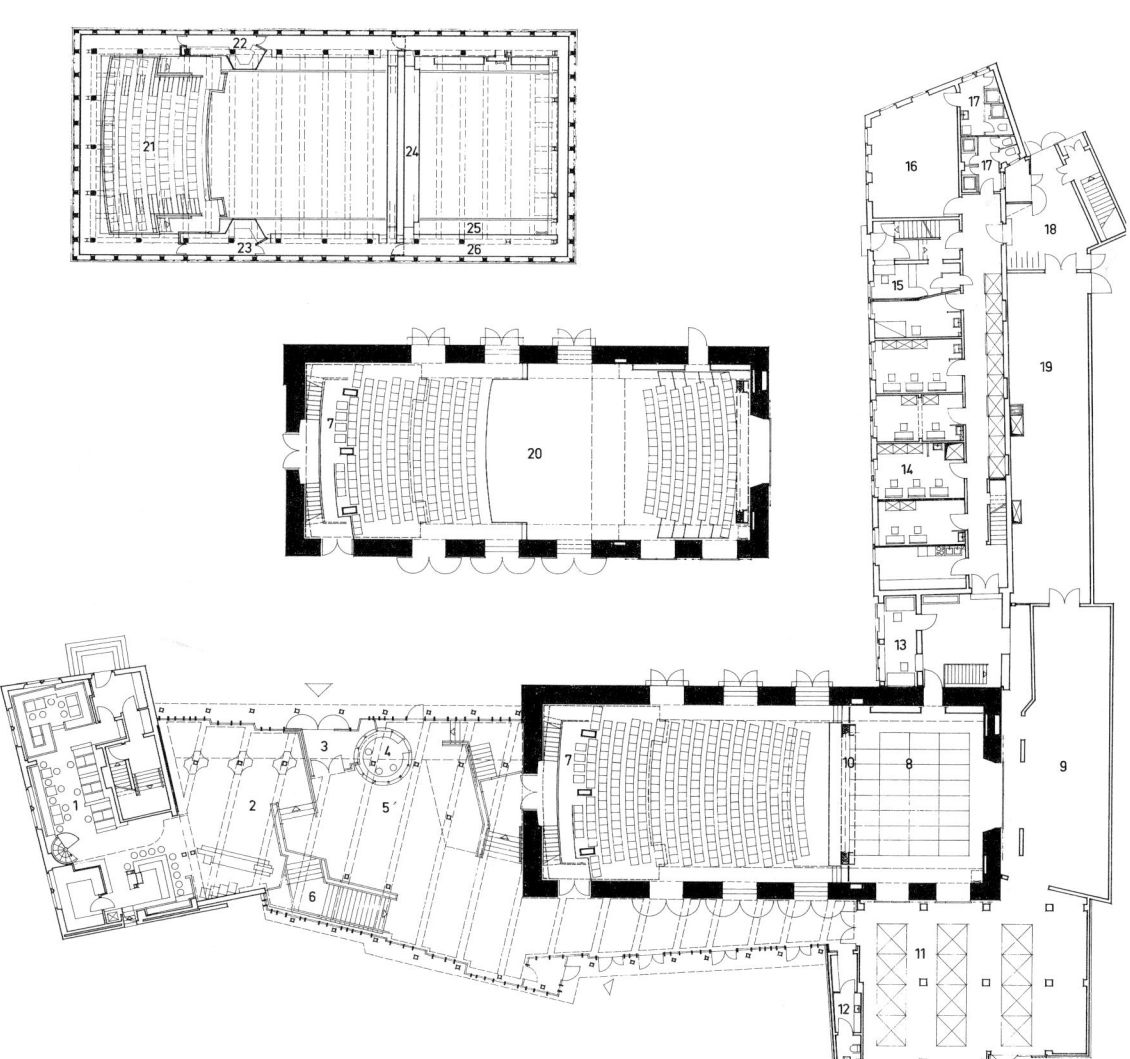

Typical seventeenth-century covered tennis court.

The temporary theatre photographed in 1945; it remained unchanged until 1973.

The interior seen from the same viewpoint, being gutted in 1973 prior to rebuilding.

The new theatre of 1975, again from the same viewpoint, arranged with stage rostra to form an arena layout.

Cost: DM 6.5 million

Primary use: drama

Seats: total 407 (main floor 299, gallery 104 and 4 handicapped)

Furthest balcony seat from stage front (end stage layout): 19m (62ft)

Proscenium opening: 7.7m (25.25ft) wide, 5.5m (18ft) high.

Stage: variable; typical end stage layout: width 11.5m (37.75ft), depth to stage front 10m (33ft), height to grid underside 9m (29.5ft)

Flying system: 24 single purchase counterweight sets and 2 motor sets for the end stage, plus 16 motor sets over the central stage, movable to any position

Orchestra pit: 25 musicians (variable depth)

Volume: 3000 cub.m (100,000 cub.ft)

Reverberation time: 1.2 secs. at mid-frequencies with full audience

Maximum background noise level: 30dB(A)

The arena stage seen from the gallery.

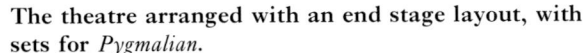

The theatre arranged with an end stage layout, with sets for *Pygmalian*.

The foyer, surrounding the stone walls of the former tennis court. Occasional dramatic events are staged here also.

In the seventeenth and eighteenth centuries, redundant tennis courts were frequently converted into theatres, and this recent conversion of a covered tennis court built in 1649 into an experimental studio theatre is a unique modern-day equivalent. The result is architecturally and theatrically one of the most interesting and successful contemporary German auditoria. The Ballhof (literally 'ball-house') is typical of numerous such examples throughout Europe from the sixteenth to eighteenth centuries. It has an exposed roof construction and measures nearly 11m (36ft) by 30m (98.5ft) by 10m (33ft) high inside. It was later used for various purposes with different internal arrangements, and after surviving the devastating bombing of the Second World War it served as Hanover's temporary drama theatre until 1973. Since the conversion of 1975 it has been the principal theatre of Hanover and home of the state drama company.

The building with its ancillary accommodation wraps around two sides of the Ballhof Platz, adjacent to the Historisches Museum on the Burgstrasse. The tennis court was originally free-standing and enclosed within its stone walls a single large space with an open framed gallery. The present conversion has preserved the exterior appearance of the original building, with extensions which provide support facilities that are entirely modern in style and avoid historical pastiche. These include a foyer, a side stage and store rooms, while the dressing rooms occupy a narrow wing built in 1937–38. The structural framework has been reinforced with steel, and most of the new internal elements are also built of steel, including the balcony, proscenium arch, and lighting bridge and galleries.

Part of the seating is movable, and various stage arrangements can be made, including an end stage or an arena layout (although the building is too narrow for true theatre-in-the-round). By placing both stages together, a single flat floor can be created. The stages are built of 1m by 2m (3.3ft by 6.6ft) removable sections—the end stage has 32—and there is a variable proscenium arch which can be stored upstage against the wall or alternatively can

The exterior of the Ballhof in 1939.

The exterior after restoration, with new glazed foyer entrance.

be used at an intermediate position to create a larger forestage. There are two forestage lifts side by side, which can form an orchestra pit, either together or singly to one side of the stage or the other. Alternatively, they can become part of the seating area, or, for the arena layout, part of the central stage. Besides a counter-weighted flying system for the end stage, there are electrically driven lines over the central area for use with the arena stage. In addition, the gridiron extends over the entire auditorium so that pulleys can be installed at any point. Above the proscenium is a lighting bridge and, extending the length of the auditorium, are two lighting galleries on each side, 3m (10ft) and 5m (16.5ft) high. Air for the heating and ventilation system is fed below the seats from ducts contained in an underfloor plenum.

The interior adopts the 'black box' approach, with dark brown walls and woodwork, to highlight both actors and spectators. (The original tennis court was also painted dark to enable the players to see the white balls.) The seating is beige coloured and the balustrades and foyers deep red. The building is entirely lit at night by spotlights. The principal design problem during the conversion work was to meet the exacting fire and other safety requirements for theatres, while preserving and exposing as far as possible the historic building fabric. An octagonal rehearsal room, studio and administrative offices are currently being planned to extend the theatre's facilities.

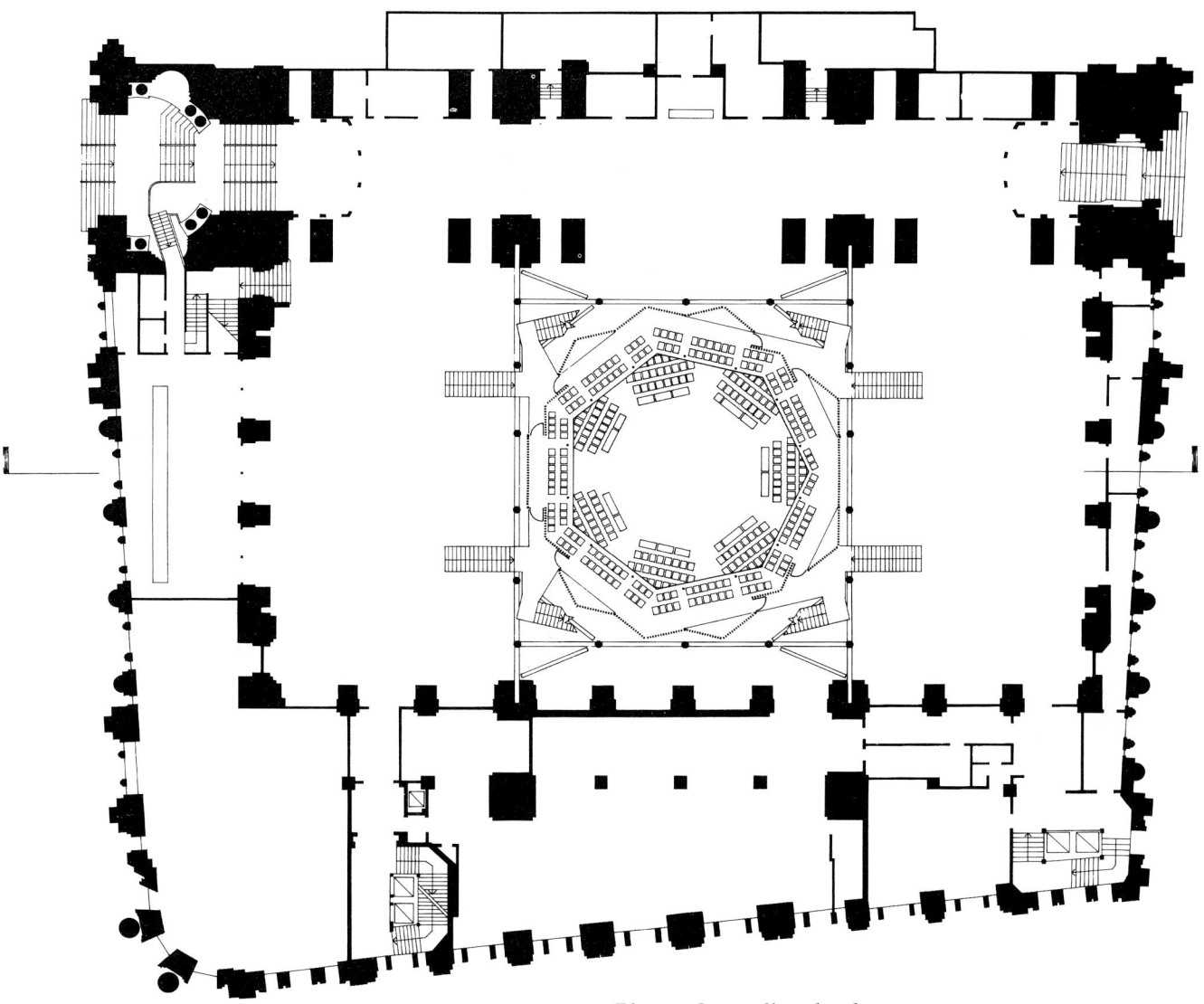

Plan at first gallery level.

Royal Exchange Theatre, Manchester

Owner: Royal Exchange Theatre Company

Architects: Levitt Bernstein Associates

Theatre design consultant: Richard Negri (Royal Exchange Theatre Company)

Theatre technology consultants: Theatre Projects Consultants Ltd

Acoustic consultant: D. K. Jones

Structural engineers: Ove Arup & Partners

Mechanical engineers: Max Fordham & Partners

Quantity Surveyors: Monk Dunstone Associates

Main contractor: J. Jarvis and Sons Ltd

Opened: 1976

Cost: £800,000

Principal use: drama; also used for classical, jazz and folk concerts, poetry recitals, one-man shows, puppets, television broadcasts

Seats: total 700, main floor 450, galleries 250

Furthest balcony seat from front of acting area: 13m (42ft)

Acting area: 7.3m (24ft) diameter, height to underside of structure 7.5m (24.5ft)

In 1970 a group of former London theatre directors and designers, who had formed the provincial '69 (formerly '59) Theatre Company, conceived the idea of building what they called a theatre 'module' as the company's permanent home, like a 'glass lantern' within the huge cathedral-like central hall of Manchester's old Royal Exchange. The historically listed building, which had closed its doors as a cotton exchange in 1968, was

Section through auditorium.

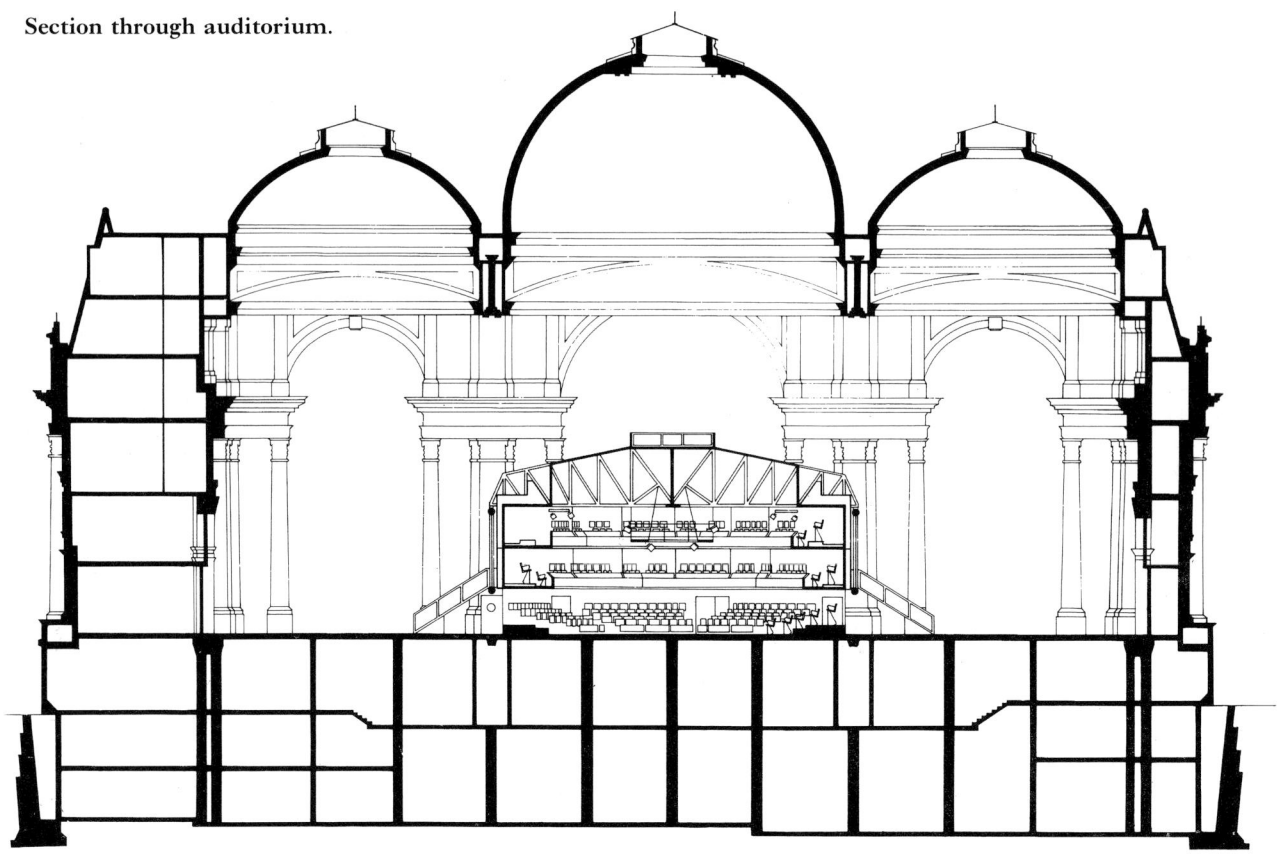

Isometric projection showing the structure spanning
between the four massive brick piers.

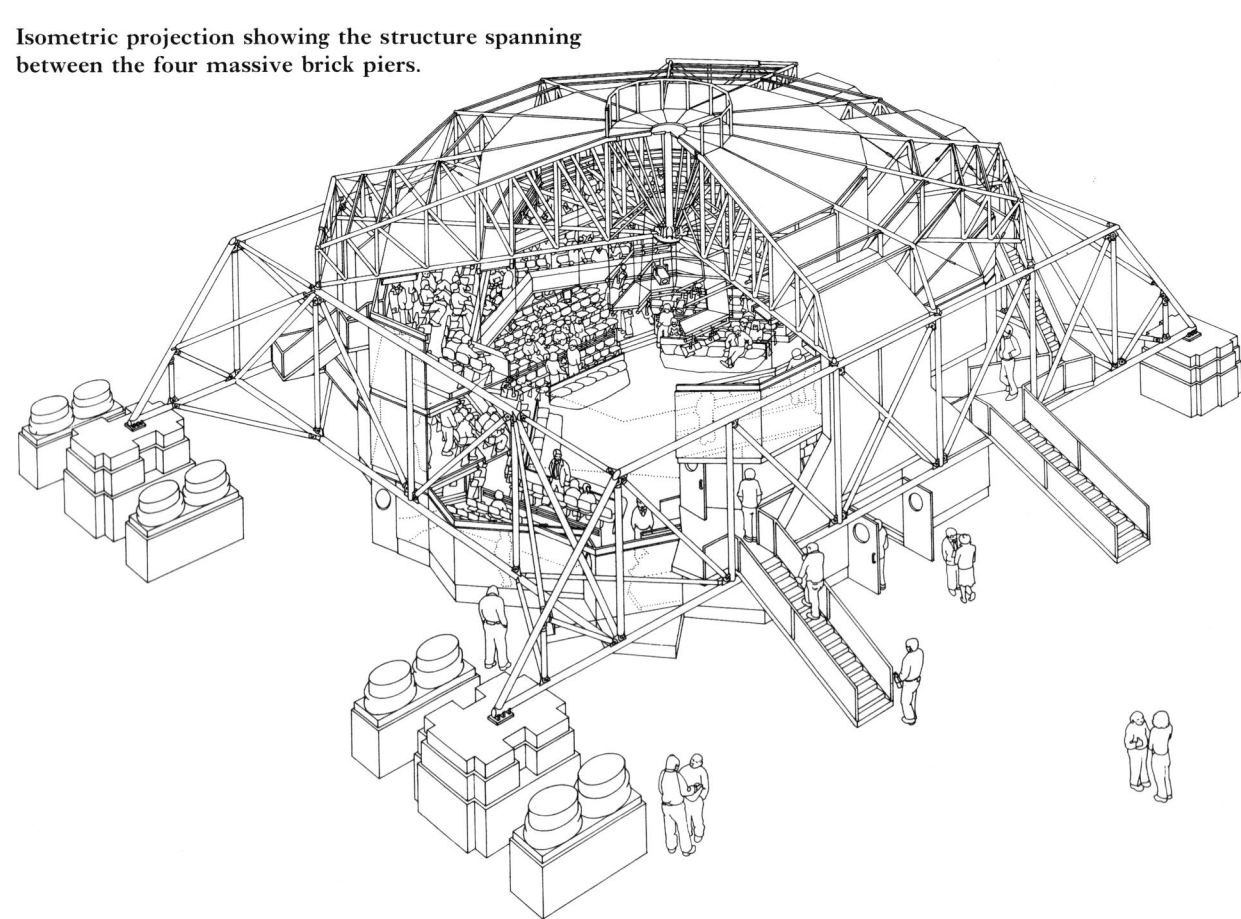

The theatre is free-standing within the great hall, which serves as a foyer for the audience, an assembly area for the actors and a reverberation chamber for battle and thunder effects.

Bridge-like tubular steel trusses 4.7m (15.5ft) deep support a series of radial roof trusses from which the galleries are suspended. The theatre is clad in corrugated metal and glass.

originally the result of a design competition in 1901, and, when completed in 1921, contained the largest commercial space in the world.

With the requirement that the design was to be specifically for the company, not for 'posterity', the users demanded close involvement with the design and even the detailing process. (Ironically, an original but over-costly proposal for a purpose-built theatre above a shopping centre, as was fashionable at the time, would have been far less related to the company's actual needs, and probably subsequent success.) Negri saw the entire theatre within the old building as being like a stage set. He visualized a circular, polychromatic scaffolding structure with a transparent skin, containing a theatre-in-the-round—'but with some direction'—built on several levels and seating about 700 people. It was built much as it was conceived, except that an idea for a continuous access ramp around the outside proved impractical.

The structure consists of a square steel frame spanning 30m (98.5ft) like a bridge between the four massive brick piers that support the dome of the Exchange, as the floor could not support the structural loading directly. A series of 14 radial trusses span between the bridge elements, from which the seating galleries are hung to enable their structural depth to be minimized. To accommodate possible deflection in the structure, the cladding, door posts and other components are all designed with compressible joints or members. The auditorium has a seven-side plan to avoid parallel surfaces, which could cause acoustic flutter echoes or coloration, and the walls are chevron-shaped for acoustic diffusion. Around a 7.3m (24ft) acting arena, which is simply the wood block floor of the original building, are placed 450 of the 700 seats, with the remainder on two gallery levels above, equally on every side, and all within 13m (42ft) of the

The balcony fronts are of perforated metal, acoustically transparent to utilize the sound-absorptive effect of the audience.

arena edge. The geometry of the galleries is rotated at each level so that a corner always sits over a flat side, giving a dynamic feel to the theatre. For events with smaller audiences, the top gallery is not used so that the auditorium appears full.

Within the centralized layout the plan has an axis orientated in the same direction as the existing building. The end bank of seats can be removed for inserting larger stage sets, and the front two rows of arena seats are partly or wholly removable to extend the acting area (occasionally, the front seating is rebuilt for the audience to sit on as part of the set). Seating in the gallery is also removable for television cameras, as the theatre is often used for broadcasting chamber music and late night concerts, and the balcony front corners can be removed for installing steps or ladders down to the arena if required for the drama. The balcony fronts are in perforated metal, so as to be acoustically transparent, to avoid the galleries being acoustically shielded and to maximize the important acoustically absorptive effect of the audience, as the auditorium is constructed entirely of hard materials. (This is because the realization of the designers' image of a steel building relied on a relaxation of the fire regulations which would normally have required the steelwork to be fire-protected; in return for this concession, all materials had to be non-combustible or highly flame retardant.) Lighting catwalks are hung from the trusses, together with a seven-sided central lighting gallery which is suspended lower over the arena. Additional, low-angle lighting is attached to the balcony fronts.

The stage machinery is simple and flexible, consisting of scaffold tubes and pulleys which are clamped to the structural steel sections as required, for suspending props or lowering people. Counterweights are located, and visible, outside the theatre enclosure from where the pulleys are operated. The company accepts that theatre-in-the-round has limitations against a fully equipped stage for certain productions, and its designers work around these; for instance, in the absence of traps or bridges, the grave in *Hamlet* is represented with tape on the floor. On the other hand the intimacy of the auditorium gives opportunities for the audience to be involved—for *Moby Dick*, the whole theatre became the boat. The proximity of the audience to the acting area means also that the sets must be of good quality, and that the available money goes into a smaller number of finely finished items.

Besides being a foyer at intermission, the great hall of the old building is also the back of house during the performance, where actors await their entrance. The 'building within a building' also presents the possibility of the vast space being visually and acoustically linked to the auditorium, as the walls are glazed with toughened glass and the structure outside may be illuminated for a sense of 'space beyond' or for theatrical lighting effects. (The transparent skin was also considered important for fire safety.) An interesting idea for gaining some acoustical variability is the series of shutters in the auditorium skin at top gallery level, which are designed, when open, to link the short reverberation time within to the cathedral-like 7.5 second reverberation time of the outer hall. Effective for cavalry charges, thunder and certain types of music, this is an amusing reversal of Wallace Clement Sabine's concept of perfectly sound-absorbing 'open window units'. As one would expect, however, the lightweight skin of the enclosure is itself partly transparent to sound, and the acoustics are less than ideal, although there is no problem with speech clarity, even when the actor is facing away from the listener, as the auditorium dimensions are so small. But it is, as Bernard Levin has said, 'the theatre with an echo'.

The cellular rooms around the perimeter of the existing building are converted into workshops, a restaurant, a cafe-bar, greenrooms and washrooms at ground level, and offices, plant rooms and dressing rooms at first floor level.

The seven-sided, entirely symmetrical theatre has only the simplest stage machinery, but has the advantage that all audience members are extremely close to the performers.

Schaubühne am Lehniner Platz, Berlin

Owner: The City State of Berlin

Architect: Jürgen Sawade (original design, 1927, by Erich Mendelsohn)

Theatre consultants and mechanical and electrical engineers: Klaus Wever, Rudolf Biste

Structural engineer: Hans-Jürgen Peschlow

Construction manager: Walter Hötzel

Opened: 1981

Cost: DM 82 million

Principal use: drama

Seats: 2000 maximum (can be partitioned into three auditoria seating a maximum of 700, 500 and 300 respectively)

Stage: totally adaptable and non-predetermined within the overall auditorium enclosure of 33m (108.25ft) by 68.5m (224.75ft)

Ceiling height: 6–12m (19.75–39.5ft) at the sides, 9–12m (29.5ft–39.5ft) in the centre, depending on floor elevation

Flying system: collective spot line equipment

Volume: 79,000 cub.m (2,800,000 cub.ft)

Reverberation time: variable between approximately 1 sec. and 3 sec. at middle frequencies

Maximum background noise level: 30 dB

This remarkable theatre is the home of the Schaubühne, a company whose performances are based around experimental spatial arrangements and the integration of audience and performers. Their previous accommodation was an old clubroom on the second floor of a building in the Kreuzberg district of Berlin, which had become wholly inadequate for their purpose. Consequently, the Schaubühne since 1972 had ventured from time to time—with accompanying difficulties over workshop and rehearsal space—into the exhibition halls near the radio tower in Berlin and the film studios at Berlin-Spandau. From this experience, the company sought by the mid-1970s permanent accommodation in a neutral hall-type building where the spatial shape and

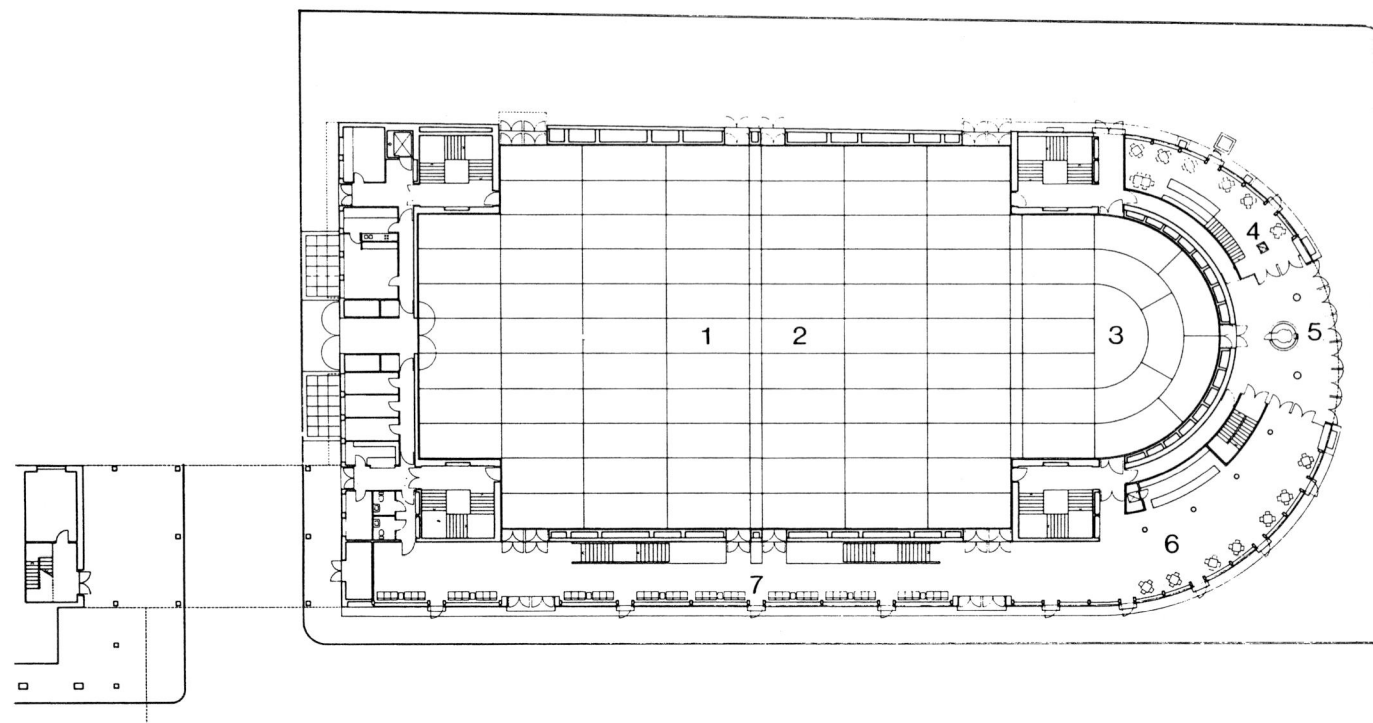

Ground floor plan. Key: 1 auditorium I, 2 auditorium II, 3 auditorium III, 4 restaurant, 5 entrance and box office, 6 bar, 7 foyer

Cross sections, showing different seating arrangements, and, below, a longitudinal section through the theatre.

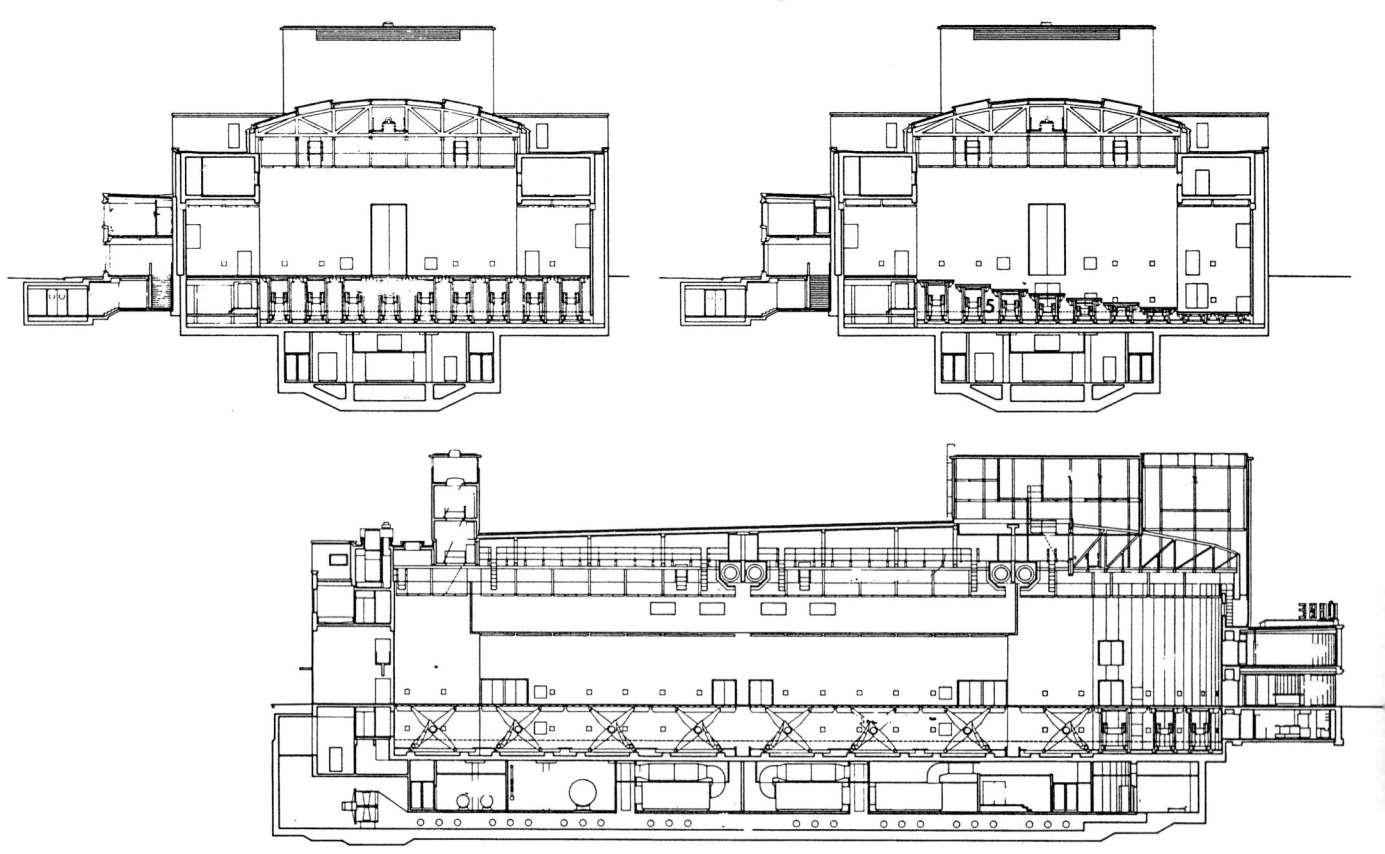

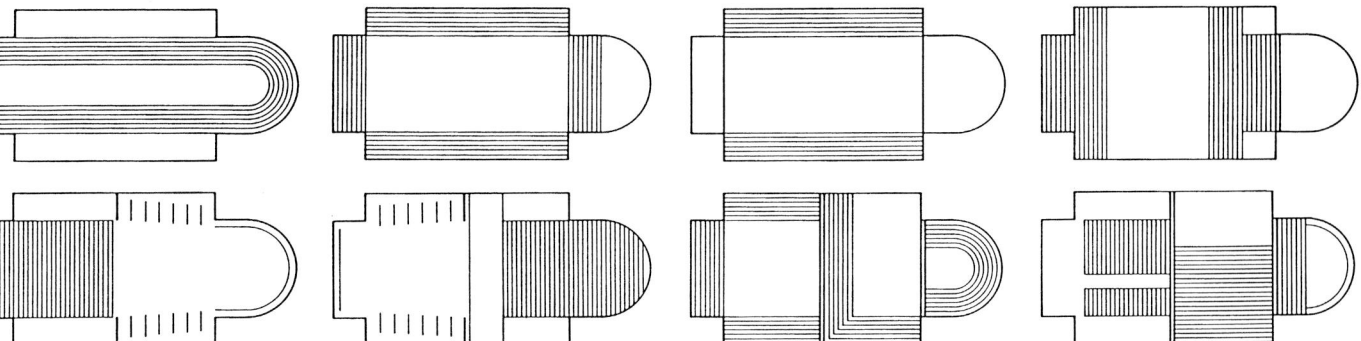

Some of the possible seating arrangements: (*left to right, top*) longitudinal arena with 1500 seats, large arena stage with 1500 seats, transverse stage with 1200 seats, lateral transverse stage, (*left to right, bottom*) 1200 seat proscenium theatre, 1200 seat proscenium theatre with orchestra pit, three theatre arrangement with apron, 'knossos angle' and apron stages, three theatres with kabuki, end stage and semi-circular stages.

character could be radically altered according to the performance, and where alternating and parallel productions could take place. After considering aircraft hangars and other structures, no adequate existing building could be found in the Berlin area, nor suitable sites for the alternative proposal—a new industrial shed. At that point the Berlin Senate was persuaded of the viability of purchasing for conversion to a theatre the former Universum cinema, a highly interesting architectural monument of the Modern Movement, built in 1927–31 by Erich Mendelsohn during his productive period in Germany just before the rise to power of the National Socialist Party. The building is situated in Lehniner Platz at the upper end of Kurfürstendamm,

and originally formed part of a complex which included a theatre, cabaret, hotel and apartment block and which became an artistic and theatrical focus in pre-war Berlin, and a centre for film and exhibitions just after the Second World War. Damaged in the war, the building was later crudely converted into two cinemas, so that much of the original interior had been damaged.

Because of the condition of the original cinema, the entire interior could be gutted to convert the building to the needs of the Schaubühne. A new basilica-like single volume was then constructed inside, almost filling the entire original shell. This enormous rectangular box has a semi-circular apse at one end, and is constructed of stark, board-marked in-situ concrete, with no intermediate columns, and with holes cast in the wall at one metre intervals for supporting sets. A demountable ceiling grid—which can be walked upon as an access deck— conceals lighting, ventilation and hoist beams with rolling pulley equipment. The space can be divided into three by means of heavy steel doors which retract into the

The restored exterior of the former cinema. The new lettering is in the style of the original.

Set for Shakespeare's *Hamlet*.

Set for the *Agamemnon* by Aeschylus.

Set for *La Dispute* by **Marivaux**.

floor when not in use. These provide fire separation of one and a half hours at 1000°C and an acoustic reduction of about 60 decibels. This gives the option of using either the large volume (sections A + B + C), or the two-section arrangement A + B or B + C, or the three separate sections A, B, C. The spaces can be used in parallel, enabling, for instance, a set to be retained while a touring company uses one of the other spaces, or they can be used simultaneously. The movable partitions and their storage were the greatest single design problem to be overcome, as well as the most expensive single element in the building. Continuous lighting and sound mixing galleries extend along the sides of the auditorium at high level.

Within this primary structural box, the entire floor area is divided into seventy-eight 7m by 3m (23ft by 10ft) hydraulic platforms, floored in Oregon pine, which are capable of supporting 1500 kg/sq.m. These can be lowered up to 3m (10ft) downwards from the entrance level, enabling the topography of the floor to be infinitely variable, and to achieve virtually any form of theatrical arrangement—historical or experimental—of stage, platform, apron, seating rake, tower or terrain. The seating arrangements may range from a tiny space for 50 seats within the semi-circular apse, to an auditorium for 2000 spectators.

Over the 'rough topography' formed by the movable floor sections, a 'detailed topography' is then laid, consisting of lightweight, adjustable height platforms, six per floor section, which can be easily dismantled, moved and stacked as required. Each platform is designed to take a row of four seats—simple black tubular steel chairs which lock together.

Perhaps more than any other theatre in Germany, the entirely neutral and totally adaptable 'primitive' structure provided here, giving the basic tools of space and technology, provides the director with complete freedom to manipulate and integrate the actors and audience. It is important to note that the concept for the building was only possible through a general relaxation (in return for adequate exiting and other precautions) of normal safety and fire requirements. This is with respect to furnishings, stage props and sets, and to the various uses, seating arrangements and simultaneous operation of the theatre spaces. This dispensation gives the necessary production freedom and enables any desired relationship of the acting and spectator areas within the given space. German theatres normally must receive dispensation through lengthy authorization processes for any deviation from stipulated uses, as well as any change to the predetermined routes of egress within the auditorium.

In plan the theatre is offset to one side of the central axis of the Mendelsohn outer shell, and the apse and the curved end of the building are therefore nonconcentric. The transitional zone in between contains a long foyer, a bar and a restaurant, all clad in sleek metal finishes, reflecting in a contemporary form the restrained elegance of the 1920s interior, and completing the link with the original artistic character of Lehniner Platz.

Queen Elizabeth II Theatre, Winchester

Owner: Winchester College

Architects: Edward Cullinan Architects

Theatre consultant: Tim Foster

Structural engineers: Felix J. Samuely & Partners

Quantity surveyors: Stern & Woodford

Main contractor: Mason & Co. (Winchester) Ltd

Opened: 1982

Cost: £140,947

Primary use: educational drama

Seats: 250

Furthest balcony seat from stage front: 11m (36ft)

Proscenium opening: 8.3m (27.2ft) wide and 4.7m (15.5ft) high

Stage: width 11.5m (38ft), depth 7m (23ft) from pit to cyclorama wall (variable)

Volume: 1800 cub.m (63,560 cub.ft)

Reverberation time: 0.9 sec. at middle frequencies with full audience (estimate)

This is a simple school theatre converted from a redundant brick gymnasium built in 1880, possibly designed by William Butterfield. There was a fencing gallery at one end and changing rooms alongside; the gymnasium itself had often been used as a drama workshop in the past. A new entrance with steps and double doors was formed through the gable end of the building, which faces onto a previously little-used garden court with a circular driveway. This leads to a small foyer with the theatre beyond. The interior retains the original brick walls and robust exposed roof trusses. Steeply

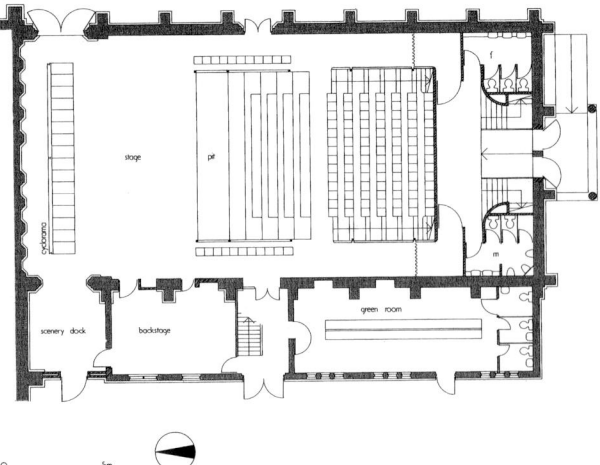

Ground floor plan. The raked seating connects with the upper gallery. Note the pit in the existing floor.

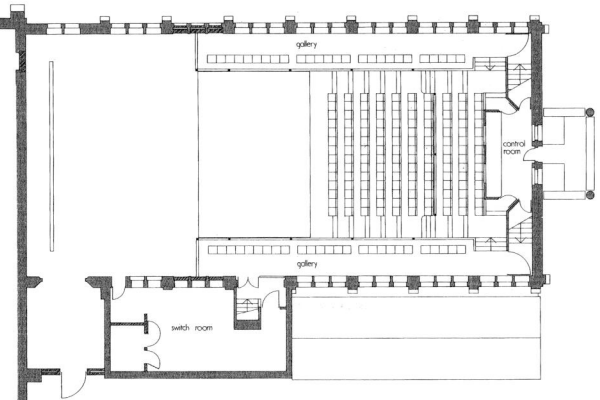

Upper gallery level plan.

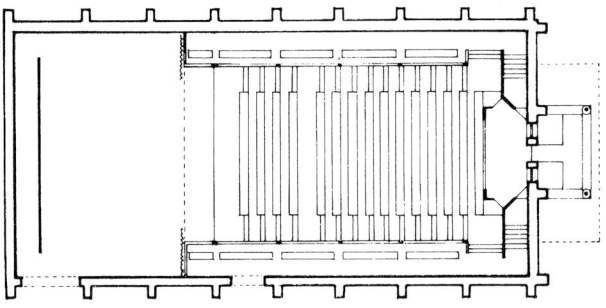

Proscenium or end stage layout, with seating units filling the forestage area.

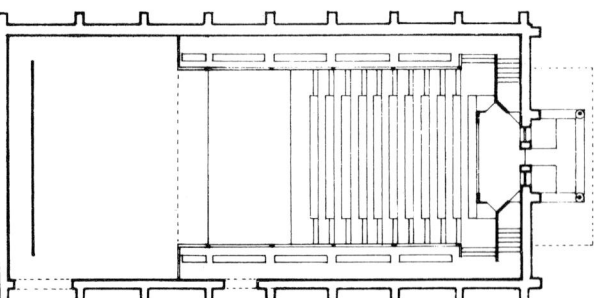

Proscenium stage with orchestra pit, rostrum units removed from pit.

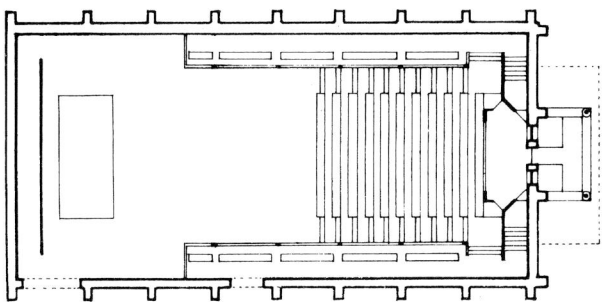

Pit infilled with rostrum units to form the maximum size stage.

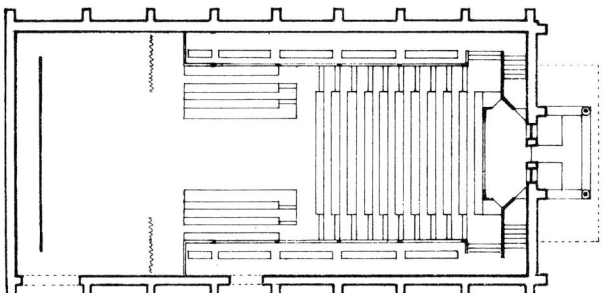

Thrust stage format with sideways seating.

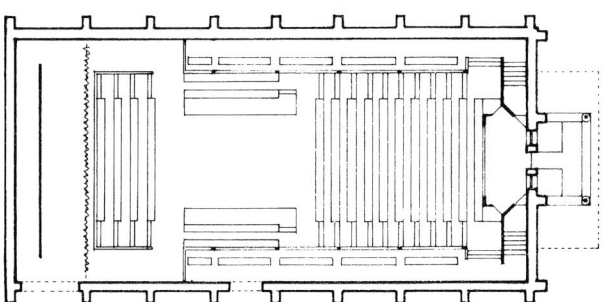

Seating units added to form a theatre-in-the-round.

Perspective section. Note the adaptable pit, shown filled with four rows of seats, and also the cyclorama wall. The 'Juliet balcony' to the extreme right can be used for outdoor performances.

raked stalls seating springs from the old gymnasium floor level to connect with newly inserted side galleries at the upper level. This layout, necessary for good sightlines particularly when the acting area is extended as a thrust towards the seating, creates a kind of hybrid between the 'courtyard' theatre form with a more or less flat floor, and the conventional raked theatre with an end stage.

The stage is simply the original floor level of the gymnasium, defined by a pedimented arch to the profile of the roof trusses. A white cyclorama wall to the rear of the stage also creates a cross-over passage for actors. In addition, there is provision for suspending scenery, and scaffold bars are attached to the underside of the roof trusses to give a broad choice of lighting angles. The forestage area can be adapted to several different formats. A large pit is cut out of the original floor, which can be used for an orchestra or for a forward extension of the seating, or—with a smaller orchestra—for both, all within the proscenium arrangement. It can be filled with a thrust stage, or it can be completely covered over with rostrum units to form a dance floor. With movable seating units, a thrust stage with sideways seating can be created, and with seating at the rear, a theatre-in-the-round. It is also waterproofed so that it can be filled with water for theatrical effects.

The side galleries, accessible both from the seating rake and from the foyer, also connect directly with the green rooms which occupy the former changing rooms, to allow actors to enter or leave through the audience. The galleries also connect with an external 'Juliet balcony' over the front entrance. This is sheltered by a very large overhanging gable formed as an extension of the existing ridge of the building, creating a monumental entrance porch 'in the historic manner of temples and theatres'. The balcony and entrance steps are intended for outdoor performances, bands, banners and preproduction gimmicks.

The theatre will eventually form part of a fine arts centre which will include two other existing buildings, and the newly created entrance court will be part of a series of routes to be established between the historic meadow and Kingsgate Street with its ancient walls.

The theatre has simple bench seating and galleries. At the bottom left, the rostrum units can be seen extending into the pit.

Villanueva Concert Hall, Prado Museum, Madrid

Owner: The Prado Museum

Architect: José Garcia de Paredes (collaborators: J. Lafuente, M. Cuadrado, I. Prieto, architects, and Gustavo Torner, painter)

Acoustic consultant: Garcia BBM

Structural engineer: Julio Martinez Calzón

Mechanical and electrical engineers: Acoysa & Tecelsa

Main contractor: Cubiertas & MZOV

Opened: 1984

Cost: pts 155 million

Uses: chamber music, recitals, lectures, conferences

Seats: total 402, main floor 323, gallery 79

Stage: 40 sq.m (430 sq.ft)

Volume: 2300 cub.m (81,190 cub.ft)

Reverberation time: 1.55 sec. at middle frequencies with full audience

This elegantly restrained and timelessly classical small concert and conference hall is inserted into the ground floor of Juan de Villanueva's Prado Museum, on the axis of the great central entrance portico and rotunda vestibule, directly beneath the famous Velazquez Room. The hall was seen as vital to the cultural and educational role of a modern museum; however, the architect's delicate task was to create a contemporary intervention which avoided pastiche yet which represented the neoclassical spirit of the building and also did not destroy elements of the original architect's work.

Villanueva's plan of 1785 for this area beyond the main entrance portico was for a double height rectangular galleried hall or *Salón de Juntas* (meeting room). A later (undated) design altered this to a more narrow hall with a semi-circular apse, of which only the foundations were laid when the architect died in 1811. The area remained an open court until it was eventually enclosed as the 'Sala Reina Isabel', by Narciso P. Colomer in 1853, creating a gallery level with a central light-well. In 1890 Francisco Jareño closed the central opening by inserting a steel-framed floor, creating the present Velazquez Room on the upper level. The new auditorium is thus built within the walls of Narciso P. Colomer, on Villanueva's foundations, with the ceiling being Jareño's floor.

In the new hall, twin columns and roof beams, shaped to diffuse sound, replace a colonnade which previously supported Jareño's floor structure above. The columns

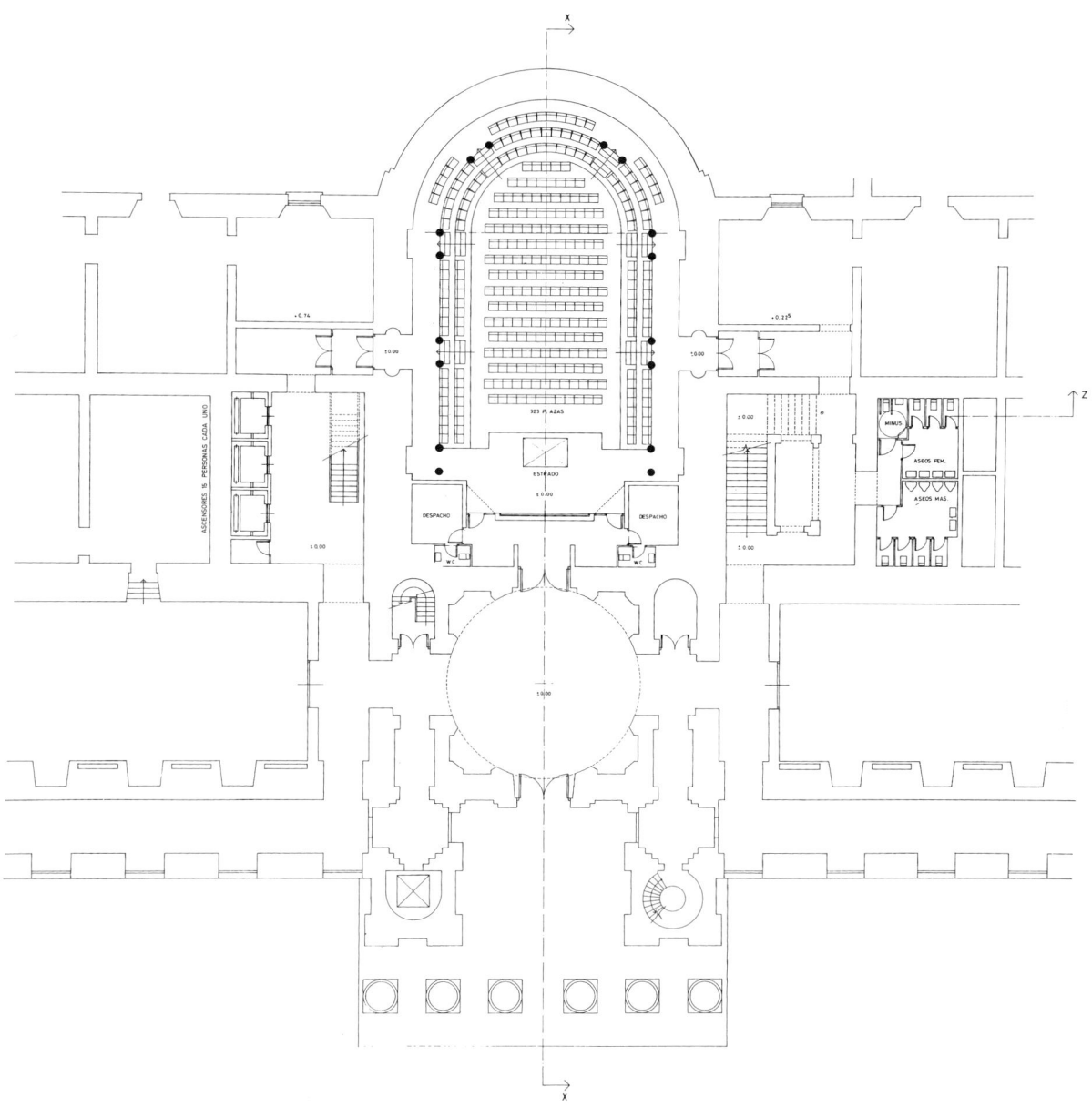

Ground floor plan. The new hall sits within the apsidal space conceived by Villanueva around 1811, which remained unexecuted when he died and was subsequently altered several times.

continue around the apse along with a balcony which recalls, despite the lower ceiling height, Villanueva's original idea for a lofty, galleried room. Five large windows in the apse, also in the original scheme, have also been opened up; these are double-glazed with a black-out system. The interior is understated and deliberately austere. The entire stage surround, the cylindrical columns and the gallery fronts are clad in Colmenar stone. Upholstery is avoided for reasons of acoustics and durability, and the seating is shaped from palisander plywood. The hard, sound-reflecting floor finish is of matching-coloured linoleum. Groups of translucent spherical light fixtures mark the main lines of architectural structure, and additional lighting is provided over the stage.

The expected orientation of the hall, with a sequential entry along the central axis, is reversed, as the stage faces the museum's front portico, with audience access through existing side entrances. This is to avoid windows in the apse being behind the stage, with resulting glare, and also to relate the stage to the backstage facilities: dressing rooms on the ground floor, and radio, television, lighting, recording and translation booths upstairs. Either side of the central axis outside the new concert hall, Villanueva's design of 1785 suggests a pair of staircases, the right hand of which was eventually built by Pedro Muguruza in 1924. Part of the present conversion involved solving the circulation problems that the large number of visitors—unthinkable in Villanueva's day—have now created inside the museum. It was decided to complete the symmetry by installing three 15 person elevators in the location intended for the second staircase. The concert hall and its related areas can be used independently of the museum, which can be closed off when required.

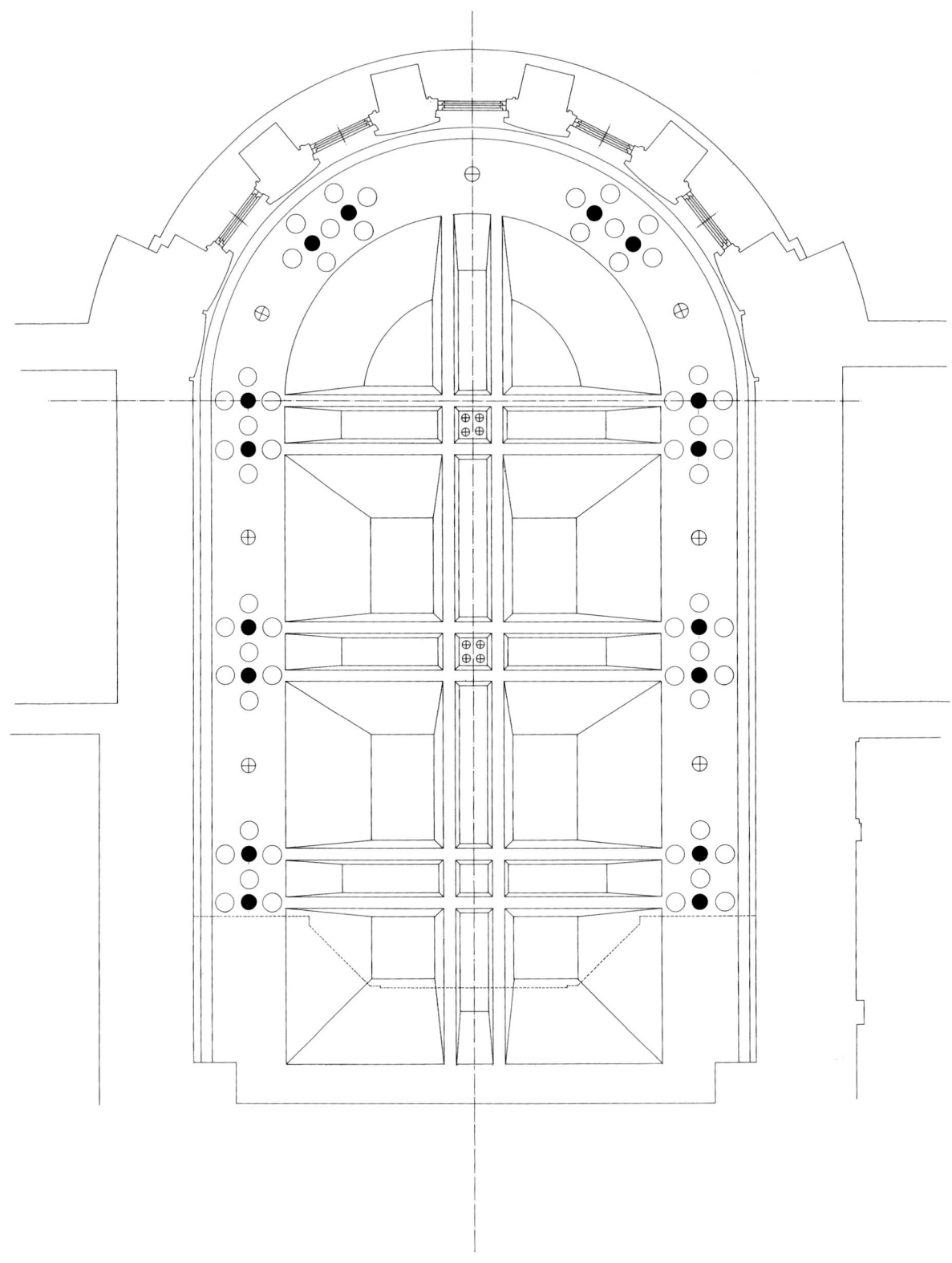

Reflected ceiling plan. New ceiling beams sit on twin
columns and are profiled for the optimal distribution
of reflected sound.

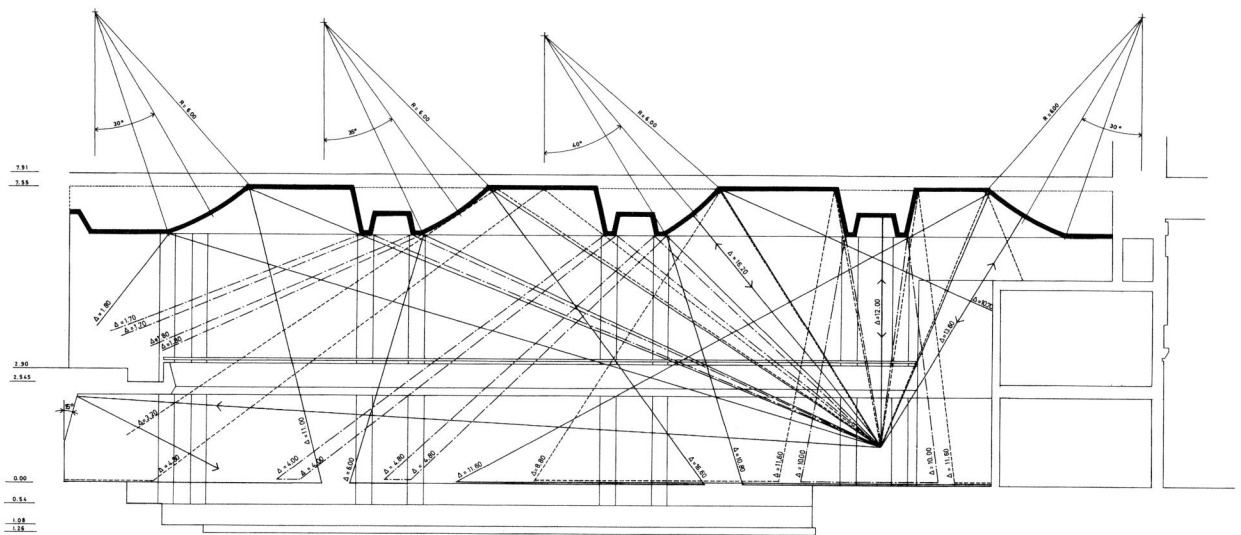

Sections with reflected sound pattern.

Interior of the auditorium. Note the amphitheatre seating on the main floor.

Interior looking towards the stage. The hall is
orientated so that the stage is related to the backstage
facilities.

CHAPTER 7

Mobile and Outdoors

Short Life, Loose Fit

Some theatre companies in recent decades have taken the view that conventional auditorium structures are theatrically inhibiting, and have turned to holding performances out of doors, in make-shift accommodation, or in temporary, mobile structures. Along with some symphony orchestras, they felt that traditional buildings give a sense of enshrinement and inaccessibility and that it was necessary to 'take the performance to the audience'. On a practical level also, ideas for mobile theatres arose out of permanent theatres being inadequate for touring companies, or simply unavailable, in many areas.

Architecturally, the most basic form of drama is simple street theatre, the origins of which range from medieval troupes of strolling players to elaborate public pageants and parades, royal entrances and religious festivals. The architectural and scenographic preparation for such events may be minimal, or there may be elaborate transformations of the existing urban setting. In the past, enormous temporary architectural structures were sometimes erected, as for example when the sixteenth-century Archduke Ernst of Austria entered Antwerp, for which occasion a great 'Theatre of Peace' was said to have been constructed.

Mobile theatre structures have their origins in travelling sideshows, circuses, and the booth theatres of the Middle Ages. These would normally have used canvas tents, and carts for transportation. However, 'temporary' theatres could be more permanent than this. On the royal estate at Balmoral there is a demountable private theatre and ballroom which was commissioned by the Prince Consort from the Eagle Foundry of Manchester at the Great Exhibition of 1851. The building took a week to construct, and it has 16 cast iron columns with foliated capitals, wrought iron roof trusses, and galvanized corrugated iron walls and roof. Today's temporary, mobile theatres, typically with about a ten year life, may be tensile or inflated structures, or perhaps be enclosed by a geodesic dome, using plastic-coated skins and with sophisticated structural joints and junctions. The trucks that transport the structure can double as backstage accommodation, and it has even been proposed that they could form structural anchors for the tent.

Another architectural solution is the idea of a floating theatre. The last project of the architect Louis Kahn was for a floating concert hall, the construction of which was completed in time for the bicentenary of American Independence. This comprises a bandshell for the orchestra on the deck of a steel barge, which plays to its audience on the riverbank. Also on board is a 100-seat children's theatre. The Venice carnival traditionally used floating structures, and in 1979 the Italian architect Aldo Rossi built a floating 200 to 250 seat 'Teatro del Mondo' as part of the Venice Biennale.

Temporary theatres that were adaptable to individual sites or performance requirements were especially popular in the 1960s, particularly as student projects. At the time, some advanced architects rejected conventional buildings altogether in favour of a highly-serviced architecture of total flexibility, mobility—and fun. Many of the ideas for the new architecture were in themselves highly theatrical, using elements such as balloons, tents, pylons, movable escalators, cranes and other variable components. Examples of projects are Peter Cook's Plug-in City of 1964, Instant City of 1968 and Ideas Circus of 1969 by the Archigram group, and the series of Fun Palace projects of 1961 and later, devised by the theatre director Joan Littlewood and the architect Cedric Price. Since that era, some theatre companies, such as the Bubble Theatre Company, London, have continued to require a high degree of mobility and adaptability, while others since the 1960s have settled into permanent accommodation. Interestingly, the Royal Exchange Theatre Company, Manchester (see Chapter 6), commissioned a demountable replica of its permanent theatre for touring use.

There is, however, a continuing strong tradition, at least in North America, for outdoor musical concerts, where again there are various possible degrees of permanence and enclosure. Concert facilities may range from the permanent music pavilion in the tradition of the classical Greek amphitheatre, to the temporary bandshell made of plastic, cardboard or canvas, erectable in city parks. Most famous in North America are the pre-Second World War examples of the Hollywood Bowl, the Chicago Symphony Orchestra's summer home at Ravinia, and the Boston Symphony Orchestra's summer home of Tanglewood Music Shed at Lennox, Massachusetts. In Great Britain there are no facilities of this sort, apart from the somewhat quaint tradition of the brass band pavilion with deckchairs in the public parks. In the eighteenth century, however, the English pleasure garden, of which music was an integral part, was an amenity that was exported to every part of Europe and beyond. Of the various large-scale events of this kind that have taken place in recent times, most have been greatly successful. For instance, in 1974, frustrated by the lack of provincial large-scale theatre facilities, the Royal Ballet hired a huge circular tent seating 1200, which toured to Plymouth, Battersea Park and Newcastle.

Open air concerts before very large audiences usually require electronic sound amplification or assisted resonance systems. However, although canvas tent structures provide no significant sound insulation from outside noise, such enclosures can substantially improve the acoustics for the sound within, compared with the open air: canvas reflects the upper frequency sound, aiding musical clarity and speech intelligibility and, for circuses, making whip cracks especially effective.

Festival Theatre, Caesarea

Owner: The Israeli Government Department of National Parks—Yaacov Yannai, director

Acoustical, structural and mechanical designers: George C. Izenour Associates, Inc.

Associate designer: Arnon Adar

Construction engineer: Gideon Kreiser

Supervising engineer for Department of National Parks: David Kissin

Opened: 1968

Uses: symphonic music, smaller musical groups and soloists, opera, dance and drama

Seats: 3300

Furthest seat from the stage: approximately 45m (150ft)

This Roman theatre in Israel, half way between Tel Aviv and Haifa, is one of the major buildings of the ancient maritime city of Caesarea Judea, founded by King Herod the Great in the first century BC. The theatre was excavated by an Italian team in 1958–60, and the site became used for evening performances by leading musicians. In the mid-1960s the seating was rebuilt with precast concrete units to the same profile as the original

Site photograph from the air showing ruined state of the building before restoration work began. The wall in the foreground is built of material taken from the theatre, and is a portion of a later Byzantine fortress which also incorporated the seating bank of the theatre.

Aerial photograph of the canopy in the playing position, with 95 per cent of the intended restoration complete.

seats and using rubble from the excavation as aggregate, and the stage was rebuilt in marble, with a resilient plywood finish. The concerts, however, faced almost intolerable acoustical difficulties, being for the most part events that would normally take place indoors, for besides being in the open air the theatre is adjacent to a beach with a prevailing onshore wind, carrying with it the noise of surf. The problem was overcome—without the use of electro-acoustic amplification—by constructing a shell structure around the stage, to enable the musicians to hear each other and to collect and redirect the sound energy into the auditorium. The archaeologists had

stipulated, however, that the shell must be removable and stored out of sight when not in use, as the site is a popular tourist attraction by day.

The solution to these difficult requirements was to design a three-legged canopy mounted on four flange wheels. When not required, the entire structure is winched sideways to stage right on two tracks, one set in the stage, the other set in a drainage ditch behind the stage, for about 100m (330ft) into the revetment of a low hill adjacent to the excavation. The canopy was built in Israel from imported weathering steel. The sound-reflecting membrane is constructed of 18 gauge dampened sheet steel—a mass of 10–15kg per sq.m (about 2–3lb per sq.ft) being desirable for efficient energy reflection in acoustical shells. The supporting skeleton is a triangulated kite-like space frame built of 40mm and

Aerial view of the Festival Theatre, Caesarea.

The New York Philharmonic Orchestra conducted by
Leonard Bernstein on opening night.

Plan of the Festival Theatre seating bank and concert
shell.

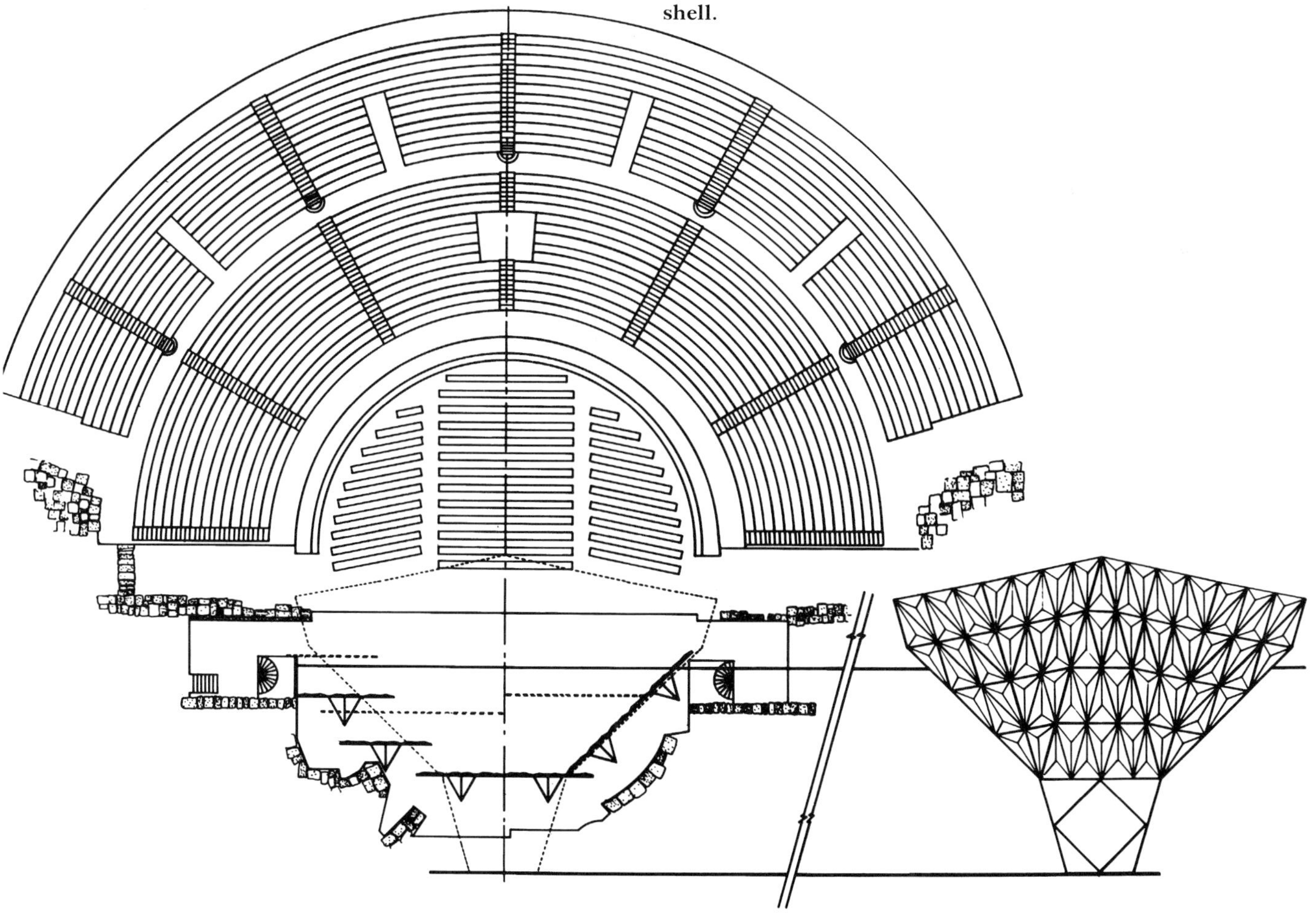

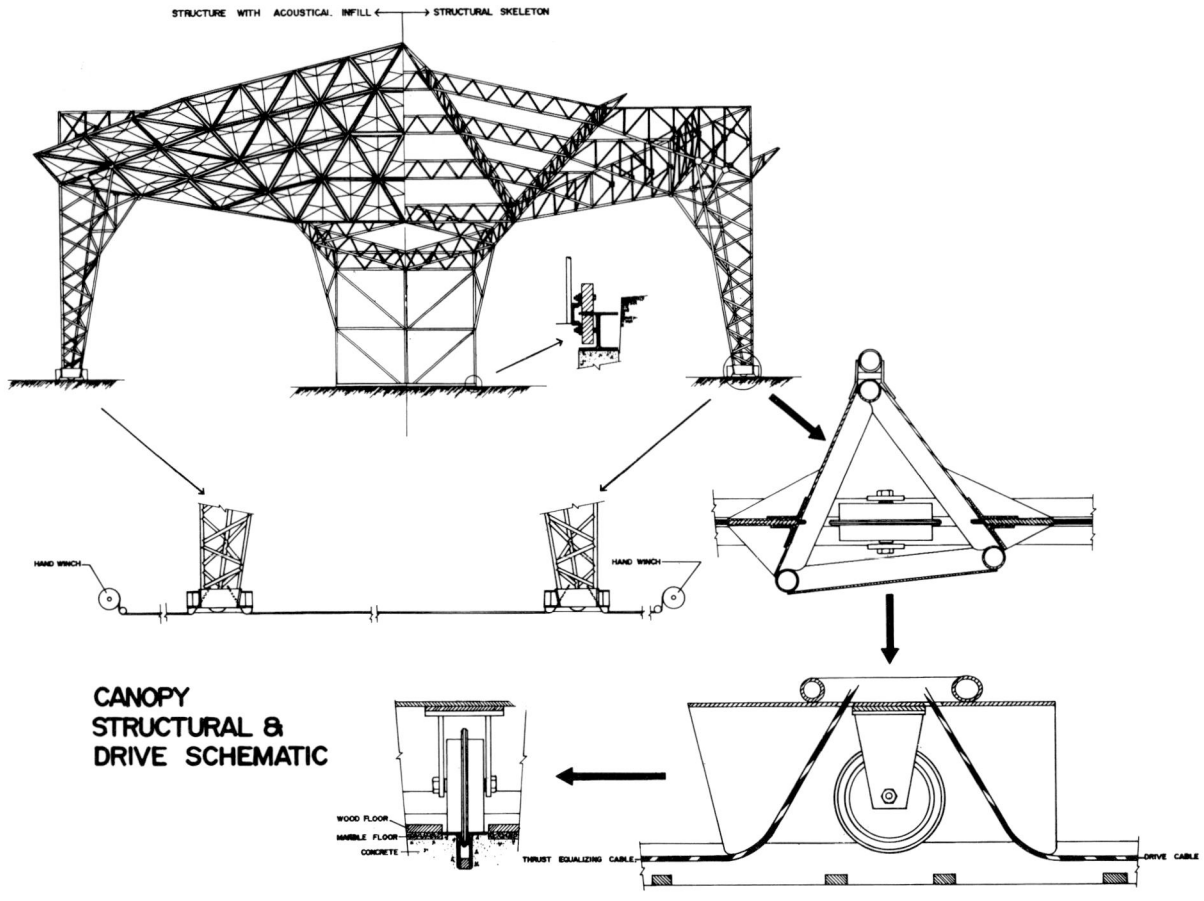

STRUCTURE WITH ACOUSTICAL INFILL ←——→ STRUCTURAL SKELETON

CANOPY
STRUCTURAL &
DRIVE SCHEMATIC

The structuring of the canopy and method of
movement.

50mm (1.6in and 2in) steel pipe. The sides and rear of the
canopy are enclosed by pivoting wall units—six in all—
similarly structured and infilled, which can form either a
sound-reflecting surface around the orchestra or a wing
stage for dramatic presentations. The sidewalls weigh a
total of 7 tons and the canopy weighs 22 tons. The shape
of the canopy was designed from ray diagrams: the sound
was concentrated within a 90 degree spread, and because
of the steep seating rake, the direct and reflected sound
arrives to all seats within 30 milliseconds. The canopy
was inaugurated at the final concert of the 1968 Caesarea
festival, with the New York Philharmonic conducted by
Leonard Bernstein in a performance of Mahler's Fifth
Symphony. The occasion was a success, the sound
energy arriving in the audience having been approximately doubled compared with the previous conditions,
while the musicians could hear themselves, without
electro-acoustic amplification.

The New Bubble Theatre Project, London

Client: The Bubble Theatre Company

Architect: Pentagram Design, Ron Herron, with
Peter Rice

Designed: 1977–78 (unbuilt)

Estimated cost: £100,000

Uses: mobile theatre

Seats: 350

Floor area: 416 sq.m (4480 sq.ft)

The New Bubble was designed as an inflatable structure
for the Bubble Theatre Company, a professional mobile
theatre group of about ten players founded in 1972 and
funded by the Greater London Arts Association and the
Greater London Council. It holds workshops, informal
performances and various events in summer (and, since
1984, all year) in parks and other temporary venues. Its
aim is to introduce theatre to London neighbourhoods
where permanent theatre premises do not exist.

The mobile theatre was to replace an existing smaller
tent structure, using the principle of the pneumatic tyre.
This provides a rigid freestanding structure which is
rapidly demounted and transported. The basis of the
structure is a series of three primary high-pressure ribs
which create a semicircular internal space with a 16m
(52.5ft) span with no additional means of internal or
external support. These are supplemented by smaller
ribs that form half domes to enclose the ends. The areas
between the ribs are infilled by low-pressure air cushions.

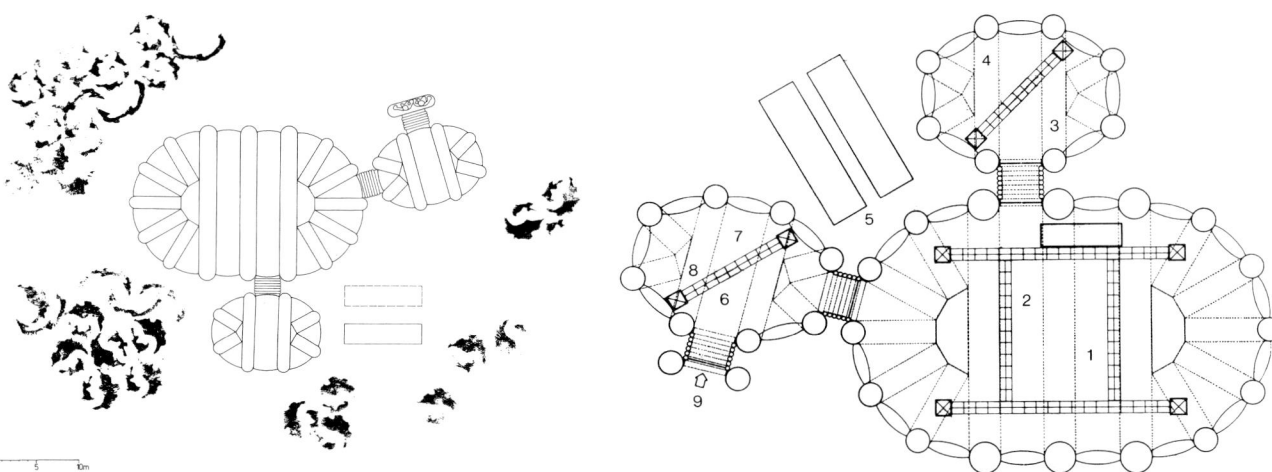

Roof plan.

Plan. Key: 1 theatre, 2 stage, 3 dressing room,
4 green room, 5 trailers, 6 display, 7 bar, 8 tickets,
9 public entrance

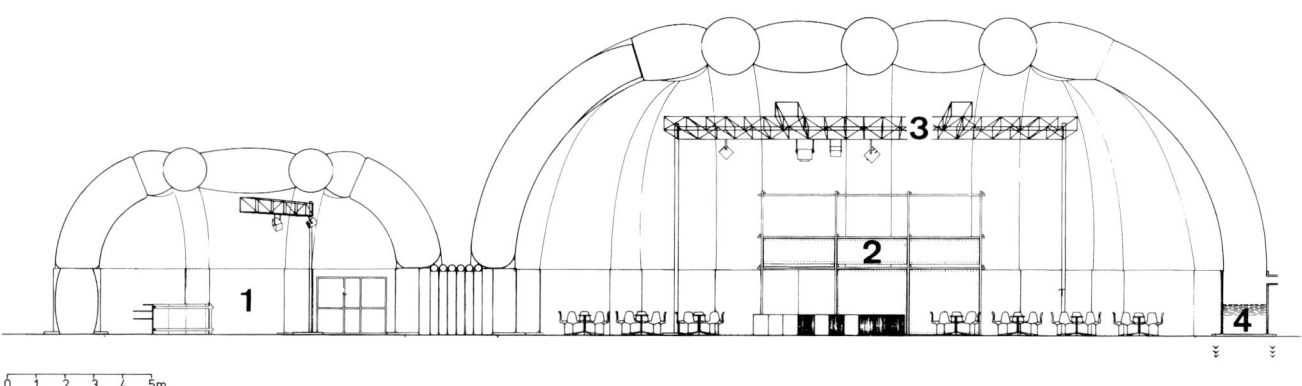

Section. Key: 1 foyer, 2 theatre, 3 lighting rigs, 4 solid
anchors staked into the ground

Exterior view.

Two identical but smaller structures form the foyer/bar and the dressing/green room, which can be attached to the main structure at any point. All the ribs and air cushions break down for ease of handling and transportation, and are joined on site by nylon zips with straps and buckles. The only extra requirement was for a method of anchoring the structure to the ground. For this, the ribs are enclosed in solid tubs which are anchored by conventional stakes. The structure can be inflated by six air pumps in about 30 minutes. Two of the pumps then operate intermittently to maintain air pressure. A blue and yellow neoprene-coated nylon fabric was selected as the main material, which was resistant to flame, abrasion, puncturing, creasing, tearing, stretching and loss of colour.

Seating is in a table and chair arrangement to give an intimate cabaret-style theatre atmosphere. To comply with safety regulations it is designed as units of small circular tables with five attached swivel chairs each. The stage is of small hexagonal units which can be fitted together into various shapes and sizes. These can be placed anywhere, as fire exits can be located between any two ribs and therefore do not require fixed gangways.

Demountable extension project to the Lyric Theatre, Hammersmith

Client: Lyric Theatre Company

Architects: Ron Herron Associates

Designed: 1982–83 (unbuilt)

Estimated cost: £150,000

Uses: Rehearsal, experimental theatre, conferences, wedding receptions, etc.

Seats: 200–300

Floor area: 20.3m by 8m (67ft by 26ft), 162.4 sq.m (1748 sq.ft)

In contrast to the mobile New Bubble project, the design for the Lyric, Hammersmith, was for a permanent location but, because of statutory regulations, it had to be a temporary, demountable structure. In practice its life would be limited by the fabric—perhaps 15 to 20 years—though this could be renewed. The site was a terrace at the side of the Lyric Theatre. The brief was to make a space for rehearsal and experimental productions for audiences of 200–300, which could also be used for other events such as wedding receptions, conferences, a Saturday market and an extension to the foyer restaurant.

The structure is a light steel frame with an integral lighting grid and a raised, serviced floor. It is clad with removable zipped-in inflatable cushions. The side cushions can be raised to make an open sided structure for summer use. The steel frame is extended vertically to form lighting columns and to provide support for 'sails' which are intended to prevent rain drumming into the cushions and to add the possibility of changing and adapting the interior space for the range of uses envisaged so that 'theatre' becomes an integral part of the architecture—the architecture of change.

Plan. Key: 1 zip-in inflatable cladding, 2 steel nets, 3 lighting poles, 4 metal steps and ramp, 5 interchangeable floor panels, 6 lighting rig, 7 electrical duct, 8 mobile screens, 9 plug-in mobile servery

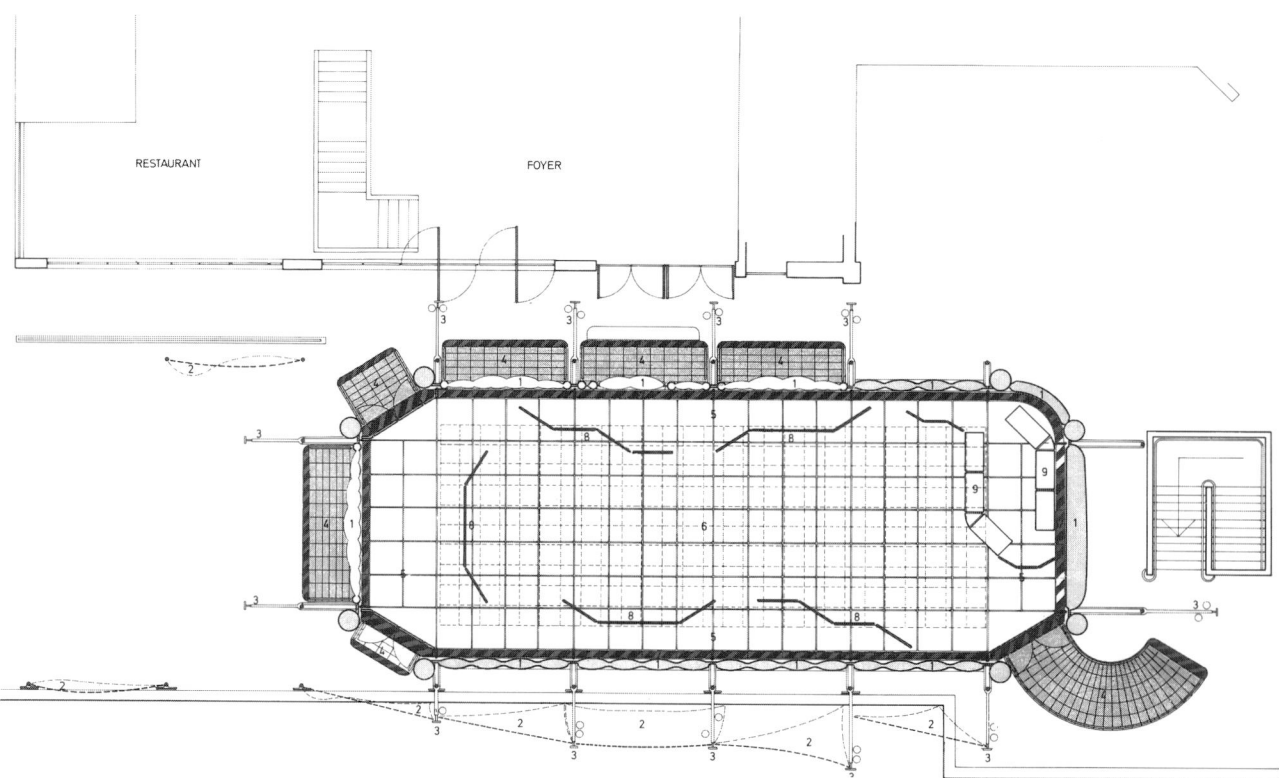

RESTAURANT   FOYER

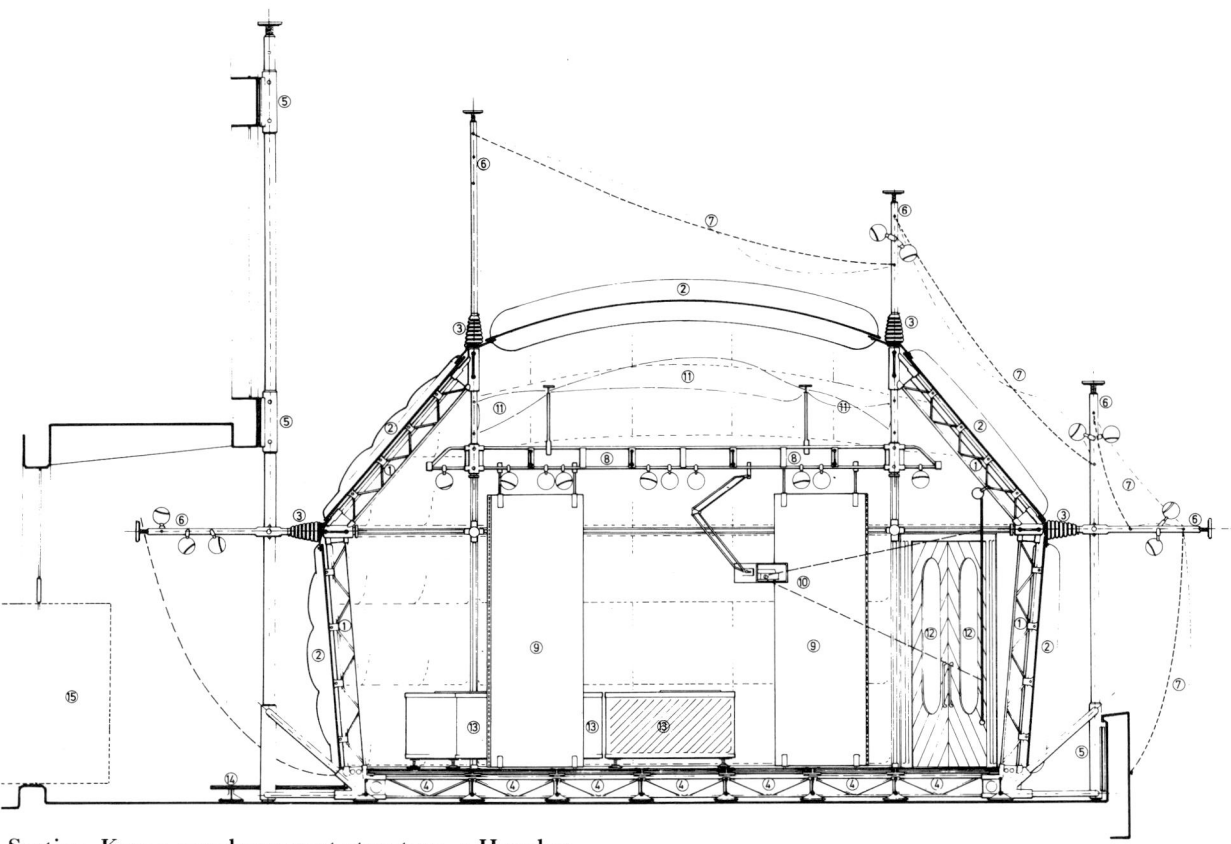

Section. Key: 1 panels support structure, 2 Hypalon inflatable panels, 3 neoprene seal, 4 interchangeable floor panels, 5 steel anchor structure, 6 external lighting poles, 7 external netting, 8 lighting rig, 9 set screens, 10 projection facilities, 11 acoustic baffles, 12 entrance doors, 13 mobile servery units, 14 metal grip step, 15 new doors to foyer

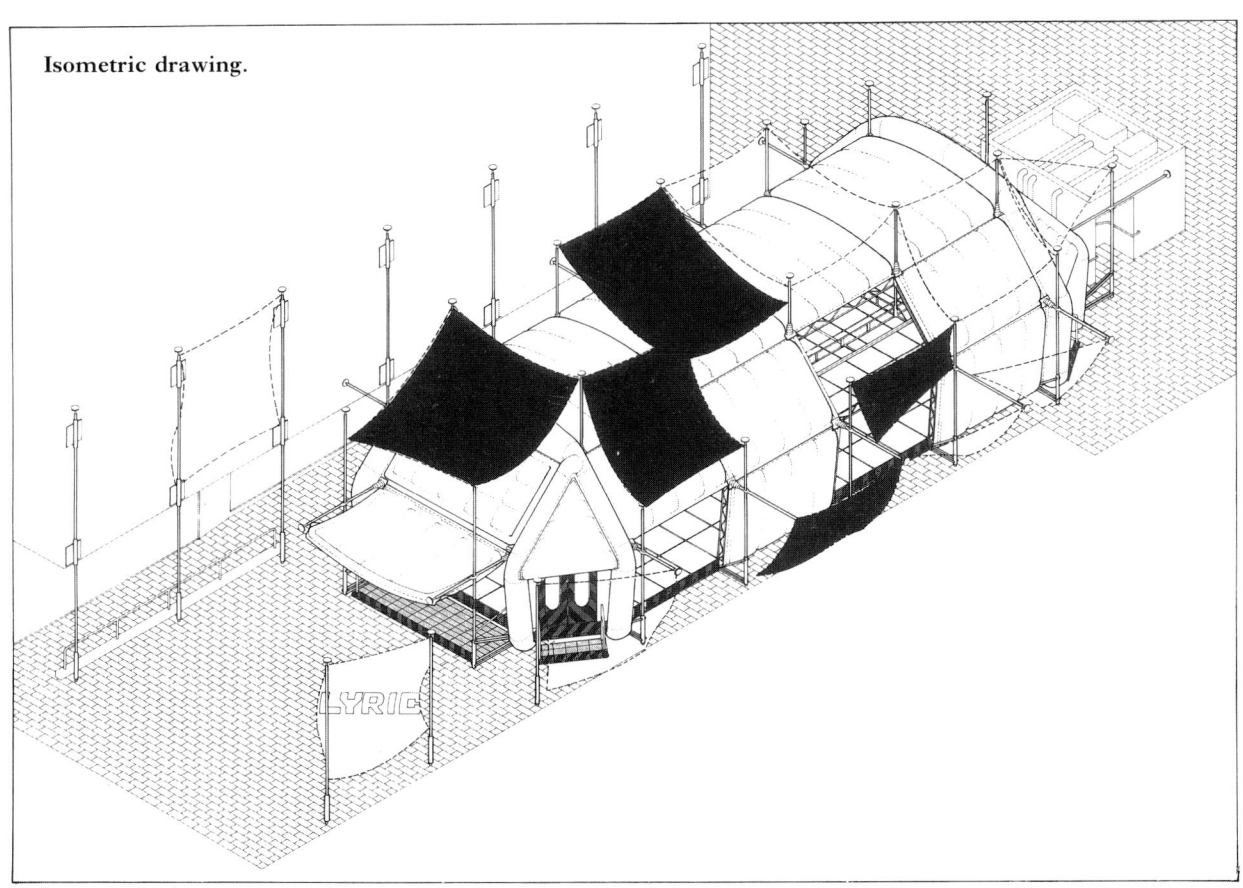

Isometric drawing.

Section: reception format.

Section: rehearsal mode.

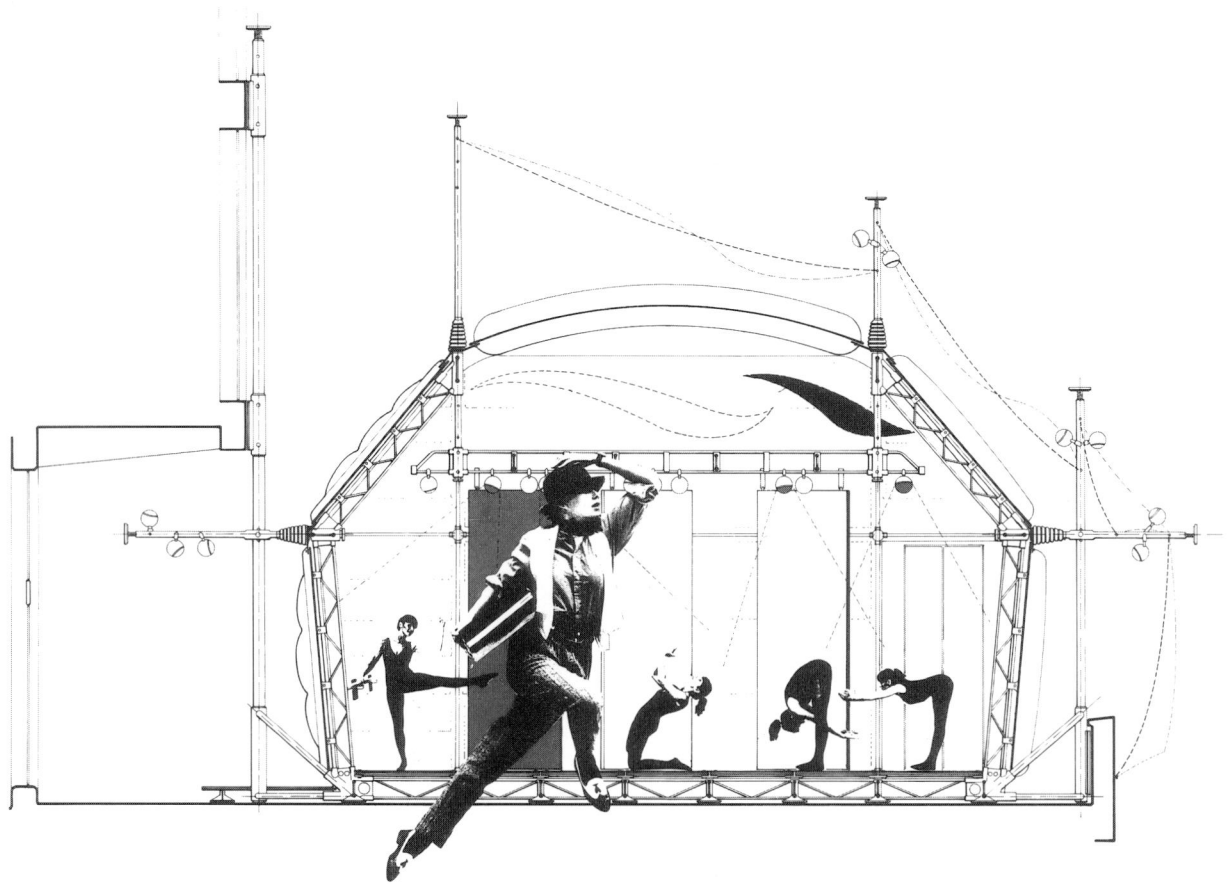

Concord Music Pavilion, California

Owner: City of Concord, California

Architects: Frank O. Gehry & Associates

Acoustic consultant: Jaffe Acoustics Inc.

Structural engineer: Garfinkel & Kurily

Mechanical engineers: John Kerr & Associates

Electrical engineers: Irving Schwartz & Associates

Main contractor: F. A. Lathrop Construction Co.

Opened: 1975

Cost: $30,600,000

Primary uses: symphony, opera, ballet, rock, jazz, school performances, graduations, meetings

Seats: 3500 under canopy, 6000 seating on lawn

Furthest seat from stage front: 29m (95ft)

Stage: diameter 17m (55.5ft), area 225 sq.m (2420 sq.ft)

Concord began to be a musical centre in 1969 with the inauguration of a summer festival of jazz which took place in a neighbourhood park. The Jazz Festival grew in reputation and popularity until it became clear that a permanent home was called for, though the pavilion now serves a variety of purposes. The circular amphitheatre is set in a bowl-shaped lawn against the background of Mount Diablo in the San Francisco Bay area. The stage is offset from the centre, beneath a vast square roof canopy. This spans between the backstage wall and the rear of the seating where it is supported on two giant columns. From the roof is hung a circular catwalk, control booth, lighting grid and an array of reflecting panels which return sound to the orchestra and, on the periphery of the array, direct sound outwards to the audience. A further 6000 listeners can sit on grass slopes which surround three sides of the arena.

While such an audience capacity is excessive by present-day standards for conventional indoor concert

Site plan.

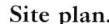

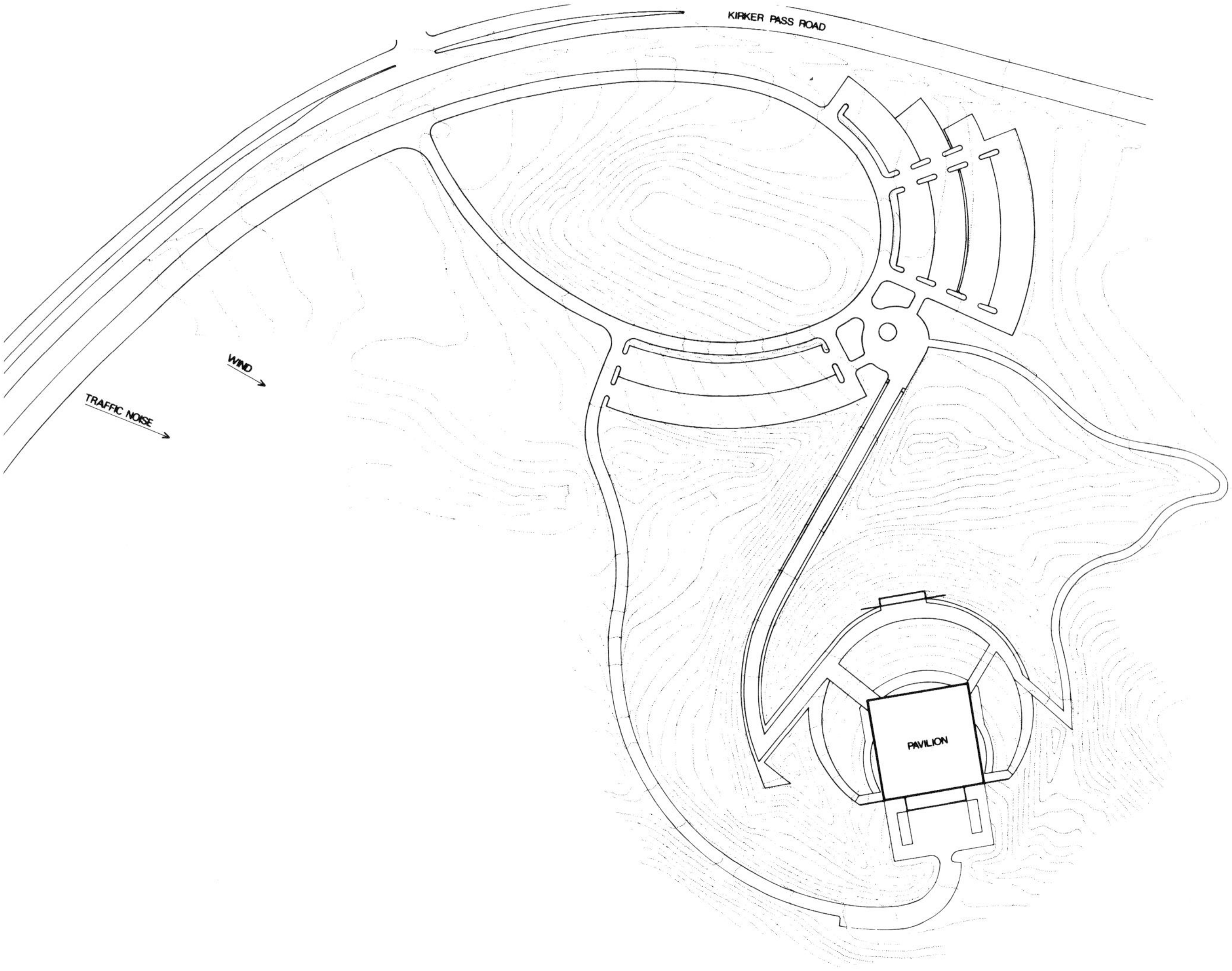

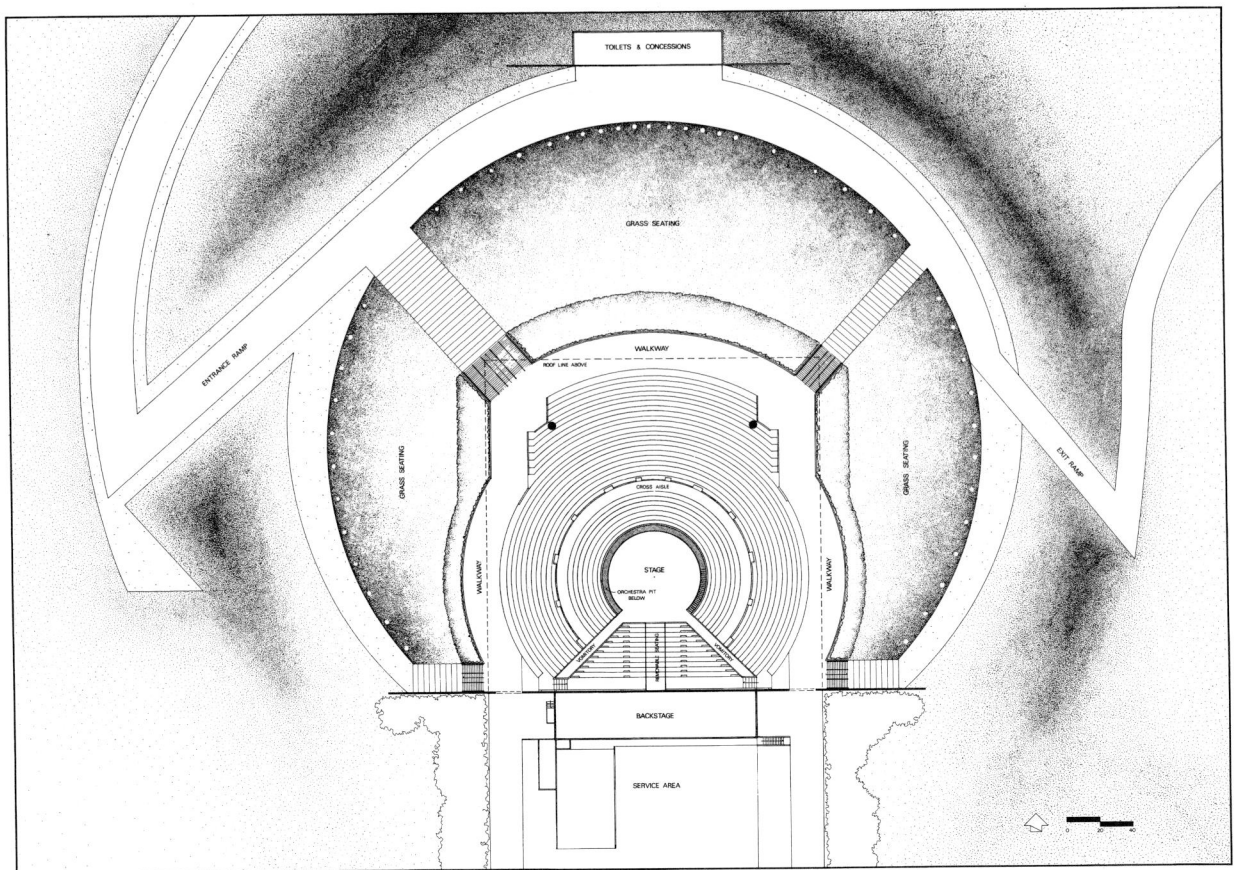

Bowl plan.

Section looking south.

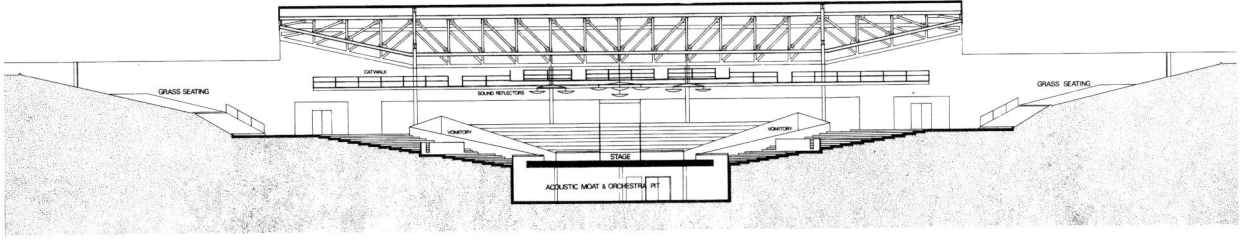

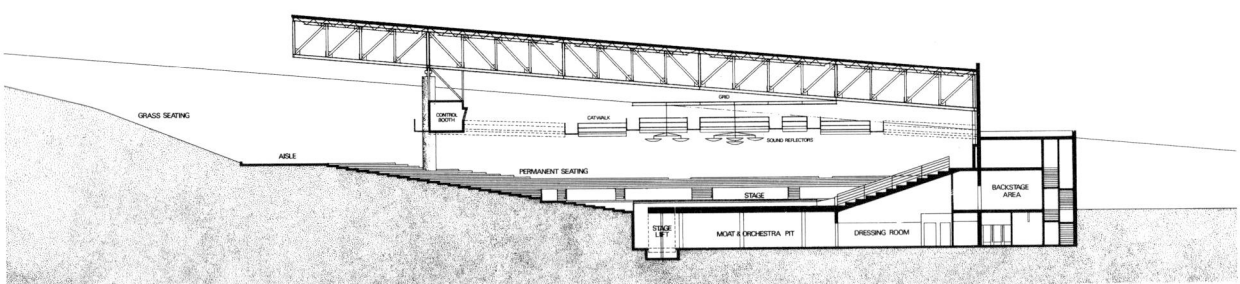

Section looking east.

halls, the surround plan accommodates this number without extreme visual remoteness from the orchestra. However, the centralized location of the orchestra, on the other hand, provides no opportunity for a shell to reinforce its sound energy, and of course there are no sidewalls to generate some reverberant warmth to the orchestra's tone. To help compensate, the acoustician devised a reverberation chamber beneath the stage whereby the vibration of the orchestra platform induces energy within the chamber. This is then reintroduced into the auditorium as late-arriving low frequency sound through an opening or 'moat' around the platform. (This device was reapplied at Boettcher Hall, Denver—see page 48).

The grassy slopes of the bowl form an extension to the auditorium, where a further 6000 listeners may sit.

The 3000 seat auditorium, although requiring a sound reinforcement system, is relatively intimate for its capacity.

Around the stage is the acoustical moat, which is designed to introduce low frequency reverberant energy into the open air auditorium.

In addition, an assisted resonance system was installed, with a series of frequency-selective microphones and resonators around the catwalk, and loudspeakers above the canopy. Articulating loudspeakers are also used for soloists and, in addition, five loudspeakers are mounted along the edge of the roof to provide time delayed sound reinforcement for the listeners outside. The difficulty of providing for a vast audience, and without a conventional rigid auditorium enclosure, necessitates sound amplification and makes a wholly natural sound impossible to achieve. This is one case where the designer, 'having broken one rule, might as well break others'.

Royal National Eisteddfod Mobile Theatre, Wales

Owner: The Royal National Eisteddfod of Wales

Architect: John Dangerfield Associates

Structural engineers: Buro Happold

Theatre consultant: John Franklin Robbins

Fabricator: Clyde Canvas Ltd

Completed: 1983

Cost: £150,000

Building area: 900 sq.m (9688 sq.ft)

Principal use: drama

Seats: proscenium/end stage 406, thrust stage 348, theatre-in-the-round 540

Furthest seat from the stage: 15.5m (51ft) (end stage layout)

Preliminary design model of the theatre.

The exterior of the tent.

Proscenium opening: width 8m (26.25ft), height 5.0m (16.4ft)

Stage: proscenium stage 12m (39.5ft) wide, 8m (26.25ft) deep, including a 2m (6.5ft) thrust beyond the proscenium, thrust stage identical to proscenium layout but with semi-circular forestage addition, radius 4m (13ft), theatre-in-the-round, circular stage radius 4m (13ft)

Eisteddfod means 'a session' in Welsh, and the name has been given to the national gathering of Welsh bards since at least the Middle Ages. The Royal National Eisteddfod of Wales is nowadays an arts festival that takes place annually in a different town, and a competition was held in 1982 to design a mobile theatre for it. After the competition, the brief was broadened to include the possibility of the tent being rented by theatre companies when not required for the Eisteddfod (though this has not happened to date). For it to be viable for normal productions, roughly double the original audience capacity was required, and this was achieved in the

The interior, showing the rostra being assembled to form a thrust stage.

The seating system can form a trapezoidal layout with access aisles; lighting bars span between the aluminium masts that support the tent membrane.

The tent being transported within its container. When the mobile theatre is constructed the trailer is linked to the tent by a PVC cover to become the dressing and green rooms.

winning design without radically changing the original idea and with only small changes to the plan area and headroom height. Apart from the extreme mobility and elegant simplicity of the tent structure which the engineers developed, the theatre is also interesting because it can be used in different stage configurations: end stage/proscenium, thrust stage, and theatre-in-the-round (the latter will not be attempted until the purchase of extra seating).

The enclosure is designed for a 10 year life-span—which could be extended with maintenance—and is constructed in polyester fabric, triple-coated with PVC to provide a white external skin, a blackout layer and an internal coloured lining in light red to provide a theatrical atmosphere. The membrane is supported by aluminium masts and dismantles into two three-quarter ton sections, with lifting cradles for handling by a fork lift truck. Erection and dismantling is usually carried out by local labour under the direction of the original fabricator. Installation of the tent takes one day. The tent, of course, is not good at excluding noise, but by situating it in a quiet part of the Eisteddfod field, noise levels are tolerable. Speech clarity inside is remarkably good, as the double-curved fabric surfaces reflect and diffuse the upper frequency sound efficiently. Also, there is no noise from flapping canvas, etc., as with a conventional marquee, because of the tension of the fabric (the Eisteddfod sites are often exposed to wind).

There is natural ventilation, with louvres at the mastheads, but no heating as the tent is for summer use. Electricity is provided from the mains supply. (Performances were initially in the daytime, but are now also held in the evening.) There is a suspended lighting grid over the stage, and lighting bars over the auditorium suspended between the masts. On either side of the central mast there is a platform, one for the lighting control panel and the other for a television camera. A further television camera platform is available at either side, although in practice a hand-held camera has generally been used from the aisles. (Nearly all the Eisteddfod productions here are televised and, in addition, Harlech Television (HTV) has rented the theatre for its own productions.)

The competitions proposal included simple bleacher seating, but the requirement for the larger audience capacity necessitated the development of a standard seating unit in trapezoidal bays to enable a more compact radial plan. For accommodating full length three act plays the seats were also required to be more comfortable. The stage is built of simple rostrum sections constructed from steel framing and boards. Between performance venues the stage and seating are generally stored and delivered to the part of Wales where it is required, and erected by semi-skilled local labour. The tent itself is transported in an adapted 12.2m (40ft) standard steel goods trailer, which converts during the festival into dressing and green rooms. When parked behind the theatre, the nearside face of the trailer is dropped into the horizontal position to form an additional wardrobe storage area which also becomes, with a PVC cover, a link to the main tent.

Arena Theatre, International Garden Festival, Liverpool

Owner: Merseyside Development Corporation

Architects and landscape architects: Cass Associates, Liverpool

Structural engineers: Ward, Ashcroft & Parkman, Liverpool

Services engineer: Clifford and Partners, Chester

Quantity surveyors: McGill & Partners, Liverpool

Main contractors: Norwest Holst (Projects) Ltd (managing), Tysons Ltd (construction)

Opened: 1984

Cost: £220,000

Uses: concerts and other outdoor events

Seats: 1500

Furthest seat from stage front: 25.6m (84ft)

Stage: width 17m (56ft), depth 8.5m (28ft), semi-circular

The auditorium was built as a low-budget theatre for Liverpool's International Garden Festival, to be handed over later for community use. It is a semi-circular 'Greek amphitheatre', sunk into a manmade hill landscaped with Mediterranean planting. The theatre is 50m (164ft) across and accommodates its audience on 17 rows of simple benches made from slabs of greenheart salvaged from a 70-year-old jetty in the Mersey. Behind the stage and extending across the diameter of the theatre is a *periaktoi* screen wall of free-standing upended concrete sewer pipes of various heights up to 6m (19.7ft). These are topped with planting and spiky cactus-like sculptures. The effect is to create, out of this unlikely material, memories of classical columns. Access to backstage is between the columns through pedimented *aedicula* doorways, painted with curious *trompe l'oeil* panels. The theatre is built on unsteady soil conditions, 13m (42.6ft) of unconsolidated domestic refuse, and the stockade of pipes continues as a retaining wall—filled with soil and planted—around the perimeter arc of the seating, creating stability yet with the ability to move differentially.

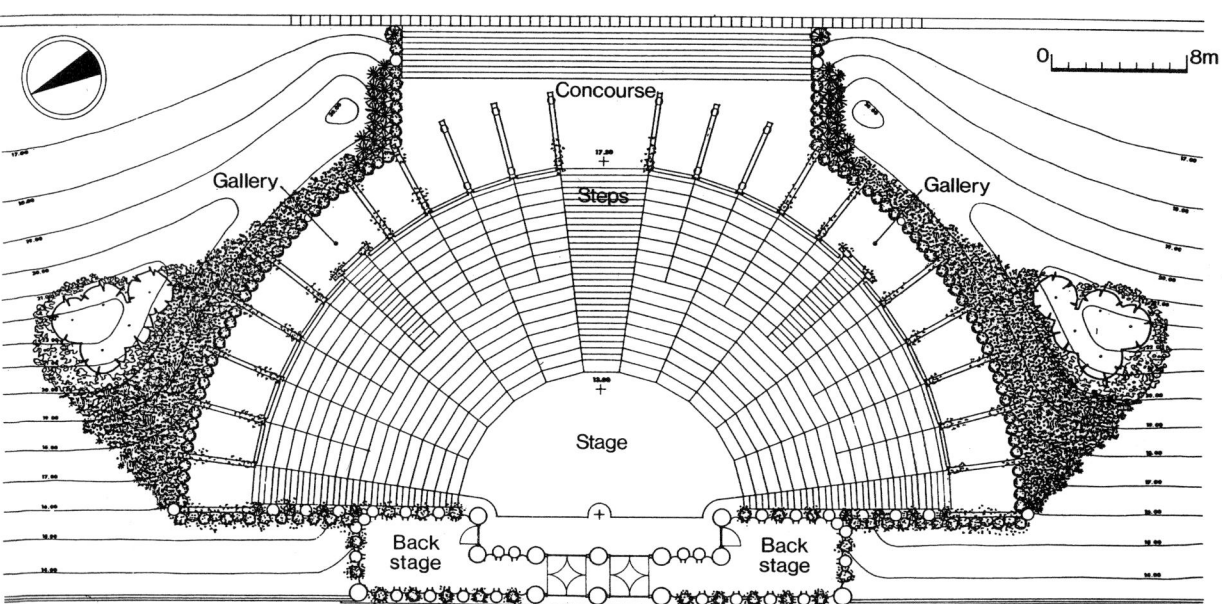

Plan of the amphitheatre.

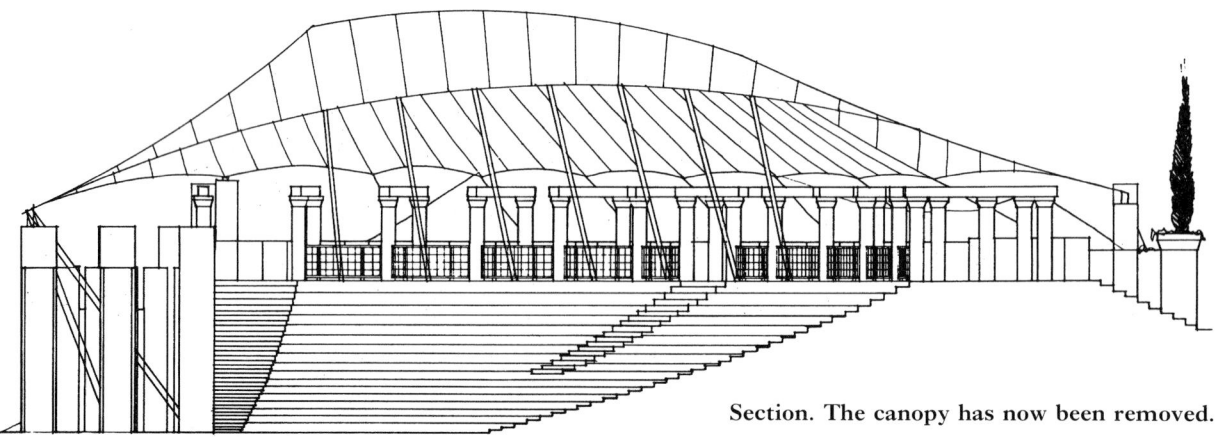

Section. The canopy has now been removed.

The auditorium, with its informal bench seating.

Between the retaining wall and the rear seats is a double colonnade (another Vitruvian feature) of smaller, 300mm (11.8in) standard concrete drain pipes resting on concrete pads. With the spigots upward, Doric fashion, these support a pergola of heavy timber cross beams. A lightweight temporary roof (with Building Regulations approval for six months) sheltered the arena during the festival, like a high-tech velarium. This was tied back to the concrete columns and held in tension by a series of steel struts that could be jacked up in the event of ground settlement.

Against the usual drawbacks of the northern climate with possibilities of wind, rain and cold, and with minimal backstage facilities and limited stage lighting, the theatre has enjoyed robust success, with a striking combination of 'ad hocism', historical allusion and high-tech design. Since the Festival, the canopy has been dismantled as required by the statutory approval, while the theatre continues to thrive. At the time of writing, its future is unknown, as it is uncertain whether or not the City Council will take over the Festival site from the present owners as a permanent amenity, as originally planned.

The concrete drainage pipes create a remarkably
effective allusion to the colonnade around Vitruvian
theatres.

The stage, with pedimented entrance doorways
painted with *trompe l'oeil* designs.

Useful Addresses

Principal English-speaking architectural societies

AMERICAN INSTITUTE OF ARCHITECTS, 1735 New York Avenue North West, Washington D.C 20006

NEW ZEALAND INSTITUTE OF ARCHITECTS, P.O. Box 438, Wellington C1

ROYAL ARCHITECTURAL INSTITUTE OF CANADA, 151 Slater Street, Ottawa 4, Ontario

ROYAL AUSTRALIAN INSTITUTE OF ARCHITECTS, 118 Alfred Street, Milson's Point, New South Wales

ROYAL INSTITUTE OF BRITISH ARCHITECTS, 66 Portland Place, London WIN 4AD

IOSTAT *(International Organization of Scenographers, Theatre Architects and Technicians);* OISTAT *(Organisation Internationale des Scénographes, Techniciens et Architectes de Théâtre); and affiliated societies*

AUSTRIA	Austrian Centre of the OISTAT, c/o Professor H. B. Gallée, Hochschule Mozarteum, Mirabellplatz, 1, A-5020 Salzburg
BELGIUM	Association Belge des Scénographes et Techniciens de Théâtre/ABSTT/Section Belge de l'OISTAT, 45 Rue de Flandre, 1000 Bruxelles
BULGARIA	Centre Bulgare de l'OISTAT, c/o Centre national de l'IIT, rue Pop Andrei 1, Sofia C
CANADA	Associated designers of Canada, 12 Birch Avenue, Suite 205, Toronto, Ontario M4V ICB
CZECHOSLOVAKIA	Centre tchécoslovaque de l'OISTAT, Dielny SND, Mliekarenská cesta 6, 815 86 Bratislava, Ružová dolina
DENMARK	Danish Centre of the OISTAT, c/o Faelles-Forbundet for Teater, Film, OG TV, Sankt Knüdsvej 26, 1903 Copenhagen
EGYPT	D Mostafa Ramzi, 104 Street No. 37, apartment 5, Maadi-Cairo
FEDERAL REPUBLIC OF GERMANY	OISTAT Secretariat Bundesrepublik Deutschland, c/o Hellmut Himstedt-Alexander, Feldbrunnenstrasse 74, D-2000 Hamburg 13
FINLAND	Finnish Centre of the OISTAT, Maneesikatu 4 C, 00170 Helsinky 17
FRANCE	Association Française des Scénographes et Techniciens de Théâtre/AFSTT/Section française de l'OISTAT, 6, rue Lalande, 75014 Paris
GERMAN DEMOCRATIC REPUBLIC	Sektion DDR der OISTAT, Leipziger Strasse 112, 1080 Berlin
GREAT BRITAIN	Association of British Theatre Technicians, OISTAT, 4 Great Pulteney Street, London WIR 3DF

HUNGARY	OISTAT National Centre, c/o Optical Acoustical and Filmtechnical Society/OPAKFI/Ankerköz 1, H-1061 Budapest	NORWAY	OISTAT Section Norge, c/o Riksteatret, Kongensgt.1, Oslo 1 Postboks 724, Sentrum
ISRAEL	Israeli Centre of the OISTAT, c/o Israeli Centre of the ITI, 227 Dizengoff St, Tel Aviv	POLAND	Polskie centrum OISTAT, Teatr Wielki, ul.Moliera 3/5, 00-076 Warszawa
ITALY	Centre Italien de l'OISTAT, Teatro Municipale, Reggio Valli, Piazza Martiri 7 Luglio, 42 100 Reggio Emilia	RUMANIA	Central Roman OISTAT, prof.Traïan Nitescu, rue Hatmanul Arbore 3-7, esc.4, et.1. ap. 5, 71226 Bucuresti
JAPAN	OISTAT National Centre, 1-8-14-505, Ebisu, Shibuya-ku, Tokyo 150	SOVIET UNION	Centre Soviétique de l'OISTAT, c/o Giproteatr, M. Levshinsky Per.7, build.3, 119 034 Moskva
MEXICO	Mexican OISTAT Delegation, Francisco Sosa 396, Coyoacan 21, D.F., Mexico 1	SWEDEN	Svensk Teaterteknísk Förening-OISTAT, 45003 Box, 104 30 Stockholm
NETHERLANDS	Netherlands Centre of the OISTAT, c/o Vereiniging voor Podiumtechnologie, Van Speyckstraat 177/III, 1057 G 2 Amsterdam	SWITZERLAND	Association Suisse des responsables techniques de théâtre—OISTAT, Notkerstrasse 19, 9000 St Gallen
NIGERIA	National Centre of the OISTAT, c/o James Olu Aborisade, Dept. of Theatre Arts, University of Ibadan, Ibadan	UNITED STATES OF AMERICA	US Centre of the OISTAT, c/o US Institute of Theatre Technology, Inc., 330 W. 42nd Street, Suite 1702, New York, NY 10036
		GENERAL SECRETARIAT	Celetná 17, 110 01 Praha 1
		SECRETARY GENERAL	prof. Josef Svoboda, Filmařská 53, 150 00 Praha 5-Barrandov

Further Reading

Of the numerous publications on auditorium architecture and all its aspects, many modern works have become outdated over the last decade or so. This is because of technical developments, for instance in stage lighting, advances in acoustical knowledge, and changes in the designer's attitude, concerning, for example, the actor-audience relationship in theatres. The following is a selected list of books on different areas.

On the technical aspects and design and management of auditoria:

BERANEK, LEO L., *Music, Acoustics and Architecture*, Wiley, New York, 1962, reprinted Krieger, Huntingdon, New York, 1979. A classic worldwide survey of 54 concert halls with valuable data on acoustics. However, the relative importance which acousticians would now place on some of the acoustic criteria has since changed, especially with regard to the importance of lateral sound reflections.

CREMER, LOTHAR, and HELMUT A. MULLER, *Principles and Applications of Room Acoustics*, 2 vols, Applied Science Publishers, London and New York, 1982 (original German edition 1978). The most complete technical reference work on room acoustics in English for the specialist.

HAM, RODERICK, *Theatre Planning*, Architectural Press, London, announced for 1987. A technical and architectural design guide, updated from the original edition of 1972.

IZENOUR, GEORGE C., *Theater Design*, McGraw-Hill, New York, 1977. Contains much technical and bibliographical information and excellent architectural drawings, biased towards the fan-shaped hall. As such, the book is more a record of the recent past than a reflection of present trends.

LORD, PETER, and DUNCAN TEMPLETON, *The Architecture of Sound*, Architectural Press, 1986.

LORD, PETER, and DUNCAN TEMPLETON, *Detailing for Acoustics*, Architectural Press, 1983.

PILBROW, RICHARD, *Stage Lighting*, Cassell, London, second edition 1979.

REID, FRANCIS, *The Stage Lighting Handbook*, Adam and Charles Black, London, second edition 1982.

REID, FRANCIS, *The Staging Handbook*, Pitman Publishing Ltd, London, and Theatre Arts Books, New York, 1978, reprinted Adam and Charles Black, 1983.

REID, FRANCIS, *Theatre Administration*, Adam and Charles Black, London, 1983.

TEMPLETON, DUNCAN, and DAVID SAUNDERS, *Acoustic Design*, Architectural Press, 1987.

On musical instrument acoustics, as related to the performing ambience:

MEYER, JURGEN, *Acoustics and the Performance of Music* Verlag das Musikinstrument, Frankfurt-am-Main, 1980. An important and up-to-date study of this subject.

On the history of auditoria:

BAUR-HEINHOLD, MARGARETE, *Baroque Theatre*, Thames and Hudson, London, 1967 (first German edition, 1966).

FORSYTH, MICHAEL, *Buildings for Music: The Architect, the Musician, and the Listener from the Seventeenth Century to the Present Day*, The MIT Press, Cambridge, Mass./Cambridge University Press, Cambridge, 1985. A history of concert halls and opera houses which relates their acoustics to the evolution of musical style.

HARTNOLL, PHYLLIS, (ed.), *Oxford Companion to the Theatre*, Oxford University Press, London, fourth edition 1983.

LEACROFT, RICHARD, *The Development of the English Playhouse*, Methuen, London, 1973.

LEACROFT, RICHARD and HELEN, *Theatre and Playhouse*, Methuen, London and New York, 1984. Both books are illustrated with fine drawings by the late Richard Leacroft.

SACHS, EDWIN O., *Modern Opera Houses and Theatres*, 3 vols., London, 1896–98, reprinted Benjamin Bloom, New York, 1968. A superbly illustrated *parallèle* of late nineteenth century theatres.

WICKHAM, GLYNNE, *A History of the Theatre*, Phaidon, Oxford, 1985.

Theatres of the period immediately prior to those in this book are shown in:

ALOI, ROBERTO, *Architetture per lo Spettacolo*, Hoepli, Milan, 1958.

BENTHAM, FREDERICK, *New Theatres in Britain*, Rank Strand, London, 1970. Case studies from 1958.

SCHUBERT, HANNELORE, *The Modern Theatre*, Pall Mall Press, London, 1971 (original German edition, 1971). A thorough documentation of postwar German theatre-building.

The following journals on theatre design and technology, and on acoustics, often include articles on architectural subjects:

Actualité de la Scénographie, Paris
Acustica, Stuttgart
Applied Acoustics, Barking, Essex
Bauten der Kultur, Berlin (GDR)
Bühnentechnische Rundschau, Zurich
Cue, London
Journal of the Acoustical Society of America, New
   York
Journal of Japanese Institute for Theatre Technology,
   Tokyo
Journal of Sound and Vibration, London and New
   York

Kép- és Hangtechnika, Budapest
Podium, Nijmegen
Proszenium, Zurich
Sightline, London
Stsenicheskaya Teknika i Teknologia, Moscow
Svensk Teaterteknisk Förening, Stockholm
Színháztechnikai Fórum, Budapest
Theatre Crafts, New York
Theatre Design and Technology, New York

Architectural magazines which frequently illustrate new theatres and concert halls include:

A & U (Architecture & Urbanism), Tokyo
Architect (formerly *RIBA Journal*), London
Architects' Journal, London
Architectural Record, New York
Architectural Review, London
Architecture d'aujourd'hui, Paris
Arkitektur DK, Copenhagen
Arkitektur, Stockholm
Baumeister, Munich
Building, London
Canadian Architect, Don Mills, Ontario
Casabella, Milan
Domus, Milan
Progressive Architecture, Stamford, CT
Werk, Bauen und Wohnen (formerly *Bauen und
   Wohnen*), Zurich

Index

M

A

$(3 + 13)$